PRINCIPLES OF

REAL ESTATE LAW

Principles of

REAL ESTATE LAW

By

PAUL G. CRETEAU, LL.B.
Member of the Maine
and New Hampshire Bars

Castle Publishing Company
P. O. BOX 188, PORTLAND, MAINE 04112

Library of Congress Catalog Card Number: 76-52549

ISBN 0-9603372-0-2
Second Printing . . . January, 1980

PRINTED IN THE UNITED STATES OF AMERICA

SUMMARY OF CONTENTS

TABLE OF CONTENTS

CHAPTER 1. REAL AND PERSONAL PROPERTY

CHAPTER 2. HISTORICAL BACKGROUND

CHAPTER 3. ESTATES IN LAND

CHAPTER 4. LANDLORD AND TENANT (LEASES)

PAGE

CHAPTER 5. DOWER, CURTESY, AND THE HOMESTEAD EXEMPTION

CHAPTER 6. CO-OWNERSHIP

PAGE

CHAPTER 7. EASEMENTS

CHAPTER 8. ADVERSE POSSESSION

CHAPTER 9. WILLS AND DESCENT

PAGE

CHAPTER 10. DEEDS

PAGE

CHAPTER 11. MORTGAGES

PAGE

CHAPTER 12. RECORDING AND TITLE EXAMINATION

CHAPTER 13. CONTRACTS

PAGE

CHAPTER 14. REAL ESTATE BROKERAGE

PAGE

CHAPTER 1

REAL AND PERSONAL PROPERTY

"Property and law are born together, and die together. Before laws were made there was no property; take away laws and property ceases."

Bentham: The Theory of Legislation

INTRODUCTORY STATEMENT

The subject of real estate enjoys a happy combination of attributes: it is practical; it is important; it is interesting. It is practical because probably no other field of endeavor offers such a variety of activity and so much potential in financial rewards. It is important because it directly affects all of us and concerns the nation's largest asset: land. It is interesting because to a large extent, it tells a fascinating story: the history of man.

Chronologically the story really begins with the *next* chapter: Historical Background. However, before our thousand-year plunge into the Dark Ages, when all this began, we should first consider the *anatomy* of our subject matter. We must, at the outset, carefully distinguish real property from personal property, for the laws governing each differ widely.

IN GENERAL

"Property" commonly denotes everything which is the subject of ownership, whether tangible or intangible. It is divided into two broad classifications: *real* property and *personal* property.[1] *Real* property pertains to land and all the things which are more or less permanently attached to it, while *personal* property consists of property of a personal or movable nature not attached to the land, such as furniture, automobiles, livestock and the like. An article of personal property is also referred to as a "chattel," derived from the word cattle, a most important item of possession during the Middle Ages.

The term *land* includes not only the soil but everything attached to it, whether attached by nature, such as trees and water, or by man, such as buildings, fences, and shrubs. It includes not only the surface of the earth but also the space beneath and above the surface. "Whoever owns the land owns the buildings above and the minerals below."

The classical concept that ownership of a parcel of land includes not only the surface but extends infinitely upward and downward has been modified in recent times; otherwise a property owner could prevent aircraft from flying over even at high altitudes. Today, although "ownership" of land includes the space above and below the surface, it does so only to the extent necessary for the enjoyment and exploitation of the property. Under this concept, a temporary invasion of the airspace by aircraft, when it does not interfere with the owner's use and enjoyment of the surface, does not constitute a trespass.

1 The terms "real" and "personal" are a product of the old common law rules of procedure. *Res* is Latin for "thing" or "object" as opposed to the Latin word *persona* which refers to persons or actions. One who had been wrongfully deprived of an interest in land could, in a legal action, recover the very land itself—called a "real" *(res)* action. However, a person who had been wrongfully deprived of goods or chattels was relegated to an action for money damages—the pecuniary value of the object—against the other person *(persona)*. The two classes of actions were accordingly said to "sound in realty" or "sound in personalty," respectively. Very basically the distinction is between movable and non-movable items; personal property is property of a movable nature, not substantially affixed to the land, while real property consists of the land, buildings, and those things more or less substantially attached to them. And personal property may be tangible, such as livestock, furniture, and jewelry, or it may be intangible, such as stocks, bonds, bank deposits, and royalties.

TREES AND CROPS

The ancient common law rule that whatever is attached to the land is part of the land usually applies to trees and crops. "Emblements," crops that require annual planting and cultivation, are usually treated as personal property; but in some situations they are considered part of the realty. For instance, the *tenant* of a farm ordinarily becomes the owner of the crops and may sell or mortgage them as personal property. He may, before his lease terminates, harvest the crops which he planted; and if the lease is of an uncertain duration, he is allowed a reasonable time after the termination of the tenancy to enter upon the land and harvest the crop. However, when land is sold or mortgaged, the growing crops pass with the land unless the parties expressly except them from the transaction.

Growing trees are considered part of the land on which they stand and pass with the land upon its transfer; but when they are cut, they become personal property.

Sometimes trees grow so close to the property line that their branches extend beyond it and over the land of the adjoining owner. Although such trees belong entirely to the owner of the land on which the trunk stands, the adjoining owner may cut the overhanging limbs and encroaching roots without any liability for resulting damage to the tree. Where the trunk of a tree, sometimes referred to as a "line tree," grows directly on the property line, the general rule is that the adjoining owners are tenants in common[2] of the tree. They each have an undivided interest in the whole tree, and neither one may destroy it without being liable to the other for half the damage. This rule creates the peculiar result that the tenant in common of the tree has less right to cut off its branches than he would if it belonged wholly to the adjoining owner.[3]

2 As to the nature of a tenancy in common, see the chapter on Co-ownership.

3 5 AMERICAN LAW OF PROPERTY § 19.15 at 63 (Casner ed. 1952).

FIXTURES

To anyone dealing with real estate, a basic knowledge of the law of "fixtures" is absolutely essential. A fixture is an article of personal property which, while retaining its separate physical identity, has become so connected or attached to the realty as to become a part of it.

The real question in the law of fixtures is whether a particular thing has become so integrated with the land as to become part of it. It is not always easy to determine whether a specific item is realty or personalty; the manner in which it is attached to the land is only one of the factors to be considered. There are many borderline situations where an article has attributes of both real and personal property; and often the courts must resolve the issue.

To assist in determining whether a particular article is personalty or realty, a body of court decisions has set out general rules or "tests" to be employed in any given case. Under the early English cases, a chattel was not considered a fixture unless it was actually attached to the land by bolts, screws, or other such device. However, the American courts early rejected the "annexation test" as inconclusive and adopted the so-called "intention test." Under the intention test if the person who affixed the article did so with the *apparent intent* of permanently improving the land, then the thing annexed is considered a fixture and becomes part of the real estate.

REALTY OR PERSONALTY?—TESTS

Intent

Unfortunately there is no universal test by which it can be determined in every case whether a chattel has become so affixed to the realty as to become part and parcel of it. For personal property to lose its character as a chattel and become a fixture, it must be physically or constructively *annexed* to the realty; it must be appropriated to the *use* of the realty; and it must be *intended* as a permanent part of the realty.

Under the modern rule, the controlling factor or "test" for determining whether an object has become a fixture is the *intention* with which it was affixed to the realty. The manner and extent of physical annexation are chiefly valuable as *evidence* of such intention. If the article was attached with the apparent *intent* to make it a permanent addition to the realty, it will ordinarily become a fixture; on the other hand, if the annexation was not intended to be permanent, the chattel will ordinarily not be deemed a fixture.

By "intention" is meant not the initial intention at the time of procuring the article, nor the secret intention with which it is affixed; it is the objective or manifest intention—the intention as evidenced by all the facts and circumstances, including the relationship of the parties.

In some states, stoves and refrigerators installed in an apartment house are considered fixtures and thus are part of the realty. The basis of these decisions is that such appliances are ordinarily installed with the *intent* that they remain there permanently, since they increase the rental value of the apartments, and because the custom is to include stove and refrigerator with rental units. However, other states have taken a contrary view, holding that the installation of such appliances in an apartment house does *not* sufficiently indicate an intention to permanently annex them to the building.

Whether an article was affixed with the *intent* to make it a permanent part of the realty is a mixed question of law and fact, depending upon the circumstances in each particular case. In determining intent, the court will consider the manner in which the article is attached, the adaptability of the article to the realty and the annexing person's relationship to the realty.

Method of Annexation

In applying the test of *annexation*, the general rule is that a chattel does not become a fixture unless it is in some way physically or constructively attached to the realty. If the article is affixed in such a manner as to induce a reasonable person to believe that it is part of the real estate, then it will ordinarily be considered a fixture. Thus, when an item of personal property is so affixed to the realty that it cannot be detached without doing material damage either to the article or to the realty, it is generally considered to be a fixture and therefore part of the realty.

However in order to be merged in the realty, it is not necessary that a chattel should be physically fastened to the realty at all times; there may be *constructive* as well as actual annexation. Some articles of personal property are so essential to the use of the real estate that although they are not physically attached to it at all times, they are nevertheless considered part of the realty. The most common example is to be found in the case of storm windows and storm doors which are ordinarily considered to be part of the realty although removed and stored in the spring.[4]

According to the law of fixtures, unless otherwise stated a grantor of real estate ordinarily "intends" whatever is necessary for the operation and enjoyment of the property to pass with it. And the courts, in effectuating such "intention," take into account what things the ordinary person would consider as part of the whole. Thus in a leading Maine case[5] the court held that a logging chain, which could be removed simply by lifting it from a hook, should pass with the sale of a sawmill because the mill could not operate without it. In that case the court said:

[4] A building is generally considered to be part of the realty even though it is not physically anchored to the land; it may be set on skids or held down by the force of gravity alone.

[5] Farrar v. Stackpole, 6 Me. 154 (1829).

> "Although the being fastened or fixed to the freehold is the leading principle in many of the cases in regard to fixtures, it has not been the only one. Windows, doors and window shutters are often hung but not fastened to a building; yet they are properly part of the real estate and pass with it; because it is not the mere fixing or fastening, which is regarded, but the use, nature and intention."

Adaptability to the Realty

Where the article is essential, or where it is particularly adapted to or used with that part of the realty to which it is attached, it is usually presumed to be a fixture; and this is true even though the article can be severed from the realty without injury to it or to the realty. This presumption is based upon the fact that where an article is especially fitted to or usable with the realty to which it is attached, the person making the annexation must have *intended* it as a permanent improvement. Thus the sale of a farm will ordinarily include the usual and necessary buildings, even though they are built on skids or are portable, and it will also include the engines used to turn farm machinery. The conveyance of a store building will ordinarily include the shelves, counters, and showcases. The sale of a residence usually includes electric light fixtures, wall-to-wall carpeting, and the storm windows and screens. The conveyance of an apartment house has included "in-a-door" beds, which are not physically attached but are necessary for the occupancy of an "efficiency" apartment.

Relationship of the Parties

In determining the intention with which an article is annexed to the realty, the court will also consider the *relationship* of the parties. As stated above, it is not the unrevealed, secret intention that is important, but rather the intention as indicated by the attendant facts and circumstances, including the relationship and conduct of the parties. The intention should be inferred from all these.

Since the criterion is " the apparent intention to permanently improve the land," whether or not an article is a fixture may well depend upon whether the relationship of the parties was that of landlord-tenant, mortgagor-mortgagee, or vendor-purchasor. What a typical owner might intend under the circumstances might be quite different from what a typical tenant might intend.

Landlord—Tenant

There is a strong presumption that a tenant who affixes chattels to leased land does so for his own benefit and *not* with the intent to enhance the landlord's realty. Consequently, if a tenant, for purposes of his trade, for ornamental or domestic use, or for agricultural purposes, affixes a chattel to leased land, he may under the "trade fixtures" doctrine[6] remove it at any time before the expiration of his term, provided the removal would not materially injure the realty.

The trade fixtures doctrine was adopted because it encourages trade and because it is seldom the *intention* of a tenant to make his fixtures permanent annexations to the land and thereby donate them to the landlord. Hence, as a general rule *any* fixture made by a tenant for his own comfort, convenience or pleasure, may be removed by him at any time during the term of his lease, provided the same can be removed without serious damage to the real estate.[7]

Where a tenant affixes an article that would merge with the realty if attached by an *owner*, the article is still

6 Articles so affixed by a tenant are known as "Trade Fixtures."

7 Where a chattel is so affixed that it cannot be removed without doing material damage to either the chattel or the real estate there is a natural presumption that the intention was not to remove it. Thus in a case where a tenant built a cold storage plant into a rented warehouse building he was not allowed to remove it. The court held that the cold storage plant was not a removable trade fixture since it could not be dismantled without reducing it to a worthless mass. The court reiterated the well-established principle that ". . . the right of removal can only be exercised when it causes no material injury. . . ." Squire v. City of Portland, 106 Me. 234, 76 Atl. 679 (1909).

technically a fixture. The trade fixtures doctrine merely allows the tenant the *privilege* of removing it, provided that he does so prior to the expiration of his lease and provided that its removal will not cause material injury to the real estate or destroy the fixture itself.

Where the tenancy is for a fixed and definite period, the tenant's right to remove his trade fixtures will be lost, provided there is no agreement to the contrary, unless they are removed before the termination of his tenancy. If the term is of uncertain duration, or if it is a tenancy at will, the tenant is allowed a reasonable time after the termination of his tenancy to remove the fixtures. If he fails to remove them within the permitted time, they become the property of the land owner.

Under the trade fixtures doctrine, tenants are permitted to remove a great varity of fixtures, so long as removal is within the time limits and will not cause substantial damage to the realty or virtually destroy the fixture itself. For example, tenants have been allowed to remove partitions, air conditioners, beautician's equipment, bar fixtures, a brick kiln and lumber shed, refrigeration systems, underground tanks, boilers, bowling alleys nailed to the floor, gas fixtures screwed upon gas pipes of a room, water pipes fastened by hooks driven into the walls, a portable iron furnace connected by hot air pipes, hot water heaters, and various agricultural fixtures.

Mortgagor—Mortgagee

As between mortgagor and mortgagee, the general rule of fixtures applies, whether the owner installs the chattel and *later* executes a real estate mortgage, or whether the chattel is installed *after* the mortgage is executed; the apparent intention of the annexor at the time he installs the chattel is still the determining factor. In such cases the chattel becomes part of the realty which is subject to the lien of the mortgage, and it cannot thereafter be removed by the landowner without the mortgagee's consent.

Vendor—Purchaser

Often times a person who has contracted to purchase real estate will take possession of the property before actually receiving the legal title. If a prospective purchaser in possession affixes articles to the land with the apparent intent to make them permanent additions, such articles ordinarily become fixtures and thereafter belong to the owner of the land. Consequently if the prospective purchaser for some reason is unable to perform his part of the contract, and therefore fails to acquire the title, the fixtures will remain part of the realty and may not be removed. But if the seller repudiates the contract and the purchaser is not at fault he may reclaim the fixtures he installed.

Licensees

Where a person having no legal interest in the land obtains permission of the owner to install fixtures thereon, he is said to be a *licensee.*[8] Such licensee is generally privileged to take off whatever he has installed or erected, subject to an obligation to pay damages for any resulting injury to the realty. The logic of the rule is based upon the *intention* criterion; a mere licensee would not usually "intend" to make his annexations a permanent part of the realty and thereby donate them to the landowner.

The rule is different where a third party purchases or takes a mortgage on property upon which a licensee has placed his fixtures. If chattels are attached to the realty in such a manner as to indicate that they are fixtures, but under an agreement between the owner of the chattels and the owner of the realty that they are to remain personalty and not become part of the real estate, they will nevertheless pass by a deed or a mortgage of the real estate to any purchaser or mortgagee who is *without notice* of such an agreement.

[8] In real property law a license is a mere right or privilege to enter upon or do acts upon another person's land, which right or privilege may be revoked at any time; it is a personal privilege and not an interest in the land.

Trespassers

Where a trespasser on another person's land annexes fixtures to the realty, they at once become the property of the owner of the land. This is generally the law even where the trespasser has acted in good faith, under an honest, if mistaken, claim of right. The harshness of this rule has been relaxed somewhat in a few states by so-called "betterment acts" allowing some compensation to a trespasser who has mistakenly and in good faith made improvements to another person's realty.

Agreements As To the Thing Annexed

The parties may enter into a special agreement as between themselves whether an article shall retain its character as personal property or assume the status of a fixture. When the parties enter into such an agreement the legal tests for determining whether the article is a fixture do not apply; the agreement itself will control the status of the article.

However, special agreements fixing the status of property as realty or personalty are binding only upon the contracting parties and persons who have knowledge of the agreement; they are not binding upon innocent parties who are without notice of the agreement. So the general rule may be stated thusly: Chattels attached to the realty in such a manner as to indicate that they are fixtures will pass with the realty to an *innocent* purchaser or mortgagee, *notwithstanding* an agreement between the owner of the chattel and the owner of the realty that the chattels were not to become part of the real estate.

In the last few decades it has become usual to purchase chattels on an installment basis. Typically the buyer and seller enter into a contract which stipulates that ownership of the article shall remain in the seller until the purchase price is paid (a conditional sales contract), or that the seller will hold a chattel mortgage on the article sold as security for his payment. In both cases it is contemplated that the article sold shall remain personal property to be repossessed by the seller if the agreed payments are not made. But what happens if, under such an arrangement, the purchaser annexes the chattel to his land? Even if a chattel is so affixed to the realty that it would ordinarily become part of it, it will, *as between the parties*, remain personalty if, at the time the article is annexed, there is an *agreement* to that effect between the owner of the chattel and the owner of the land, and if its removal will do no substantial injury to the realty. Since in such cases the parties, in effect, agree that the article shall remain personal property and not become a fixture until fully paid for, the seller retains the right to repossess the article if the landowner fails to make the payments.

However, in many states prior to the adoption of the Uniform Commercial Code, any such agreement to preserve the chattel character of property affixed to real estate was ineffective as against a *mortgagee* of land *unless* he agreed to it. In other words, the fixtures became subject to the mortgage and could not be removed without the mortgagee's consent, in spite of any agreement between the owner of the land and the seller of the chattel. The title to fixtures passed to the mortgagee, and his title was superior to that of a conditional seller, even if the chattels were annexed *after* the execution of the mortgage. The mortgagee automatically acquired a lien on any "after affixed" chattels.

Under the new Uniform Commercial Code, adopted in nearly every state, a person selling an article on an installment basis, which has been or will be attached as a *fixture*, may now protect his security in such article by executing a *security agreement* which replaces the old chattel mortgage and conditional sale contract. Notice of the existence of this *security agreement* is made by filing a document, called a *financing statement*, in the registry of deeds. The recording of the financing statement gives notice to all that a security interest exists in the article which will prevail over subsequent purchasers and mortgagees of the real estate. If the purchaser of the article fails to make his payments, the secured party may repossess it and remove it from the real estate, even if such removal causes material injury to the realty. The security holder, however, must reimburse the owner or encumbrancer for any damage resulting from the removal of the article.

SUMMARY

"Property" is classified as either *real* or *personal.* Real property pertains to land and all things which have been more or less permanently attached to the land, either by man or by nature. Property of a personal or movable nature, sometimes referred to as "chattels," is personal property or "personalty."

A "fixture" is an article of personal property which, while retaining its separate physical identity, has become so attached to the real estate as to become part of it.

For a chattel to become a fixture, it must be physically or constructively *annexed* to the realty; it must be appropriated to the *use* of the realty; and it must be *intended* as a permanent part of the realty.

Where it is questionable whether or not an item is a fixture, the court will consider the *intention* with which the article was annexed, the *method of annexation*, its *adaptability* to the realty, and the *relationship of the parties.*

Where a *tenant* affixes a chattel to leased realty for purposes of his trade, he may, under the *trade fixtures* doctrine, remove it prior to the expiration of the lease, provided removal will not cause material injury to the real estate.

As between mortgagor and mortgagee, the general rule of fixtures applies; the apparent intention of the annexor is the determining factor.

When a person in possession of land under a contract to purchase installs fixtures thereto, they become part of the realty and thereafter belong to the owner of the land unless the seller defaults on the contract.

A licensee is generally allowed to remove fixtures that he has installed, provided no damage to the realty will result. However, the title to such fixtures will pass by a deed or a mortgage of the real estate to any purchaser or mortgagee who is *without notice* of the license privilege.

Generally when a trespasser affixes articles to another person's land, such articles at once become the property of the owner of the land even though the trespasser acts in good faith.

The parties may agree as between themselves that an article affixed to the realty shall nevertheless retain its character as personal property. However, such agreements are binding only upon the parties thereto; they are not binding upon innocent purchasors or mortgagees who are without notice of the agreement.

When an article to be attached as a fixture is sold on an installment basis, the seller may protect his security interest in the article by executing a *security agreement* with the buyer and recording a *financing* statement in the registry of deeds.

CHAPTER 2

HISTORICAL BACKGROUND

"The history of what the law has been is necessary to the knowledge of what the law is."

Oliver Wendell Holmes, Jr.
The Common Law

INTRODUCTORY STATEMENT

Most students of real estate are concerned with matters of present day law—the law of real property as it exists in the United States today. However, before rushing headlong into the subject we should pause, if just briefly, to consider the past; it is not possible to truly understand or appreciate modern real estate law without some idea of how it first came to be. On this subject, "A page of history is worth a volume of logic."

HOW THE LAW BEGAN

Although man walked the earth long before laws[1] ever came into existence, the conduct of primitive peoples was, nevertheless, governed by an ancient sociological force—certain things were "taboo."[2] Early clans or tribes developed ways of conduct called "folkways," based in part upon the accumulated experience and knowledge passed down from one generation to another. Eventually these folkways developed into established customs and were observed by all members of the family or group, in many cases long after the original

1 The word "law" has many definitions but for our purposes we shall simply consider it to mean the established rules of human conduct prescribed and enforced by members of a society for its own benefit and protection.

2 The word "taboo" comes from the Polynesian word *tapu* meaning sacred, restricted, or prohibited.

purpose of the custom had vanished in the murk of centuries. So the conduct of primitive man was governed, to a large extent, by the "rules" or customs of the tribe; conduct which violated established custom was taboo, and the deterrent was fear—fear based upon superstition or fear of incurring the wrath of the tribe or clan.

To trace the "lineage" of American law we must look back over a span of more than a thousand years—to that period when England was a province of a crumbling Roman Empire. As the power of Rome faded, leaving the island defenseless, the onslaught of invading hordes began. The barbarians came in waves, from Jutland, the Danish Islands, and from the northern and central parts of modern Germany. The invaders landed along the English coast and easily fought their way inland against a people grown soft under centuries of Roman military occupation. The mass Germanic invasions began at about the middle of the fifth century, and continued for more than five hundred years.[3] The highly organized government and advanced culture which the Romans had nurtured for over four centuries were obliterated, and the long night of the Dark Ages closed in.

> "England was once again a barbarian island. It had been Christian, it was now heathen. Its inhabitants had rejoiced in well-planned cities, with temples, markets, academies. They had nourished craftsmen and merchants, professors of literature and rhetoric. For four hundred years there had been order and law, respect for property, and a widening culture. All had vanished. The buildings, such as they were, were of wood, not stone. The people had lost entirely the art of writing. Some miserable runic scribblings were the only means by which they could convey their throughts or wishes to one another at a distance. Barbarism reigned in its rags, without even the stern military principles which had

3 1 POWELL, REAL PROPERTY 41 (1973).

> animated and preserved the Germanic tribes. The confusion and conflict of petty ruffians sometimes called kings racked the land. There was nothing worthy of the name nationhood, or even tribalism."[4]

Yet it was from the rubble of this five-century long nightmare that the seed of the Common Law germinated—out of the folkways and customs of the Germanic tribes, eventually to emerge as the dominant legal philosophy in the Western Hemisphere.

FEUDALISM

The fall of the Roman Empire and the resulting total collapse of Western civilization ushered in an era of confusion, carnage, waste, and illiteracy.

> "It was not just the fall of a single state but the disintegration of all law and order. It became once again as the dawn of history, a world of disorganized individuals who looked to their own might for the minimum essentials of life. Unfortunately, we can best visualize the scene by realizing that we live on the brink of a similar precipice. A total nuclear war could reduce modern society to the same horrendous condition . . . ."[5]

During this period man's time was mostly occupied with the task of staying alive. Since there was no government and so no authority, the law of the jungle prevailed; bands of marauding chieftains would confiscate lands and divide the plunder among their most favored and valued followers to reward them for their support in the past and to insure their continued loyalty in the future. This was the beginning of a political institution known as feudalism which, born of the violence of the times, had its roots in the land.

The early feudal organization consisted "of a series of

[4] 1 CHURCHILL, A HISTORY OF THE ENGLISH SPEAKING PEOPLES; THE BIRTH OF BRITAIN 70 (1958).

[5] CRIBBET, PRINCIPLES OF THE LAW OF PROPERTY 27 (1962).

military alliances between neighboring chieftains, culminating in the ruler of the particular country. Each petty leader organized his own domain on the same lines as the kingdom, so that each leader's domain and the organization thereof was a replica of the principal organization, the feudal state. The neighborhood chieftain organized his military force and provided for the maintenance of the agricultural economy by which he lived by parcelling out portions of land to his followers in return for their services.''[6] The alliance between the leader and his followers eventually resulted in the personal relationship of lord and man.[7] Such was the general structure of the English society on the eve of the Norman Invasion.

WILLIAM THE CONQUEROR

For all practical purposes the year 1066 marks the beginning of the history of American property law. In the autumn of that year the fleet of William, the Duke of Normandy, put in at Pevensey Bay in Sussex. With an army of knights, archers, and men-at-arms William defeated and killed King Harold in the famous Battle of Hastings, a victory which was to profoundly affect the lives and liberties of men for centuries. The invading army continued to cut a swath of devastation toward London, and on Christmas day William the Conqueror was crowned King of England and supreme lord of the land.

With the victory secured, the new king, like a modern political boss, began the distribution of available patronage—land. The land holdings of the defeated Saxon nobility became ''forfeited'' and available for distribution to the Conqueror's men as a reward for their past services and to form the new Norman aristocracy. The mass peasant

6 LAWLER & LAWLER, A SHORT HISTORICAL INTRODUCTION TO THE LAW OF REAL PROPERTY 2 (1940).

7 "Landowners were easy prey for any roving band of invaders who descended upon them. They were therefore obliged to seek protection where they could find it and pay whatever was demanded. Thus a powerful landowner with a retinue of fighting men could force his weaker neighbors to become his dependents in return for his protection." LINTON, THE TREE OF CULTURE 373 (1955).

population were not disturbed in their small holdings—they merely acquired new Norman overlords to whom they would render the ancient services. It was out of the land holdings of numerous members of the Saxon nobility that William granted immense holdings to his closest military followers. To less than a dozen of his associates went about one-fourth of England, with smaller holdings allocated to lesser barons.[8] The great land redistribution did not destroy the existing feudal structure but rather, the English and Norman land holding patterns were merged, resulting in a new ruling class and a new system of land holding.

From the standpoint of property law, the most significant aspect of the new feudal structure was *tenure*. The dictionary defines "tenure" as having to do with the manner in, or the period for, which anything is had and enjoyed. And in the setting of the feudal society it implied exactly that—a mode of holding or possessing land. As there was virtually no money economy during the first years following the Conquest, it was through land tenure that the members of the new Norman society provided for their basic needs.

The most pressing need after the Conquest was security; the new regime had to be protected against rebellion from within and invasion from without. William's act of bestowing land grants upon his followers not only served to repay them for their support in the great venture, but it was also the means by which the new king "financed" his royal army. A grant by the king did not carry with it "ownership" of the land in the modern sense of the word; but rather, the lord or baron receiving the land "held" it "of" the king[9] much as a tenant. In return for the land the tenant was obliged to furnish a specified quota of knights for the king's army, the number usually depending upon the grant. Such a land holding arrangement between the king and baron was known as tenure by *knight service*, sometimes called military tenure.

8 MOYNIHAN, INTRODUCTION TO THE LAW OF REAL PROPERTY 3 (1962).

9 Those holding directly of the king were known as "tenants-in-chief."

There were also three other types of land tenure utilized, each for the purpose of filling one of the basic needs of the times: The fundamental need for subsistence gave rise to *socage* tenure. Those who held lands by this type of tenure were required to furnish annually a specified quantity of some product of the soil. From the pomp and ceremony of medieval aristocracy rose the need for splendor; the maintenance of large households required a variety of services ranging from those of a dignitary nature to the more humble duties of cooking and sewing. These services were "purchased" with land and *serjeanty*[10] tenure resulted. The spiritual need for salvation gave rise to *frankalmoign* tenure. Frankalmoign, meaning "free alms," was the type of tenure which arose from a grant of land to a church or religious body in return for services of a religious nature, such as saying masses or prayers.

So the four basic needs of the times were fulfilled by the use of four principal types of land grants, each creating a tenurial relationship characterized by the nature of the services required in return for the land. Military tenure solved the immediate need for *security*; socage tenure arose out of the great need for *subsistence*; serjeanty tenure provided the personal *services* demanded by the aristocracy; and frankalmoign tenure resulted from the desire for *salvation*. Thus, by distributing land in military tenure, William the Conqueror provided for his "national"army, and through grants in socage, serjeanty, and frankalmoign tenures he also provided for his subsistence, services, and salvation.[11]

Feudal tenure did not end simply with the relationship between the king and his tenants-in-chief. The tenants-in-chief, who occupied the highest social level in the feudal aristocracy, also had needs to fulfill; as great land barons they also maintained large households, and so required subsistence and a variety of services. Most of the tenants-in-chief held

[10] Serjeanty is derived from the medieval Latin word *serientia*, meaning service.

[11] 1 POWELL, REAL PROPERTY 48 (1973); CRIBBET, PRINCIPLES OF THE LAW OF PROPERTY 29 (1962).

their land by knight service and so were required to furnish a specified quota of knights. In order to fulfill the conditions under which they themselves held the land, such tenants-in-chief would grant portions of their land to others, also by knight tenure, the terms of the grant being that the grantee serve as a knight with the chief tenant whenever called upon. Thus was created a relationship between the tenant-in-chief and his own tenant known as "subtenure"—something like the modern sublease. The number of individuals to whom the tenant-in-chief granted land in this way corresponded to the quota due the king. In this way the tenant-in-chief not only satisfied the obligations under which he himself held the land, but by similarly granting out parcels to others in socage tenure, serjeanty tenure, and frankalmoign tenure, he took care of his personal needs as well. Although the creation of these subtenures resulted in the tenant-in-chief's becoming both tenant and lord at the same time, it in no way affected his already existing tenure with the king.

After making the above grants, the tenant-in-chief would retain a choice portion of the land for his own use and possession which would serve as the site for his castle or manor house. This constituted a typical organization called a *manor*, in which the tenant-in-chief, the lord of the manor, had made provision for most of his needs by virtue of grants he had made to others. The manorial lands were worked by a low class of peasants, known as *villeins*, whose social position was substantially that of the American Negro before the Civil War. The villeins were attached to the manor and, under the arbitrary will of the lord, performed the many menial tasks associated with medieval farming. In return for this service the lord provided shelter for them and made available small plots of land for their own personal use. The considerable territory of a typical manor constituted the basic unit of the feudal system and dominated life in medieval England.

From the parcel of land which a subtenant received, he would, in turn, allot smaller tracts to others, also upon condition that specified services be rendered him, thereby creating another subtenure. This process of creating subtenures was repeated in a descending scale until the actual user of the land was reached.

Each grant created a relationship of lord and tenant, with the result that as many as three or four "middle lords" stood between the king and the lowest man in the feudal structure—the serf, who actually tilled the soil. The land so held by one as tenant of another was known as his feud or fief, later to become our modern word "fee." All persons between the king at the top and the peasants at the bottom held their land in a dual capacity—they were tenants of those above and lords with respect to those below.[12] And although, in this way, several individuals came to have simultaneous interests in the land, they obviously could not use and occupy the same land at the same time; the person at the bottom of the pyramid actually farmed the land, whereas the overlords received the feudal services.[13]

The feudal society was organized in the form of a giant

12 MOYNIHAN, INTRODUCTION TO THE LAW OF REAL PROPERTY 10 (1962).

13 In addition to the regular tenurial services required of the tenant by virtue of the terms of the grant, there were also further rights and obligations due the lord known as *incidents* of tenure. For instance, at the beginning of his tenure a tenant took the oath of *fealty* in which he promised to be loyal to the lord; a breach of this obligation was a serious offense, called a felony, which resulted in a forfeiture of the land. When land later became inheritable, if a tenant died leaving a minor heir, the incident of *wardship* entitled the lord to *all* of the profits of the land until the heir became of age, at which time the heir was required to pay the lord a sum called *relief* for the privilege of succeeding to his ancestor's land—much like the modern inheritance tax. However, when the tenant died without leaving heirs, the land reverted or *escheated* to the lord. And due to the great rivalry between the English land barons it became important that no minor tenant be allowed to form a marital alliance with a family hostile to the lord. This gave rise to the incident of *marriage* by which the lord had the right to arrange a suitable marriage for his minor wards. For about two hundred years after the Conquest the tenant could not transfer his holding to someone else without the lord's consent which, if granted, required from the tenant a money payment called a *fine*. The incident known as *aids* arose out of the close personal bond which existed in the early feudal tenures. *Aids* were financial contributions made to the lord to assist him in times of difficulty, such as to ransom his person if he were captured, to contribute to the knighting of his eldest son and to the dowry of his eldest daughter upon her marriage.

pyramid with the king at the top and the serfs at the bottom, while the middle tiers were occupied by lords of various degrees of importance. Rights in land flowed down the pyramid while a variety of services and obligations moved upward.

So with every acre in the country held of someone under some form of service the landed pyramid rose up, tier by tier to the king.[14] And the connecting chain which bound it all together was tenure. Such was the law of the feuds—a legacy of the Dark Ages and more accurately custom than law.

THE COMMON LAW

The Norman who became lord of the manor not only assumed control of the economy in the area, he also assumed *legal* jurisdiction over his tenants as well. He sat as judge in his manorial court, deciding controversies and dispensing his own brand of justice. The quality of justice dispensed by these manorial courts depended upon the temperament of the lord and the customs of his particular manor. Consequently the law throughout the country was not consistent—there was no law common to all England.

The accession of Henry II in the year 1154, however, marked the beginning of a new legal system which was to dominate England and eventually reach the New World. In order to curb the growing independence and power of the great land barons, Henry established a system of royal courts. He appointed judges who went on circuit throughout the provinces to administer the "king's justice." Trial by jury became available to anyone seeking justice in these royal courts which gradually came to take the place of the manorial courts. The establishment of this "national" court system began the growth of the *Common Law*, a term which implies a law *common to all men*, geographically and socially. With the

14 1 CHURCHILL, A HISTORY OF THE ENGLISH SPEAKING PEOPLES; THE BIRTH OF BRITAIN 174 (1958).

establishment of these royal courts, giving the same justice throughout the realm, the old diversity of local law was broken down and "a law common to the whole land and to all men took its place."

The great mass of the Common Law, referred to as "the unwritten law," developed out of the decisions of actual trials. The early judges, in effect, "created" much of the Common Law by interpreting and applying the ancient, unwritten customs of the land. Their early decisions or "opinions" were eventually recorded annually in books, called *Year Books*, and lawyers ascertained what the law was by reading and studying them. The decisions were based upon the unwritten customs of the land—it was the customs that were unwritten, not the law.

As the number of decided cases grew, the Common Law became more established and therefore more predictable. This was a consequence of the policy or doctrine of *stare decisis*, which is a Latin phrase meaning to "stand by decisions." This rule or policy of following the rules of law already laid down in previous decisions resulted in what is popularly known as "case law," which made it possible for a lawyer to determine or predict what the law would be in a given situation by finding a decision handed down involving substantially the same facts. The law of the Middle Ages was dominated by the land law—a mass of uncertain and conflicting customs which eventually developed into a definite and systematic body of rules.[15]

When the early Colonists first settled the New World, it was considered, not only by the settlers but by the judges and lawyers of England, that they brought with them, as part of their heritage, as much of the English Common Law as was applicable to their new situation. Of course the Colonists did create and establish some new rules of law specially adapted to their needs; but by and large they developed a legal system

[15] 1 AMERICAN LAW OF PROPERTY § 1.2 (Casner ed. 1952).

based on the law with which they had come in contact in England.

This, then, is the Common Law—a unique body of rules evolved from ancient tribal customs. It spread to the New World, and though modified to meet the needs of a new country, it has become the basis of the legal institutions of all the United States except Louisiana. Much of it, even now, remains unchanged from the original form as expressed by the early English judges.

THE DECLINE OF FEUDALISM

Originally all landholding was limited to the lifetime of the tenant. The reason for this was that the early feudal notion of landholding was based upon the *personal* status of an individual; presumably the land had been granted to a particular tenant because of the services he could render to the lord. Consequently, if the tenant died, the land would "revert" to the lord who would then replace the services by regranting the land to a new and acceptable tenant. The fact that the deceased tenant left "heirs" was hardly a significant factor; a man held land because he was a brave knight or a good cook, and it didn't necessarily follow that his heirs would also be so endowed.

However, by the thirteenth century the pressures of a changing society began to exert their influence upon the law of the feuds. After a century of tenure by knight service, it became apparent that a regular army of paid professional soldiers would be an improvement over a feudal militia which required so much time to answer the call to arms. By the end of the twelfth century, tenants holding land by knight service made money payments, called *scutage*, in lieu of military service. Later, most services due under socage tenure were also commuted to money payments—rent. With the substitution of money payments for personal services there was no longer any valid objection to allowing a tenant's heirs to succeed to the land, and land became inheritable.[16]

In the year 1290 a statute[17] was passed which prohibited any further lengthening of the feudal chain of tenures[18] and gave tenants the full right to make a complete transfer of the land to another without permission of the overlord and without paying a fine. Not until the thirteenth century did the personal status of the hapless villein begin to improve. Gradually he was given a slight measure of protection by the customary law of the manor, and in the fourteenth century the terrible Black Death created a scarcity of agricultural labor which improved his bargaining power—if he survived. In the fifteenth century the royal courts gave him further protection against the lord of the manor and eventually the last remnants of this lowly station in life disappeared.[19]

The tenures and feudal incidents developed out of the basic needs of the times.[20] However, with the passage of years their continued existence became increasingly difficult to justify. With the assertion of a strong central government able to give adequate protection to life and property, the incidents became completely unjustified and were finally abolished by the Statute of Tenures in the year 1660.[21] This statute not only abolished all the incidents except *escheat* but, for all practical

16 Even then land often escheated to the overlord for lack of an heir, and it wasn't until the passage of the Statute of Wills in 1540 that the tenant gained the power to control the disposition of his land by will.

17 The name of the statute was *Quia Emptores* which took its name from the first two words of the body of its Latin text: "Because purchasers. . . ."

18 It was to the benefit of the land barons to prevent a further lengthening of the feudal chain since it simplified the feudal structure; enforcement of the feudal obligations became increasingly complicated with the lengthening of the tenurial chain.

19 CASNER & LEACH, CASES AND TEXT ON PROPERTY 262 (1951).

20 For example, in early times the protection given a minor child of a deceased tenant against marauders and murderers may well have justified the overlord's free use of the land until the child was old enough to care for himself. And if a tenant's land descended to his surviving unmarried daughter it was, perhaps, reasonable that the lord should have some say in the choice of her husband, who would, according to the law of that time, assume control of her land upon marriage.

21 MOYNIHAN, INTRODUCTION TO THE LAW OF REAL PROPERTY 24 (1962).

purposes, it converted all tenures into *socage* tenure and signaled the end of the feudal period. Finally the English Property Acts of 1925 removed the last traces of feudalism as a system of land holding, and in England today all land is held directly of the king by socage tenure (payment of taxes) and the services and incidents have disappeared.

Feudalism never really existed in the United States, although in some of the early American Colonies a few manors were established following the English manorial system, and some of the early charters called for the payment of a nominal rent under *socage* tenure. The American Revolution ended whatever tenurial relationship may have existed between England and America; today, in this country, all land is "allodially" held, that is, absolutely and in one's own right, free from the rendition of services to a superior (except for the obligation to pay taxes, of course).[22]

Undoubtedly the question in your mind now is: If the feudal system has long ceased to exist in England and never did exist in this country, how does it concern our study of modern American property law? The answer is that although feudal tenure no longer exists, the effects of tenure endure, for they are the basis of the English concept of *estates,* a concept which was received into American property law practically in its entirety and which is the very foundation of our present system of land ownership.

SUMMARY

The *common law* comprises a body of rules and principles which derive their authority from ancient usages and customs, as interpreted by the early English judges. The early colonists of the New World brought with them as much of the English common law as was applicable to their new way of life. In the United States the phrase refers to that part

22 1 AMERICAN LAW OF PROPERTY § 1.41 (Casner ed. 1952).

of the common law of England which was in force here at the time of the Revolution; it is the basis of the legal institutions of all the United States except Louisiana.

For all practical purposes the Norman Conquest marks the beginning of American property law. Our modern land law evolved from the English feudal system. Under the feudal structure the king "owned" all the land in England. Much of it he granted to others in return for stipulated services. The relationship between the king and his grantees (tenants-in-chief) was called *tenure*, of which there were four basic types:

(1) *Military tenure* or knight service.

(2) *Serjeanty tenure*, characterized by services of a personal nature.

(3) *Frankalmoign tenure*, characterized by services of a religious nature.

(4) *Socage tenure*, characterized by services of an agricultural nature or money rental.

Besides the obligations attached to the grant by virtue of the tenural relationship, there were additional obligations imposed upon the tenant known as *incidents* of tenure.

Tenants-in-chief granted portions of their holdings to others, also in return for stipulated services, thus creating *subtenures*. The subtenants likewise granted still smaller portions to others in a descending scale, down to the actual user of the land. This process of creating subtenures, known as *subinfeudation*, resulted in three or four "middle lords" standing between the king and the user of the land.

The feudal structure was in the form of a pyramid, with the king at the top and the serfs at the base, while the middle tiers were occupied by lords of various degrees of importance—all bound together by some form of tenurial relationship. Although feudal tenure no longer exists, it has an important effect on us; it is the basis of our modern concept of land ownership.

CHAPTER 3

ESTATES IN LAND

INTRODUCTORY STATEMENT

The latter part of the feudal period was characterized by a deepening conflict of interests between lord and tenant, the lord demanding as many benefits as he could get and the tenant wishing to give as little as possible in return for the land. In this struggle between the "haves" and the "have-nots" the ground rules of feudal tenure were established, culminating in the law of the feuds; and out of the law of the feuds was forged the unique doctrine of estates.

The *estate concept*, said to be one of the most remarkable aspects of English land law, forms the blueprint of our modern American landholding system. And though a legacy of a social system long dead, the doctrine itself has probably improved with age, its features almost unmarred by the toll of centuries.

THE ESTATE CONCEPT

In chapter two we took a brief look at the structure of the English feudal system and considered the various kinds of tenure by which land was held under that system; we also considered those other rights and obligations attached to tenures—the incidents of tenure. In other words, we considered the feudal relationship *between the parties*. Now we shall consider the relationship of the parties *to the land*—the various *interests* they actually had in the land. These "interests" were called ESTATES.

The word "estate" comes from the Latin word *status*. In the early days of the feudal system a man's position or status in the community was determined by the quality and quantity of his landholding. Later the term lost its significance in respect to personal status, and eventually the word "estate" came to refer to the extent and character of any person's *interest in land*. Today in modern legal parlance, an *estate* in real property refers to the *interest* which a person has in land. An estate in land has been defined as "the degree, quantity, nature, or extent of interest which a person has in real property," which may vary from absolute ownership down to mere naked possession.

When the average person considers "ownership," he usually thinks of the article itself; if the "ownership" involves real estate, he thinks of the land and the buildings; he envisions the tangible, physical property itself. But ownership is a concept; it is really the relationship among people in regard to the land. So, to properly understand the estate concept, you should always keep in mind that when it is said that a person "owns" land, what is more precisely true is that the person has an *interest in* the land—an interest called an estate; the estate and the land are two separate things.

You will recall the structure of the English feudal system: the king granted land to close associates who, in turn, allotted smaller tracts to others, and so on down the scale. Each person in the tenurial chain more accurately owned an estate *in* the land rather than the land itself. And so, today, *several* persons may each have some type of estate in the same parcel of land, for an estate is an interest *in* the land which is separate from the land itself.

Before considering the various types of estates, you might find it helpful to visualize our modern theory of land ownership as compared to a bundle of sticks wherein each stick represents a distinct and separate right or privilege of ownership. One who holds the complete[1] bundle of sticks

[1] Actually, to say that one holds the "complete" bundle of sticks is not quite accurate. No person enjoys *unrestricted* rights to his property since private rights and privileges are always subject to the needs of society. For instance,

with respect to a given parcel of land is said to hold a "fee simple absolute" estate in the land—the largest quantum of interest a landowner can possibly have. From the virtually absolute ownership represented by the fee simple absolute estate, estates are catalogued down to holdings amounting to mere naked possession, as in the case of a tenant who wrongfully remains in possession of premises to which he no longer has legal rights.

Estates are classified according to *time,* that is, according to how long they might possibly last. And this "time" element may be measured in terms of years, by one or more person's lives, or by specified events of certain or uncertain occurrence. An estate in land is a time in land, or *land for a time.* If this concept sounds strange to you, consider the following example:

Assume that H has an estate in fee simple absolute (the largest estate known to the law—the whole "bundle of sticks") in a parcel of land. H has a wife and one young son. H would like the son to have the land eventually, yet he wants to provide for his wife during her lifetime. He may accomplish both results by carving his fee simple absolute estate into two new estates—by giving his wife the land for her lifetime (a life estate) and the "remainder" in fee simple absolute to his son. The moment the deed is delivered (or the moment H dies, if a will is employed), H's title to the land will pass from him, and his estate in fee simple absolute will "split" into two new estates: a *life estate* in the wife, and a *remainder* in fee simple absolute in the son.[2] The wife and son will then each have a present estate in the land; the wife's life estate will entitle her to the possession, rents, and profits of the land during her lifetime. The son will also have a

private rights in property are always held subject to governmental powers of taxation and eminent domain. And private property rights are also subject to *regulation* (through the exercise of governmental police power) in the interest of the public's safety, health, morals, and general welfare.

2 H could do this by either delivering a *deed* during his lifetime or by leaving a will which would become effective upon his death.

present existing estate (remainder in fee simple); but before becoming entitled to the right to the possession and profits, he will have to "wait" until the prior life estate in his mother comes to an end.

Of course the physical real estate will not change—only the *estates in the land* will change. *Both* estates will come into existence simultaneously, even though the son's estate cannot become possessory until the death of his mother, the life tenant. And when the mother dies, the son will not inherit his estate in the land from her—it will have been his as a remainder in fee simple since the transfer by H.[3]

Now that you are beginning to think of estates as interests in land which are separate from the land itself, we are ready to consider each of the estates as they exist today, little changed from their original common law form.

The estates which finally evolved out of the English feudal system to become part of our present landholding system are:

FREEHOLD ESTATES	The fee simple absolute The fee simple determinable The fee simple subject to a condition subsequent The fee simple subject to an executory limitation The fee tail The estate for life
NON-FREEHOLD ESTATES	Estates for years Periodic estates Estates at will The tenancy at sufferance

Those estates listed above the broken line are classified as *freehold* estates and are the subject of this chapter; those

[3] CRIBBET, PRINCIPLES OF THE LAW OF PROPERTY 23 (1962).

listed below the broken line are classified as *non-freehold* estates, the subject matter of chapter four. Although significant from an historical standpoint, the distinction between the terms freehold and non-freehold is of little practical importance. The term "freehold" comes from the fact that under the early feudal system of William the Conqueror, freehold estates were estates of dignity; they were held by "freemen," who were entitled to the full protection of the king's court.

Holders of non-freehold estates were not so fortunate. Non-freehold estates were not really part of the feudal pattern at all; they were independent rights in the use of the land and were not considered by the feudal society as constituting an actual *interest in* the land. And so non-freehold estates, such as leases (which are estates for years), were and are still today, classified as personal property and not realty.

THE FEE SIMPLE ABSOLUTE

The estate in *fee simple absolute* is the largest estate known to the law and the most common of all the estates. It is an absolute and wholly unqualified estate in the land—the complete "bundle of sticks." The holder of this type of estate has the largest quantum of interest possible under the law.[4]

The fee simple absolute estate, usually shortened to "fee simple" or "fee," is an absolute estate in perpetuity. That is to say, its duration is potentially infinite. The holder of such an estate may, during his lifetime, sell the land, or he may give it away; he may leave it by will to anyone he pleases;[5] and if he dies without a will, the estate will pass on to his

4 Although the fee simple absolute estate represents the ultimate in land ownership, the rights of the owner of such an estate are, of course, subject to the legal rights of adjacent owners, zoning and subdivision laws, the laws of eminent domain, and in some instances the use of the land is limited by restrictive covenants (deed restrictions) imposed by former owners.

5 Subject, however, to the statutory rights of a surviving spouse, a matter to be considered in Chapter 5.

legal heirs.[6] He may convey (transfer by deed) or devise (leave by will) the entire estate (in which case the estate will continue along in the new owner), or he may grant out lesser estates from it. The duration of this type of estate is potentially infinite in time in that it will come to an end *only* in the event that the owner dies without having left a valid will and without heirs.[7]

Creation of the Fee Simple Absolute

At early common law, in order to create a fee simple estate by conveyance (in a deed)[8] it was absolutely essential that the deed be made to the grantee "and his heirs." That is, if A wished to convey a fee simple estate in land to B, the deed would have to contain the words "to B *and his heirs*"; any substitute words would not suffice, regardless of how clearly they expressed the intention to convey a fee simple estate.[9] Thus a conveyance using the words "to B" or "to B forever," or even "to B in fee simple absolute" would pass only a life estate to B. This may seem odd to you at first but the reason for the verbal ritualism is to be found in the early feudal structure.

You will recall that early feudal tenure was limited to the *lifetime* of the grantee for the reason that landholding was based upon the *personal* status of an individual; a tenant was granted land because of the services he could render to the lord. And when a tenant died the land would revert to the lord who would replace the services by re-granting the land

6 "Legal heirs" include both the *direct* descendants of the deceased and those persons related to him *collaterally*.

7 In which case the land will *escheat* to the state.

8 A "conveyance" is a transfer of title to real property from one living person to another by *deed;* when an estate in land is transferred by *will* it is called a "devise."

9 However, the common law rule requiring words of inheritance ("and his heirs") to create a fee simple estate never applied to *wills*. Hence, in a *devise* of land, as distinguished from a *conveyance,* a fee simple estate could be created without the use of the magic word "heirs," provided the will showed an intent on the part of the testator to leave such an estate. A "testator" is a person who dies leaving a valid will.

to another acceptable tenant; the lord was not obliged to accept a deceased tenant's heirs.

However, the eventual substitution of money payments for services lessened the importance of the personal relationship between lord and tenant; accordingly the objection to allowing a tenant's heirs to succeed to the land began to disappear, and gradually land became inheritable. Nevertheless, the heirs of a tenant were not permitted to succeed to the land unless the grant to the tenant signified, in advance, a willingness on the part of the lord to accept the heirs. This the lord did by including the words "and his heirs" (words of inheritance) in his grant to the tenant. So if the lord wished to grant to his tenant an inheritable estate, the conveyance was made to the tenant "and his heirs," thereby giving formal notice that the tenant's heirs would be allowed to inherit the land. Over the years the words "and his heirs" became indispensable words of art; no other phrase would suffice to create an inheritable estate.

With the establishment of inheritable estates through the use of the words "and his heirs" in the original conveyance, another question arose: Did the words "and his heirs" confer any actual interest on the tenant's presumptive heirs? The words "to B and his heirs," if interpreted literally, would *appear* to give the presumptive heirs an interest in the land as well as the tenant. Should B then, be allowed to convey the land to a third person and thereby defeat the future inheritance of his heirs apparent? For about the first hundred years the answer was thought to be *no*; the presumptive heirs were regarded as taking an interest by virtue of being mentioned in the original grant to the tenant. However, by the beginning of the thirteenth century the courts decided that the words "and his heirs" created no interest in the would-be heirs. It became the settled rule of law that the words "and his heirs" in a conveyance "to B and his heirs," merely indicated that B was given an estate in fee simple, and B's heirs took no interest by virtue of the conveyance. The courts construed the words as being "words of limitation"—that is, words which merely establish the *quantum* of the estate—an estate in *fee simple.* So the words "and his heirs" became the equivalent of "fee simple"—nothing more.

By the end of the thirteenth century the tenant had finally established for himself the absolute freedom of alienation—the freedom to convey to others through sale or by gift, without obtaining anyone's consent. Today this right is such a basic characteristic of the fee simple estate that any attempted restriction of alienation by anyone granting such an estate will be declared void by our courts as contrary to public policy. The holder of land in fee simple may convey all or part of it during his lifetime, or he may grant lesser estates out of his fee simple; but he cannot restrict its free transferability.

The common law rule requiring the technical words "and his heirs" to transfer a fee simple estate by deed has been abolished in England and in nearly all of the United States. Most state statutes specifically provide that the terms "heirs," "assigns," "forever," or other technical words of inheritance shall not be necessary to create a fee simple estate. So today, a grantor who wishes to convey a fee simple estate may do so by any language (in the deed) which indicates an intention to transfer such an estate.[10]

QUALIFIED FEES

A fee simple estate may be absolute or qualified. It is *absolute* (a fee simple absolute) when it is not subject to termination *unless* the owner dies without heirs and without having left a valid will.[11]

10 Although just about all of the states have dispensed with the common law rule requiring technical words of inheritance, such words are still generally used throughout the country to describe a fee interest.

11 Don't confuse this situation with a *conveyance* of the estate by the owner during his lifetime. When the owner of such an estate makes a conveyance of it he is merely voluntarily transferring the legal title from himself to another—it is not a "termination" of the estate; the estate will "go on" in the new owner.

However, the law does allow some qualifications or conditions to fee simple estates. A fee simple estate with a condition or a qualification attached to it is called a *defeasible* or *qualified* fee simple. It is called a defeasible or qualified fee simple because although its duration is potentially infinite it may come to an end by the happening or non-happening of some event specified in the conveyance or will creating the estate.

The three types of qualified fee simple estates are:

(1) The fee simple determinable.
(2) The fee simple subject to a condition subsequent.
(3) The fee simple subject to an executory limitation.

THE FEE SIMPLE DETERMINABLE[12]

The fee simple determinable estate is one which has been created to last or endure *only* until the happening of a named event.[13] It is an estate in fee simple with a provision that the estate shall *automatically* expire upon the happening of a stated event. Such an estate is a fee simple because it *may* last forever; but it is not an "absolute" fee—it is a *determinable* fee because it may end by the happening of the event named.

Example:

A, owning Blackacre in fee simple absolute, transfers it "to B and his heirs *so long as the said Blackacre is used for public school purposes.*" B has an estate in *fee simple determinable.*

Example:

A, owning Blackacre in fee simple absolute, transfers it "to B and his heirs *so long as no commercial building is erected upon the land.*" B has an estate in fee simple determinable.

12 The fee simple determinable estate is also referred to variably as a "fee upon limitation," a "determinable fee," or a "modified fee."

13 This estate, like any other estate, may be created by deed or by will.

> Or ". . . so long as the premises are not used for the sale of liquor,"
>
> or ". . . so long as said lot shall be occupied for a meeting house or house of public worship,"
>
> or ". . . so long as said park shall be used for . . ." a designated purpose.

The fee simple determinable estate has all the characteristics of a fee simple absolute except one—its *duration* is not infinite because it will terminate upon the happening of the stated event.[14] And the "stated event" (upon the occurrence of which the estate is to automatically expire) can be either the *happening* or the *non-happening* of a specified occurrence, as for example, "so long as" or "during the time while," the land is used for specified purposes, or "until" a specified event occurs.

Creation of the Fee Simple Determinable Estate

The words which qualify the estate, that is, limit its duration until the happening or non-happening of a stated event, are called *words of special limitation.* The traditional words used to create a special limitation are "until," "during," "while," or "so long as," although no particular words are necessary, provided they show an intent on part of the person transferring the estate that it shall *automatically* expire upon the happening of a stated event.

What if the stated event actually happens? For example, A, owning Blackacre in fee simple absolute, transfers it to B and his heirs *"so long as the property is used exclusively for religious purposes."* B has a fee simple determinable estate in Blackacre. What happens when the property is no longer used exclusively for religious purposes? In that case B's

14 When the owner of a fee simple *absolute* estate grants a fee simple *determinable,* he does not part with the complete "bundle of sticks," and so he retains a type of "future interest" in himself called a "possibility of reverter," that is, there is a possibility that the property will revert to him or his heirs *if* the stated event takes place.

estate *automatically* ends and the property (the estate) reverts to A (or A's heirs if A is not living at the time) who will then own it in fee simple absolute again.

The owner of a fee simple determinable estate has all the rights and privileges that an owner in fee simple absolute would have. He may convey the estate during his lifetime or he may dispose of it by will; and if he dies without leaving a will, the estate will descend to his heirs. However, the determinable quality of the fee follows the transfer; that is to say, the new owner would hold the estate subject to losing it if the stated event occurred; a mere transfer of the estate will not destroy the determinable feature of it.

THE FEE SIMPLE SUBJECT TO A CONDITION SUBSEQUENT[15]

A fee simple subject to a condition subsequent is an estate in fee simple with a provision that *upon the happening of a stated event* the grantor shall have the *power to terminate* the estate granted.

Example:

> A, owning Blackacre in fee simple absolute, transfers it "to B and his heirs, *but on condition that if liquor is sold on the premises conveyed, then the grantor or his heirs may re-enter and repossess the premises.*" B has a fee simple subject to a condition subsequent. If B sells liquor on the premises A (or A's heirs if A is dead at the time) will have the option of terminating the estate.[16]

The fee simple determinable and the fee simple subject to a condition subsequent are obviously quite similar,[17] but there

15 The estate is also called a "fee on condition subsequent," or an "estate on condition."

16 This *right* in a grantor to terminate the granted estate upon the happening of a stated event is a type of "future interest" called a *right of entry for condition broken.*

17 Occasionally, even the courts use the terms "fee simple subject to a condition subsequent" and "fee simple determinable" interchangeably. This looseness in the use of the terms creates much confusion and should be avoided. The two estates are fundamentally different; the fee simple determinable estate ends *automatically*

is a fundamental difference between the two. The fee simple determinable *automatically* comes to an end and reverts to the grantor upon the happening of the stated event; the fee simple subject to a condition subsequent does not automatically terminate upon the happening of the stated event—it does not terminate until the grantor effectively *exercises* his right to terminate the estate. In other words, the estate *continues* despite the breach of the specified condition until there is an affirmative act of re-entry by the grantor, or until he brings a legal action to recover the land. Or to put it another way, in the case of the fee simple determinable, the candle just burns out; in the fee simple upon condition subsequent the candle must be snuffed out by the holder of the right of entry.[18] Until forfeiture of the estate is enforced by re-entry, the holder of a fee simple subject to a condition subsequent may convey or devise the property; and upon his death intestate (without a will), it will descend to his legal heirs. However, the condition remains attached to the land.

Creation of the Fee Simple Subject to a Condition Subsequent

As in the creation of the fee simple determinable, there are no particular or formal words necessary to create a fee simple subject to a condition subsequent; it is a question of the grantor's intention, to be gathered from the deed or the will. The words traditionally used are "upon express condition that," or "upon condition that," or "provided that," usually coupled with a provision that if the stated event occurs, the grantor "may re-enter and repossess the premises." The condition may call for the performance of an act, as for instance, "on condition that the grantee provide and maintain the grantor's son until he reaches the age of majority," or "providing the grantee maintains and provides for the grantor for life," or "provided the land be improved for park

upon the happening of the named event, whereas, in the case of the fee simple subject to a condition subsequent, the estate ends only at the *option* of the grantor.

18 4 THOMPSON, REAL PROPERTY § 1874 (repl. 1961).

purposes,'' or ''upon condition that the grantee support the grantor and his wife for life.''

An estate may be either a fee simple determinable or a fee simple subject to a condition subsequent, *depending upon the particular words used.* For example, a conveyance to B and his heirs ''so long as the premises are not used for the sale of liquor,'' would create a *fee simple determinable* estate in B, whereas a conveyance to B and his heirs ''upon express condition that if liquor is sold on the premises conveyed, then the grantor may re-enter and terminate the estate,'' would create a fee simple subject to a condition subsequent. Sometimes the language used in the deed or will is ambiguous and the courts are called upon to resolve the question; just which type of estate has been created is a question of the grantor's intention to be gathered from the language used in the deed or will.

A mere provision stating the motive or purpose of the conveyance, or an expression that the property is to be used for a particular purpose, will not of itself convert a fee simple absolute into a qualified fee. Thus, a devise or conveyance of real estate '' to A and his heirs, *to be used as a parsonage''* does not create a qualified fee and A takes an estate in fee simple absolute. Similarly, a deed stating that the land is being conveyed ''for school purposes,'' without more specific qualifying language, does not import a condition and the grantee takes an unqualified estate.

Even where the deed or will recites that the property is to be used for a particular purpose *only* and for no other purpose, the majority of states hold that such language does not of itself create a qualified fee. Thus where the deed provided that the premises were ''intended for a burying ground and to be used for no other purpose,'' the court, reflecting the general rule, held that the words did not create a condition subsequent but ''import merely the purpose of the parties when the conveyance was made—and their intention as to the future use to which the lot should be devoted.'' The court said that at most the words imposed "but a moral obligation" to use the premises for no other purpose than for burial, and the grantee took a fee simple absolute.[19] So in order to create a qualified fee the intent must be expressed in clear, specific, and unambiguous language.

THE FEE SIMPLE SUBJECT TO AN EXECUTORY LIMITATION[20]

A fee simple subject to an executory limitation is an estate in fee simple with a provision that *upon the happening of a stated event* the property shall pass from the grantee to some *third person.* In other words, if and when the stated event actually happens, rather than the estate reverting to the grantor, as in the case of a fee simple determinable, or giving the grantor a right of entry for condition broken, as in the case of a fee simple subject to a condition subsequent, the estate *automatically* goes over to a *third person.*

Example:

> A, owning Blackacre in fee simple absolute, transfers it "to B and his heirs, *but if B should die leaving no children surviving him, then to C and his heirs.*" B has an estate in fee simple subject to an executory limitation.

Example:

> A, owning Blackacre in fee simple absolute, transfers it "to B and his heirs *for so long as the land is used exclusively for school purposes, then to C and his heirs.*" B has an estate in fee simple subject to an executory limitation.

It should be noted at this point that qualified estates are not confined to the fee simple category which we have discussed up to now. There can be determinable *life estates,* as for example, "to B for *life,* or so long as she uses the property as her residence." And there can be an *estate for years* (a

[19] Phinney v. Gardner, 121 Me. 44, 115 Atl. 523 (1921).

[20] This estate is also called a "fee simple upon conditional limitation."

leasehold) subject to a power of termination in the lessor, as for example, "To B for five years, on condition that liquor is never served on the premises, and in the event that liquor is ever served on the premises the lessor shall have the right to terminate the lease."

Before considering the next estate it should be pointed out that not *all* conditions or limitations on an estate are allowable at law. A grantor may not attach a condition to his grant if such condition is illegal or is contrary to public policy. So a provision requiring the grantee to perform an illegal act is void. An attempted restraint of alienation is void as against public policy; for example, a condition in a conveyance that the land is not to be sold, leased, or rented to persons other than of the Caucasian race is a direct restraint upon alienation and void as against public policy. And a condition which would have the effect of placing a *total* restraint upon marriage is generally held by the courts to be contrary to public policy and void, although a reasonable, partial restraint on marriage is considered valid. For example, conditions placing a restraint on the marriage of the grantee during his or her minority, or which prohibit marriage to a particular person or a person outside of a particular religious faith, are considered not contrary to public policy; and a condition against *remarriage* imposed upon a widow is valid.

THE ESTATE IN FEE TAIL

The oddly fascinating *estate in fee tail* survives today as a kind of feudal museum piece. It was designed by the landed aristocracy in England for the purpose of keeping the land in the family. In feudal times the family estate was not only the symbol of status but also the real basis of wealth; the attempt on part of the aristocracy to keep this family wealth intact gave rise to the estate in fee tail.

You will recall that a grant "to B and his heirs" created in B an estate in fee simple absolute with complete freedom of alienation, that is, B had the right to devise the land, to sell it, or to give it away. By holding such an estate, "B" would be in a position to squander the family fortune and leave nothing for the next generation. And if "B" happened to be a not overly intelligent chap, or irresponsible, the family fortune would be placed in jeopardy as soon as "B" came into his "inheritance." The estate in fee tail was designed to prevent any dissipation of the family estate by making the grant not to "B and his heirs" but rather "to B *and the heirs of his body.*"[21] In this way, B got an estate for his lifetime only (a life estate), followed by a life estate in his eldest son, followed by a life estate in *his* eldest son, and so on down, generation after generation; it was merely a *succession of life estates.*[22]

So by being granted land in fee tail, the grantee never got more than a life estate, and neither did his son, nor his son's son, etc. It was an estate of inheritance confined to the heirs *of the body*—the estate would endure as long as there were lineal descendants of the grantee; and if the line ran out, the land would revert to the original grantor or his heirs. Through the use of the estate in fee tail, a grantor could "plant" the estate in the "biological family" and thus head off its eventual depletion by that invariably frivolous "younger generation."

Because the estate in fee tail had been tailored for the landed aristocracy in England, its reception in early America was not good; the settlers felt that it impaired the free alienability of land and so was not compatible with the new democratic philosophy. Beginning late in the eighteenth century, states began abolishing or emasculating the estate in fee tail, and in most states the fee tail has been eliminated or drastically modified by statute. Although this ghost of the

21 At a time when, under the system of primogeniture, there could be only *one* heir at a time (the eldest son), the words "heirs of his body" necessarily meant successive *generations,* not several heirs of the body in the same generation. CASNER & LEACH, CASES AND TEXT ON PROPERTY 277 (1951).

22 The *fee tail* is an estate "carved" out of a fee simple estate—it has been "cut down" to the lineal heirs. In fact, the word "tail" comes from the French word *tailler* (to carve).

past is infrequently encountered and is of little real significance today, it continues to haunt us—a vestige of feudal ingenuity.

THE ESTATE FOR LIFE

The last estate classified in the family of freehold estates is the *estate for life.* A life estate is just what you would expect it to be—an estate that will last only for the period of a lifetime. Except for the estate in fee simple absolute, the life estate is the most common freehold estate today. No particular words are necessary in the creation of a life estate so long as the language used shows an *intent* to create such an estate; and a grantor of a fee simple estate may *reserve* a life estate in himself.

The duration of the life estate may be measured by the life of the grantee himself, or it may be measured by the life of a person or persons *other* than the grantee. Thus if A, the owner in fee simple, transfers (by will or by deed) "to B for life," or "to B until he dies," or "to B during his natural life," in each case B will get an estate for his own life. However, where A, the owner in fee simple, transfers "to B for the life of C," B has a life estate, but its duration is measured by C's life. Of course C, whose life is merely used as the measuring stick, takes nothing. This is known as an estate *pur autre vie* (for the life of another.) Sometimes several people's lives are used as the measuring stick, as for example, "to B for the lives of X, Y, and Z," in which case B's estate will last until the death of the survivor of the three.

The life estate, of course, is not an estate of inheritance since it must come to an end upon the death of the life tenant[23] or the death of the person whose life has been designated as the measuring stick. A life tenant may sell his interest,[24]

23 Life estates, as well as fee simple estates, may be *defeasible* upon the happening of some event, and so, may terminate *before* the death of the life tenant. For example, a grant "to B for life, so long as she continues to live on the land," would give B a *determinable life estate* which would come to an end *before* B's death in the event she ceased to live on the land.

24 Where B, the life tenant, conveys his interest to C, C has an estate measured by *B's* life.

although, as a practical matter, a life estate is not a very marketable commodity; or he may convey lesser estates out of it, for instance, by granting an estate for years (a leasehold),[25] regardless of the number of years. Of course the life tenant cannot convey an estate *greater* than the one he has, that is, one that extends beyond the life named.

A life tenant has the right to the undisturbed possession of the land and the right to receive the rents and profits; for all practical purposes he is the "owner" of the land, except that he is not entitled to commit "waste," that is, use the land in such a way as to unreasonably reduce the value of the "following" estates or interests in the land owned by others. A life tenant who commits "waste" is liable for damages to the person having the next immediate estate. The excessive cutting of timber or the removal of earth or minerals from the land could constitute "waste."[26]

The life tenant is obligated to keep the premises in a reasonable state of repair,[27] but he is under no duty to make improvements or major repairs, or to keep the buildings insured, or to rebuild structures destroyed through no fault of his own. And the life tenant must pay the current taxes, the interest on any mortgage[28] or other encumbrance on the property, but only to the extent of the gross income of the property, or its fair rental value if he personally occupies it.

FUTURE INTERESTS

IN GENERAL

As we have seen, land "ownership" is really a concept. It is a *relationship* among people in regard to the land. A person who "owns" land is a person who has an interest *in* the

25 The lease would necessarily come to an end upon the death of the life tenant.

26 Legal "waste" is the doing of acts by one in rightful possession which cause permanent or lasting damage to the realty. Any destruction done or permitted, by the life tenant, to the lasting injury of the inheritance is "waste."

27 Failure to do so constitutes "permissive waste."

28 But he is not obligated to make payments on the principal.

land—an interest called an *estate.* And when the estate is one in fee simple absolute, the owner has the complete "bundle of sticks," or "total ownership," which he may carve into other lesser estates. But when this is done, only one of the estates will be *possessory;* as to the others the privilege of actual possession will or may be had at some time in the *future.* Accordingly, an interest in land in which the enjoyment of possession will or may be had in the *future* is called a "future interest."

The estates we have considered up to now relate to "present" interests in that they each carry the privilege of present possession; now we shall round out our study of estates by considering those interests in land in which the privilege of possession is *future* rather than present. These "future interests" are classified as follows:

(1) The Reversion
(2) The Possibility of Reverter
(3) The Right of Entry for Condition Broken
(4) The Remainder
(5) The Executory Interest

REVERSIONS

A *reversion* is simply that estate "left" in a person who transfers out *less* than his entire interest;—it is the "residue" of his estate, so to speak. So whenever an owner fails to dispose of all of his estate, there will be a reversion left in him,[29] since whatever a man does not dispose of remains in him and his heirs.

Example:

A, owning Blackacre in fee simple absolute, transfers it "to B for life," with no further provision as to disposition of the land. B has a life estate in possession. A has a future interest called a *reversion,* or a *reversonary*

[29] If A, owner in fee simple absolute, transfers to B in fee simple absolute, there can be no reversion, of course, since A transferred the complete "bundle of sticks."

interest. When B dies the land will "revert" to A.

Since A, in the above example, did not dispose of his entire interest, the reversion arises automatically—no express words are necessary to create it. Technically a reversion is not an estate that truly "reverts" but rather an estate that "remains" in a grantor; it is the *right to possession* that "reverts" to the grantor, and hence, the name of the estate. The grantor is, in effect, merely "waiting" to again possess the land. And because his right to actual possession is postponed to some future time (when the life estate ends), the reversion is called a "future interest."

For a reversion to arise, the grantor need not have a fee simple; a life tenant may also have a reversion. For example, if A has a life estate and grants to B an estate for years (a leasehold), A would have a reversion, since an estate for years (regardless of the number of years) is a lesser estate than a life estate.[30]. And if B, in turn, transfers an estate for a lesser number of years (a sublease), B would also have a reversion.

In all states reversions are alienable (transferable by deed), devisable, (transferable by will), and descendable (capable of being inherited), and the owner of a reversion may maintain an action for waste.

THE POSSIBILITY OF REVERTER

A *possibility of reverter* is the interest which is left in a person who creates a fee simple determinable estate. You will recall that a fee simple determinable is an estate which is to last only until the happening of a named event.

Example:

> A, owning Blackacre in fee simple absolute, transfers it "to B and his heirs, so long as the premises are used exclusively for religious purposes." B has an estate in fee simple determinable. If the premises ever cease to be

[30] Of course, when the life estate comes to an end the estate for years will automatically terminate, regardless of the fact that, according to its terms, there would be several years left to run.

> "used exclusively for religious purposes," B's estate will *automatically* come to an end and the property (the estate) will revert to A. A is left with a future interest called a *possibility of reverter*. It is called a possibility of reverter because there is a possibility that, sometime in the future, the estate will cease to be used exclusively for religious purposes, in which event, the estate will *automatically* revert to A (or to A's heirs if he is no longer living at the time).

In most states a possibility of reverter is freely transferable. However, a minority of states take the view that a possibility of reverter is not an estate at all but rather a mere *possibility* of becoming an estate at some future time, and as such it is not transferable by deed. In just about every state a possibility of reverter will descend to the holder's heirs, but a few states do not allow it to be devised.

THE RIGHT OF ENTRY FOR CONDITION BROKEN

A *right of entry for condition broken*[31] is the interest which is left in a person who creates an estate subject to a condition subsequent. The right of entry is not technically a "right" but rather a *power to terminate* the granted estate upon breach of the condition.

Example:

> A, owning Blackacre in fee simple absolute, transfers it "to B and his heirs upon the express condition that if liquor is sold on the premises, the grantor or his heirs may re-enter and repossess the premises." B has a fee simple subject to a condition subsequent and A retains a future interest called a *right of entry for condition broken.*

Upon a breach of the condition (the sale of liquor) the estate in B will continue until A (or A's heirs if he is not living at the time) elects to terminate B's estate by making an entry on the

[31] The right of entry for condition broken is also called a "power of termination."

land or by bringing an action to recover it. Thus A has the *power to terminate* B's estate, or what is called a *right of entry for condition broken.*

In a majority of states the right of entry for condition broken is not transferable by deed.[32] Moreover, in some states any attempt to transfer a right of entry will extinguish it. However, according to the majority rule a right of entry is both descendable and devisable, although a few states do not even allow it to be devised.

Over the years both the *possibility of reverter* and the *right of entry for condition broken* have created considerable difficulty in determining the status of land titles. Both of these "future interests" can continue for an indefinite period of time, and so they have a tendency to clog up titles and impede land development. Consequently several states have passed statutes limiting the *duration* of these interests. These statutes of limitation usually vary from thirty to forty years. Their effect is to convert the fee simple determinable and the fee simple subject to a condition subsequent into fees simple *absolute* after the prescribed period of time.

THE REMAINDER

A *remainder* is an interest which is created in a person *other than* the grantor (or testator); it is a "future interest" because the right to actual possession must "wait" until the estate "ahead of it" comes to an end. Thus a transfer from A "to B for life, then to C and his heirs" would create in C a future interest called a *remainder;* C's right to actually possess and enjoy the land must "wait its turn" until the termination of B's life estate.

You will note that the future interests considered up to now (the reversion, possibility of reverter, and right of entry for condition broken) arose because the grantor had transfered

[32] However, both the possibility of reverter and the right of entry for condition broken may be *released* to the holder of the defeasible fee, thus giving him a fee simple absolute by way of "merger" of the present and future estates.

less than his entire interest, and so the "residue" of the estate stayed with him. The *remainder,* on the other hand, is an interest created in favor of someone *other than* the grantor—in favor of a *third person.*

Example:

> A, owning Blackacre in fee simple absolute, transfers it "to B for life, then to C and his heirs." B has a life estate and C has a *remainder in fee simple.* C's future interest is called a *remainder* because upon the expiration of B's life estate the property, or more accurately, the residue of the estate, will *not* revert to A but will *remain away* from him—it will go to C who is called a "remainderman." The estate "remains away" from the grantor.

Remainders are classified as being either *vested* or *contingent.* A remainder is "vested" if there is no uncertainty as to the identification[33] of the taker (remainderman) and there are no conditions to be fulfilled before the remainderman can take possession, other than the termination of the prior estate.[34] However, if there is an uncertainty in respect to the identity of the remainderman or the right to possession is dependent upon some event which is uncertain to happen, or

33 The identification may be uncertain because the remainderman is either unborn or because some event, such as survival to a certain time, must occur before it can be determined who is to take the remainder. Example: "To B for life, then to B's first child and his heirs." B is childless at the time of the grant. There is a *contingent* remainder in B's yet unborn first child; upon the birth of the child, he (the child) will have a *vested* remainder.

34 "Vested" remainders are classified as either being (1) *absolutely vested,* (2) *vested subject to partial divestment,* or (3) *vested subject to complete divestment.* A remainder is absolutely vested when it is to an identifiable person and has no condition attached to it, as for example, "A to B for life, remainder to C and his heirs." C's remainder is absolutely vested. A remainder is vested subject to being partially divested when the remainderman's *share* is subject to being *diminished* in favor of others. Thus a devise from A "to B for life, then to the children of X." At the time of A's death X has one child. The child has a vested remainder *subject to partial divestment* because he will have to *share* the gift with any later born brothers or sisters. A remainder may be vested but subject to being totally divested, as for example, "to B for life, then to C and his heirs, but if C is not lawfully married at the time of B's death, then to X and his heirs."

upon a condition which may not be performed, the remainder is *contingent.* In other words a remainder is vested when there is nothing to interfere with the remainderman's taking possession immediately upon the termination of the prior estate. A contingent remainder is one that has a contingency attached to it.

Example:

A, owning Blackacre in fee simple absolute, transfers it "to B for life, then to C and his heirs." C has a vested remainder in fee simple since no condition has to be fulfilled for C's estate to "fall in," other than the death of B.[35]

Example:

A, owning Blackacre in fee simple absolute, transfers it "to B for life, then to C and his heirs, *if C marries X.*" C has a *contingent* remainder in fee simple. It is called a contingent remainder because it is contingent upon C marrying X. If and when the marriage between C and X takes place, C's contingent remainder will become a "vested" remainder and he will be entitled to immediate possession upon B's death.[36] And now you know how the land barons provided for their less attractive daughters.

Example:

From A "to B for life, remainder to the first son of C who reaches the age of twenty-one, and his heirs." C is childless at the time. Here *both* contingencies must be met: (1) A son must be born to C, and (2) the son must live to be twenty-one years of age. When both conditions are met the remainder will *vest* in the son but not before. If the contingencies are not met the estate will revert to A

35 If the transfer had been "to B for life, remainder to C *for life,*" C would have a vested *life* estate in remainder.

36 As long as C's remainder is contingent there will be a *reversion* in A; but the "vesting" of C's remainder operates to destroy the reversion in A. And if C dies before B, his *vested* remainder will pass to his heirs or devisees, unless C transfers it during his lifetime.

or his successors in title.

Vested remainders have always been transferable by deed or by will, but under the early common law a *contingent* remainder was considered to be a mere naked possibility and, as such, was not transferable. However, over the centuries the rule slowly changed in favor of the transferability of contingent future interests, and in most states today the owner of a *contingent* remainder may transfer it by will or by deed. In several states there are statutes which specifically provide for the transfer of contingent interests.

THE EXECUTORY INTEREST[37]

You will recall that when we took up the estate known as the *fee simple subject to an executory limitation* one of the examples used was: "To B and his heirs, but if B should die leaving no children surviving him, then to C and his heirs." This gave B an estate in fee simple subject to an executory limitation. But what interest does C have? C has a future interest in the land known as an *executory interest.*[38] Of course, if B dies leaving children, C's "future interest" will be extinguished forever. But if B dies leaving *no* surviving children, the estate will "shift over" to C.[39]

Since C's right to receive the land is "contingent" upon B's dying *without* children, you are probably now wondering what the difference is between an *executory interest* and a *contingent remainder.* Although the distinction is of little practical significance today, the remainder, you will recall, is an interest which must "wait" until the estate "ahead of it" comes to an end. The executory interest, on the other hand, *displaces* or "cuts short" the estate ahead of it.

37 Sometimes called an "executory *limitation.*"

38 When the transfer is by deed C's interest is called an executory interest; when the transfer is by will, C's interest is called an executory *devise.*

39 An executory interest may be limited to take effect on the expiration of a fee simple *determinable,* as for example, "to B and his heirs so long as the land is used for residential purposes, and if during B's lifetime the land is not so used, then to C and his heirs." B has a fee simple determinable and C has an executory interest.

It will be recalled that a transfer "to B for life, then to C and his heirs if C marries X" gives C a *remainder,* contingent upon his marrying X; but even if the marriage takes place and the remainder becomes "vested," C's possession and enjoyment would have to "wait" until the termination of B's life estate. Now compare that situation with a transfer "to B *and his heirs,* but if B dies leaving no surviving children, then to C and his heirs." Here C's interest is *not* a remainder—it is an *executory interest* which displaces or cuts short B's *fee simple* estate.[40]

In most states today executory interests are transferable by deed, devisable by will, and descendible on the death of the owner intestate.

SUMMARY

Our modern system of land "ownership" is patterned after the English theory of *estates.* The word "estate" refers to the nature and extent of a person's *interest in land;* a person who "owns" land is a person who has an interest *in* the land—an *interest* called an *estate.*

Estates are classified according to their potential duration, measured in terms of years, lives, or events; an estate in land is "land for a time."

The present landholding system in the United States is comprised of the following estates:

FREEHOLD ESTATES
- The fee simple absolute
- The fee simple determinable
- The fee simple subject to a condition subsequent
- The fee simple subject to an executory limitation
- The fee tail
- The estate for life

---

40 One of the distinctions between a remainder and an executory interest is that a remainder follows a life estate or less, while an executory interest follows a *fee* (a fee simple subject to an executory limitation).

NON-FREEHOLD ESTATES	Estates for years Periodic estates Estates at will The tenancy at sufferance

The *fee simple absolute* estate is an unqualified estate of potentially *infinite* duration. At early common law, to create this type of estate by *deed* it was essential that the deed be made to the grantee " and his heirs." However, the common law rule requiring the technical words "and his heirs" to transfer a fee simple estate by deed has been abolished in nearly all of the United States.

The *fee simple determinable* is an estate in fee simple created to last only until the happening of a stated event. If the stated event occurs, the estate will *automatically* revert to the grantor.

The *fee simple subject to a condition subsequent* is a fee simple which is subject to the grantor's power to terminate the estate upon the happening of a stated event. If the stated event occurs, the estate will continue in the grantee until the grantor *exercises* his power of termination.

The *fee simple subject to an executory limitation* is an estate in fee simple with a provision that, upon the happening of a stated event, the property shall automatically "shift over" to some *third person.*

The *fee tail* is an estate which is "cut down" or restricted to the grantee and his lineal descendants. In most states today the fee tail estate has either been abolished or drastically modified by statute.

An estate for *life* is an estate having a duration measured by the life or lives of one or more persons. The life tenant is entitled to the exclusive possession of the property and its income; however, a life tenant who causes permanent damage, or *waste,* to the freehold is liable for damages.

The estates considered above relate to "present" interests

in that the owners of such estates enjoy the privilege of *present possession.* Interests in land in which the privilege of possession will or may be had in the *future* are called "future interests," and are classified as follows:

(1) The reversion

(2) The possibility of reverter

(3) The right of entry for condition broken

(4) The remainder

(5) The executory interest

A *reversion* is that estate "left" in a person who transfers out *less* than his entire interest. Such person is said to retain a future interest called a "reversion" because at some future time the right to possession will *revert* to him.

A *possibility of reverter* is that interest which is left in a person who creates a fee simple determinable estate. There is always the *possibility* that, at some time in the *future,* the stated event will occur, causing the estate to automatically revert to the grantor—hence, the term "possibility of reverter."

A *right of entry for condition broken* is that interest which is left in a person who creates an estate subject to a condition subsequent. There is the *possibility* that, at some time in the *future,* the stated event will occur, thus giving the grantor the right to re-enter and repossess the property if he wishes to do so.

A *remainder* is an interest (created by a transferor in favor of a third person) which *follows* the natural termination of a prior possessory estate; the "remainderman's" right to actual possession must "wait" for the prior estate to end. If there are no conditions to be fulfilled (other than the termination of the prior estate) before the remainderman can take possession, the remainder is said to be *vested;* a remainder with a condition attached to it is called a *contingent* remainder.

An *executory interest* is an interest created in favor of a third person which, upon the happening of a stated event, will displace or cut short the prior possessory estate and vest in the third person.

line 896

CHAPTER 4

LANDLORD AND TENANT (LEASES)

INTRODUCTORY STATEMENT

In chapter three we considered the various estates in land which make up our present landholding system: the estates in fee simple, fee tail and estates for life. Those estates were, and still are, classified as *freehold* estates. The term "freehold" is thought to derive from the fact that under the early feudal system such estates were considered to be estates of dignity; they were held by "freemen" who were entitled to the full protection of the king's court. We now turn our attention to the so-called *non*-freehold estates, generally referred to as "leaseholds." Leasehold estates were not really considered part of the feudal landholding pattern at all; they were merely contractual rights in the *use* of land as opposed to creating an actual *interest in* the land. In fact, leasehold estates were, and are still today, classified as personal property and not realty.

A leasehold estate arises when an owner of an estate in land transfers possession of the property to another for a period of time. The transaction, called a lease, creates the relationship of landlord and tenant and the parties are referred to as lessor and lessee. Leaseholds involve two areas of law: the law of real property and the law of contracts. In a way a lease is both a conveyance and a contract; it conveys a possessory interest in the land and it also creates a contractual relationship between the landlord (lessor) and the tenant (lessee).

CLASSIFICATION OF LEASEHOLD ESTATES

There are four basic types of leasehold estates, classified according to the period of their potential duration. They are:

(1) Estates for Years
(2) Periodic Estates
(3) Estates at Will
(4) The Tenancy at Sufferance

Estates for Years

The estate for years is one which is to continue for a fixed or definite period of time, regardless of the length of the period; it may be for a day, a month, a year or a thousand years—it is still called an *estate for years*. The fact that it is called an estate for *years* may be somewhat misleading since the duration of the estate may be for years or it may be for a period less than a year. The criterion is simply that the term must be fixed and certain; it must have a fixed beginning and ending. Thus any lease for a definite period is called an estate for years, regardless of the length of the period.

As in the case of estates in fee simple and for life, estates for years may be qualified—that is, they may be made subject to termination *before* the term expires upon the happening or non-happening of a specified event. Thus, there may be a determinable estate for years, or there may be an estate for years subject to a "condition subsequent" or an executory limitation. In fact, most estates for years *are* created subject to a condition subsequent, allowing the lessor the right to terminate the lease upon the breach of any of the conditions specified in the lease.

No technical or formal words are necessary to create a leasehold estate. Any language by which the possession of land is transferred for a specified term at a stipulated rental is in effect a "lease." Under early common law a leasehold estate could be created verbally no matter how long the term. However, the original English Statute of Frauds (1677) changed this by providing that all leases for a period of more than three years must be in writing to be enforceable. Any lease of more than three years which was not in writing was treated as a *tenancy at will*, terminable at the will of either party at any time. Today, in most states, leases for a term of *more than one year* must be in writing. A few states permit oral leases for a term up to three years, yet a few other states in effect prohibit oral leases by providing that an oral lease for any period creates only a tenancy at will. Nearly all states have statutes requiring that leases for longer than a specified period (usually two to seven years) be recorded in the registry of deeds.

Since an estate for years is a lease for a fixed term, it cannot be terminated (except by mutual consent) before the expiration of the term, unless of course there is a provision or an option contained in the lease providing for termination. Upon expiration of the term the estate for years will terminate without notice. The estate for years does not terminate upon the death of the tenant. In such case the leasehold estate passes to the personal representative of the lessee and his estate remains liable under the terms of the lease.

Periodic Estates

A periodic estate (also referred to as an estate from period to period) is one that continues for successive *periods* until it is terminated by proper notice. The period may be a year or a fraction of a year. The most common type of periodic estate is the estate from year to year. Other types are the estate from month to month and from week to week, depending upon the particular unit of duration. The chief characteristic of the periodic estate is the element of continuity. Unlike the estate for years, which automatically ends at the expiration of its specified term, the periodic estate, once created, does not terminate at the end of any particular period of time; it continues along indefinitely for successive periods until one of the parties elects to terminate the tenancy by giving proper notice.

Periodic estates may be created by an express agreement between the parties,[1] as for example where A leases land to B "to hold as a tenant from year to year." This would expressly invest B with a periodic estate—an estate from year to year. Or a lease for a fixed term may be followed by a periodic tenancy. For example, if A were to lease land to B "for a term of three years, to continue from year to year thereafter," this would create a lease for a fixed term of three years (an estate for years) to be followed by a periodic estate (from year to year).

Mostly, however, periodic estates arise by implication. For example, where the lease fails to specify the duration of the tenancy but the rent is payable on a monthly basis, the result would be a tenancy from month to month. In other words, where the premises are leased for an indefinite time but the rent is payable periodically—yearly, quarterly, monthly etc.—the way the rent is paid determines the period.

Example:

> A leases his residence to B for an indefinite period with the rent payable monthly. This would ordinarily create a periodic tenancy by implication and B would be a tenant from month to month.

Occasionally a lessee will take possession under a lease which is invalid, either because it does not comply with the statute of frauds or because of some other reason. In such cases only a tenancy at will (discussed later) arises. However, in most states, upon the payment of rent by the tenant, the tenancy at will becomes a periodic tenancy by implication, the period determined by the way the rent is actually paid.

Example:

> A leases Blackacre to B for a term of ten years. However, the lease is invalid because it was not witnessed and recorded in accordance with the local statutory

1 In fact, in a few states this is the *only* way they can be created.

requirement. However, B makes his first quarterly rental payment under the terms of the lease. In most states the acceptance of the rent by A would convert the tenancy at will into a periodic estate, and a tenancy from quarter to quarter would result.[2]

Periodic estates quite frequently arise by implication when a tenant "holds over" after the expiration of an estate for years. A "holdover" tenant is one who continues in possession after his lease has expired. When a tenant "holds over" the landlord has an option: he may treat him as a trespasser and evict him, or he may continue to consider him as a tenant. If the landlord elects to recognize the holdover as a tenant (usually by accepting rent from him) a periodic tenancy arises by implication. In most states such holdover tenancies are converted into estates from year to year if the term of the original lease was for a year or longer. However, if the original lease was for a term *less* than a year, the period is determined by the manner in which the rent was actually payable; if payable monthly, then the tenancy would be one from month to month, etc.

Example:

A leases Blackacre to B for a term of three years. After the expiration of the three-year term B continues in possession of the premises. Thereafter A continues to accept monthly rental payments from B. B is a tenant from year to year.[3]

Example:

A leases land to B for a period of ten months, rent payable monthly. At the expiration of the ten-month period B continues to occupy the land with the consent of A. B is a tenant from month to month.

[2] In a few states oral or invalid leases can create only a tenancy at will, regardless of how the rent is paid.

[3] In a *few* states the term of the periodic tenancy is *entirely* governed by how the rent was payable under the original lease; if the rent was payable monthly, then the holdover tenant becomes a tenant from month to month.

We have defined a periodic estate as one that continues for successive periods until it is terminated by proper notice. But what constitutes "proper notice"? The early common law required a six-month notice to terminate a tenancy from year to year; and where the period was for less than a year a notice equal to the length of the period was required. Thus a tenancy from month to month required a month's notice, a tenancy from week to week required a week's notice, etc. However, today the length of notice required to terminate a periodic tenancy is generally governed by the statutes of the various states. The length of notice required to terminate an estate from year to year varies considerably from state to state, ranging from a minimum of thirty days to a maximum of six months. For tenancies involving lesser periods the required notice is generally thirty days, although there is some variation among the states here also.

Whatever the required notice may be, it must be such as to terminate the estate at the *end* of a period and not some intervening date. For example, in Maine a notice of six months is required to terminate a tenancy from year to year.[4] Thus, in that state a year-to-year tenancy which began on, say, January 1 could only be terminated by notice given no later than the preceding July 1; a notice given on July 15 to terminate on January 15 would not be effective. In other words, to be effective the giving of the notice must precede the *end* of the term by the length of the notice period required by statute. Although in a few states only the landlord is required to give notice, in most states whichever party wishing to terminate must give notice in order to terminate a periodic tenancy.

As in the case of the estate for years, a periodic tenancy does not terminate upon the death of either the landlord or the tenant.

4 State v. Fin & Feather Club, Me., 316 A2d 351 (1974).

Estates at Will

An estate at will (tenancy at will) is an estate which may be terminated at the will of either the landlord or the tenant and which has no specified period of duration. Although an estate at will lasts only while both parties wish to continue it, it is classified as an estate because, while it exists, the tenant has the exclusive right to possession; he may bring an action for trespass against persons (including the landlord) interfering with his possession.

Estates at will may be created by express agreement that the tenancy shall exist only so long as both parties wish it to, as where A transfers possession of the premises "to B at the will of A." However, a tenancy at will is seldom created by express agreement; almost invariably it arises by legal implication. For example, where a tenant takes possession for an indefinite period and without any specific agreement as to the payment of rent, a tenancy at will arises. However, upon the payment of rent by the tenant the tenancy at will would (in most states) be converted into a periodic tenancy for a term equal to the rent-paying period. And where a lessee takes possession under an invalid lease, he usually does so as a tenant at will, at least until he commences his rental payments, at which time he would (in most states) become a tenant from period to period.

Another situation in which a tenancy at will may arise by implication is where a purchaser of land enters into possession before he receives the legal title; until the purchaser receives the legal title he is generally considered to occupy as a tenant at will. Tenancies at will are also created by legal implication as a result of various state statutes. For example, some state statutes provide, in effect, that any person in possession of real estate with the consent of the owner is presumed to be a tenant at will until the contrary is shown. And in a few states, by statute, all leases not in writing create only a tenancy at will, regardless of how the rent is paid. In these states a tenant who continues to occupy the premises with the consent of the lessor after the expiration of a written lease is a tenant at will, and the payment of rent will not convert it into a periodic tenancy as it would in most states.

Under common law an estate at will could be terminated without any notice whatever. The tenant was allowed just enough time to remove his personal belongings. Today, however, most states require that either party wishing to terminate a tenancy at will must give some advance notice in writing, usually equal to the rent-paying period or at least thirty days. The purpose of notice statutes is to prevent breaches of the peace which often result from abrupt terminations; they allow the tenant a reasonable time to find other accommodations, and also seasonably advise the landlord of the tenant's intention to vacate so that another tenant might be engaged.[5]

In addition to termination through statutory notice, an estate at will terminates automatically upon the death of either the landlord or the tenant. Also, a sale or lease of the premises by the landlord usually terminates an estate at will. In such cases the tenancy comes to an end by operation of law and the statutory notice is not required. However, it should be pointed out that there is considerable variation among the states with respect to the termination of tenancies at will; in each case the applicable state statute must be consulted.

The Tenancy at Sufferance

The tenancy at sufferance is a possessory interest in land which arises when a person who previously held an estate in land *wrongfully remains* in possession after the termination of his estate. For example, a tenant for years who wrongfully

[5] The typical lodging agreement, as in the case of a hotel guest, does not create a tenancy at will and the lodger is not a tenant, even though his stay may be a long one and he pays on a weekly or monthly basis; his right to occupy the room or rooms may be terminated without notice. However, where a room is rented under circumstances where the occupant retains exclusive possession and control, the relationship of landlord and tenant will arise. But where the owner of the building retains keys to the room in order to have access for the purpose of supplying maid service and other services, he has control and the occupant is a mere lodger.

continues in possession after the expiration of the lease is a tenant at sufferance; and a tenant at will whose tenancy has been terminated either by the prescribed statutory notice in writing or by operation of law (death of the landlord or sale or lease of the premises) becomes merely a tenant at sufferance. Thus a tenant at sufferance is sometimes referred to as a "holdover" tenant. He is not really a tenant at all but is one step removed from a trespasser; he differs from a trespasser only in that his *original* entry into possession was lawful.

Although the tenancy at sufferance has always been included in the catalogue of estates, this flimsy interest is really no "estate" at all; it is only naked possession, without right. In the case of a tenant at sufferance the landlord may elect one of the following options: (1) he may treat him as a trespasser and evict him forthwith (in which case the tenant is not even entitled to a notice to vacate the premises) or (2) he may continue to recognize him as a tenant (usually by accepting rent) and thereby create (in most states) a periodic tenancy by implication.

ESSENTIALS OF A VALID LEASE

The relationship of landlord and tenant is created by an express or implied contract[6] between the parties—a contract called a lease. No technical or formal words are necessary so long as the intent to establish the relationship is clear. Keep in mind, however, that statutes in most states require that leases for *more than one year* must be in writing.[7] Although the

6 An *express* contract is one in which the terms have been expressly stated in distinct and explicit language, either verbally or in writing. An *implied* contract is one in which the terms are not expressly stated in words but which may be inferred from the *conduct* of the parties and the circumstances surrounding the transaction.

7 As to the formalities of executing a written lease, the various states differ. A few states require that they be executed with the same formality as deeds. And some states require that leases for longer than a stipulated period (usually two to seven years) must be recorded in the registry of deeds. However, as a substitute for recording the entire lease itself, a few of these states permit the recording of a brief *memorandum of lease*. The recording of such memorandum constitutes notice to the public of the existence of the lease just as effec-

writing need not be in any particular form, it is essential that it contain at least the names of the *parties*, an adequate *description*[8] of the leased premises, the *term*[9] of the lease and the amount of *rent* to be paid.

In addition to the essential terms mentioned above, most leases (especially long-term leases) generally contain a wide variety of other provisions dealing with such subjects as taxes, insurance, repairs, fixtures, restrictions on the use of the premises, assignment and subleasing, renewals, extensions, options to purchase, etc. The growing complexities of our modern society and the increasing use of long-term leases as a device for financing and to minimize income taxes have given a new dimension to the importance of leasehold interests. The modern lease can be and often is a highly complex multi-page document, bristling with provisions, covenants and conditions in the attempt to provide for all possible and foreseeable contingencies.

RIGHTS, DUTIES & LIABILITIES OF LANDLORD & TENANT

As to the Use of The Premises

tively as if it had been recorded in full, but without disclosing facts of a confidential nature, such as the amount of the rental, etc.

8 The lease must describe the premises with sufficient certainty as to indicate what is being leased. As a general rule of law, oral evidence will not be permitted to add to, vary or contradict the terms of a written lease; when a lease is reduced to writing there is a legal presumption that the writing contains the whole agreement. For example, testimony relating to an oral agreement purporting to include more or different premises than was described in the written lease would not be admissible in evidence. However, if the written lease appears on its face to be ambiguous or incomplete, or if it is uncertain from the language used what premises are included in the description, then oral evidence is admissible for the purposes of identifying the premises leased. Thus where the premises leased are referred to merely by street number or by the name of an apartment building, oral evidence is admissible to establish the extent of the premises leased.

Ordinarily a lease of a building, unless the lease states otherwise, includes the land on which the building stands together with so much of the surrounding real estate as is necessary for the use of the property as intended.

9 The "term" of a lease (the period for which it is to run) should be specified precisely. The lease must fix the date the term is to begin and its duration.

During the term of the lease the tenant, for all practical purposes, is the owner of the premises. He has the sole and exclusive right to possession and the landlord has no authority to enter the premises or otherwise disturb the tenant. If the landlord enters the leased premises without the consent of the tenant he is a trespasser.

The tenant has an implied obligation to use the premises in a tenantlike manner and to exercise reasonable care to prevent damage to the landlord's reversion. The tenant must not use the property in such a way as to cause any permanent or lasting damage to the realty. To do so constitutes "waste" for which the tenant will be liable in damages.

A tenant may not make material alterations to a leased building merely to suit his own taste or to adapt the building to a use different from that for which it was originally constructed or used.[10] Some states take the view that any material alteration of a building by a tenant constitutes "waste" even though the value of the premises is increased thereby.[11] Other states hold the view that to constitute "waste" the alterations must be such as to actually diminish the value of the property. Of course, where the lease contains express provisions regarding alterations by the tenant such provisions will control. Subject to the above qualifications the tenant may put the premises to any reasonable use he wishes, provided the use is not illegal[12] or prohibited by the terms of the lease.

10 Of course the tenant may decorate the premises in accordance with his own taste and needs so long as he does no permanent damage to them.

11 This is known as "meliorating" waste.

12 A lease made for an illegal purpose (for example, the illegal sale of liquor, prostitution, etc.,) is void from the beginning because it is against public policy. But what if the purpose was legal at the time the lease was executed but became illegal sometime thereafter? If the lease expressly restricts the tenant to *one* particular use which subsequently becomes illegal, the lease terminates on the ground that performance has become legally impossible. However, if only one of several uses subsequently becomes illegal the lease does *not* terminate. In order for a lease to terminate on the ground that the use to which the premises can be put has become illegal, the illegality must

The landlord of course has a right to control his own property and may, by a restrictive clause in the lease, limit the tenant's use of the premises or prohibit certain designated uses. And this is so even though the restrictions imposed may be unreasonable; it is not for the tenant to say what is reasonable and what is not. However, the law does not favor restrictions upon the use of land, so for a restrictive covenant to be effective it must be explicit and unambiguous. Any doubt as to the meaning of a restrictive clause in a lease will be resolved in favor of the tenant and against the landlord. Thus where the lease merely states the purpose for which the property is leased, the tenant will not be restricted to that particular use. Such clauses are generally regarded by the courts to be "descriptive" or "permissive" rather than restrictive. In order for the landlord to effectively limit the use of the rented premises, the lease should clearly stipulate that the premises are to be used for a specified purpose only, *and for no other purpose.*

AS TO THE CONDITION OF THE PREMISES

There is no implied warranty on part of the landlord that the leased premises are fit for occupation or that they are adaptable to the purposes for which they were rented, or even that they are in any way suitable for habitation. In the absence of an express warranty in the lease the tenant takes the premises as he finds them. In other words, unless the lease expressly so stipulates the landlord is not obligated to put the premises in a habitable condition or to make repairs. Nor is he liable for injuries resulting from the defective condition of the premises. Thus, even if the premises are wholly unfit for

relate to the *principal* business or use to which the tenant is restricted.

Example:

L leases premises to T "to be used only as a dancehall and for no other purpose." If subsequent zoning regulations effectively prohibit such use the lease will terminate.

Example:

L leases premises to T "to be used only as a restaurant and bar and for no other purpose." Subsequently the sale of liquor on the premises becomes illegal. The lease is not terminated and T remains obligated to pay the rent.

occupancy at the time they are rented, or become so later, the tenant remains liable for the rent during the full term of the lease. The reason for this is based upon the concept that a lease is a transfer of an estate in land and the tenant, like any other purchaser, must inspect, judge and test the premises for himself; either that or insist that an express warranty of fitness be included in the lease. The rule of *caveat emptor* applies: let the buyer beware.[13]

There are a few exceptions to the rule that there is no implied warranty by the landlord that the premises are in safe condition and fit for occupancy: In the case of the rental of a furnished house or apartment, or where the premises are being leased only for a short term, thereby indicating an immediate occupancy, there *is* an implied warranty that the premises shall be reasonably fit for use and occupancy. This rule derives from an old English case[14] which involved the leasing of a furnished dwelling for a short term. When the tenant was forced to abandon the premises because they were infested with bugs, the court held that he was justified in not paying the rent. The reason for *implying* a warranty of habitability and fitness in the case of furnished dwellings is that in such cases the parties usually intend an immediate occupancy, without allowing the tenant sufficient time to adequately inspect the premises.

Example:

L leases to T a furnished dwelling recently occupied by a person suffering from a serious contagious disease. Upon discovering this fact T would be justified in

13 However, with the changing conditions of our society there is now a definite trend away from the traditional common law doctrine of *caveat emptor*. About a dozen states have discarded the ancient doctrine that a landlord is under no duty to maintain the premises in a habitable condition; in its place they have adopted the position that there *is* an implied warranty of habitability in *all* leases of *residential* property. The enactment of housing codes and consumer protection laws appears to be sounding the requiem to the old doctrine of *caveat emptor* as it applies to residential leases.

14 Smith v. Marrable, 11 M. & W. 5, 152 Eng. Rep. 693 (1843).

repudiating the lease on the ground that the premises are not reasonably safe for human habitation.

In a leading Massachusetts case, the general rule and the reasons therefore are stated thusly:

> "It is well settled, both in this Commonwealth and in England, that one who lets an unfurnished building to be occupied as a dwelling house does not impliedly agree that it is fit for habitation. In the absence of fraud or a covenant, the purchaser of real estate, or hirer of it, for a term however short, takes it as it is, and determines for himself whether it will serve the purpose for which he wants it. He may, often does, contemplate making extensive repairs upon it to adapt it to his wants. But there are good reasons why a different rule should apply to one who hires a furnished room or a furnished house for a few days, weeks or months. Its fitness for immediate use of a particular kind, as indicated by its appointments, is a far more important element entering into the contract than when there is a mere lease of real estate. One who lets for a short term a house provided with furnishings and appointments for immediate residence may be supposed to contract with reference to a well understood purpose of the hirer to use it as a habitation. An important part of what the hirer pays for is the opportunity to enjoy it without delay, and without the expense of preparing it for use. It is very difficult, and often impossible, for one to determine on inspection whether the house and its appointments are fit for the use for which they are immediately wanted, and the doctrine of caveat emptor, which is ordinarily applicable to the lessee of real estate, would often work injustice if applied to cases of this kind. It would be unreasonable to hold, under such circumstances, that the landlord does not impliedly agree that what he is letting is a house suitable for occupation in its condition at the time."[15]

15 Ingalls v. Hobbs, 156 Mass. 348 (1892).

Another exception to the general rule that there is no implied warranty that leased premises are reasonably fit for habitation involves the lease of a building for a particular use and which is still under construction. Where the lease is executed before the construction or the alteration of the premises is completed, there is an implied warranty that the premises will be suitable for the intended use. The reason for this exception to the rule is that until the construction is sufficiently complete the lessee has no opportunity to ascertain by inspection whether the premises are in fact suitable for the intended use.

Although there is no implied warranty on part of the landlord that the leased premises are in reasonably fit condition suitable for occupancy (other than in those situations mentioned above), the landlord is under a duty to inform the tenant of any *hidden* defects which would make the premises dangerous. If he fails to do so he will be liable to the tenant, his family and guests, and to other invitees as well, for any injuries resulting from the defective condition. However, in order for the landlord to be liable for injuries resulting from hidden defects, it must be shown (1) that the landlord had actual knowledge of the defect, (2) that he failed to inform the tenant, and (3) that the defect was one which the tenant could not be expected to discover upon a reasonable inspection of the premises.

The Duty to Make Repairs

The landlord is under no obligation to make repairs unless the terms of the lease require him to do so, or unless a statute imposes such a duty.[16] The reason for this is that the leased premises are in the exclusive possession of the tenant and the landlord ordinarily has no right to enter, even for purposes of

[16] The law of landlord and tenant evolved from an agricultural society at a time when the land was the primary consideration and the structures were relatively unimportant. However, today in many states landlords are required by statute to make necessary repairs and to keep the premises in a condition reasonably fit for human habitation.

inspection. However, the rule that the landlord is under no duty to make repairs does not apply to those parts of the building used in common by different tenants, such as hallways, porches, stairways, elevators, walks, fire escapes, etc. Since the landlord normally retains control over these "common parts" he has the duty to exercise reasonable care to maintain them in a safe condition. If he is negligent in this regard he will be liable for any resulting personal injury to a tenant or any other person lawfully on the premises.

Although the tenant has no obligation to make substantial repairs to the leased premises, he does have the duty to make minor repairs to the extent necessary to protect the building from the elements. Thus it is the tenant's duty to keep the premises reasonably weathertight—to repair such things as broken windows and leaky roofs, and to otherwise take whatever steps are necessary to keep the premises from falling into a state of decay or dilapidation. Beyond this the tenant is not obligated to make repairs. For instance, he is not obligated to rebuild or restore any part of the premises which may have been destroyed by fire or other casualty without his fault.[17] However, the tenant does have the duty to use the premises in a tenantlike manner and to deliver them up in substantially the same condition as they were at the beginning of the term, ordinary wear and tear excepted. Thus there is a continuing duty on part of the tenant not to expose the premises to decay or ruin. Neglect of this duty constitutes *waste.* In fact any act or omission of duty by a tenant which causes permanent or lasting damage to the premises is waste. There are two types of waste: *voluntary* (sometimes called "commissive") waste and *permissive* waste. Voluntary waste involves the commission of some destructive act such as the tearing down of a structure, the removal of fences or ornamental trees, or the cutting of timber.[18] Permissive waste

17 However, if the premises are materially damaged due to the negligence or willful misconduct of the tenant, he will be liable to the landlord for the resultant damages.

18 Unless specifically allowed under the terms of the lease, any substantial

consists of mere neglect or omission to do what is necessary to prevent the property from deteriorating for lack of repairs.

As has been said, the landlord is under no obligation to make repairs unless he agrees to do so, or unless the duty to repair is imposed upon him by statute. The tenant, on the other hand, is obligated to make minor repairs but only to the extent necessary to keep the premises from falling into a state of decay or ruin. However, the parties may, and often do, expressly stipulate in the lease as to who shall make repairs. Covenants[19] concerning repairs may be expressed in any form so long as the intent of the parties is clear. For example, the lease may simply place the duty of making repairs either upon the landlord[20] or the tenant; or the lease may impose upon the the landlord the duty to make outside repairs and the tenant the duty to make inside repairs; or the lease may obligate one of the parties to make the repairs but provide for a sharing of the expense. A covenant on part of the tenant to surrender the premises in as good condition as when he received them is in effect a covenant to repair.

In some states a covenant to make repairs imposes upon the

alteration of the premises by the tenant may constitute waste even though such alteration enhances the value of the premises.

19 A "covenant" may be defined as any written agreement between two or more parties to do or not to do some specified act. There is a distinction between a "covenant" and a "condition." When a covenant is broken the remedy is an action for damages against the person who made the promise. However, a breach of a *condition* subjects the estate to forfeiture. Whether a provision in a lease is a covenant or a condition is a matter of the intention of the parties. Where the lease clearly provides that in the event of a breach the landlord may re-enter and declare a forfeiture of the estate, the clause is usually construed as a condition rather than a covenant. Whenever possible, however, courts tend to construe the language in leases as creating covenants rather than conditions. The reason for this is that courts do not favor forfeitures.

20 Ordinarily a covenant obligating the landlord to make repairs is accompanied by an express provision allowing him the privilege of entering the premises, both for the purpose of inspection and to make the necessary repairs. And since the tenant is usually in the best position to know the condition of the premises he has a duty to notify the landlord of the need for repairs, unless of course, the landlord has actual knowledge that repairs are in fact needed, in which case a notice to repair is not necessary to render the landlord liable upon his covenant to repair. However, the tenant has no duty to notify the landlord of the necessity for repairs to those portions of the premises over which the landlord retains control.

person making the covenant an obligation to *rebuild* the premises in the event they are destroyed by fire or other catastrophe, even though he is without fault. However, other states take the more reasonable view that the word "repair" does not mean "rebuild", and that a covenant to repair imposes no duty to reconstruct the premises if they are substantially destroyed by fire or the elements.[21]

If the landlord covenants to make repairs and fails to do so, the tenant is not automatically relieved from the duty to pay rent. However, he has an option: he may sue the landlord for damages[22] or he may make the necessary repairs himself and deduct the cost thereof from the rent due. Moreover, if the landlord's failure to repair renders the premises untenantable, the tenant may abandon the premises and avoid liability for future rent on the ground of constructive eviction. (The subject of constructive eviction will be discussed later in this chapter.)

Liability for Injuries to Persons on the Premises

As a general rule of law a person who has the custody and control of real estate owes a legal duty to all persons who are rightfully on the premises to maintain them in a reasonably safe condition. However, the duty extends only to invited persons; there is no duty to keep the premises safe for trespassers and others who enter without invitation.

Since under the general rule a landlord is not obligated to keep the premises in a safe or habitable condition, or to make

21 In those states where a covenant to repair does *not* impose a duty to rebuild in the event of total destruction, such an obligation may be created simply by including in the lease a covenant to *rebuild* or *restore* the premises in the event they are destroyed by fire, flood or other catastrophe. Conversely, in those states where a covenant to make repairs *does* impose the duty to rebuild in the event of destruction, this liability may be avoided by simply excepting from the covenant to repair those damages resulting from fire or the elements, etc.

22 The measure of damages is usually the difference between the rental value of the premises as they actually are and their value if they had been in the condition in which the landlord agreed to keep them. However, where the cost of the repairs is relatively slight in comparison to the rent, the measure of damages is the reasonable cost of making the repairs.

repairs, he is ordinarily not liable for injuries to persons on the premises resulting from the negligent condition of the premises. It is the tenant's responsibility to ensure the safe condition of that part of the premises over which he has exclusive possession and control. However, there are some instances where the landlord remains liable for injuries suffered by persons on the premises even though the tenant is in possession: As stated above, the landlord will be liable to the tenant and his invitees[23] for any injuries sustained as a result of concealed defects which were known to the landlord and about which he failed to notify the tenant. And, of course, the landlord continues to be responsible for the safe condition of those portions of the premises which remain under his control and which are used in common by all the tenants. Thus the tenant is not responsible to others for the safe maintenance of the common stairways, hallways, walks etc., or any other area under the landlord's control.

As to whether the landlord is liable for personal injuries sustained by the tenant and others as a result of the landlord's failure to perform his *agreement to repair*, the states are sharply divided. Most states hold that there is no liability. However, there is a growing number of states which hold that a landlord who has agreed to keep the premises in repair *is* liable to the tenant and to his invitees as well for any injuries sustained by them as a result of the landlord's failure to perform his agreement.[24]

In just about every state, a landlord who has not agreed to make repairs but who nevertheless undertakes to do so and does the job *carelessly* is liable for any resulting injury to the tenant or his invitees.

23 "Invitees" include guests and all persons entering the premises under an express or implied invitation to conduct business.

24 The duties owed by a landlord to a tenant's family, his guests and invitees, are the same as those owed to the tenant himself. Persons rightfully on the premises by the consent of the tenant stand in his shoes; such persons have no greater rights as against the landlord to recover for injuries due to the defective condition of the premises than the tenant himself would have. If the tenant could not maintain an action against the landlord, then neither can they.

The fact that the landlord may have expressly covenanted to keep the premises in repair is no defense in an action against the tenant by a person injured because of the negligent condition of the premises; the tenant remains liable. But to hold either a landlord or a tenant liable for an injury sustained on the premises it must be shown by the injured party that the landlord or tenant was at fault in that he failed to exercise due care to prevent the injury. Moreover, the injured party must himself have been free of contributory negligence when he sustained the injury.

Exculpatory Clauses

Leases often contain clauses purporting to excuse the landlord from any liability for property damage or personal injuries sustained by a tenant as a result of the condition of the premises. These are known as *exculpatory* clauses and the states are in nearly hopeless disagreement as to their validity. Some states refuse to enforce such clauses on the ground that it is against public policy to allow a person to contract away his liability for his own negligence. Other states uphold them on the theory that the landlord and tenant relationship is a private affair and the parties should be free to contract as they wish. Perhaps the safest course of action for the landlord is to carry appropriate types of liability insurance.

Tenant's Obligation to Pay Rent

The word "rent" derives from the Latin *reditus*, meaning the return from the use or occupation of real estate. The rent need not be payable in money; it may be in the form of goods or services, such as a share of the crops or the performance of labor or other specified services. However, its most common form is money payable at a specified time.

Where the lease fails to specify the *time* of payment, the rent does not become due and payable until the end of the term. And if the lease provides for the rental to be paid monthly, quarterly, or yearly, but fails to specify any particular time of payment during such periods, the rent is not due and payable until the *end* of those respective rental periods. However, most leases stipulate that the rent shall be payable *in advance*, usually on a monthly or quarterly basis. In a few states (by statute), unless the lease expressly provides otherwise, all rent is due and payable in advance. Where the rent is payable on a certain day, the tenant has until midnight of that day in which to make payment. If the date on which the rent is payable falls on a Sunday, the general rule is that the time for payment is extended to the following Monday. Where the lease fails to stipulate the *place* at which the rent is to be paid, it is payable at the leased premises.

Of course the parties are free to stipulate as to the amount of the rental and when it is to be paid. With respect to the manner in which the rent is determined, there are three basic types of leases: the *gross* lease, the *net* lease and the *percentage* lease. A "gross" lease is one in which the tenant pays a fixed rental and the landlord pays the taxes and insurance and all other costs of operating and maintaining the property. Under a "net" lease the tenant, in addition to paying the rent, assumes responsibility for all costs of operating and maintaining the property, including taxes and insurance; thus the rental income is "net" to the landlord. In the case of a "percentage" lease (designed to allow the tenant to adjust to fluctuating business conditions) the rental is based upon some specified percentage of gross sales or net profits received by the tenant from a business conducted on the leased premises, usually in addition to a flat minimum rental. Under a percentage lease the tenant has an implied duty to maintain accurate business records and to make them available to the landlord. Percentage leases require careful drafting, especially with respect to such terms as "gross sales," "net earnings" etc.

When Premises Are Destroyed By Fire

At common law and in most states today, unless the lease

provides otherwise a tenant is not excused from paying rent if the buildings on the land are accidentally destroyed by fire or other casualty. The reason for this rule is that during the term of the lease the tenant is considered to be the owner of an estate in land and as such he should suffer the risk of loss as any "owner" must. Another reason for the rule is that although the use of the building may be the principal element of value, the lease is actually a lease of *land*, and as long as the tenant is able to enjoy the exclusive possession of the land his obligation to pay rent continues.[25]

The rule that the accidental destruction of the building does not excuse the tenant from paying rent does not apply to the lease of a single room or an apartment. The destruction of a building will terminate the lease of a room or an apartment therein because in such a case the destruction of the leased premises is *complete*; nothing remains in existence for the tenant to occupy. For the same reason a lease of a building which expressly excludes the underlying land is terminated upon a total destruction of the building.

Several states have refused to follow the majority rule that liability for rent continues if the building is destroyed through no fault of the tenant. In these states where a substantial portion of the building is destroyed or rendered untenantable

25 Does the receipt of insurance money by the landlord following a destruction of the leased premises have any effect upon the tenant's liability to pay rent? There are two rules: Some states support the view that the tenant must continue to pay rent and cannot compel the landlord to use the insurance money to restore the premises; and this is so even though the tenant was obligated under the lease to keep the premises insured for the benefit of the landlord. Under this view, after the premises have burned down and the landlord has collected the insurance, the tenant nevertheless remains obligated to pay the rent, even though the landlord refuses to rebuild, provided the landlord is under no duty to repair. Other states take a different view, however, holding that where the tenant has agreed to keep the premises insured for the benefit of the landlord, and the premises are destroyed, the tenant is absolved from further liability to pay rent. However, the results can be controlled by the terms of the lease. For example, the lease could obligate the landlord or the tenant to keep the buildings insured against fire or other casualty and upon damage or destruction to use the proceeds to rebuild. The covenant imposing the duty to insure should specify the amount of insurance and the disposition to be made of the proceeds.

through no fault of the tenant he is relieved of further liability for rent; or if the tenant remains in possession of the premises after a partial or total destruction of the building, the rent will be proportionately reduced.

In view of the hardship of the majority rule holding the tenant liable for rent even if the building is accidentally destroyed by fire or other casualty, most leases expressly provide for such a contingency; the parties usually include a stipulation releasing the tenant from liability for rent in the event the premises are totally or partially destroyed as to be unfit for occupancy.

Landlord's Remedies for Non-payment of Rent

At common law the landlord could enforce the payment of rent by seizing the tenant's chattels and holding them as security until the rent was paid. The remedy had its origin in the feudal tenures and was known as the landlord's right of *distress*. "Distress" is the taking of another's personal property for holding or sale in order to satisfy a claim for overdue rent. The right to "distrain" for rent was never looked upon with favor in the United States, mostly because of the opportunity it affords for injustice and oppression. In most states the old common law remedy of distraint has either been abolished completely or modified by statute, and today the landlord's remedy for nonpayment of rent is governed almost entirely by the various state statutes.

Modern statutes generally prohibit the landlord himself from seizing the tenant's property and vest that authority in some public official. Also these statutes often list certain exemptions and usually restrict the right of distress to include only property located on the leased premises and which is owned by the tenant himself, specifically excluding chattels belonging to third persons. The most effective method of protecting the landlord against the non-payment of rent is through a covenant in the lease conferring upon the landlord the power to terminate the tenancy in the event the tenant defaults on the rent.

ASSIGNMENT AND SUBLEASE

Distinction Between Assignment and Sublease

As we have seen, the landlord and tenant relationship arises when the holder of an estate in land (the lessor) transfers to another (the lessee) the exclusive possession of the property for a certain period of time. Unless prohibited by the terms of the lease, the lessee may also transfer all or part of *his* interest in the premises.[26] This may be accomplished either by an assignment or a sublease. If the lessee transfers his interest in the property to another for the entire unexpired balance of his term, the transaction is called an *assignment*; the lessee is referred to as the *assignor* and his grantee (the new tenant) is referred to as the assignee. However, if the lessee transfers his interest in the property for any period *less* than the unexpired balance of his term (thus leaving a reversion in himself) the transaction is a *sublease*. To state it another way, a sublease occurs when the lessee leases the premises to another for a shorter term than he himself has. The test is whether the lessee parts with his entire estate or retains a reversion. If the lessee transfers the entire balance of his term, the transaction is an assignment, but if the lessee retains some reversionary interest, however small, it is a sublease.

26 However, because a *tenancy at will* may be terminated by either party at any time it generally cannot be transferred and any attempt to do so will ordinarily terminate the tenancy.

Except for any formalities required by local statute (such as the necessity of a writing or the requirement of recording) no particular form need be followed to transfer a leasehold interest. Assignments and subleases are simply transfers of leasehold estates requiring no more formalities than do the leases themselves.

A few states prohibit the transfer of leasehold estates without the consent of the landlord. And in the other states an exception to the rule of free transferability is sometimes made in the case of percentage leases. Where the rental is based upon a percentage of the gross sales or profits from the tenant's business it is generally considered that the lease is personal and therefore not transferable without the consent of the landlord.

Example:

L leases Blackacre to T for a term beginning January 1, 1976 and expiring on January 1, 1978. On June 30, 1976 T transfers all his interest in Blackacre to X for the balance of the term expiring on January 1, 1978. The transaction is an *assignment* with T referred to as the *assignor* and X as the *assignee.*

Example:

L leases Blackacre to T for a term beginning January 1, 1976 and expiring on Janury 1, 1978. On June 30, 1976 T transfers all his interest in Blackacre to X for a period of one year. The transaction is a *sublease* with T referred to as the *sublessor* and X as the *sublessee.*

Example:

L leases Blackacre to T for a term of ten years beginning on January 1, 1976. T "assigns" his entire interest in Blackacre to X except for the last day of the term. The transaction is a sublease regardless of what the parties call it.

A transfer of the lessee's entire interest in only *part* of the premises for the balance of the term constitutes a *partial* assignment rather than a sublease. As to whether the reservation in a lease of a right of entry for "condition broken" stamps the transaction as a sublease rather than an assignment, there is a conflict of authority. A minority of states follow the so-called Massachusetts Rule holding that a transfer of the entire unexpired remainder of the term will nevertheless constitute a sublease if the lessee reserves in himself a right of entry for condition broken.

Effect of Assignment

Since a lease is both a conveyance and a contract it creates a dual relationship between the parties: Because the "conveyance" transfers an estate (a leasehold estate) the parties are said to enter into *privity of estate*; and as a result of having entered into a contract the relationship of the parties is also said to be based upon *privity of contract*.

"Privity of estate" simply means that the lessor and the lessee have mutually exclusive interests in the same land. Privity of estate is the basis for enforcing those covenants in a lease which touch and concern the land. Covenants which touch and concern the land, such as the covenant to repair, to pay rent, covenants to renew or extend the lease, options to purchase etc., are said to "run with the land." If the covenant runs with the land both the benefit and the burden of the covenant will follow along with an assignment of the lease; thus covenants which run with the land are enforceable by and against assignees of the lease. If the covenant does not relate to the land but is personal in nature, such as a collateral promise to purchase goods or materials for instance, the covenant will not run with the land and so will not be enforceable by or against an assignee of the lease. However, most lease covenants are of a type which run with the land.

"Privity of contract" is that relationship which exists between any contracting parties; it means that the parties are mutually bound by the terms of the contract.

During his occupancy of the leased premises the lessee is said to hold both by privity of estate and privity of contract. However, when he assigns the lease the lessee (assignor) ceases to be a tenant and the privity of estate which existed between him and the lessor ends. The privity of contract, however, continues since a person may not transfer away his contractual obligations. The assignee (the new tenant) steps into the shoes of his assignor, thus establishing a new privity of estate between the lessor and the assignee. By virtue of the new privity of estate created between the lessor and the assignee (the new tenant), the lessor has a right of action against the assignee on the covenant to pay rent and on all other covenants running with the land. The lessor also retains his rights against the assignor (original tenant) by virtue of their privity of contract which continues to exist.

So the effect of an assignment is to place the assignee into the shoes of the assignor; in doing so both the assignor and the assignee become liable for payment of the rent and the performance of the other covenants running with the land. The assignee (new tenant) becomes liable by reason of his privity of estate; the assignor (original tenant) remains liable by reason of his privity of contract.

Example:

L leases property to T for a term of five years. Later T assigns his lease to X. The effect of the assignment is to terminate the privity of estate between L and T and create a new privity of estate between L and X. However, the privity of contract between L and T continues. If X (the assignee) fails to pay the rent or perform any of the other covenants running with the land L may sue him directly, by virtue of the privity of estate, or he may sue T by virtue of the privity of contract.[27]

In the example above if X were to make a new assignment to Y the privity of estate between L and X would cease; Y would then become liable to L for rent subsequently accruing (and also on the other covenants running with the land) by virtue of their privity of estate. X's liability would terminate upon reassignment since he would no longer be in privity of estate or privity of contract with L.

[27] If X failed to pay the rent and T were compelled to make payment, T would be entitled to indemnification against X. The reason for this is that upon acceptance of the assignment the law implies a promise on part of the assignee of a lease (X in this case) to comply with the terms of the lease. If he fails to do so and the assignor (T in this case) is required to pay the rent or other sums to the landlord, then the assignor may recover such sums from the assignee. However, an assignee's obligation to perform the covenants in a lease is limited to the time he occupies under the assignment; if he himself were to assign the lease to another, he would thereby divest himself of the privity of estate and would no longer be liable, either to the landlord or to the assignor (original tenant). In other words, the assignee is liable only during the period of his occupancy.

Ordinarily there is no privity of *contract* between the landlord and the assignee because the assignee was never a party to the original lease. Consequently an assignee may relieve himself from subsequent liability to the landlord by making a new assignment, thereby terminating the privity of estate.

Example:

> L leases to T and T assigns the lease to X. At that point X is liable to L on the covenants running with the land by virtue of the privity of estate. Later X reassigns the lease to Y. X is thereby relieved of any subsequent liability to L since there is no longer privity of estate and there never was privity of contract.

However, if the assignee expressly *assumes* the obligations of the lease his liability will not be terminated if he reassigns the lease; in such case the reassignment terminates the privity of estate but by *assuming* the obligations of the lease the assignee will create a new privity of contract between him and the main lessor.

Example:

> L leases property to T. Later T assigns the lease to X who expressly agrees to "assume and perform all covenants" in the original lease. X will remain bound by the covenants of the lease by virtue of the privity of contract even though he reassigns the lease.

Effect of Sublease

Where the lessee transfers his interest in the leased premises for a period *less* than the unexpired balance of his term (thus leaving a reversion in himself) the transaction is a sublease. In the case of a sublease there is neither privity of estate nor privity of contract between the original lessor and the sub-tenant. Consequently, a subletting in no way alters the legal relationship between the landlord and the lessee (sublessor).

A sublease creates a new estate carved out of the original leasehold, and the lessee becomes the landlord of the subtenant. The subtenant is not directly liable to the main lessor for the payment of the rent or the performance of other covenants; however, the lessee (sublessor) remains directly accountable to the landlord for payment of the rent and for performing all the other covenants in the lease. The sublessor also remains liable to the lessor for any damage to the premises caused by the negligence of the subtenant.

Of course the subtenant can acquire no greater rights in the premises than the lessee has. Thus any restrictions contained in the original lease are binding on the subtenant. Although there is no privity whatsoever between the landlord and the subtenant, the subtenant holds the premises subject to the terms and conditions contained in the original lease.

The Right to Assign or Sublease

Unless the terms of the lease expressly prohibit it the tenant may assign or sublease his interest in the premises to another without the consent of the landlord. However, leases most often do include a prohibition against assignment or subleasing without the consent of the landlord, the purpose being to ensure that the premises will be occupied by a financially responsible tenant who will use them properly. However, since they tend to restrain the free transferability of land, restrictions against assignment and subleasing are not favored by the law and are therefore strictly construed. Thus a lease which prohibits assignment does not prevent the tenant from subleasing; and conversely, a covenant against subletting is not broken by an assignment. And the taking of roomers or lodgers is not considered a breach of the covenant against subletting since such transaction does not result in a "transfer" of the leasehold. A prohibition against subleasing the "entire" premises is not violated by subletting only a portion of the premises; to prevent such a transfer the lease should contain a provision prohibiting the subleasing of the whole *or any part* of the premises.

In most states even where the lease contains a condition against assignment, if the landlord *once* consents to an assignment the condition is abrogated and the lease thereafter becomes freely assignable. This rule is based upon a seventeenth century English case, and is known to law students as the Rule in Dumpor's Case.[28] However, this rule does not apply to subleasing, so by consenting to *one* subletting the landlord does not thereby lose his right to prevent future sublettings.

Provisions which prohibit assignment or subleasing without the consent[29] of the landlord usually confer upon the lessor the power to terminate the lease in the event the lessee violates the covenant. However, such provisions are for the benefit of the landlord and may be waived by him. Thus, if the lessee assigns or subleases his interest in violation of the terms of the lease, the assignment or sublease is not considered void until the landlord takes some affirmative action to terminate the lease. The landlord may expressly or by his conduct waive the breach of the covenant not to assign or sublease. Conduct generally relied upon to establish a waiver is the landlord's acceptance of rent after knowledge of the assignment or sublease.

EVICTION

Generally

Since the tenant owns an estate he is, for all practical purposes, the owner of the premises during the existence of the lease. He has the sole and exclusive right to possession for the entire term of the lease and the landlord has no authority

28 However, the rule is easily circumvented by having the landlord condition his consent to an assignment on there being no *further* assignments without his consent.

29 Even though the lease requires the landlord's written consent to an assignment or sublease, his *oral* consent will be sufficient.

to enter or otherwise disturb the tenant. If the landlord enters the premises without the express or implied consent of the tenant he is a trespasser and the tenant may bring an action against him for damages.

The mere relationship of landlord and tenant gives rise to an implied obligation on part of the landlord not to disturb or in any way interfere with the tenant's use and occupancy of the leased premises. This is known as the landlord's covenant for quiet enjoyment. The covenant for quiet enjoyment imposes upon the landlord a contractual duty not to interfere with the tenant's possession and enjoyment of the leased premises. However, in order for the lessee to prove a breach of the covenant for quiet enjoyment he must be able to show that his use and enjoyment of the premises has been *substantially* interfered with, either by the landlord himself or by someone with a paramount title.[30]

Where the interference affects the tenant's physical possession of the premises it is referred to as an *eviction*. Thus an eviction is any act of the landlord which deprives the tenant of the beneficial enjoyment of the premises. The covenant for quiet enjoyment is breached by an eviction, of which there are two types: *actual* eviction and *constructive* eviction.

Actual Eviction

An actual eviction takes place when the landlord wrongfully deprives the tenant of possession of all or part of the leased premises. In the case of a total eviction the tenant is not liable for rent accruing during the period he is without possession; upon wrongful eviction by the landlord the tenant may either bring an action to recover possession or he may bring suit for damages for breach of the covenant for quiet enjoyment. If the eviction is of a part of the premises only, the tenant may retain possession of the remaining part and pay no

30 An eviction "by paramount title" arises when a third person establishes title to the leased premises superior to that of the landlord and thereby gains possession.

rent whatever so long as the partial eviction continues. The reason for this rule is that the landlord cannot apportion his own wrong.

Example:

After the tenant took possession of leased premises the landlord constructed a permanent brick wall on the adjoining lot. The wall encroached upon the leased land by five feet. This constitutes an actual partial eviction and the tenant's liability for the whole rent is suspended during the continuance of the encroachment.

Constructive Eviction

To constitute an actual eviction the tenant must have been wrongfully deprived of all or part of the possession of the leased premises; a mere disturbance or interference by the landlord does not constitute an *actual* eviction and does not discharge the liability for rent. However, if the disturbance or interference by the landlord is so substantial as to render the premises unfit for occupancy the tenant may abandon possession and terminate his liability for future rent. Abandonment under such conditions amounts to a *constructive* eviction, provided the tenant vacates the premises within a reasonable time after the occurrence. A landlord's failure to comply with his covenant to furnish heat, or to make repairs,[31] or to furnish elevator service or provide other essential services is usually grounds for a constructive eviction.

To constitute a constructive eviction the interference or omission by the landlord must be grave and substantial. And no matter how great the interference or omission, there is no

31 As a general rule the landlord's failure to perform a covenant to repair is not grounds for a constructive eviction unless the failure to repair results in the premises becoming uninhabitable. However, before the tenant can claim a constructive eviction for failure to make repairs he must give reasonable notice to the landlord and afford him the opportunity to make the necessary repairs.

constructive eviction if the tenant remains in possession.[32] Constructive eviction is effective only from the time the tenant abandons possession of the premises. A constructive eviction suspends the tenant's obligation to pay rent while he is out of possession. Upon a wrongful eviction the tenant may bring an action to recover possession or he may treat the lease as terminated and sue for breach of the covenant for quiet enjoyment.

TERMINATION OF LEASES

A lease for a definite period ordinarily terminates at the expiration of the term, specifically on midnight of the last day. Leases are sometimes drafted so as to automatically terminate upon the happening of a specified contingency; or the lessor may reserve the option to terminate the lease upon the occurrence of a certain event, such as the insolvency of the lessee or his ceasing to occupy the premises, or upon a sale of the premises or their destruction by fire or other casualty.

A lease may be terminated by *surrender*, which is a termination by *mutual agreement*; it is a yielding or giving back of the premises to the landlord with his consent before the expiration of the lease. A surrender releases the tenant from further liability to pay rent. A surrender may be by express agreement or by operation of law. A surrender by operation of law is one in which mutual consent is implied from the conduct of the parties. For example, if the tenant abandons the leased premises before the expiration of the lease and refuses to pay the rent the landlord can, in most states, allow the premises to remain idle and sue for the rent. But if following abandonment by the tenant, the landlord unqualifiedly resumes full possession and control of the premises, then there is a surrender by operation of law. And if the landlord, with the consent of the tenant, gives a new lease

32 The tenant must vacate the premises within a reasonable time after the occurrence or he will be deemed to have *waived* the claim of constructive eviction.

of the premises to a third party, that also is a surrender by operation of law.

A lease will also terminate when the leased premises are taken by eminent domain, or if the lessee becomes bankrupt, or by foreclosure of the lessor's reversionary interest where the lessor's estate was subject to a prior mortgage.

SUMMARY

A leasehold estate arises when an owner of real estate transfers possession to another for a period of time. The transaction, called a lease, creates the relationship of landlord and tenant and the parties are referred to as lessor and lessee. A lease is both a conveyance and a contract; it conveys a possessory interest in the land and it also creates a contractual relationship between the landlord (lessor) and the tenant (lessee).

There are four basic types of leasehold estates:

(1) Estates for Years
(2) Periodic Estates
(3) Estates at Will
(4) The Tenancy at Sufferance

The estate for years is one which is to continue for a fixed or definite period of time, regardless of the length of the period; it may be for a day, a month, a year or a thousand years. Upon expiration of the term the estate for years will terminate without notice.

A periodic estate is one that continues for successive periods until it is terminated. The period may be a year or a fraction of a year. The periodic estate, once created, does not automatically terminate at the end of the period but continues indefinitely for successive periods until one of the parties elects to terminate the tenancy by giving proper notice.

An estate at will (tenancy at will) is an estate which may be terminated at the will of either the landlord or the tenant and which has no specified period of duration. Under common law an estate at will could be terminated without any notice whatever. Today, however, most states require some advance notice in writing, usually equal to the rent paying period or at least thirty days.

A tenancy at sufferance is a possessory interest in land which arises when a person who previously held an estate wrongfully remains in possession after the termination of his estate. A tenant at sufferance differs from a trespasser only in that his original entry into possession was lawful. In the case of a tenant at sufferance the landlord has an option: he may treat him as a trespasser and evict him forthwith, or he may deal with him as a tenant (usually by accepting rent) and thereby create either a periodic tenancy or a tenancy at will.

No technical or formal words are necessary to create a leasehold estate. Any language by which possession of land is transferred for a specified term at a stipulated rental is in effect a "lease." In most states leases for a term of more than one year must be in writing. And in nearly all states leases for longer than a specified period (usually two to seven years) must be recorded in the registry of deeds. Although a lease need not be in any particular form it is essential that it contain at least the names of the *parties*, an adequate *description* of the leased premises, the *term* of the lease and the amount of *rent* to be paid.

During the term of the lease the tenant is for all practical purposes the owner of the premises, and the landlord has no authority to enter or otherwise disturb the tenant. The tenant may put the premises to any reasonable use he wishes, provided the use is not illegal or prohibited by the terms of the lease. However, the tenant has an implied obligation to use the premises in a tenantlike manner; he must not alter or use the property in such a way as to cause permanent damage to the realty. To do so constitutes "waste" for which the tenant will be liable in damages.

Unless the lease so stipulates the landlord is not obligated to put the premises in a condition fit for occupation. The tenant takes the premises as he finds them and the rule of *caveat emptor* applies. However, there is a definite trend away from the traditional common law doctrine of *caveat emptor*, and several states have now adopted the position that there *is* an implied warranty on part of the landlord that the premises are fit for occupation in all leases of residential property.

There are two exceptions to the general rule that there is no implied warranty by the landlord that the premises are in safe condition and fit for occupancy: (1) In the case of the rental of a furnished house or apartment, and (2) the lease of a building which is still under construction.

Although in most states there is no implied warranty on part of the landlord that the leased premises are fit for occupancy (other than the exceptions mentioned above), the landlord is under a duty to inform the tenant of any *hidden* defects which would make the premises dangerous. If he fails to do so he will be liable to the tenant and to his family and guests for injuries resulting from the defective condition.

The landlord is under no obligation to make repairs unless he agrees to do so or unless the duty to repair is imposed upon him by statute. The tenant, on the other hand, is obligated to make minor repairs but only to the extent necessary to keep the premises from falling into a state of decay or ruin. However, the parties may, and often do, expressly stipulate in the lease as to which party shall make repairs and to what extent. If the landlord covenants to make repairs and fails to do so, the tenant has an option: he may sue the landlord for damages or he may make the necessary repairs himself and deduct the cost thereof from the rent due.

As a general rule the landlord is not liable for injuries to persons resulting from the negligent condition of the premises. It is the tenant's responsibility to ensure the safe condition of that part of the premises over which he has exclusive possession and control. However, the landlord is responsible for the safe condition of those portions of the premises used in common by all the tenants such as the common stairways, hallways, walks, etc. And as stated above, the landlord will be liable for injuries sustained as a result of hidden defects which were known to him and about which he failed to notify the tenant. In order to hold either the landlord or the tenant liable for injuries sustained on the premises, the injured party must prove that the landlord or tenant failed to exercise due care to prevent the injury and that the injured party was himself free of contributory negligence.

Where the lease fails to specify the time of payment, the rent does not become due and payable until the *end* of the term. And where the lease provides for the rental to be paid monthly, quarterly, or yearly, but fails to specify any particular time of payment during such periods, the rent is not due and payable until the *end* of those respective periods. However, most leases stipulate that the rent shall be paid *in advance*, usually on a monthly or quarterly basis. Where the rent is payable on a certain day the tenant has until midnight of that day in which to make payment. If the date on which the rent is payable falls on a Sunday, the general rule is that the time for payment is extended to the following Monday. Where the lease fails to stipulate the *place* at which the rent is to be paid, it is payable at the leased premises.

With respect to the manner in which the rent is determined, there are three basic types of leases: the *gross* lease, the *net* lease and the *percentage* lease. A ''gross' lease is one in which the tenant pays a fixed rental and the landlord pays the taxes and insurance and all other costs of maintaining the property. Under a ''net'' lease the tenant, in addition to paying the rent, assumes responsibility for all costs of maintaining the property, including taxes and insurance. In the case of a ''percentage'' lease the rental is based upon a specified percentage of gross sales or net profit received by the tenant from a business conducted on the leased premises.

Under common law and in most states today, unless the

lease provides otherwise a tenant is not excused from paying rent if the buildings on the land are accidentally destroyed by fire or other casualty. However, the destruction of a building will terminate the lease of a room or an apartment therein because in such case the destruction of the leased premises is complete. For the same reason a lease of a building which expressly excludes the underlying land is ordinarily terminated upon a total destruction of the building.

Under common law the landlord could enforce the payment of rent by seizing the tenant's personal belongings and holding them until the rent was paid. This remedy was known as the landlord's right of *distress*. The right to "distrain" for rent was never looked upon with favor in the United States and today the landlord's remedy for nonpayment of rent is governed almost entirely by the various state statutes. The most effective method of protecting the landlord against the nonpayment of rent is through a covenant in the lease giving the landlord the power to terminate the tenancy in the event the tenant defaults on the rent.

Unless prohibited by the terms of the lease, the lessee may transfer all or part of his interest in the leased premises. This may be accomplished either by an *assignment* or a *sublease*. If the lessee transfers his interest in the leased property to another for the *entire* unexpired balance of his term, the transaction is an *assignment*; the lessee is referred to as the assignor and his grantee (the new tenant) is referred to as the assignee. If the lessee transfers his interest in the property for any period *less* than the unexpired balance of his term the transaction is a *sublease*. In other words if the lessee transfers the entire balance of his term the transaction is an assignment, but if the lessee retains some reversionary interest, however small, it is a sublease. A transfer of the lessee's entire interest in only *part* of the premises for the balance of the term constitutes a *partial* assignment rather than a sublease.

The effect of an assignment is to place the assignee (new tenant) into the shoes of the assignor (original tenant) whereupon *both* the assignor and the assignee become liable for payment of the rent and the performance of the other covenants running with the land. The assignee (new tenant) becomes liable by reason of his privity of estate; the assignor (original tenant) remains liable by reason of his privity of contract.

The effect of a sublease is to create a new estate carved out of the original leasehold, whereupon the lessee becomes the landlord of the subtenant. Consequently, a subletting in no way alters the legal relationship between the landlord and the lessee (sublessor) who remains directly accountable to the landlord for payment of the rent and for performing all the other covenants in the lease. Of course the subtenant can acquire no greater rights in the premises than the lessee has, and any restrictions contained in the original lease are binding on the subtenant.

Unless the terms of the lease expressly prohibit it the tenant may assign or sublease his interest in the premises without the consent of the landlord. However, leases most often contain a prohibition against assignment or subleasing without the consent of the landlord.

The relationship of landlord and tenant gives rise to an implied obligation on part of the landlord not to disturb or in any way interfere with the tenant's use and occupancy of the leased premises. This is known as the landlord's covenant for quiet enjoyment. Any act of the landlord which deprives the tenant of the beneficial enjoyment of the premises is an *eviction.*

The covenant for quiet enjoyment is breached by an eviction, of which there are two types: *actual* and *constructive.* An "actual" eviction occurs when the landlord wrongfully deprives the tenant of physical possession of all or part of the leased premises. In the case of a total eviction the tenant is not liable for rent during the period he is without possession, and he may either bring an action to recover possession or sue for breach of the covenant for quiet enjoyment. If the eviction is of a part of the premises only, the tenant may retain possession of the remaining part and pay no rent whatever so long as the partial eviction continues.

A mere disturbance or interference by the landlord does not constitute an *actual* eviction and does not discharge the liability for rent. However, if the disturbance or interference by the landlord is so substantial as to render the premises unfit for occupancy the tenant may abandon possession and terminate his liability for future rent. Abandonment under such conditions amounts to a *constructive* eviction, provided the tenant vacates the premises within a reasonable time after the occurrence. To constitute a constructive eviction the disturbance or interference by the landlord must be grave and substantial. And no matter how great the disturbance or interference, there is no constructive eviction if the tenant remains in possession. A constructive eviction suspends the tenant's obligation to pay rent while he is out of possession. Upon constructive eviction the tenant may bring an action to recover possession or treat the lease as terminated and sue for breach of the covenant for quiet enjoyment.

A lease for a definite period ordinarily terminates at the expiration of the term, specifically on midnight of the last day. Leases are sometimes drafted so as to automatically terminate upon the happening of a specified contingency; or the lessor may reserve the option to terminate upon the occurrence of a certain event. A lease may also be terminated by *surrender,* which is termination by mutual agreement. And a lease will terminate when the premises are taken by eminent domain, or if the lessee becomes bankrupt, or by foreclosure of the lessor's reversionary interest.

CHAPTER 5

DOWER, CURTESY, AND THE HOMESTEAD EXEMPTION

DOWER AND CURTESY

Introductory Statement

A husband and wife, at common law, were considered as one person, and the *one* was the *husband.* A married woman was incapable of acquiring or disposing of property. This early concept that marriage made husband and wife "one flesh" may have a romantic appeal to some, but legally it placed women in the same class as infants and idiots. Upon marriage a woman lost all power to control or deal with her own property; she could not acquire property nor could she dispose of it—even by will. She was not permitted to bring a legal action except in conjunction with her husband, even in cases of personal assault upon her. Property-wise a woman's position was one of complete subjection to the male.[1]

However, this grim state of affairs was probably tempered somewhat by the availability of many of those subtle, "extra-legal" techniques universally employed by wives in the influencing of husbands. And during the violent years of the early feudal period the husband's function as *physical protector* may have justified his complete rule of the roost. Yet women resented their servile status and a change in the law was inevitable.

[1] CASNER & LEACH, CASES AND TEXT ON PROPERTY 283 (1951).

So the great legal pendulum of marital rights began to swing—from a position of almost total male superiority to its present place of virtual legal equality between the spouses. And there are some who are of the opinion that the pendulum has not yet come to rest—that a kind of social momentum is carrying it to the opposite extreme, where complete female dominance will replace the already well-shattered male empire. But this is for the sociologists to ponder. The fact is that the inexorable erosion of husband's "rights" is the process by which our modern law was shaped.

The Estate by the Marital Right

Since at early common law the wife's legal identity was merged in that of her husband, by the mere fact of marriage a husband became entitled to the *exclusive* possession and profits of all of his wife's property, both real and personal. This interest was known as his *estate by the marital right* which lasted until the marriage was dissolved by death or divorce.[2]

Eventually the courts relaxed the harshness of this situation by allowing property to be conveyed in such a way as to enable a wife to retain the use and profits free from her husband's control. And the so-called "Married Women's Property Acts" of the nineteenth century further reduced the husband's control over his wife's real estate; in England and most of the United States today a wife has almost unlimited control over her real and personal property.

Curtesy

As we have seen, at common law a husband acquired, upon marriage, an exclusive right to the use and profits of all of his wife's real estate. This estate by the marital right lasted only as long as the marriage lasted; if the wife died or there was a divorce the husband's interest terminated.

[2] It was also known as the husband's estate *jure uxoris* (by right of the marriage).

However, if a *child were born of the marriage,* the husband's estate by the marital right was *enlarged* to an estate for his own life, and upon the death of the wife he would continue to hold the land for his life as tenant "by the curtesy of England." Curtesy was an estate measured by the husband's life alone; it attached to *all* estates in fee simple which the wife held at any time during the marriage, provided that a child had been born of the marriage. Until the death of the wife, this life estate in the husband was called curtesy *initiate*; upon the death of the wife the surviving husband's estate became curtesy *consummate.*

For *curtesy* to attach, it was essential that the child be born alive during the marriage. It made no difference if the infant did not survive, but he or she must have been born alive "and heard to cry within the four walls."[3]

Dower

From very early times the English law also gave a wife certain rights in her husband's land if she survived him. For more than a thousand years these rights have been known as *dower.*

Dower existed long before the Norman Conquest; its origins go back to a period in history when the bridegroom made a payment to the family of the bride, in return for the rights over her which he acquired by the marriage, and gave to her a morning-gift for her support if she outlived him.[4]

From its early beginnings as a precarious, ill-defined interest, dower emerged into a definite estate; it became established that a widow was entitled, on the death of her husband, to a *life estate* in an undivided *one third* of all the lands of which he had been seized (owned) *at any time during the marriage.* It was an interest given to the widow for her support and maintenance, and it was not necessary that issue be born of the marriage for dower to attach.

3 CASNER & LEACH, CASES AND TEXT ON PROPERTY 287 (1951).

4 1 AMERICAN LAW OF PROPERTY § 5.2 (Casner ed. 1952).

During the husband's lifetime the wife's dower interest was a mere expectancy (dependent upon her surviving her husband) called *inchoate* (contingent) dower.[5] But this expectancy was protected in that the husband could not defeat the right of dower by conveyance or by will, nor could the interest be impaired by the husband's creditors.[6] If the husband wished to convey or mortgage the land free from any possible claim for dower, a *release* of the wife's inchoate dower interest was necessary. This was accomplished by having the wife join in the deed or mortgage; without her signature on the conveyance her inchoate dower interest remained outstanding and the husband could not convey a marketable title.

After the death of the husband the wife's inchoate dower became *consummate* (completed) and she became a *dowager*, entitled to have her dower *assigned* to her. The "assignment" involved the actual physical division of one-third of the lands to which her dower interest had attached and not been barred or released. Once dower had been assigned her status became that of "a tenant in dower" with an *estate for life* in the land assigned.

In comparing curtesy and dower note the difference between them: although both were estates for *life*, curtesy extended to *all* of the wife's realty whereas dower extended to only *one-third* of the husband's realty; and curtesy depended upon the birth of issue but the widow was entitled to dower even though no issue resulted from the marriage.

Dower and curtesy are a product of the social conditions of the Middle Ages. Their function was to provide some economic security for the spouse; and in an age when agriculture was the chief source of wealth that security was to be found in the *land*.

5 Inchoate dower attached to *all* estates in fee simple owned by the husband during the marriage.

6 Once attached, dower could be barred only by the death of the wife before the husband, by divorce for the fault of the wife, or by a release of the dower interest by the wife.

Marital Rights Today

With the advent of the industrial revolution, dower and curtesy became obsolete as a system of "marital social security." As the economy changed from agricultural to industrial the chief form of family wealth also changed—from land to savings accounts, stocks, bonds, and life insurance. Consequently, state legislatures have attempted to adopt statutory substitutes for dower and curtesy. Today dower and curtesy, in its common law form, have been abolished in most of the states and replaced by broader and more substantial statutory rights.

Modern statutes generally give to a spouse, as a substitute for dower or curtesy, an outright fractional share (rather than a life interest) in all the real estate which the other spouse had owned at any time during the marriage. However, dower and curtesy or their statutory substitutes are seldom exactly the same in any two states. Some states have expanded dower and curtesy into an outright share in fee simple as opposed to merely a life interest. In some states the share is one-third; in others it is one-half. In some states dower is limited to land owned by the husband at the time of his death; in other states dower attaches to all land owned by the husband at any time during the marriage.[7] In some states the widow or widower may elect to take an intestate share[8] or some other designated share in fee simple in lieu of dower or curtesy. And in some states the community property system regulates the property

7 Where dower is limited to land owned by the husband *at the time of his death,* the husband is free to convey his land during his lifetime without obtaining his wife's signature on the deed. However, where dower attaches to all land owned by the husband *at any time during the marriage,* the husband must secure his wife's signature to any conveyance of his realty in order to release her dower interest and thus convey a clear title.

8 An *intestate* share is that share to which the surviving spouse would be entitled had the deceased spouse died without having left a valid will. The estate of a person who dies without having left a valid will is distributed according to statutes of descent and distribution, also referred to as the laws of *intestate succession.* The subject of intestate succession will be considered in Chapter 9.

rights of husband and wife.[9] About a dozen states have retained something very close to common law dower and curtesy, but in the case of curtesy a few of these states have abolished the requirement that a child be born of the marriage. In some states curtesy has been abolished in favor of an interest similar to dower.[10] In each case the particular state statute must be consulted.

So-called "Married Women's Acts," enacted in most states, have expanded the rights of married women to own, possess and control their own property. In most states a husband acquires no right to control his wife's property by mere virtue of the marriage; the right to the exclusive possession and control of her property remains in her after marriage as fully as before. Today a married woman may own, manage, sell, mortgage, convey and devise by will her real and personal property with the same freedom as that of a married man.

The early common law concept of spousal inequality is fast disappearing. The modern tendency is to treat husband and wife alike with respect to their shares in each other's property. But this is a tendency only. Usually the widow receives greater protection than the widower. However, the Equal Rights Amendment to the Federal Constitution should finally balance the scales.

THE HOMESTEAD EXEMPTION

Most states have enacted laws designed to give some protection to the family as a unit by allowing a householder or the head of the family a limited exemption against the claims of his creditors. These laws are known as *homestead laws,*[11] and

9 The community property system will be discussed in Chapter 6.

10 Divorce terminates dower and curtesy and their statutory substitutes, although in some states a divorce bars only the party at fault.

11 Do not confuse the homestead exemption with the term "homestead" as used in connection with federal homestead laws. Under federal homestead laws, designed to promote the settlement and development of the West, one who occupied unappropriated

the land with respect to which such exemption applies is known as a "homestead"; it usually comprises the dwelling house and adjoining land of the head of the family.

The primary purpose of homestead exemption laws is to place the homestead beyond the reach of creditors while it is occupied as a home. By protecting the householder from being picked clean to the bone by his creditors the family is afforded at least some small measure of security. The homestead exemption is designed not only for the protection of the husband or head of the family, but also for the benefit of the wife and children as well. The homestead exemption is not a product of the common law but is strictly an American contribution to the law of real property. The first homestead statute was enacted by the Republic of Texas in the year 1839.

To be entitled to a homestead exemption a person must qualify as a *householder* or *head of a family*. Ordinarily the husband is the head of the family, although the wife may become such if she is the sole or chief supporter of the family. Most states require that the person claiming a homestead exemption must have a family, but it is not necessary that the claimant be a married person. A "householder" or "head of a family" is generally considered to be anyone who has residing with him persons for whom he has a legal or moral obligation to support.[12]

In most states, the "homestead" to which the exemption applies consists of the dwelling house and adjoining land actually occupied as a residence by the head of the family. The premises must be occupied primarily as a family residence but the householder need not be the owner in fee simple; he may occupy as a life tenant or as a tenant under a lease and still be entitled to the exemption. Of course, a termination of the

public land as a "homestead" for a specified period of time obtained title to the land without payment.

12 A bachelor with no children or other persons dependent upon him is not the "head of a family" within the homestead statutes although he may keep house and is, in that limited sense, a householder.

householder's interest in the homestead property automatically terminates his homestead rights therein.

The actual amount of the homestead exemption varies from state to state. It is generally expressed in terms of money (usually from about $1,000 to $10,000), or land area, or a combination of both. Only that dollar value or land area which exceeds the statutory amount is reachable by creditors.

In many states, to be entitled to the homestead exemption, the householder must file a formal *declaration of homestead* indicating his intention to claim certain land as his homestead. Ordinarily, the declaration must aver that the claimant is the head of a family; it must briefly describe the land and buildings and must be acknowledged and recorded as required by statute. Once perfected the exemption will, in most states, last for the lifetime of the householder, and after his death it will continue for the benefit of his surviving widow for her lifetime, and for the benefit of his children until they reach majority. Thus the homestead exemption, in some respects, is analogous to a life estate.

The homestead exemption is not absolute; there are certain claims against which the homestead is *not* exempt. For instance, the homestead is not exempt from debts incurred prior to its establishment as a homestead. And in most states the exemption is not allowed against a mortgage given to finance all or part of the purchase price (the owner should not be allowed to purchase the homestead and then avoid payment by setting up the exemption), nor against any mortgage on the homestead which was properly executed by *both* spouses. Nor does the exemption apply to debts contracted for the repair or improvement of the homestead property, or to the payment of the property taxes on the homestead.

The owner of a homestead has an absolute right to sell or mortgage the property. However, the conveyance or mortgage of homestead property will not be effective unless the householder's spouse joins in the deed or mortgage, and some states require, in addition, a formal release or renunciation of the homestead right.

The basic purpose of homestead legislation is the protection of the family. Thus most state statutes provide that upon the death of the householder or head of the family, his or her surviving spouse shall be entitled to the homestead, and that it shall be exempt from the same debts as it was during the householder's lifetime. And most statutes extend the protection to include the dependent minor children of the marriage as well. However, in a few states a surviving spouse must make an election between dower or curtesy and homestead rights, but most states permit the surviving spouse to claim the homestead exemption *in addition* to dower or curtesy.

SUMMARY

At common law a husband and wife were considered one person, and *he* was the *one*; a married woman was incapable of acquiring or disposing of property. A husband, by right of the marriage, became entitled to the exclusive possession and profits of all of his wife's property for the duration of the marriage. And if a child were born of the marriage the husband's marital right was *enlarged* to a life estate in him which he held "by the curtesy of England."

At common law a widow was entitled, on the death of her husband, to a *life estate* in an undivided *one-third* of all the lands of which he had owned at any time during the marriage. It was an interest given to the widow for her support and maintenance, called *dower.* During the husband's lifetime the dower interest (called *inchoate* dower) was protected in that the husband could not defeat it by conveyance or by will; nor could it be impaired by the husband's creditors. After the death of the husband, the wife's dower became *consummate* (completed) and the widow was entitled to have her dower assigned to her, at which time her status became that of a "tenant in dower" with an estate for life in the land assigned.

In most of the United States dower and curtesy have either been abolished or materially altered. As a substitute for dower and curtesy modern statutes generally give to a spouse an outright fractional share of the other's property, both real and personal.

Today a married woman may own, manage, sell, mortage, convey and devise by will, her real and personal property with the same freedom as that of a married man.

Most states have enacted laws designed to give some protection to the family as a unit by allowing a householder or the head of the family a limited exemption against the claims of his creditors. These laws are known as *homestead laws*, and the land with respect to which such exemption applies is known as a "homestead"; it usually comprises the dwelling house and adjoining land of the head of the family.

The primary purpose of homestead exemption laws is to place the homestead out of the reach of creditors while it is occupied as a home.

To be entitled to a homestead exemption a person must qualify as a *householder* or *head of a family.* A "householder" or "head of a family" is generally considered to be anyone who has residing with him persons for whom he has a legal or moral obligation to support.

The actual amount of the homestead exemption varies from state to state. It is generally expressed in terms of money (usually from about $1,000 to $10,000), or land area, or a combination of both. Only that dollar value or land area which exceeds the statutory amount is reachable by creditors.

In many states, to be entitled to the homestead exemption, the householder must file a formal *declaration of homestead* indicating his intention to claim certain land as his homestead. Ordinarily, the declaration must aver that the claimant is the head of a family; it must briefly describe the land and buildings and must be acknowledged and recorded as required by statute.

The basic purpose of homestead legislation is the protection of the family. Thus most state statutes provide that upon the death of the householder or head of the family, his or her surviving spouse shall be entitled to the homestead, and that it shall be exempt from the same debts as it was during the householder's lifetime.

CHAPTER 6

CO-OWNERSHIP

INTRODUCTORY STATEMENT

In chapter three we considered the various types of estates which comprise our system of land "ownership." You will recall that a person who "owns" land is a person who has an *interest in* the land—an interest called an estate. And two or more persons may each have an estate in the same parcel of land. For instance, we know that a transfer "to B for life, remainder to C and his heirs" creates two estates in the land—a *life estate* in B and a *remainder in fee simple* in C. But although B and C each have present estates in the land, they are not co-owners, since their *right to possession* is not concurrent; B is first entitled to the exclusive possession for his lifetime; C's right to possession must "wait its turn" until B's life estate ends. Thus the interests of B and C are said to be *successive* in character—that is, one estate succeeds or "follows" the other. The subject of this chapter is the concept of co-ownership—a type of ownership where two or more persons have *simultaneous* interests in the same property rather than successive interests; that is to say, all of the co-owners are entitled to possession of the same parcel of real estate at the same time.

Since the days of the feudal system the law has recognized the idea of two or more persons being simultaneously the owners of the same land. Out of this "simultaneous ownership" idea there evolved the four types of concurrent estates recognized at common law: JOINT TENANCIES, TENANCIES IN COMMON, TENANCIES BY THE ENTIRETY, AND ESTATES IN COPARCENARY. Of these four common law forms of co-ownership only the first three still survive today, the estate in coparcenary having become virtually obsolete in the United States and seldom even mentioned as a form of ownership.

JOINT TENANCY

THE NATURE OF JOINT TENANCIES

Joint tenancy is a form of co-ownership which exists between two or more persons who hold title together as a fictitious unity. Joint tenants own *one* interest *together*, and each joint tenant has exactly the same rights in that interest as his cotenant or cotenants.

The essence of a joint tenancy is the quality of unity—unity of ownership and a community of interest between the cotenants. Thus, in order for a joint tenancy to be created or to continue to exist, four essential elements or "unities" must be present: TIME, TITLE, INTEREST, and POSSESSION.

The unity of *time* means that the interests of all joint tenants must be acquired at the same time.

Unity of *title* means that the cotenants must receive their interests by the same conveying instrument, that is, the same deed or will.

Unity of *interest* means that the parties must have identical interests, both as to the type of estate[1] and the amount of the share; one cotenant cannot have a fee simple absolute and the other a life estate, nor can one have a one-fourth interest and another a three-fourths interest.

Unity of *possession* means that all the joint tenants have an equal and undivided right to possession, and not divided

[1] An estate in joint tenancy may be created in fee simple, for life, for years, or in remainder.

interests in separate parts; each joint tenant is entitled to the possession, use, and enjoyment of the *whole* property, during his life, subject to the equal rights of his cotenants.[2]

Each joint tenant stands exactly in the same position as each of the others; anything which creates a distinction either severs the joint tenancy or prevents it from ever arising. In other words the four unities must be present if a joint tenancy is to exist; the tenants must have one and the same interest, accruing by one and the same conveyance, commencing at one and the same time, and held by one and the same undivided possession. With that in mind consider the following common situation: A, a bachelor, owns a parcel of land in fee simple absolute. He marries B and then decides he wants ownership in himself and B as joint tenants. To effectuate this he executes a deed to himself and his new bride, using language clearly indicating an intent to create a joint tenancy. At common law the attempt to create a joint tenancy would fail because two of the four unities—time and title—are missing. At common law a person could not convey property to *himself*—such a conveyance was a nullity. Consequently, when A conveyed to himself and B, the conveyance *as to himself* was ineffective. Thus B received her interest at a different *time* and by a different *instrument* than A; although the intent was clear the result was a tenancy in common and not a joint tenancy. In order for an owner of property to create a joint tenancy between himself and another, it was necessary for him to first convey the title to a third party (straw man) who would then convey the title back to the original owner and his intended joint tenant, thereby preserving the four unities necessary for the creation of a joint tenancy. This is still the law in some states even today.

To avoid the necessity of using a straw man, several states have enacted statutes permitting a direct conveyance from a grantor to himself and other persons as joint tenants.

2 The unity of possession is not peculiar to joint tenancies; all co-owners have a common right to share, possess, and enjoy the property.

However, notwithstanding such enabling statutes it is surprising how many attorneys still persist in the use of a straw man in such cases.

The Right of Survivorship

The most important characteristic of a joint tenancy is the *right of survivorship*, historically referred to as the "Grand Incident of Survivorship." Upon the death of a joint tenant, his interest does not descend to his heirs or pass by his will, but rather, the entire ownership *remains* in the surviving joint tenant or tenants. Note that the deceased joint tenant's share does not "pass to" the surviving joint tenant or tenants, as property is usually thought of as "passing" by will or descent. The joint tenancy concept is "oneness"—the joint tenants own the whole together. Consequently, when one joint tenant dies, his interest does not technically "pass" to the surviving joint tenant or tenants—it is *extinguished* and the whole estate continues in the surviving joint tenants,[3] freed from the rights of the deceased joint tenant. The surviving joint tenants, in theory, get nothing which they did not already have; it was theirs from the beginning.[4]

Because of the automatic survivorship feature, the joint tenancy is a popular form of co-ownership; a great majority of married couples in the United States own property in joint tenancy. Property owners frequently use the joint tenancy as a substitute for a will, usually to avoid the necessity for probate proceedings or because of an erroneous belief that death taxes can be eliminated.[5] Although the joint tenancy may serve a useful purpose, especially in the case of small estates, the

[3] The *last* surviving joint tenant, of course, owns the whole estate in *severalty* (exclusively) since he no longer shares the estate with his former cotenants.

[4] Thus dower and curtesy do not attach to jointly held property, except in the case of the *last* surviving joint tenant who thereby becomes the sole and exclusive owner.

[5] The principal attribute of a joint tenancy is that when one joint tenant dies the surviving joint tenant succeeds immediately to the entire ownership without the necessity of any probate or other action upon his part.

parties should clearly understand the legal implications of this type of co-ownership before creating it.

Simultaneous Death

The automatic survivorship feature of the joint tenancy makes it important to determine the order of death where joint tenants perish in a common disaster, such as in an automobile accident; in such cases the order of death is often impossible to determine. This occurrence is becoming increasingly common on our highways, and nearly all states have adopted the so-called Uniform Simultaneous Death Act. This statute provides that where two joint tenants die under circumstances where their deaths were either simultaneous or the order of death is impossible to determine, the property held in joint tenancy shall be distributed, one half as if one had survived and one half as if the other had survived, meaning that the property descends one half to the heirs of each. The statute, in effect, treats the parties as having died as tenants in common with proportionate shares.[6]

Tax Treatment

Since the estate or "share" of a deceased joint tenant does not, in legal theory, actually "pass to" the surviving joint tenant or tenants, shouldn't such estate or share be exempt from death taxes? You might think so. However, our vigilant and resourceful tax administrators plugged this apparent loophole several years ago. The federal estate tax statutes, for taxation purposes, ignore the survivorship theory; they treat the property as having actually "passed" at death, but only to the extent of the deceased joint tenant's actual *contribution* to the value of the joint interest. And if the joint tenants acquired the property by gift, a share proportioned to the

[6] The Uniform Simultaneous Death Act provides that "Where there is no sufficient evidence that two joint tenants died otherwise than simultaneously, the property so held shall be distributed one half as if one had survived and one half as if the other had survived. If there are more than two joint tenants and all of them have so died the property thus distributed shall be in the proportion that one bears to the whole number of joint tenants."

number of joint tenants is includable in the estate of the deceased joint tenant for estate tax purposes.[7] Many state inheritance and estate tax statutes follow the same theory with some modifications.

Termination of a Joint Tenancy

Although the essence of a joint tenancy is unity, each joint tenant may, during his lifetime,[8] dispose of his undivided interest; and this is accomplished by a simple conveyance, with or without the permission of the other cotenants. Such a transfer ends the joint tenancy (and the right of survivorship) insofar as the share conveyed is concerned, because the unities of time and title are destroyed; the grantee becomes a *tenant in common* with the other joint tenant or tenants, since he takes his interest at a different time and by a different conveyance.[9]

Where there are only two joint tenants and one conveys his interest to a third person, the breaking of the unities ends the joint tenancy; the grantee of the share conveyed and the remaining cotenant become tenants in common in equal shares.[10] For example, if A and B are joint tenants and A conveys his interest to X, B and X will hold as tenants in common in equal shares.[11]

7 Int. Rev. Code of 1954, § 2040.

8 Of course a joint tenant cannot *devise* his interest since at death the incident of survivorship is already operative.

9 Whenever one of the unities is severed as a result of a transfer by a joint tenant of his interest, the grantee holds an undivided, inheritable share *in common* with the remaining cotenants, free from the incident of survivorship; the only unity essential to a tenancy in common is the unity of *possession*.

10 Since dower and curtesy do not attach to property held in joint tenancy, a joint tenant may convey his interest without the necessity of obtaining his spouse's signature on the deed. Dower and curtesy do, however, attach to land held *in common* with others.

In most states a *divorce* in and of itself does not affect the joint tenancy of husband and wife; the right of survivorship continues to exist after the divorce as before. However, if the husband and wife enter into a stipulation calling for a division of the jointly held property, and the stipulation is made part of the divorce decree, the joint tenancy will be converted into a tenancy in common.

11 Since there is no right of survivorship between tenants in common, the share of a deceased tenant in common passes to his heirs or devisees.

Where there are *more* than two joint tenants, a conveyance by one does not destroy the right of survivorship between the others, who will, as between themselves, continue to hold their shares in joint tenancy.

Example:

A, B, and C are joint tenants. A conveys his interest to X. B and C remain joint tenants, as between themselves, in an undivided two-thirds of the estate; X holds an undivided one-third as a tenant in common with B and C. If B dies without having disposed of his interest during his lifetime, C will end up with an undivided two-thirds interest, X would have an undivided one-third interest, and the relationship between them would be as tenants in common.

Where there are more than two joint tenants and one conveys his interest to one of his cotenants, the cotenant grantee holds the share conveyed as a tenant in common but continues to hold his original share in joint tenancy.

Example:

A, B and C are joint tenants. A conveys his interest to B. B then becomes a tenant in common with respect to the one-third interest conveyed by A; however, B and C remain joint tenants as to the other two-thirds interest. And upon the death of B his one-third interest in common will descend to his heirs or pass under his will, but C will end up with the other two-thirds interest as surviving joint tenant.[12]

TENANCY IN COMMON

The tenancy in common is a type of co-ownership in which *only* the unity of *possession* is involved. In fact, the only difference between holding property as a tenant in common

12 MOYNIHAN, INTRODUCTION TO THE LAW OF REAL PROPERTY 221 (1962).

with others and holding it separately as sole owner is that in the case of the tenancy in common there is a blending of possession.

Unlike joint tenants, each tenant in common holds a separate and distinct, though undivided, fractional share in the property. But all tenants in common share one single right to the equal use and possession of every part of the whole property, as though sole owner, subject to the same right in the other cotenants;[13] in this respect only is the tenancy in common like the joint tenancy.

Since there need be no unity of time, title, or interest, tenants in common may acquire their shares at different times and by different instruments of conveyance; they may hold unequal shares, and the quantum of their estates may differ. Thus A, owning land in fee simple absolute, may convey a one-half interest to B and his heirs by *deed* and later *devise* a one-fourth interest to C for life and a one-fourth interest to D and his heirs. The result would be a tenancy in common between B, C, and D with B holding an undivided one-half interest in fee simple absolute, C holding an undivided one-fourth interest for life, and D holding an undivided one-fourth interest in fee simple absolute.

Like joint tenants, a tenant in common may dispose of his interest during his lifetime with or without the consent of his cotenants. However, unlike the joint tenancy situation, there is no right of survivorship between tenants in common. When a tenant in common dies, his interest descends to his heirs or passes in accordance with the terms of his will; and a spouse's dower or curtesy will attach to the interest of a tenant in common.[14]

13 And one cotenant may not bar another cotenant from his proportionate share of the profits, for cotenants have the duty to account for rents and profits received in excess of their proportionate share.

14 Unless, of course, the estate so held is a mere *life* estate.

Partnership Realty

Under the common law a partnership[15] was not recognized as a legal entity and for that reason it could not take and hold the legal title to real estate used for partnership purposes; the title to such real estate was held by the partners themselves as tenants in common. And although the partners held the realty as tenants in common, they held it in trust for partnership purposes, to be first applied, if necessary, to the payment of partnership obligations, including the payment of any balance due a partner on final settlement.

However, under the Uniform Partnership Act, now in force in nearly all states, the partnership is treated more as an entity. The Uniform Act provides that real estate may be acquired and conveyed in the partnership name, and that the partners are co-owners holding as "tenants in partnership" rather than as tenants in common. When a partner dies the Uniform Act declares that his interest in the partnership property is not subject to dower or curtesy but vests in the surviving partner or partners.

CREATION OF JOINT TENANCIES AND TENANCIES IN COMMON

Although the idea of two or more persons having simultaneous interests in the same land existed at a very early date, the old common law favored joint tenancies rather than tenancies in common. Consequently, a conveyance or devise to two or more persons created a joint tenancy *unless* the terms of the instrument specifically indicated that a tenancy in common was intended. Thus a conveyance "to A and B," or "to A and B equally," created, at common law, a joint tenancy.

The reason for the common law presumption favoring the creation of a joint tenancy, with its right of survivorship, is

[15] A "partnership" is generally defined as an association of two or more persons to carry on as co-owners a business for profit.

purely historical; when one joint tenant died there was always someone immediately available to render the feudal services due the over-lord. Also, the landholding class wished to avoid as much as possible the splitting of feudal services among several heirs; an over-lord preferred to have one responsible tenant from whom to receive the feudal services and incidents rather than be faced with the administrative burden of collecting from several cotenants.[16]

The survivorship feature of the joint tenancy often worked a hardship since the interest of a deceased joint tenant remained in the surviving joint tenant or tenants, to the exclusion of the family and heirs of the decedent and often contrary to the intent of the parties. But as the feudal system waned, so did the justification for the survivorship principle, and the legal presumption in favor of the joint tenancy began to shift in favor of the tenancy in common. Courts began to construe transfers to two or more persons as creating a *tenancy in common* rather than a joint tenancy, *unless* the intention to create a joint tenancy was clearly spelled out. This judicial turnabout was motivated by a desire to preserve the rights of the spouse and family of a deceased co-owner; the courts took the view that the ultimate ownership of property should not depend upon the mere accident of survivorship unless such intent was clearly indicated by the conveying instrument.

Today the presumption in favor of tenancies in common has been crystallized by legislation. In a few states joint tenancies have been abolished; in most states they continue to exist but their creation is controlled by statute. These statutes provide, in substance, that a conveyance or devise to two or more persons shall be construed to create a tenancy in common and *not* a joint tenancy *unless* the intent to create a joint tenancy is clearly expressed in the creating instrument.[17]

16 This was also the basis for the English rule of *primogeniture* whereby the eldest male heir inherited real property to the exclusion of other heirs of equal degree.

17 When two or more persons take property as heirs by intestate succession, they take as tenants in common.

The estate in joint tenancy has become increasingly popular as a method of holding property in the case of husband and wife or persons in close relationship. Indeed, it may be said that in most states, for many practical reasons, joint tenancies are looked upon with favor rather than with disfavor. However, in order to create a joint tenancy a clear intent to do so must be expressed. What are the appropriate words necessary to create a joint tenancy? The statutes do not specify the exact technical language necessary, but for many years the legal profession has utilized the words "as joint tenants and not as tenants in common," or "as joint tenants with rights of survivorship as such, and not as tenants in common." However, any language clearly indicating an intention to create a joint tenancy will be sufficient.

Partition

Simultaneous ownership in real estate sometimes proves impracticable, either because the cotenants cannot agree as to the use to which the property should be put or simply because of personal friction which often arises when there is a blending of possession. If the closeness of the relationship proves too unpleasant, a joint tenant or a tenant in common can compel a *partition*, that is, a physical division of the land into separate parcels, each parcel wholly owned by one of the erstwhile cotenants.[18]

The right of a cotenant to compel a partition is regulated by statute and the procedure varies from state to state. Partition provides a means by which people can free themselves of an unwanted common ownership arrangement; if a voluntary partition cannot be effected, a party is ordinarily entitled to partition as a matter of law, and his reasons for seeking partition are not material. Actual physical division will be ordered by the court if the land is capable of such division and if injustice to the other cotenants will not result; otherwise the

18 If the co-owners can *agree* on a division of the property, they can accomplish a partition by an exchange of deeds.

property will be ordered sold and the proceeds divided. Where there is a physical partition but division into exactly equal shares is not practicable, the court may order the favored cotenant to compensate the others by a money payment called *owelty*.

Joint Bank Accounts

The various types of co-ownership discussed in this chapter can exist in all forms of *personal* property as well as in realty. Because of the survivorship feature there are three classes of personal property which are frequently held in joint ownership: United States government bonds, corporate securities, and bank deposits.

Probably the most common form of co-ownership in personal property today is the joint bank account. A joint bank account is a bank account in the names of two or more persons payable to either or to the survivor. Although joint bank accounts, both savings and checking, are often created merely for purposes of convenience, it is the survivorship feature that is most appealing to the public—the idea that the surviving co-depositor automatically succeeds to the ownership of the account without the necessity of a will or the expense and delay of probate proceedings. Over the years there has been an increasing tendency on the part of the public to utilize the joint bank account as a substitute for a will; indeed, the joint bank account is often referred to as "the poor man's will." However, since the legal rules governing joint bank accounts vary substantially from state to state, the practice of keeping money in such accounts, as a substitute for a will, can lead to unpredictable and often undesirable consequences.

The reason for the great divergency of opinion among the states in this area of the law stems from the fact that, from a legal standpoint, the joint bank account is sort of a square peg in a round hole. The typical joint bank account situation is not a "true" joint tenancy because the four common law unities of time, title, interest, and possession are lacking; deposits and withdrawals are made at different *times,* and there is no unity of *title* or *possession* since either joint depositor can withdraw the entire amount and appropriate it to his own use. In order to uphold the desired survivorship feature in joint bank accounts, courts have found it necessary to rely upon various legal theories, none of which is entirely satisfactory. For example, assume that A deposits $10,000 of his money in the bank, making the account payable to either A or B or to the survivor. If B survives, on what theory can he claim title to the account?—he has contributed nothing. In such cases as this, where money belonging to one person is deposited to the account of himself and another, the relationship created usually depends upon the *intention* of the depositor. The depositor may have placed the money in the account merely for convenience of withdrawals, or he may have intended to establish a true joint interest in the account. But which is it? In some states the burden of proving that a joint interest in the account was actually created would fall upon B, the non-contributing survivor, whose claim would of necessity rest upon one of three theories: (1) that the deposit constituted a *gift* to B, or (2) that the deceased depositor had established a *trust* for B's benefit, or (3) that the deceased depositor had entered into a *contract* with the bank for the benefit of B. Unless B, the surviving depositor, were able to establish title to the account under one of these three theories his claim would fail.

Since, from a legal standpoint, all three theories have technical pitfalls, the adoption of any one of them usually involves at best a judicial union of the square peg with the round hole. Consequently several states have discarded the "gift," "trust," and "contract" theories and have passed statutes known as "joint tenancy statutes." The typical joint tenancy statute provides that any bank account established in the names of two or more persons, payable to either or to the survivor shall be deemed to create the full equivalent of a common law joint tenancy with the right of survivorship. These statutes dispense with the necessity of the four common law unities of time, title, interest and possession. However, the effect given these statutes varies from state to state. Some of the states hold that all accounts in the names of two or more persons payable to either or to the survivor shall be *conclusive* evidence of the depositor's intention to establish a joint tenancy and thereby vest title in the survivor; other states hold to the view that such accounts establish only a presumption that the depositor intended to create a joint tenancy, which presumption may be rebutted by clear and convincing evidence. Where the presumption is rebutted (usually by the deceased depositor's estate) survivorship rights must be established, if at all, in accordance with one of the three theories mentioned above, and this is not always possible.[19]

The joint bank account is being used more and more as a convenient and inexpensive vehicle for transferring savings upon death while yet retaining control during the donor's lifetime. However, joint bank accounts are often the subject of considerable misunderstanding among lay people, partly because of the diversity of state banking laws[20] and partly because the banking industry has failed in many instances to adequately explain to the public the legal consequences of joint ownership of bank accounts.

Until joint bank accounts are put on a basis of equality with other forms of joint ownership their frequent misuse as a method of property disposition will no doubt continue. In the meantime the responsibility for properly enlightening depositors as to the effect of our various joint bank account laws

19 The banks themselves are usually protected by statute when they pay any part of an account to a co-depositor, whether the other be living at the time or not. A few states have taken the position that the sole purpose of joint tenancy statutes is to relieve the banks of the responsibility for determining the relative interests of the depositors; other states have declared such statutes to be both for the protection of the banks *and* to establish survivorship interests.

20 For instance, in some states in order to create a joint bank account with the right of survivorship all the depositor need do is so specify in writing; yet other states flatly prohibit or severely limit the survivorship feature in joint bank accounts except where the co-depositors are husband and wife or closely related.

must fall upon the bankers; whether they are currently meeting this responsibility is questionable. The point of the discussion here is to caution against the casual use of the joint bank account as a substitute for a will. State banking laws differ considerably. Local statutes must be consulted.

TENANCY BY THE ENTIRETY

The tenancy by the entirety is a form of co-ownership between husband and wife which evolved from the common law fiction that husband and wife were one person. At common law a transfer of land to grantees who were husband and wife resulted in a tenancy by the entirety; since in the eyes of the law they were *one* they took but one estate—the entirety—with the right of survivorship. In a tenancy by the entirety the estate is held by husband and wife together as a *whole* rather than in undivided shares, and if one spouse dies the entire estate belongs to the other by virtue of the right of survivorship.[21] Like the joint tenancy, the tenancy by the entirety is characterized by the four unities of time, title, interest, and possession, plus an additional unity—the unity of husband and wife.[22] It is really a joint tenancy between husband and wife with some modifications.

A tenancy by the entirety differs from a joint tenancy in that a tenancy by the entirety cannot be terminated without the consent of *both* husband and wife. Thus, tenants by the entirety have no *individual* interest which they can convey; although both spouses may join in a conveyance of the property to a third person, neither alone can transfer his interest, create a severance, compel a partition, or otherwise defeat the right of survivorship in the other spouse.

Under common law any conveyance of land to a man and

21 Where tenants by the entirety die simultaneously or the order of their deaths is impossible to determine the estate is distributed as if they had been tenants in common.

22 A *divorce* destroys the unity of husband and wife and transforms a tenancy by the entirety into a tenancy in common.

wife created a tenancy by the entirety unless a contrary intent was clearly expressed. In those states which still recognize the tenancy by the entirety this is still pretty much the rule today. In such states a conveyance or devise of real estate to a husband and wife without specifying the type of estate intended is generally presumed to create a tenancy by the entirety. For example, a transfer to husband and wife "jointly," or even as "joint tenants," will ordinarily create a tenancy by the entirety in those states which recognize it.[23] At the present time the tenancy by the entirety, with various statutory modifications, is recognized in less than half of the United States.[24]

COOPERATIVES AND CONDOMINIUMS

Two forms of co-ownership which are relatively new to this country are the cooperative apartment and the condominium. They are both a type of home ownership in a multi-family structure. The origin of the cooperative apartment, or "co-op" as it is generally called, has been traced to France and England and as far back as Ancient Rome. In this country the co-op form of ownership first made its appearance in New York nearly a hundred years ago—before the advent of the condominium. The increasing population created a necessity for a more efficient use of land through high rise multi-family dwellings. Co-ops developed out of a need to share the rising costs of land and building construction among a group of

[23] However, a transfer to husband and wife as "tenants in common" will create a tenancy in common rather than a tenancy by the entirety.

[24] THE ESTATE IN COPARCENARY: Also classified as a type of cotenancy under the common law was the estate in coparcenary. However the estate in coparcenary is all but extinct in this country today. It arose out of the English rule whereby lands descended to the eldest son, to the exclusion of younger sons—the rule of *primogeniture*. If there were no sons to succeed to the estate it descended to the female heirs who took as coparceners. Collectively they took a single estate with unities of time, title, and possession, but their interests could be unequal. Like the tenancy in common there was no right of survivorship among coparceners. Although the term "coparceners" is still sometimes used to describe heirs who take land by descent (intestacy) the tenancy is virtually obsolete and such heirs inherit as tenants in common.

individuals. The co-op form of ownership became especially popular during the housing shortage following the First World War.

Co-ops are usually organized on a corporate basis. That is, a corporation is formed which holds title to the land and buildings. The corporation then leases the various apartments to the individual stockholder members of the co-op, who are referred to as tenant-stockholders. The lease, which is referred to as a "proprietary lease," entitles the tenant-stockholder to occupy a specific apartment.[25] The participants in a cooperative association—the tenant-stockholders—do not actually "own" their apartments; they have no fee interest in the real estate at all. They merely own shares of stock in the corporation, which shares entitle them to a long-term proprietary lease. Thus a participant in a co-op has been described as being something more than a tenant and yet something less than an owner.

The term *condominium* is usually defined as "a system of separate ownership of individual units in a multiple-unit building." The term is believed to have originated in Ancient Rome; it meant joint domain or co-ownership. The condominium is simply another form of cooperative ownership except that the owner of a condominium actually owns his apartment outright, holding a fee simple[26] title thereto, plus an undivided interest as a tenant in common in those areas of the property used in common by all the unit[27] owners.

The idea of separate ownership of parts of a building is not new to the law. The condominium concept existed in England and in various parts of Europe during the Middle Ages. Although the condominium is barely ten years old in this country it is fast becoming our most prevalent form of new housing. Increased demand for homes, high prices and a

25 The "proprietary lease" is usually a long-term lease containing the usual clauses and conditions found in many ordinary apartment leases.

26 Ownership of condominium units may be in fee simple absolute or any other estate in real property recognized by law.

27 The word "unit" as used here is synonymous with "apartment".

scarcity of land have given impetus to this ancient form of ownership. Economists predict that within twenty years half of the population in the United States will be living in some form of condominium.[28]

The condominium concept is established by the use of three basic documents: (1) the declaration, (2) the bylaws, and (3) the individual apartment deed. Of these three basic documents the *declaration*, sometimes referred to as the "master deed," is the most important. It enables the condominium to come into existence and contains the covenants, conditions and restrictions which establish the condominium regime. The declaration also contains the legal description of the land, a legal description of each of the individual units, and of the common elements[29] as well.

The *bylaws* set out the rules governing the internal operation of the condominium. They usually provide for such matters as the use and maintenance of the common elements, the method of selecting a board of co-owners, the rules for conducting meetings, the rights and responsibilities of the unit owners, the collection of monthly charges and assessments, rules for the use and maintenance of recreation facilities, etc. Condominium living is a cooperative way of life; unit owners must live by the rules of the association.

The *individual apartment deed* is the vehicle used to actually transfer the fee simple title to a particular unit, together with an undivided interest in the common areas. The deed designates which of the units is being conveyed by specific reference to the recorded declaration. Since the declaration

[28] Cooperatives and condominiums are not limited to residential uses; they are equally adaptable to commercial uses as well. Nor are they confined to high-rise structures. Although many cooperatives and condominiums built today are in the form of high-rise apartments, they may also be built as attached town houses, or simply as a cluster of detached buildings.

[29] The common elements include those areas and facilities shared by all of the unit owners, such as the underlying land, the foundation, hallways, lobbies, stairways, basements, elevators, swimming pool, parking areas, exterior walls, roof, storage spaces, etc. The common elements consist of all portions of the condominium property *except* the units.

already contains the legal description[30] of all of the units, the individual apartment deed need only refer to the recorded declaration and identify the unit as it is architecturally delineated therein.

It is the consensus of opinion that there are more advantages to the condominium form of ownership than there are to membership in a cooperative association. For instance, as we have seen, the members of a co-op do not own their own apartments—they have no fee interest in the real estate; all they actually "own" is a share in a cooperative venture which entitles them to a proprietary lease. Thus in actuality they are mere tenants, subject to the laws of landlord and tenant. The owner of a condominium, on the other hand, holds the legal title to his apartment. Consequently he enjoys the same income tax advantages as any other homeowner. He may deduct from his income the interest paid on his mortgage and also the real estate taxes. These deductions are not available to a mere tenant.

Also, in a typical cooperative organization, financing is accomplished by having the corporation place one or more mortgages on the entire property. Such mortgages and other encumbrances on the property are amortized through periodic rental payments which are made by all of the tenant-stockholders. Thus not only are the tenant-stockholders of a co-op committed to one plan of financing, they are all dependent upon the continued solvency of their fellow members. If one member of the cooperative is unable to meet his monthly carrying charges each of the other members must underwrite the deficiency or place his own equity in jeopardy. The unit owner of a condominium project, however, does not

30 The "legal description" of a condominium usually consists of a three-dimensional drawing of the entire structure, depicting each of the units therein, their elevations and locations with reference to the boundaries of the underlying land, plus the dimensions of the interior surfaces of each unit. The area of space enclosed by the apartment walls, floors and ceilings constitutes the "unit" which is owned outright in fee simple. The remainder of the property —both the land and building but excluding all other units—is owned by all the members as tenants in common.

suffer the disadvantage of such financial interdependence. Each condominium owner may finance his own unit independently, and so his title is not endangered by any failure on the part of other owners to meet their share of the mortgage and tax payments. A condominium owner is taxed separately and is responsible only for the mortgage indebtedness on his own unit. The condominium form of ownership may also have some psychological advantage over the cooperative apartment in that the condominium owner enjoys the satisfaction of owning his own home, whereas the member of a co-op is essentially a tenant.

COMMUNITY PROPERTY

The institution of *community property* is a system of co-ownership between husband and wife which exists in only eight states: Arizona, California, Idaho, Louisiana, Nevada, New Mexico, Texas, and Washington. It originated in Spain and France shortly after the decline of the Roman Empire.

The basic principle of community property is that while the material contributions of each spouse may be unequal, the efforts of both husband and wife are equally necessary to the success of the marriage—that since marriage is a "community," husband and wife should share equally as to the property acquired during the marriage.[31] The community property system replaces the common law interests of dower and curtesy. Under this system husband and wife become equal co-owners of all property acquired *during* the marriage by their joint efforts. In some respects their interests are analogous to a tenancy in common or a partnership.

However, not everything is considered as community property; property owned by either spouse *before* marriage, property acquired by gift or inheritance after marriage, together with income from such property, is considered to be the separate property of the spouse concerned.[32] And the

31 4A POWELL, REAL PROPERTY 722 (1975).

32 CRIBBET, PRINCIPLES OF THE LAW OF PROPERTY 89 (1962).

spouses may, by mutual consent, convert community property into the separate property of either the husband or the wife. In the case of divorce, community property is generally divided equally between husband and wife, although the share may be fixed by agreement of the parties.

Traditionally the husband is considered to be the head of the community, and for that reason the management and control of community property is generally placed in him. However, as managing agent the husband cannot transfer or encumber community property without the wife's consent. It would appear that with the advent of equal rights legislation the concept of the husband as manager will soon be disappearing.

SUMMARY

Since the early days of the feudal system the law has recognized the concept of co-ownership—a type of ownership where two or more persons have concurrent interests in the same property.

There were four types of concurrent interests recognized under common law: *joint tenancies, tenancies in common, tenancies by the entirety*, and *estates in coparcenary*.

The joint tenancy is a form of co-ownership which exists between two or more persons who hold one interest together as a unit; each person has exactly the same rights in that interest as his cotenant or cotenants. Joint tenants have one and the same interest, accruing by one and the same conveyance, commencing at one and the same time, and held by one and the same undivided possession.

The outstanding characteristic of the joint tenancy is the inherent *right of survivorship*; when one joint tenant dies his interest does not descend to his heirs or pass by his will, but rather, the entire ownership *remains* in the surviving joint tenant or tenants. However, property held in joint tenancy is subject to federal and state inheritance taxes notwithstanding the survivorship feature.

Under the Uniform Simultaneous Death Act, where two joint tenants die under circumstances where the order of death is impossible to determine, the property held in joint tenancy is distributed, one half as if one had survived and one half as if the other had survived.

A joint tenant may, during his lifetime, transfer his undivided interest by a simple conveyance, with or without the consent of the other cotenants; such a transfer ends the joint tenancy insofar as the share conveyed is concerned, and the grantee becomes a *tenant in common* with the remaining joint tenant or tenants.

The tenancy in common is a type of co-ownership in which only the unity of *possession* is involved. Like joint tenants, tenants in common have an equal and undivided right to possession, but unlike joint tenants, tenants in common hold separate and distinct shares in the property.

Tenants in common may acquire their interests at different times and by different instruments of conveyance; they may hold unequal shares, and the quantum of their estates may differ.

Like joint tenants, a tenant in common may dispose of his interest during his lifetime, with or without the consent of his cotenants. However, there is no right of survivorship between tenants in common; when a tenant in common dies his interest descends to his heirs or passes in accordance with the terms of his will.

The Uniform Partnership Act provides that real estate may be acquired and conveyed in the partnership name, and when a partner dies his interest in the partnership property vests in the surviving partner or partners.

Most states have statutes which provide, in substance, that a transfer to two or more persons shall be construed to create a tenancy in common and not a joint tenancy *unless* the intent to create a joint tenancy is clearly expressed.

A co-owner may compel a *partition*, which is a physical division of the land into separate parcels. Actual physical division will be ordered by the court if the land is capable of such division and if injustice to the other cotenants will not result; otherwise the property will be ordered sold and the proceeds divided. Voluntary partition may be accomplished by an exchange of deeds.

Co-ownership may exist in *personal* property as well as in realty. Probably the most common form of co-ownership in personal property is the joint bank account. However, in some states joint bank accounts are not on the same basis with other jointly held property. Since banking laws vary substantially from state to state, the joint bank account should not be utilized as a substitute for a will without first consulting local statutes.

Under common law a transfer of land to a man and wife created a tenancy by the entirety. It differs from a joint tenancy in that tenants by the entirety cannot separately transfer their interest to another person, compel a partition, or otherwise defeat the right of survivorship in the other spouse. The tenancy by the entirety is still recognized in nearly half of the United States today.

The common law estate in *coparcenary* was like a joint tenancy in that the coparceners held a single estate together; but, as in the case of tenants in common, there was no right of survivorship among coparceners. Although the term "coparceners" is still sometimes used to describe persons who take land by descent, the tenancy itself is obsolete.

Cooperatives and condominiums are a form of home ownership in a multi-family structure. The participants in a cooperative association do not actually "own" their apartments; they merely own shares in a corporation which entitles them to a long-term lease. The condominium is simply another form of cooperative except that the owner of a condominium owns his apartment outright, plus an undivided interest in the common areas of the property.

The condominium concept is established by the use of three basic instruments: (1) the *declaration,* (2) the *bylaws,* and (3) the *individual apartment deed.* The declaration contains the covenants, conditions and restrictions which establish the condominium regime, plus the legal description of the entire property. The bylaws set out the rules governing the condominium. The individual apartment deed transfers the title to the various units together with an undivided interest in the common areas. There are more advantages to the condominium form of ownership than there are to membership in a cooperative association.

Community property is a system of co-ownership between husband and wife under which they become equal co-owners of all property acquired during the marriage by their joint efforts. It exists only in Arizona, California, Idaho, Louisiana, Nevada, New Mexico, Texas, and Washington.

CHAPTER 7

EASEMENTS

THE NATURE OF EASEMENTS

An easement is a right, privilege, or liberty which one has in land owned by another; it is a right to a limited use in another's land for some special and definite purpose. It is a non-possessory interest in land since the owner of an easement does not possess the land itself—he merely has the right to do certain acts on the land of *another.* However, it is more than a mere personal privilege; it constitutes an actual interest in the land and is regarded as realty.[1] Typical easements involve rights of way across another's land, the right to lay pipes underneath another's land, or the right to flood it or string power lines across it.

Easements may be *affirmative,* such as those mentioned above, or they may be *negative.* An affirmative easement is one which allows the holder of the easement to do certain acts on another's land; a negative easement is one which allows the holder of the easement to *prevent* an owner from doing certain acts on his *own* land.

Easements are either *appurtenant* or *in gross.* If the easement was created for the purpose of benefiting *other land*

[1] Another nonpossessory interest in land very similar to an easement is a *profit.* A profit is the right to take, from land of another, a portion of the soil or some product of the land. For example, a profit may consist of a right to take gravel, coal, timber, water, or minerals. Since the same legal principles apply to both easements and profits there is no necessity for treating them separately.

owned by the holder of the easement, it is *appurtenant*—that is, appurtenant to the land benefited.

Example:

> A has an easement to lay drain pipes across a portion of B's land for the purpose of draining surface water from A's land. The easement is *appurtenant* because it benefits land owned by A.

An easement appurtenant inheres to the land benefited—it is "fixed" to it and cannot exist separate from it; such an easement attaches to and "runs with the land." This means that when the land is transferred, the easement follows along with it—*even if the deed does not mention the easement.* Thus, in the example above, if A conveys his land, the right to continue to maintain drain pipes across B's land will accrue to A's grantee, since the easement "runs with the land" as the title passes from one person to another.

The land which is benefited by the easement is referred to in legal parlance as the *dominant tenement;* the land burdened by the easement is referred to as the *servient tenement.*[2]

An easement *in gross* does not benefit any other land; it exists independently of other land, and is a mere personal interest in or right to use the land of another. In other words, there is a servient tenement but no dominant tenement. For instance, a public utility company's easement to place and maintain power lines across another's land is an example of an easement in gross.[3]

2 It may help you to remember the terms if you think of the land being benefited as the "ruling" or "dominating" (dominant) parcel, which is "served" by the servient tenement.

3 At common law an easement *in gross,* because of its personal nature, was not transferable or inheritable—it died with the individual holder. However, a *profit* was, and is today, a transferable and inheritable interest. Since it is the right to a portion of the soil or some product of the land of another, it is treated as an estate or interest in the land itself.

The general rule in the United States today with respect to easements in gross is that if they are commercial in character, such as railroad or public utility easements, they are transferable; a non-commercial easement in gross is transferable only if such intention is indicated in its creation, such as by the use of the words "heirs and assigns".

CREATION OF EASEMENTS

BY EXPRESS GRANT

The most commonly used method of creating easements is by an express conveyance.[4] The deed must describe the interest correctly and it must comply with the formalities necessary for the transfer of any interest in land. (As to the formal requirements of a *deed,* see chapter 10.)

BY RESERVATION OR EXCEPTION

Easements may also be created by express reservation or exception in the deed of conveyance. For example, A may convey a parcel of land to B but *reserve* or *except* a right of way across the land conveyed in order to retain access to other land owned by A.

BY IMPLICATION

The general rule of law is that when an owner of a tract of land conveys *part* of it to another, he is said to grant with it, *by implication,* all "easements"[5] which are apparent and obvious, and which are reasonably necessary for the fair enjoyment of the land granted.

Example:

A is the owner of two lots, 1 and 2, adjoining each other. There is a dwelling house situated on each lot but

[4] Although it is not common practice, easements may also be created by *will.*

[5] Since by definition as easement is a right, privilege, or liberty which one has in the land of *another,* a person can never have a true easement in his *own* land. However, an owner often uses one part of his land in such a way as to benefit another part, as for example, when one part contains drainage pipes, or sewers, or roadways which increase the usability of the other part. Such use of one part of the land for the benefit of another part creates what is referred to as a "*quasi*-easement"; the part benefited is the *quasi*-dominant tenement and the burdened part the *quasi*-servient tenement. And if the common owner conveys away that portion of the land benefited (the *quasi*-dominant tenement) the grantee will be entitled to an easement in the land retained by the grantor (the *quasi*-servient tenement). This *implied* easement will correspond to the use indulged in by the original owner, but the *quasi*-easement must have been apparent, permanent, and reasonably necessary for the enjoyment of the *quasi*-dominant portion, otherwise an easement by implication will not arise.

the water supply for both dwellings is piped from a driven well located on lot 1. This situation is apparent and obvious.[6] A conveys lot 2 to B, nothing being said about the water supply or an easement. According to the general rule, B is entitled to an easement in the form of a right to continue to draw water from the well on the land retained by A, even though such right was not specified in the deed from A to B. B, having seen how A used the property, can reasonably expect a continuance of the former manner of use. B's easement is said to arise by implication, based upon the probable intention of the parties.

When the owner of a tract of land has made use of one part for the benefit of another part of the tract, and the portion benefited is conveyed away, as in the example above, the general rule is that the grantee will be entitled to an easement by implication in the land retained by the grantor—but *only* if such use (*quasi*-easement) was *apparent, permanent,* and *reasonably necessary* for the enjoyment of the conveyed land.

The requirement that the *quasi*-easement must have been "apparent" at the time of title severance has been interpreted by some states to mean "readily visible." However, most states hold that it is sufficient if the *quasi*-easement was discoverable by careful inspection of the property by one conversant with the potential uses of the land. According to the majority rule, the *quasi*-easement must be apparent in the sense of being indicated by objects which are necessarily seen or would be ordinarily observable by persons familiar with the premises.

If the *quasi*-easement was neither visible nor discoverable upon reasonable inspection of the property, then an easement by implication will not arise. For example, a *quasi*-easement consisting of a sewer line which is completely underground

6 This would give rise to a *quasi*-easement with lot 2 as the *quasi*-dominant tenement and lot 1 as the *quasi*-servient tenement. It would be a "quasi" easement because a person cannot have a true easement in his own land.

and with no visible cleanout pipes, vents, or other visible indications of its existence, would probably not be sufficiently "apparent" to give rise to an easement by implication.

The requirement that the *quasi*-easement must have been "permanent" means that it must be permanently adapted to the use of the land and not merely occasional or temporary.

The rule in most states is that the *quasi*-easement must be "reasonably necessary" to the use and enjoyment of the land conveyed. Mere convenience, however great, is not sufficient. The general *test* of necessity is whether the party claiming the right can, at reasonable cost, create a substitute. A few states hold that an easement by implication will not arise unless it is *strictly* necessary to the beneficial use of the land conveyed.[7]

By Estoppel

An easement may be created by *estoppel.* The word "estop" means to stop, to prevent, or to prohibit; an estoppel is an estopping. In legal parlance an estoppel is a bar raised by the law which precludes a person, *because of his conduct,* from asserting rights which he might otherwise have—rights as against another person who in good faith relied upon such conduct and was led thereby to change his position for the worse. The name "estoppel " was given "because a man's own act stoppeth up his mouth to allege or plead the truth."

[7] Under the English common law doctrine of "ancient lights" it was held that where one who is the owner of two adjoining lots of land, on one of which is a building with an apparent and continuous right of light and air through its windows over the other lot, conveys away the lot with the building, retaining the vacant lot, there is, in the absence of an express provision to the contrary, an implied grant by him of the right to the light and air which has been enjoyed through the windows over the other property, and he cannot build any structure on such retained property so as to materially interfere with the enjoyment of light and air through those windows.

Although still adhered to in England, the "ancient lights" doctrine has not been followed in the United States. Thus there is no natural right of one landowner to receive a flow of light and air across another's land; any landowner may erect structures on his own land that will cut off the light, air and view of his neighbor. 1A THOMPSON, REAL PROPERTY § 238 (repl. 1964).

Example:

A, the owner of land abutting a lake, sells part of it to the city of X *knowing* that the purpose of the city is to use the water from the lake to supply the inhabitants with drinking water. A will be estopped from using his remaining lake frontage as a bathing beach which would pollute the lake water.

BY NECESSITY

Easements may be implied by *necessity,* regardless of the prior use of the land, if the existence of the easement is necessary for the beneficial use of the land conveyed or retained. The most common type of easement by necessity is a right-of-way; if the only means of access is over land sold or land retained, an easement by necessity will be implied in favor of either party in order to prevent the creation of a landlocked parcel.

Example:

A, owning a tract of land bounded on three sides by lands of others and on the fourth by a public highway, sells the inner portion of the tract to B, with the result that B's only access to the highway is either over land of adjacent owners[8] or over the land retained by A. There is no language in the deed indicating an intention to create a right-of-way in favor of B over the land retained by A. Nevertheless, under these circumstances B has an easement by necessity in the form of a right-of-way to the highway across the land retained by A.[9]

Similarly, an easement by necessity will be implied when the owner of land *retains* the inner portion after conveying the

[8] Under no conditions will a right of way over lands of the *adjacent owners* be implied by necessity or otherwise.

[9] Unless this were the case the land conveyed to B would have little use, except by helicopter, "and helicopters were not a factor in the thinking of the centuries in which this law crystallized." 3 POWELL, REAL PROPERTY 430 (1975).

balance to another, across which he must go for ingress and egress.

Example:

> A conveys to B that portion of his land which is contiguous to the highway, leaving himself landlocked with no means of access to the highway except either over lands of strangers or over the land conveyed to B. A has an easement by necessity over B's land.

Easements implied by necessity are based upon the presumed intention of the parties. When a person conveys a portion of his land to another, the law will not presume it to have been the intention of the parties that the grantee should derive no benefit thereof because of its being inaccessible from the highway, or that the other portion should, for like reason, prove useless to the grantor.

The states differ as to the *degree* of necessity required before a right-of-way by necessity will be implied. Some states maintain that a "reasonable necessity" or a "practical necessity" is sufficient grounds for implying an easement by necessity; other states require "strict" or "absolute" necessity. But in all cases the test is *necessity* and not mere convenience. Thus some states have held that no right-of-way by necessity exists across the remaining land of a grantor where the land conveyed borders on the ocean, although access by water may not be as convenient as access by land.[10] However, "necessity," as applied to a way by necessity, does not mean absolute physical impossibility of access. Where a right-of-way exists, but the expense of utilizing it is grossly in excess of the total value of the land itself, an easement of necessity is usually recognized.

By Prescription

Easements may be acquired by *prescription,* that is, by long continued use of another's land for purposes in the nature of

10 But where such access by water is rendered virtually impassable due to a perilous surf or other reason, a way of necessity will usually be implied.

an easement. Historically the doctrine of prescription was based upon the presumption of a lost grant, the idea being that since the use had continued for such a long period of time (since the time when "the memory of man runneth not to the contrary") it must have been based on a grant which had become lost or destroyed.

In most states the period necessary to acquire an easement by prescription is fixed by the statute of limitations applicable to the acquisition of title to land by adverse possession.[11] Depending upon the particular state statute, the period varies from five to thirty years, with periods of fifteen years or longer generally prevailing in those states east of the Mississippi.

For an easement by prescription to arise, certain conditions must be met: (1) the use must have been exercised under a claim of right adverse to the owner, (2) the adverse use must have been *continuous and uninterrupted* for the statutory period or longer, and (3) the adverse use must have been exercised with the owner's *knowledge and acquiescence,* or by a use so *open and notorious* that his knowledge and acquiescence will be presumed.[12]

Use Must Be Adverse

To give rise to a prescriptive right the use must be adverse as distinguished from permissive. To be adverse the use need not be hostile; it will be sufficiently adverse if made in such a way as to indicate indifference to the rights of the owner. And where the use has been open and notorious for the statutory period or more, with the knowledge and acquiescence of the

11 The acquisition of title to land by adverse possession is the subject matter of Chapter 8.

12 But one may not acquire an easement by prescription in the flow of light and air across another's land, nor to the prospect of view to a building, no matter how long the structure has stood. Thus, one may erect structures on his own land that will cut off the light, air, and view of his neighbor. However, in some states, by statute, the erection of a "spite fence" may be prevented. The typical "spite fence" statute provides, in effect, that any fence or other structure in the nature of a fence, unnecessarily exceeding a specified height, maliciously kept and maintained for the purpose of annoying the occupants of adjoining property shall be deemed a private nuisance.

owner of the land, the use will be *presumed* to have been adverse unless contradicted or explained. But acts in subordination to the rights of the owner are not adverse. Thus, one crossing the land of another by permission of the owner, and as a matter of accommodation, cannot gain a prescriptive right, since the use is not adverse. However a use which began in permission can *become* adverse; for instance, a continuance of a permitted use after the permission has been revoked becomes adverse.

Use Must Be Continuous and Uninterrupted

For a use to be continuous it is not necessary that it be constant or be made every day; a use may be continuous even though the specific acts of use are periodical or only occasional. Thus an easement may be acquired by a summer resident who makes use of the property only during the season. It is sufficient if the repeated acts of use are of such a character and at such intervals as to constitute *reasonable notice* of the adverse claim. What is essential is that there be no break in the adverse attitude of the user. Such a break would occur if the use were abandoned or if the user acted in subordination to the owner's rights, as by paying for the privilege of continuing the use.

For a prescriptive right to arise the use must not only be continuous—it must be uninterrupted.[13] This means that there must be no break in the use brought about by an act of the owner; if the owner of the land causes a discontinuance of the use, for even a brief period, there is an interruption and the prescriptive period must begin all over again.

Use Must Be With Owner's Knowledge and Acquiescence

For an easement to be acquired by prescription, the use must not only have been adverse, continuous, and uninterrupted for the statutory period, it must also have been with the

[13] The burden of proving that the use was "continuous and uninterrupted" is on the party claiming the easement.

owner's *knowledge and acquiescence.* "Acquiescence," in this context, is used in its ordinary sense. It does *not* mean license or permission in the active sense; it means passive assent or submission; it means uncomplaining or unresisting; it is consent by silence. And proof of acquiescence by the owner is essential; it raises the presumption of a grant. Where the adverse use has continued for the statutory period without interruption or denial on the part of the owner, and with his knowledge, his acquiescence is presumed. Anything which disproves acquiescence stops the running of the prescriptive period, since it rebuts the presumption that a grant was made.

The states are divided as to just what acts are sufficient to constitute non-acquiescence by an owner. Some states hold that mere protests or remonstrances are sufficient to prevent the acquisition of an easement by prescription; other states hold that acquiescence can be disproved only if the owner's protests are accompanied by a physical interference of the use, if only for a brief period of time.

Open and Notorious Use

The adverse use must have been with the owner's knowledge and acquiescence *or* it must have been so open and notorious that knowledge and acquiescence will be *presumed.* The requirement that the use must be open and notorious is for the protection of the landowner; it assures him a reasonable notice of the need to preserve his rights against the adverse user.

To be "open" the use must be made without secrecy or concealment. Thus a concealed use will not suffice *unless* the owner has *actual knowledge* of it. To be "notorious" it is not necessary that the use be actually known to the owner; it is only necessary that the use be such that a reasonable inspection of the premises would have discovered its existence.

Period of Prescription—Tacking

In computing time it is not necessary that the same individual be the adverse user throughout the statutory period.

Successive periods of adverse use by different persons may be added (tacked) together, provided there is "privity"[14] between them. For there to be "privity," there must be some connection or relationship between the successive users, such as grantor and grantee, ancestor and heir, or devisor and devisee. In other words, several periods of use by successive occupants holding by privity of estate may be counted together to make up the prescriptive period.

Example:

A and B own adjoining land in a state where the prescriptive period is twenty years. For fifteen years A adversely uses a way across B's land. A then conveys his land to X who continues the adverse use for 5 years. There exists between A and X the "privity" necessary to enable X to add the period of A's adverse use to his own in order to make out the twenty year prescriptive period.[15]

EXTENT OF EASEMENTS

What is the extent or scope of an easement once it has been created?—that is, what are the limits of the privileges of use to which an owner of an easement is entitled? The extent of an easement is generally determined by the manner in which it was created: if created by grant, it is fixed by the terms of the grant;[16] if created by prescription, it is fixed by the *use*

14 The term "privity" as used here denotes a mutual or successive relationship to the same rights in property.

15 There are special situations under which the statutory period of limitation will be extended due to the incapacity or "legal disability" of the landowner. The subject of legal disabilities will be taken up in the next chapter.

16 Where the meaning of the language in the granting instrument (the deed) is ambiguous, the court will attempt to effectuate the intent of the parties by construing the language in the light of the circumstances under which the easement was created.

If the deed creating the easement is ambiguous with respect to its *location*, the actual location used by the owner of the easement, if with the consent of the landowner, will resolve the ambiguity. The general rule of construction is that, in the absence of a specific limit on the scope of an easement created by grant, the grantee is entitled to a use which would reasonably serve the purposes of the grant.

through which it was created;[17] if created by necessity it is that extent required for the full utilization of the dominant tenement;[18] and if created by implication, the extent is determined by reference to the use which was being made of the *quasi*-dominant tenement at the time of the conveyance, and such uses as the parties might reasonably have contemplated at the time.

The passage of time often brings about changes in land use. Rural areas become housing developments; residential properties yield to commercial or industrial expansion. If the extent of an easement is generally fixed by the conditions which existed at the time of its creation, to what degree, if any, may the use be enlarged or expanded to meet such changing conditions? According to the general rule, the degree of use may be augmented, but only to the extent commensurate with the *normal development* of the dominant estate. A use in excess of the "normal development" of the dominant estate results in a *surcharge*[19] of the easement. The rule against surcharging operates to prevent unfair exploitation by the dominant owner, beyond what was originally contemplated when the easement was created.

Example:

A and B are adjacent landowners. A conveys to B an easement to take water from a well located on A's land. At the time of the conveyance B is using his land as a private residence. B changes the residence into a motel and continues to use the well to supply water to the motel,

Where the *width* of a right-of-way is not defined in the deed, it will be construed to be of such width as is reasonably necessary for the purposes for which it was granted.

17 The width and location of a *prescriptive* right of way are determined by the facts as they existed during the prescriptive period, since it is out of that use that the right by prescription arose.

18 In the case of a right of way by *necessity,* the owner of the servient estate has the first right to locate the way; and if he refuses to do so upon request, the owner of the dominant estate may locate the way. However, the location by either must be reasonable.

19 A surcharge is an overcharge—an encumbrance beyond what is just and right, or beyond one's authority or power. BLACK, LAW DICTIONARY (4th ed. 1951).

thus leaving an inadequate supply for A. This constitutes a surcharge of the easement.

The owner of the servient estate may use his land for any purpose he wishes, so long as he does not interfere with the easement. The owner of an easement has the right to do such things on the servient land as are reasonably necessary for the exercise of the right,[20] but nothing more; and the right must be exercised in a reasonable manner. The servient owner must allow the easement holder to come upon the land for the purpose of making necessary repairs, but the duty to repair rests upon the owner of the easement unless the parties have stipulated otherwise.

TERMINATION OF EASEMENTS

By Expiration

An easement (or profit) may be terminated or extinguished in a number of ways. Like any other interest in land, an easement may be potentially unlimited in duration or it may be created to last for a limited period of time, in which case the easement will expire according to its own terms. Where an easement is created for some specified purpose, it expires when the purpose is accomplished; when created by necessity, it ceases when the necessity ceases. However, most easements have a potentially unlimited duration requiring some special act to terminate them.

By Release or Merger

An easement may be extinguished by a *release* given by its owner to the owner of the servient land; but only if both parties concur. Since an easement, by definition, is a right in the land of *another,* an easement is extinguished when ownership of the dominant and the servient estates is united in the same person. This causes the easement to *merge* into the fee, since a person cannot have an easement on his own land.

20 For example, the right to take gravel would ordinarily include the right to go upon the land and make test borings for the presence of gravel.

By Abandonment

An easement may be extinguished by abandonment. "Abandonment" means more than mere non-use by the easement owner—it means conduct which indicates an intention never to exercise the right again. Non-use is *some* evidence, but it must be coupled with affirmative action by the easement owner indicating an intention to forego the right forever.

Example:

A has a twenty-foot right of way over adjacent land of B. A ceases use of the way and eventually constructs a permanent building so located as to make the use of the way impossible. In the absence of other factors, A's acts constitute an abandonment of the easement.

By Estoppel

An easement may be extinguished by the *conduct* of the easement holder, even though he had no intention of giving up the easement. To produce an extinguishment in this way, the servient owner must have changed his position in justifiable reliance upon the conduct of the owner of the easement. For instance, the *apparent* abandonment of an easement could result in its extinguishment: if the servient owner interprets mere non-use of the easement as an abandonment, and in reliance thereon makes substantial improvements upon his land, *to the knowledge of the holder of the easement,* the latter may be estopped to assert his rights.

Example:

A has a right of way across the adjacent land of B. A tells B that he intends to abandon the easement and that B may use the way as part of his farm. B, reasonably believing that A intends to abandon the easement, expends money and labor to make the way suitable for farming operations. A would be estopped from later exercising the easement.[21]

[21] RESTATEMENT, PROPERTY § 505, illustration 4 (1944).

By Prescription

An easement may be extinguished as well as created by prescription. In order for an easement to be extinguished by prescription, there must be a continuous and uninterrupted *interference* with the easement for the prescriptive period.

By Destruction of Servient Estate

A *destruction* of the servient estate usually extinguishes the easement. Thus, an easement in a structure, such as a party wall,[22] is extinguished if the structure is destroyed without the fault of the servient owner.

LICENSES

A license is a mere *revocable* right, privilege, or permission to enter upon or do acts upon another's land. To the extent that a license is a limited privilege to use land owned by another, it resembles an easement; the chief distinction between an easement and a license lies in the fact that while an easement is not revocable, a license is subject to termination at the will of the licensor.[23] An easement confers an interest in the land which may not be terminated at the pleasure of the servient owner; a license is a personal,[24] revocable[25] privilege which does not confer an actual "interest" in the land.

No formalities are essential to the creation of licenses; they may be created orally, in writing, or simply by a failure to comply with the formalities necessary for creating an easement, notwithstanding the obvious intent of the parties. And the death of the licensor, or a sale of the property, automatically terminates a license.

22 A "party wall" is a division between two connecting and mutually supporting structures, usually but not necessarily, standing half on the land of each owner, and maintained at mutual cost and for the common benefit of both parties.

23 A *licensor* is a person who grants a license; a *licensee* is a person to whom a license has been granted.

24 Being purely personal, a license is not transferable.

25 But a license may become irrevocable if it is coupled with an interest, as for instance, when the license is incidental to the ownership of a chattel. For example, the purchaser of a chattel located upon the vendor's land has an irrevocable privilege of going upon the land of the vendor for the purpose of removing the chattel.

SUMMARY

An easement is a right, privilege, or liberty which one has in the land owned by another.

Easements may be *affirmative* or they may be *negative*. An affirmative easement is one which allows the easement holder to do certain acts on another's land; a negative easement is one which allows the holder of the easement to prevent an owner from doing certain acts upon his own land.

Easements are either *appurtenant* or *in gross*. If the easement was created to benefit other land owned by the easement holder, it is appurtenant. An easement appurtenant is "fixed" to the land and "runs with the land" as title passes from one person to another. The land benefited by the easement is called the *dominant* tenement; the land burdened by the easement is called the *servient* tenement. An easement *in gross* does not benefit other land—it is a mere personal interest in or right to use the land of another.

Easements may be created by express grant, reservation or exception, implication, estoppel, necessity, or by prescription.

An easement created by *express conveyance* must describe the interest correctly and comply with the formalities necessary for the transfer of any interest in land. And a grantor may *reserve* or *except* an easement in the land conveyed.

When an owner of a tract of land conveys *part* of it to another, he is said to grant with it, *by implication,* all *apparent* easements (called *quasi*-easements) which are obvious, permanent, and reasonably necessary for the full enjoyment of the land granted. An easement by implication will not arise unless it is clearly necessary to the beneficial use of the land conveyed; mere convenience, however great, is not sufficient.

When a person is prevented, because of his conduct, from denying the existence of an easement, the easement is said to arise by way of *estoppel.*

Regardless of the prior use of the land, an easement will be implied *by necessity* if its existence is necessary for the beneficial use of the land conveyed. Some states hold that a "reasonable" or "practical" necessity is sufficient grounds for implying an easement by necessity; other states require "strict" or "absolute" necessity.

Long and continued use of another's land may give rise to an easement by *prescription.* For an easement by prescription to arise, the use must have been continuous and uninterrupted for the statutory period or more, under claim of right adverse to the owner, with his knowledge and acquiescence, or by a use so open and notorious that his knowledge and acquiescence will be presumed. In computing time, successive periods of adverse use by different persons may be tacked or added together, provided there is some connection or relationship between the users, such as grantor and grantee, ancestor and heir, or devisor and devisee.

The extent or scope of an easement is generally determined by the manner in which it was created, taking into consideration the conditions which existed at the time.

A use which is excessive or which has been enlarged or expanded unfairly and beyond what was originally contemplated at the time the easement was created constitutes a *surcharge* of the easement and may be prevented.

The servient owner may use his land for any purpose so long as his use does not interfere with the easement; the easement holder has the right to do such things on the servient land as are reasonably necessary for the exercise of the right, but nothing more.

Easements may be of potentially unlimited duration or they may be created to last for a limited time only, in which case they expire according to their own terms. An easement created for a specific purpose will expire when the purpose is accomplished, and when created by necessity, when the necessity ceases. An easement will be extinguished by a release given by its owner to the owner of the servient land or by a merger of ownership in the dominant and servient estates. Easements may also be extinguished by abandonment, by estoppel, or by a destruction of the servient estate; and an easement may be extinguished by prescription, that is, by a continuous and uninterrupted *interference* with the easement for the prescriptive period.

A license is a mere *revocable* right, privilege, or permission to enter upon or do acts upon another's land; it does not confer an actual "interest" in the land.

CHAPTER 8

ADVERSE POSSESSION

INTRODUCTORY STATEMENT

The old adage that "possession is nine-tenths of the law" is not without some merit; possession is a much older legal concept than ownership. Under the early feudal system mere possession of land, even by one who did not own it, conferred certain rights as against the rest of the world. In fact, at early common law, ownership could not exist *apart* from possession. A person who had possession of land with an intent to claim a freehold interest was said to have *seisin*—that is, he was "seised" of land. "Seisin" meant *possession* coupled with a freehold interest; it came as close to our modern idea of ownership as was possible within the feudal structure.

If one seised of land were wrongfully dispossessed (disseised)[1] by another, such wrongful possessor (called a disseisor) acquired, by mere virtue of the possession, many aspects of ownership; and until the rightful owner re-entered the land, either by self-help[2] or by a legal action (real action), he had lost his seisin. Moreover, the early English statutes *limited* the time within which the rightful owner could bring an action to recover his possession. At first this limit was established by setting a definite date beyond which the

[1] Disseisin was accomplished by excluding, evicting or ousting the owner from possession.

[2] "Self-help" is the regaining of possession without recourse to the law, as in self-defense.

claimant (the true owner) could not go; in order to recover his seisin (possession) he had to prove that he or his ancestor had been seised of the land *since* the date set by the statute. This date was changed from time to time, until finally, in 1623, a statute was passed which established the modern method of measuring the limitation—by adopting a *fixed-time* rule. The 1623 statute provided that no person could bring an action to recover the possession of land unless he commenced the action *within twenty years* from the time his right first accrued, and not afterwards.[3] Most of the statutes enacted by the various states are patterned after this old English statute, although the period of limitation varies greatly from state to state.[4]

The function of the *statute of limitations* is twofold: (1) it bars an action by an owner who has delayed too long in asserting his rights against one who is in possession claiming ownership, and (2) it confers ownership upon such possessor by extinguishing the rights of the original owner. Or to state it another way, a person in actual possession of land, claiming ownership, has a good title against all the world *except* the rightful owner; but if the rightful owner fails to assert his title by process of law *within* the period set by the statute of

[3] 21 Jac. 1, c. 16, §§ 1, 2 (1623).

[4] The *gross* statutory periods of possession required to establish title by adverse possession in the various states are as follows:

STATE	STATUTORY PERIOD
Alabama	Ten years
Alaska	Seven years
Arizona	Ten years
Arkansas	Seven years
California	Five years
Colorado	Eighteen years
Connecticut	Fifteen years
Delaware	Twenty years
D.C.	Fifteen years
Florida	Seven years
Georgia	Twenty years
Hawaii	Twenty years
Idaho	Five years
Illinois	Twenty years
Indiana	Ten years
Iowa	Ten years
Kansas	Fifteen years
Kentucky	Fifteen years
Louisiana	Thirty years
Maine	Twenty years
Maryland	Twenty years
Massachusetts	Twenty years
Michigan	Fifteen years
Minnesota	Fifteen years
Mississippi	Ten years
Missouri	Ten years
Montana	Five years
Nebraska	Ten years
Nevada	Five years
New Hampshire	Twenty years
New Jersey	Twenty years
New Mexico	Ten years
New York	Ten years
North Carolina	Twenty years

limitations, his right will be forever extinguished;[5] the adverse possessor will acquire a valid legal title as effectually as if he received a deed. Thus, the old doctrine of disseisin has been replaced by the doctrine of adverse possession—a doctrine which holds that possession which is adverse to the interests of the true owner, if continued long enough, can ripen into absolute ownership by operation of the statute of limitations.[6]

It is not enough that the possession last for the statutory period; it must also be open, notorious, adverse, continuous, exclusive, and under claim of right. The law concerning adverse possession differs from state to state, partly because the various statutes of limitation are worded differently and

North Dakota	Twenty years
Ohio	Twenty-one years
Oklahoma	Fifteen years
Oregon	Ten years
Pennsylvania	Twenty-one years
Rhode Island	Ten years
South Carolina	Ten years
South Dakota	Twenty years
Tennessee	Twenty years
Texas	Twenty-five years
Utah	Seven years
Vermont	Fifteen years
Virginia	Fifteen years
Washington	Ten years
West Virginia	Ten years
Wisconsin	Twenty years
Wyoming	Ten years

In some states the required statutory period is shortened if the adverse claimant has paid the taxes during his occupancy or if he has occupied under *color of title*. "Color of title" is a writing or instrument which has the appearance or semblance of validity, and which purports to pass the title, but which in fact is defective and does *not* pass the title. It is usually in the form of a deed or a will or some other paper or instrument which appears to be valid on its face but which in fact is invalid.

5 Under common law no title by adverse possession could be acquired against the sovereign, be it Crown or National Government or State. And this is still the rule today. The statute of limitations does not run against the government, and therefore title to public property cannot be acquired by adverse possession.

6 Do not confuse the gaining of title by adverse possession with the creation of an easement by adverse use (prescription). In the case of a prescriptive easement, the actual possession of the land continues in the owner of the servient estate, and the prescriptive right arises out of adverse *use*; in the case of title by adverse possession, the owner is ousted from possession, and title arises out of adverse *possession*.

Since an easement by prescription is based upon the presumption of a lost grant, the landowner's continued acquiescence during the prescriptive period is essential; anything which disproves acquiescence rebuts the presumption of a grant and stops the running of the prescriptive period. However, nothing short of making entry or a legal action will break the continuity of an adverse possession. And, of course, the land *interests* are different. A prescriptive easement involves a *use* or *right in land of another,* while adverse possession is concerned with the acquisition of *title to the fee.*

partly because there is a judicial difference of opinion as to what constitutes "adverse" possession. The frequently stated rule in most states is that the possession which will ripen into title must be *actual, open, notorious, hostile, continuous and exclusive, under a claim of right, for the statutory period.* All of these elements must exist.

ELEMENTS OF ADVERSE POSSESSION

Possession Must Be Open and Notorious

To establish title by adverse possession, the possession must be *open* and *notorious* during the statutory period. The purpose of this requirement is to put the owner on guard and to sufficiently enable him to take measures to recover his property and protect his title from an adverse possessor. Thus, a hidden or concealed use of the property, or one which is casual and intermittent, is not sufficient to prove title by adverse possession; the possession must be sufficiently notorious to put a man of ordinary prudence on notice that the land is being antagonistically held by another.

Actual knowledge of the adverse claim is not necessary. It is the *nature* of the possession which is controlling. But the possession must be so open, notorious, and unequivocal in character as to reasonably indicate to anyone visiting the premises that a claim of exclusive appropriation and ownership is being made; it must indicate more than the mere presence of an occasional trespasser. The possession must be so notorious that the owner may be presumed to have knowledge that it is adverse. If the owner has *actual* knowledge of the adverse claim, the requirement of notoriety is met.

Must Be Hostile or Adverse

For possession to ripen into title, it must be *hostile* or *adverse* in character; it must purport to deny the owner's title in the property. "Hostile," in this sense, does not imply ill will or hostility toward the owner, or even that there may be a dispute; it simply means an intent to hold title against the true owner.

Possession which is permissive, even if long continued, will never ripen into title by adverse possession. For example, possession under a tenancy, or otherwise in *subordination* to the title of the true owner, is not "hostile" or "adverse" and will not start the statute of limitations running.[7] However, one in permissive possession may, by unequivocal acts of hostility, cause his possession to *become* adverse.[8]

Must Be Continuous and Exclusive

Before title by adverse possession can be acquired, the possession must have been continuous for the full statutory period. When there is a break in the continuity of possession, the running of the statute stops, all rights gained are wiped out, and the statutory period must start anew. An abandonment of possession will break its continuity, but a temporary break or interruption, with no intent to abandon, will not.

For possession to be "continuous" it is not necessary that the adverse possessor should be actually upon the premises continually, but there should be some kind of continuity. For instance, continuity of possession may be established though the land is used seasonally, or only during certain periods of the year. However, there must be some regularity or

7 For instance, a life tenant in possession cannot gain title by adverse possession as against the owner of a future interest, since the possession of the life tenant is lawful and not "hostile" or "adverse."

8 But to change a permissive possession into one that is hostile there must be a clear and positive disclaimer of the title of the true owner.

Acts which would be held to be hostile and adverse if done by a stranger might not be if done by a co-tenant, since each co-tenant has the right to possession, and such possession will be presumed to be rightful rather than wrongful—at least until some positive and unequivocal act of exclusion shall have occurred.

As between co-tenants, evidence of long-continued, uninterrupted and even exclusive occupation by one co-tenant is not enough to bar the rights of the other co-tenants. There must be evidence from which an ouster—a putting out and a keeping out—of the other co-tenants can be inferred.

continuity of occupancy during the time the land is capable of use. The adverse possessor must have affirmatively and consistently acted as if he were the owner, taking into consideration the uses for which the land was suitable. Thus, there could be sufficient continuity of possession where land of a seasonal character is occupied only during the particular season and not during the rest of the year.[9] But the occupancy must be something more than intermittent or temporary; occasional or sporadic acts of dominion over the land, although extended over the statutory period, will not constitute continuous possession.

An entry upon the land by the true owner made openly and notoriously for the purpose of asserting his rights, and unequivocally indicating an intent to resume the actual possession, will interrupt the running of the statute.

The adverse possession must be of such an exclusive character as to give notice to all of the nature and extent of the claim; it must be such an exclusive exercise of dominion over the land that the true owner may be presumed to have knowledge that it is adverse. The adverse claimant must hold possession for himself, as his own, and not for another. Possession which is not exclusive but in participation with the true owner, or others, is not sufficient.

Must Be Under Claim of Right

For adverse possession to ripen into title, it must not only be open, notorious, hostile, continuous and exclusive—it must be *under a claim of right.* But that isn't to say that the adverse claimant should either believe or assert that he had a *legal right* to enter; indeed, as a trespasser, he may be very well aware that his entry is unlawful. The requirement of a claim of right simply means that he must *take possession of the lands as if they were his own,* and with the *intention* of holding them

[9] For example, where grazing land was occupied by an adverse possessor for grazing purposes and only during the grazing season each year, the possession was held to be continuous within the meaning of the rule. Kellogg v. Huffman, 137 Cal. App. 278, 30 P.2d 593 (1934).

for himself to the exclusion of all others. Thus, possession by a mere squatter or an avowed trespasser is not adverse possession; naked possession without a claim of right will not ripen into title, no matter how long continued. Regardless of how exclusive and hostile the possession may appear to be, it will not be "adverse" unless there is an actual *intent* to claim the title as owner.

Mistake as to Boundary Line

Sometimes a person will occupy land (not covered by his deed) up to a fence or other physical boundary under the *mistaken* belief that it is the true property line between his land and land of the adjoining owner. Does a person who so occupies land under the mistaken belief that he is the owner qualify as an adverse possessor? On this point the legal authorities are divided. A growing number of states follow the so-called Connecticut rule,[10] which holds that mistake is of no importance; that "claim of right" simply means an actual open and adverse possession in fact, and the mental attitude or motive of the possessor is immaterial. Under this majority rule, one who mistakenly occupies beyond his true line, without knowledge of the correct boundary, may nevertheless acquire title by adverse possession; an actual *intent* to claim title beyond the true line is not essential. In such cases it is the physical occupancy that is important, and the fact that it was done under a *mistaken* belief as to the *location* of the boundary line is immaterial.

Some states follow the rule laid down by the leading case of *Preble v. Maine Central R.R.,*[11] which holds that the actual *intention* of the possessor to claim adversely is an essential ingredient in adverse possession. In that case the claimant, for over twenty years, had occupied land up to a fence in the mistaken belief that it was the true property line. He testified that he "occupied it on account I thought it was my own

10 From a leading Connecticut case decided in 1831, French v. Pearce, 8 Conn. 439 (1931).

11 85 Me. 260, 27 Atl. 149 (1893).

land," but with no intention to claim title beyond his actual boundary, wherever that may be. The court reaffirmed the minority rule that actual *intent to hold under claim of right* is essential to the acquisition of title by adverse possession. The court said that "one who by mistake occupies for twenty years, or more, land not covered by his deed with no intention to claim title beyond his actual boundary wherever that may be, does not thereby acquire title by adverse possession to land beyond the true line." The court said that if the claimant had *intended* to claim title to the fence, *whether the fence was the true line or not,* there would have been adverse possession.[12] The distinction is this: where one occupies land up to a fixed boundary, under a mistake as to the true line but with the intention to claim title *only* to the true line, such possession is not hostile and will not ripen into title. However, where one occupies land under the mistaken belief that he owns to the fence or to some other boundary on the face of the earth, and he does so *with the intent to claim title up to such boundary, whether it shall eventually be found to be correct or not,* there is sufficient adverse possession. Thus the minority rule follows the subjective test of the adverse possessor, requiring him to *intend* to hold adversely regardless of whether the occupancy was through mistake or otherwise.

The minority rule has been strongly criticized as "unsound historically, inexpedient practically, and as resulting in better treatment for a ruthless wrongdoer than for the honest

[12] The mental attitude of the possessor is usually determined through testimony. For example, in a Michigan case (Ennis v. Stanley, 346 Mich. 296, 78 N. W. 2d 114 (1956).) the claimant testified as follows:

"Q. Now, did you have any intention to claim title to any land that was not yours, that belonged to somebody else? A. No, I don't want to claim something that belongs to anybody else.

"Q. What I am getting at is: Have you intended all these years to claim something that you did not own as your own? A. Why, no.

"Q. You intended only to claim what was your own, and you thought it was to that line? A. That's right."

Such testimony would indicate that the claimant had no intention of claiming any land not included in his deed, and so, did not occupy the land under sufficient "claim of right" to acquire title by adverse possession under the minority rule.

landowner."[13] Indeed, under the minority rule the statute of limitations seems to be reserved for those who deliberately set out to steal the land of their neighbor.[14]

EXTENT OF ACQUISITION— "COLOR OF TITLE"

Normally an adverse possessor acquires title only to that *portion* of the land actually *possessed and occupied* by him during the statutory period. Land is generally deemed to have been "possessed and occupied" when the claimant has exercised that type of dominion and control over the land that a typical, average owner would. The dominion required for adverse possession may be evidenced by continued residence on the land, the making of improvements, cultivating or otherwise making use of the land as an average owner would; the general test is that degree of control ordinarily exercised over such property by a typical owner.[15]

Some states require that the land shall be deemed to have been sufficiently possessed and occupied only if defined by a substantial enclosure, or when it has been actually cultivated or improved. Most states require only that the possession be open, notorious, and comporting with the ordinary management and use of the land. However, the possession must be so open, notorious and continuous that a typical owner viewing the land would be presumed to know of the adverse use and of its character and extent.

13 7 POWELL, REAL PROPERTY 727 (1974).

14 "Why a man without title who as an honest man admits that he wanted only what was his, and occupied in the belief that the land was his, should be worse off than the wilful wrongdoer who enters and occupies in order to get title by adverse possession is not explained in these cases." 3 AMERICAN LAW OF PROPERTY § 15.5 (Casner ed. 1952).

15 Some state statutes provide that possession cannot constitute *adverse* possession unless the claimant has also paid the taxes on the land. However, in most states the payment of taxes upon the land is not possession nor evidence of possession, but only evidence of a claim of title. The true owner could pay the taxes throughout the statutory period and still lose his title by adverse possession.

As we have seen, the adverse possessor's "claim of right" need not be based upon a contention or assertion that the claim is in any way legal or justified; an actual intent to claim the title as owner is all that is necessary to constitute adverse possession. However, where the adverse possessor claims under a *recorded instrument* which professes to pass title but which, by reason of some defect not appearing on its face, does not in fact amount to title, he is said to claim "under color of title." Color of title is that which has the appearance or semblance of title but which is in fact none. The instrument relied upon to furnish color of title is often a deed which is invalid due to lack of title in the grantor, or is defective for some other reason not apparent on its face. Color of title may be in the form of an invalid tax deed, a sales contract, or any instrument which serves to define the extent of the adverse possessor's claim. However, an instrument will not constitute color of title unless it appears valid on its face, is recorded,[16] and contains an adequate description of the land in question. Color of title is not legal title; its effect is only to define the limits of the claim under it.

Since it is not necessary that a "claim of right" should be also under color of title to constitute adverse possession, why is it necessary to make the distinction? Because the *extent* of acquisition can be much greater if possession is under color of title.[17] Title acquired by adverse possession is ordinarily limited to the physical portion of land actually used and occupied; but if the adverse possession is under color of title, the title acquired is not limited to the part actually occupied; it will extend over the *whole parcel described in the instrument.* In such cases the possession is said to constructively extend to the whole of the land described in the instrument, since the recorded instrument serves notice to the world that the claim

16 In some states the instrument relied upon as "color of title" need not be recorded.

17 Also, in some states the statutory period of possession is *shortened* if the adverse claimant has occupied under "color of title."

exists. The rule is well set out in the leading case of *Banton v. Herrick,*[18] where the court said:

> "When an entry is made upon a lot of land and a part is occupied without any recorded claim of title, a title by adverse possession is limited to the part actually occupied, . . . but when a lot of land is entered upon and part of it occupied under a recorded deed of the whole lot, showing a claim of title by record to the whole lot, the effect of such entry and occupation is not limited to the part actually occupied, but extends over the whole lot . . . Any record owner seeing any part of his land occupied by another in such manner as would give title by [adverse possession], if sufficiently long continued, is bound to ascertain from the public registry whether such occupation is under a recorded claim of title, and also the extent of that claim. If, knowing all this, he makes no effort to interrupt such occupation or claim until after [the statutory period] he has no cause of complaint that the law protects the occupant in his claim to the whole parcel."

This doctrine of *constructive possession* is based upon the ground that one in possession of land, under a recorded paper title containing a specific description, exercising control and dominion over the premises under claim of right, is presumed to be doing so *to the extent of his claim.*

THE REQUIRED DURATION—TACKING

Before title can be acquired by adverse possession, the occupancy must have been continuous for the full statutory period. And although the possession must be continuous, it need not be by one and the same individual throughout the whole statutory period. Successive periods of possession by different persons may be tacked or added together in order to

18 101 Me. 134, 63 Atl. 671 (1906).

make up the required period, provided there is "privity" between the occupants. "Privity," such as will allow the tacking of possessions, means that the successive occupancies must be connected so that each adverse possessor shall apparently hold by right of his predecessor in possession; unconnected possessions cannot be tacked. The requirement of "privity" is satisfied when the relationship between successive possessors was that of grantor and grantee, ancestor and heir, or devisor and devisee.[19] In such cases the adverse possession is "passed on" by deed, descent, or devise.

DISABILITIES

Title by adverse possession rests upon statutes of limitation which limit the time within which an owner must bring an action to recover land which is held adversely by another. It would seem, then, that an adverse possessor could always be assured of acquiring legal title immediately upon the expiration of the statutory period. There are at least two reasons why this is not so.[20] *First,* the statute of limitations will not begin to run against any individual *until* he has a legal cause of action. For example, a remainderman has no right to possession until the termination of the prior life estate; therefore the statute of limitations would not begin to run against the remainderman until that time.[21] In other words, the statute of limitations will not begin to run against the owner of a future interest until he first becomes entitled to possession, for until that time he has no cause of action. *Second,* most state statutes contain provisions which have the effect of lengthening the required period of adverse possession where the owner of the property is under a legal disability. Just what constitutes a legal disability and how it

19 A person leaving real property by will is referred to as a *devisor;* a person who receives real property by will is called a *devisee.*

20 Aside from the reason that one who claims title by adverse possession assumes the burden of proof.

21 For instance, A might occupy Blackacre for the full statutory period adversely to B, the *life* tenant. However in such case the statute of limitations would not have run at all against C, the remainderman. A would acquire, by adverse possession, only B's life estate.

functions to lengthen the period of adverse possession depends upon the particular state statute. The typical disabilities are minority, insanity, imprisonment, and absence from the country. In some states the running of the statute is *suspended* during the period of disability and not computed as part of the statutory period; in other states the owner may bring his action to recover the land within a stated period of time *after* the disability has been removed.

SUMMARY

A person in actual possession of land, claiming ownership, has a good title against everyone except the true owner; such adverse possession, if continued long enough, can ripen into absolute ownership by operation of the statute of limitations.

For possession to ripen into legal title it must be actual, open, notorious, hostile, continuous and exclusive, under a claim of right, for the statutory period at least.

The possession must be so open and notorious as to reasonably indicate to a man of ordinary prudence that the land is being antagonistically held by another. The purpose of the requirement of notoriety is to furnish the true owner with notice that he must take measures to protect his title.

The requirement that the possession must be hostile does not imply actual ill will or hostility toward the owner; "hostile," in this sense, means *adverse* to the owner's interest—it must purport to deny the owner's title in the property. Possession which is permissive or in subordination to the owner's title is not "adverse" possession.

The possession must be continuous and exclusive for the full statutory period; a break in the continuity of possession interrupts the running of the statute and the period must start again. For possession to be "continuous" there must be some regularity or continuity of occupancy in accordance with the uses for which the land is suitable; intermittent or occasional occupancy is not sufficient, even though extended over the statutory period. The possession must be exclusive in that the claimant must occupy the land for himself, as his own, and not for another or in participation with the owner.

To satisfy the requirement that the possession must be under a claim of right it is not necessary that the claimant believe or assert that he had a legal *right* to enter; it is sufficient if there exists an *intent* to claim title as owner, to the exclusion of all others.

A person who mistakenly occupies land beyond his true boundary line may, under the majority rule, acquire title by adverse possession even though he had no actual *intent* to claim beyond the true line. The majority rule holds that it is the exclusive exercise of dominion for the statutory period that is important, and the fact that it was done under a mistaken belief as to the actual location of the boundary line is immaterial. The minority rule holds that in such cases the mental attitude of the occupant is controlling—there must be an actual intent to claim title. Under this rule, one who, for the statutory period, mistakenly occupies land not covered in his deed, *with no intention* to claim title beyond his actual boundary wherever that may be, will not thereby acquire title by adverse possession to the land beyond the true boundary line. However, where one, for the statutory period, occupies land under the mistaken belief that he owns to the fence or to some other boundary on the face of the earth, and he does so *with the intent* to claim title up to such boundary, whether it shall eventually be found to be correct or not, may thereby acquire title by adverse possession. Under the minority rule the intention is the test and not the mistake.

Title acquired by adverse possession is ordinarily limited to the part actually occupied. However, where the adverse possessor claims under a recorded instrument which, although defective, professes to pass title, he is said to claim "under color of title," in which case, the title acquired will extend over the whole parcel described in the instrument.

Successive periods of possession by different persons may be tacked or added together to make up the statutory period. However, to allow tacking, there must be a connection or relationship between successive possessors, such as that of grantor and grantee, ancestor and heir, or devisor and devisee.

The statute of limitations will not begin to run against any individual until he has a right to possession, and thus, a legal cause of action. And most state statutes contain provisions which have the effect of lengthening the required period of adverse possession where the owner of the land is under a legal disability. The typical disabilities are minority, insanity, imprisonment and absence from the country.

CHAPTER 9

WILLS AND DESCENT

WILLS

DEFINITIONS AND TERMINOLOGY

A will is an instrument by which a person makes a disposition of his property to take effect after his death; it is revocable during the maker's lifetime and operative for no purpose until his death.[1] A person who dies leaving a valid will is said to have died *testate;*[2] such person is referred to as a *testator* (if a male) or a *testatrix* (if a female). A gift of real property by will is called a *devise;* the person leaving such property by will is referred to as a *devisor* and the person receiving it a *devisee.* A gift of personal property by will is called a *bequest* or a *legacy* and the recipient is referred to as a *legatee.* Although, strictly speaking, a testator "devises" realty and "bequeaths" only personal property, the terms are often used interchangeably without difference in legal effect.[3]

1 Originally the term "will" was used only in connection with *real* property, and a disposition of *personal* property was referred to as a "testament." An instrument disposing of *both* real and personal property was called a "last will and testament." Although the word "testament" is still often used in the heading of formal wills, the distinction between the terms has disappeared; the term "will" is now used to designate a testamentary disposition of *both* real and personal property. ATKINSON, WILLS 3 (2d ed. 1953).

2 If a person dies *without* having left a will, or if his will is declared not valid for some reason, he is said to have died *in*testate.

3 However, if it appears that the terms were used understandingly, their precise technical meaning will be applied. Whether the word "bequeath" means the same as "devise," when used in a will, is to be determined by the apparent *intention* of the testator. But there is no rule of law or public policy which makes any special form of words essential to the validity of a will; it is the apparent intention of the testator which governs.

Today the right to dispose of property by will is taken for granted; yet historically, the privilege was slow in coming. The common law, except by custom in some localities, did not permit owners to devise their lands by will. It was not until the enactment of the English Statute of Wills in 1540[4] that landowners gained the power to direct the disposition of their property after death. The Statute of Wills required only that the disposition be in writing; it did not specify that the writing be in the hand of the testator or even that he sign the document. The opportunity for frauds and forgeries permitted by this situation led to the passage of the fifth section of the English Statute of Frauds in 1677. This section required that the will be signed by the person making it, or by some other person in his presence and by his express directions, and further, that it be attested in his presence by three or four credible witnesses.[5] The English Wills Act of 1837 added a further requirement that the will should be "signed at the foot or end thereof," and also reduced the number of required witnesses from three to two.[6] The various American statutes of wills are patterned after these old English statutes, but they differ in detail from state to state.

WHO MAY MAKE A WILL?

Age Requirement

The minimum age for making a will is fixed by statute in every state. This age varies, from eighteen or less in some states to twenty-one in others. In some states the age is less for females than it is for males, and in a few states a married person may make a will at any age.

There is no "natural" right to dispose of property by will; the right to make a will is neither a common law nor a constitutional right, but a privilege granted by statute.

4 32 Hen. 8, c. 1 (1540).

5 29 Car. 2, c. 3, § v (1677).

6 7 Will. 4 and 1 Vict., c. 26 (1837).

Mental Capacity

It is the rule in all states that in order to make an effective will the testator must be of *sound mind*. What is meant by "sound mind"? The fact that a testator is an eccentric or abnormal person does not necessarily indicate that he is of unsound mind within the meaning of the wills statutes. In the matter of the testator's mental capacity, the word "sanity" is used in its legal and not in its medical sense. In the eyes of the law a mind is sound that can reason and will intelligently in the particular transaction being considered; and a mind is unsound or insane that cannot so reason and will.

The standard of mental capacity required to make a will is generally met if the testator can carry in his mind (a) the general nature and extent of his property, (b) a general idea of the persons who are the natural objects of his bounty, and (c) a general idea of the disposition which he is making of his property.[7]

A person may lack the faculty to transact certain business, or to execute a deed or contract and yet still be capable of making a will. Mere intellectual feebleness must be distinguished from unsoundness of mind. "Sound mind" within the meaning of the wills statutes does not mean a perfectly balanced mind, but simply the ability to recollect property and beneficiaries, and to conceive the practical effect of the will.

The time at which the testator must meet the "sound mind" test is the time at which he *executed* the will; mental incapacity may exist before or after the execution of a will without affecting its validity. When the issue is raised, most courts hold that the burden of proving the mental competency of the testator is upon the proponent of the will—that is, the party who offers the will for probate.[8] However, in several states the

7 Atkinson, Wills 232 (2d ed. 1953).

8 To "probate" a will is to establish before the probate court that it was executed by a competent testator and in the manner prescribed by law.

burden of proof as to the mental capacity of the testator is upon the contestant of the will.

FORMALITIES

WRITING

The necessary legal formalities for the execution of a valid will are governed by the various state statutes. With very few exceptions (such as the nuncupative will discussed below) the statutes require that wills shall be in writing. The "writing" may be typewritten, handwritten, or printed, and it may be in any language; it may be written in ink or pencil or both, and on one or many sheets of paper.[9] In fact it may be inscribed with any device on any substance which results in a readable and fairly permanent record.[10] And no particular form of words or expressions is necessary; of all legal documents a will is least governed by form. Any written instrument, irrespective of formality, made with the intent to effect a post mortem disposition of property, is testamentary in character, and if properly executed, is entitled to admission to probate.[11]

SIGNING

A will must be *signed* by the testator, or by some person for him at his request and in his presence. This requirement exists in every state as to formally witnessed wills; but the states are quite liberal as to what constitutes a sufficient signature. The fact that the signature is misspelled or is illegible will not affect the validity of the will; and it may be in pencil or affixed by a rubber stamp. A signature by mark is generally recognized as a sufficient substitute for the testator's signature if he makes it with the intent of executing a will. But

9 It is not necessary that the several sheets be physically fastened together. Separate sheets may be probated if they are connected by their internal sense by coherence or adaptation of parts, or if all the sheets are properly identified as having been in the room at the time of execution, and the testator intended to execute them as one will.

10 Atkinson, Wills 294 (2d ed. 1953).

11 5 A THOMPSON, REAL PROPERTY § 2606 (repl. 1957).

the signature or mark must be performed by the testator, or by some person for him at his request and under his express authority; and the signature will not be rendered invalid by the fact that another person guided the hand of the testator when he signed the will, if the signing is in any degree an act of the testator, acquiesced in and adopted by him.

Although the English Wills Act of 1837 required that the will be signed at the foot or end, the statutes of most American states require only a signature, and are silent as to its location on the instrument. In these states it is not necessary that the testator's signature be at the *end* of the will provided that it was placed where found with the intention of authenticating the instrument as his will. However, some state statutes require that the testator's signature be placed at the "foot" or "end" of the will.

WITNESSES

The English Statute of Frauds required that a will be attested by "three or four" witnesses, and the English Wills Act of 1837 reduced the number to "two or more." Most American states only require two witnesses to a will, although a few states require *three.* A will is perfectly valid if attested by more than the required witnesses, but if it has less than the statutory number it will be invalid. Consequently it is sound and common practice to have three witnesses to all wills, thereby satisfying the requirements of every state.[12]

12 What if the testator executes a will in a state requiring only two witnesses but dies while domiciled in a state requiring three witnesses. Is the will valid? In the absence of a special statute, the validity of a will of *land* is generally determined by the law of the state where the property is situated; and the validity of a will of *personal* property is determined by the law of the state in which the testator was domiciled (i.e., had his permanent home) at the time of his death. However, most states have passed statutes to the effect that a will made in another state shall be considered properly executed if done so in accordance with the law of the state where it was made. Since the law governing the execution of wills varies from state to state, the cautious practitioner will attempt to have the will executed in a manner which complies with the requirements of *all* states.

It is a requirement everywhere that the witnesses to a will shall be "credible" or "competent." A credible or competent witness is one whom the law will trust to testify before a court of justice. Statutes impose no restrictions as to age, and it is generally held that a minor may be a competent witness to a will.

Under the common law, any person who was a beneficiary under the will was disqualified from acting as an attesting witness. A will which was attested by a beneficiary was considered to be invalid. Even the spouse of a beneficiary was deemed to be incompetent to act as a witness. Later the law was changed so as to make a beneficiary "competent" to act as a witness by invalidating any provisions in the will made in his favor. In other words, a witness to a will was not rendered incompetent by reason of his being named as a beneficiary, but the devise or bequest to him was declared void. In a great majority of the states today the fact that a subscribing witness is also a beneficiary under the will does not affect its validity. However, the devise or bequest to such witness is void, *except* that if the beneficiary-witness would have received a share of the estate as an heir, had the testator died without a will, then so much of such share shall be preserved to him as does not exceed his gift under the will.

The statutory requirements governing the execution of wills are intended as safeguards and to prevent fraud and deceit. However they vary somewhat from state to state. Some states require that the witnesses actually see the testator sign the will, or that the will be signed in their presence; in most states the testator may either sign in the witnesses' presence or acknowledge to them his prior-made signature. Almost all states require the will to be attested and subscribed[13] in the presence of the testator; a few states require the witnesses to subscribe all at the same time and in the presence of each other. In some states the testator must indicate or declare to

13 "Attestation" refers to the mental act of bearing witness; "subscription" refers to the mere mechanical act of affixing one's signature as a witness.

the witnesses that the instrument is his last will and testament. In most states it is not necessary that the testator declare the instrument to be his last will and testament, nor is it essential that the witnesses be cognizant of its contents, or even that they know the instrument subscribed by them *is* a will.

The purpose of the requirement that wills must be executed in the presence of credible witnesses is to insure reliable evidence of their proper execution, and to provide security against fraud. But—to *what* must the witness bear witness? In many jurisdictions it is considered the duty of the attesting witnesses not only to witness the testator's signature but also to satisfy themselves that he is of sound and disposing mind and memory, capable of executing a will, and that he is not under restraint or undue influence. What if the attesting witnesses fail to observe the mental capacity of the testator, or are in fact unable to recall what occurred at the time of their attestation—does the will fail for lack of proper attestation? In just about every state the answer is no. Although it may be the duty of the witnesses to a will to observe the mental capacity of the testator, and to refuse to attest the will of one they believe lacking in testamentary capacity, most courts do not invalidate a will for the reason that the attesting witnesses failed to perform that duty. The true function of witnesses to wills is to prove that the will has been properly executed according to law, and that is done by the identification of the signatures of the testator and themselves.

UNDUE INFLUENCE, FRAUD, AND MISTAKE

As we have seen, a will is invalid if improperly executed or if the testator lacked the necessary mental capacity at the time the will was made. It will also be declared invalid if procured by undue influence or fraud, or if induced by mistake.

Undue influence is persuasion carried to the point of overpowering the mind; it is such a control over the testator as prevents him from acting intelligently and voluntarily, and in effect, destroys his free agency, causing him to do what he would not have done if such control had not been exercised.

A will is not invalid simply because it was made as a result of influence exerted upon the testator by other persons; the influence must have been "undue" in order to vitiate the will. Although the undue influence is usually exerted by a beneficiary under the will, if it is exerted by one not a beneficiary, the will is equally invalid. But acts of kindness and courteous attention do not constitute undue influence. To be classed as undue, the influence must be such as to destroy the free agency of the testator, or substitute another's volition for his; the influence must have been so overmastering as to place the testator in the attitude of saying: "It is not my will, but I must do it."[14]

It is the general rule that when only *part* of the will is tainted by undue influence, the remainder will be enforced; but if the court is unable to separate the good from the bad, the entire will fails. Although the burden of proof is upon the proponents of the will to show that it was properly executed, and that the testator was of sound mind at the time he made the will, the burden of proving the exercise of undue influence is upon the contestant of the will.

Although undue influence and fraud sometimes closely resemble one another, they are different. In the case of undue influence the testator is *coerced;* in the case of fraud he is *deceived.* But fraud and *mistake* have an affinity for each other, since, in each case, the testator has made untrue assumptions in the execution of his will; in the case of mistake, he himself has caused the error, whereas in fraud the misconception was due to the deceit of another. *Fraud* exists when the testator has been intentionally deceived by another

[14] Atkinson, Wills 256 (2d ed. 1953).

into doing what he would not have done except for the fraudulent deception.[15]

Although *mistakes* sometimes occur in connection with wills, not every kind of mistake will render the will invalid; in fact, most kinds of mistake have no effect upon the will's validity. For instance, if the claimed mistake consists of some *omission,* there is usually no remedy; the terms of the will must be in writing and cannot be proved by oral testimony. However, if a provision in a will was included by mistake, the court will usually probate the will minus the provision. A testator's mistake as to the legal effect of the language used is no ground for rejecting the will, and this is true even if the mistake was due to incorrect legal advice.

Mistake in the inducement will seldom invalidate a will. For example, a testator's mistaken belief that certain heirs were hostile to him, or were dead, or his mistaken ideas as to the value of his assets, or the amounts he had already given certain relatives, will not affect the validity of the will. Mistakes in the description of the property given, or of the person intended as the beneficiary, are often "resolved" by the court in construing the testator's language in the light of the circumstances existing at the time the testator executed the will.

TYPES OF WILLS

Holographic Wills

An holographic will is one written entirely by the testator in his own handwriting. Ordinarily such wills, wholly in the

[15] If the fraud involves the *execution* of the will, such as forgery or misrepresentation as to the character or contents of the instrument, it is called *fraud in the execution. Fraud in the inducement* involves deception by a beneficiary as to extrinsic facts which materially affect the disposition of the property, such as a statement that a person likely to be selected by the testator as a beneficiary has mismanaged funds, or has instituted insanity proceedings against the testator, or has been guilty of immoral conduct. The representations must be false and known to be false by the person making them; innocent misrepresentations will not invalidate a will. 7 POWELL, REAL PROPERTY 410 (1974).

One who claims that a will has been the product of fraud has the burden of proof.

testator's own hand, are valid *without* attesting witnesses; the "self-written" factor obviates the necessity of attesting witnesses. However, in several states the fact that the instrument is holographic does not dispense with any of the formalities of execution, and such wills must be properly witnessed as in the case of ordinary wills.[16]

Nuncupative Wills

A nuncupative will is an *oral* will, declared or dictated by the testator in his last sickness before sufficient number of witnesses, and afterwards reduced to writing.[17] The nuncupative will represents one of the very few exceptions to the general requirement that wills be in writing. Although rarely encountered today, nuncupative wills are allowed by statute in a majority of states, but only within certain specific limitations;[18] and as would be expected, the statutory requirements vary from state to state.

In almost all states allowing nuncupative wills, the will must have been made during the testator's last sickness and before witnesses; and some states require that the will be made in the testator's home or house where he died. Most statutes provide that such wills be reduced to writing within a designated number of days.

Joint and Mutual Wills

A *joint* will is one in which the same instrument is made the will of two or more persons and is jointly signed by them. Such will must be so worded that it can operate separately on

16 The state of Louisiana has a unique type of will known as the "mystic" will. The so called mystic or secret will is signed by the testator and presented to a notary and three witnesses in a closed or sealed envelope. The testator declares to the notary, in the presence of the witnesses, that the envelope contains his signed will; a written endorsement reciting the facts of execution is made on the cover by the notary and signed by him, the witnesses and the testator.

17 BLACK, LAW DICTIONARY (4th ed. 1951).

18 The privilege of making a nuncupative will is generally restricted to personal property not exceeding a specified value.

the death of each testator.[19] *Mutual* wills are the separate wills of two persons but containing mutual or reciprocal provisions for each other; they are referred to as "reciprocal," or "double," or "counter" wills. A will can be both joint and mutual, or joint without being mutual, or wills can be mutual without being joint. Because joint or mutual wills are frequently made pursuant to an agreement not to revoke them, they are breeders of controversy.[20]

REVOCATION OF WILLS

A will passes no interest in property until the death of the testator; until that time the maker of the will retains complete and absolute control over the property. Wills are said to be "ambulatory" in nature—that is, "moveable" or subject to change. Accordingly, a will may be revoked by the maker at any time before death. However, the same degree of mental capacity is required for the revocation of a will as for its execution; a will legally made stands until it is legally revoked.

Revocability is such a basic feature of a will that a testator cannot create an irrevocable will, even if he so intends. Thus a testator may change or revoke his will whenever he wishes, providing he uses the proper formalities. The fact that a will does not speak until death allows the testator to alter the will during his lifetime to meet changing conditions.

Just as the right to *make* a will is controlled by statute, so are the methods by which a will may be *revoked* regulated by statute. There are three methods of revoking a will; they are: (1) By some physical act done to the will, as prescribed by statute; (2) by a subsequent revoking instrument; (3) by certain changes in the circumstances of the maker's family status from which a revocation will be implied by law. Again, the law on the subject varies somewhat from state to state.

19 For example, a joint will which provides that it is not to become effective until the death of the survivor is invalid.

20 Although a will may be revoked at the pleasure of the maker, even if he has contracted with another not to do so, the other party may, upon satisfactory proof of the contract, recover damages against the estate.

Revocation by Physical Act

Most statutes provide for revocation by burning, tearing, cancelling and obliterating, while others also use the expressions "destroying," "defacing," or "cutting." However, in most situations these differences in wording are not material, since about all of the statutes include the words "destroy" or "obliterate."

It is not necessary to destroy the will completely in order to revoke it; the slightest burning or tearing of the instrument is sufficient if done by the testator (or by another in his presence and at his direction) with the intent to revoke the entire will. The physical acts provided by the statute will not, by themselves, constitute a revocation—the acts must be accompanied with the *intention* of revoking the will. There must be the intent as well as the act, and the intent must be plain and without doubt; a tearing or destruction by accident or mistake is not a revocation. The destruction or alteration of a will by a person who lacks testamentary capacity, or by one who is induced by undue influence, is ineffectual as a revocation; in such case the will stands unrevoked.

Although *partial revocation* by physical act is not permitted in some states, in most states a will may be revoked *in whole or in part,* either by cancellation or obliteration.[21]

Revocation by Written Instrument

A will may be revoked in whole or in part by a later will or a codicil,[22] or by any other writing executed with the same formalities as required for a will. The later instrument may contain express words of revocation which can apply either to the whole of the prior will or only to part of it.[23] However,

21 However, *alterations* or *additions* made by the testator after the will has been executed, without a new attestation, are of no effect; such alterations or additions do not affect the validity of the will—they are merely disregarded, and the will is probated according to the original draft, as if nothing had been done to it.

22 A "codicil" is an addition or supplement to a will; it may either add to, take from, or alter the provisions of the will. It must be executed with the same formality as a will, and when admitted to probate, forms a part of the will.

23 A revocation of all former wills extends to former codicils.

when the later will does not contain express words of revocation but disposes of all of the testator's property, the prior will is automatically revoked by implication. And if the wills are entirely inconsistent, only the later will can stand; but where there is no revocation clause and the inconsistency affects only a *part* of a prior will, the implied revocation extends only to the inconsistent parts—the earlier will remains effective except as altered by the later one.[24]

Revocation by Operation of Law

In most states the revocation of a will may also come about through operation of law resulting from changes in the condition and circumstances of the maker. In such cases the testator's intent is immaterial since the law revokes the will for him. This type of revocation is based partly upon the presumption that, because of the changed circumstances, the average testator would have desired revocation.

For example, under the common law the will of a *single woman* was revoked by operation of law upon her marriage. This rule was based upon the early common law concept that, upon marriage, a husband and wife, in legal contemplation, became *one* person—and that person was the husband; a married woman was incapable of acquiring or disposing of property, by will or otherwise. Since *after* marriage a woman could neither make nor revoke a will, it was resolved that marriage should, by operation of law, revoke any will made by her *before* marriage. In many states, by statute, this rule is applied to both men and women; that is, a will of either is revoked by a subsequent marriage. In some states the marriage revokes the entire will; in others the will is revoked only as it applies to the spouse, who becomes relegated to his or her intestate share.

[24] However, when it appears that a prior will was destroyed by a testator under the *mistaken* belief that a subsequent valid will had been executed, the revocation of the prior will is not necessarily absolute, but may be deemed to have been made "on condition" that the later will was a valid one. In such a case, the prior will may be considered as continuing in existence unrevoked. This is the *doctrine of dependent relative revocation*—the revocation of the prior will is dependent upon the validity of the later one.

The various states differ on whether a *divorce* constitutes sufficient change in the condition and circumstances of a testator as to work a revocation by operation of law. Most states hold that divorce alone, unaccompanied by a property settlement, will *not* produce a revocation by operation of law. However, where the divorce is accompanied by a property settlement, most courts hold that testamentary provisions in favor of the divorced spouse are revoked by operation of law, although the results sometimes turn upon the wording of the particular state statute.

Under common law the marriage of a *man,* of itself, did not revoke his will. However, marriage coupled with the *birth of a child* following the marriage were held to constitute such a radical change in the condition and circumstances of the maker of a will as to bring about a revocation by operation of law, and this is still the law in most states today.

Although the birth of a child alone did not, at common law, constitute a sufficient change in the testator's circumstances as to effect a revocation of his will by operation of law, this has been changed by statute in most states. Today, posthumously born children and children not mentioned in their parent's will are generally allowed by statute to take the same share of the estate as if the parent had died intestate. These statutes are based upon the presumption that the parent did not intend to disinherit his children, but the presumption is rebuttable. The statutes do not forbid disinheritance, provided it is intentional. In order to effectively disinherit a child[25] it is not necessary that the child actually receive something under the will; the mere mention of him by name in the will is sufficient.

To the extent that an afterborn or unintentionally omitted child is allowed to inherit by virtue of the statutes, there is a *partial* revocation of the parent's will; that is, the will is

25 In most states an *adopted* child occupies substantially the same legal status as that of a natural child.

revoked only to the extent necessary to provide the child with its full intestate share—otherwise the will remains intact.

Another type of partial revocation occurs when the subject matter of a specific gift under the will is disposed of by the testator prior to his death. Thus, if a testator devises a specific parcel of real estate and subsequently conveys it to another, the devise is thereby revoked by implication.[26] Since a will is not effective until the testator's death, he cannot dispose by will of what he does not own at the time of his death. This is known as revocation by *ademption.*

Ordinarily when a beneficiary named in the will dies in the lifetime of the testator, the devise or legacy must fail or *lapse.* However, in most states there are statutes designed to prevent lapse in certain cases. The provisions of these so-called antilapse statutes vary considerably from state to state. The typical antilapse statute provides that if certain designated beneficiaries under a will should die *before* the testator, the gift under the will shall not lapse but shall pass to the lineal descendants[27] of the deceased beneficiary. The purpose and effect of such statutes is to prevent a devise or bequest from lapsing by substituting in place of the deceased beneficiary, his lineal descendants or other designated heirs. By force of the antilapse statutes the designated heirs take under the will, in place of the deceased beneficiary, the same share he would have taken.

PROBATE

Before a will can become operative or effectual to pass the title to real or personal property, it must be probated—that is, it must be *proved* and allowed in the probate court of that state in which the testator was domiciled at the time of his death. Until that time the will has no force. To "probate" a

[26] The conveyance of a parcel of real estate by a testator, after he has devised the same by will, is a revocation of the will only as to the parcel thus conveyed.

[27] "Lineal" descendants are those in a direct descending blood line, as from father to son to grandson to great-grandson etc.

will is to *prove* the will—to establish before the probate court that the will was executed by a competent testator and in the manner prescribed by law.

Probate procedure varies from state to state. Generally the person presenting the will for probate files a *petition* for probate, setting forth the names and addresses of the widow or widower, and of the heirs at law and next of kin of the deceased, so far as is known to the petitioner. Notice, prescribed by the statute, is given to the heirs and to all other persons interested under the will; and the judge of probate assigns a time and place for hearing. If there is no objection to the probate, the statutes usually allow establishment of the will upon the testimony of only one of the subscribing witnesses. However, in the case of a will contest, the proponents of the will are usually required to produce all of the subscribing witnesses.[28] Generally, a will may be contested by anyone who would be pecuniarily benefited by a setting aside of the will.

After a will has been admitted to probate, it must be carried out in accordance with its terms; and the terms of a will may be clear or they may be ambiguous. The cardinal rule for the interpretation of wills is that they shall be construed so as to give effect to the *intention* of the testator, to be gathered from the language of the will when read as a whole.[29] And it is the intention of the maker of the will at the time of its execution which governs. Although a will speaks only after the maker's death, the language used in the instrument must be construed as of the date of its execution and in the light of the surrounding circumstances existing at that time.

Most states have statutes which provide for the probate of wills which have become lost or destroyed. These statutes generally provide that the due execution and contents of a

28 Often times subscribing witnesses have become physically or mentally disabled, or they have died or disappeared. The various state statutes ordinarily provide for such situations.

29 A will and codicil should be interpreted together as parts of the same instrument.

will which has been lost or destroyed may be proved by a properly identified copy thereof and by the testimony of the subscribing witnesses thereto, or by any other competent evidence establishing clear proof of the execution and contents of the will.

DESCENT

INTRODUCTORY STATEMENT

As we have seen, the power to choose one's own beneficiaries is available through the simple expediency of making a will. The power of devising by will is a legal incident to ownership; it is considered to be one of the most sacred rights attached to property. Yet many individuals die each year without ever exercising this power. Although over half of the adults in the United States leave nothing to pass on death anyway, of the balance, less than fifty percent leave wills; consequently about half of all the "propertied" Americans die intestate. Since all wealth changes hands once every generation, intestate statutes affect the disposition of approximately one-half of the national wealth about every twenty-five years.[30]

When a person dies without having left a will (or if his will is declared not valid for some reason) he is said to have died *intestate.* In such case the law determines how the estate is to be distributed. Statutes governing the intestate laws of a state are usually referred to as laws of "intestate succession" or "statutes of descent and distribution." The purpose of such statutes is to fill the vacuum created by the decedent's failure to arrange the distribution of his estate—to distribute the property in the manner the decedent would probably have done had he left a will. They provide an orderly pattern based upon the presumption that the surviving spouse, and those who stand in closest relationship to him, are the natural

[30] 7 POWELL, REAL PROPERTY 632-34 (1974).

objects of the decedent's bounty. The statutory plan is designed as a substitute for a testamentary plan—to carry out what would normally be assumed to have been the wishes of the decedent.[31]

Those persons entitled to a decedent's *realty* under the laws of intestacy are technically referred to as "heirs," while those entitled to the personal property are referred to as "distributees" or "next of kin." However, the term "heir" is now frequently used in a popular sense to designate a successor to either the real *or* the personal property of a deceased person, and regardless of whether the property passed under the intestate laws or by virtue of a will.

When a person dies intestate the court appoints a personal representative, called an "administrator," who administers the estate—that is, he collects the assets, pays the debts, and distributes the remainder of the estate among those entitled to it in accordance with the law and under the supervision of the probate court.

RULES OF DESCENT

GENERALLY

Although the statutes of descent vary from state to state, they follow a somewhat similar pattern throughout the country. Typically, the surviving husband or wife[32] takes a one-half or a one-third share in both realty and personalty,

31 Where a person dies intestate leaving property in more than one state, the general rule is that the law of the state in which the land is situated controls its descent, while the distribution of personalty is determined by the law of the decedent's *domicile* at the time of death. By "domicile" is meant that place where a man has his true, fixed, and permanent home and principal establishment, and to which whenever he is absent he has the intention of returning. BLACK, LAW DICTIONARY (4th ed. 1951). Every person must have a domicile somewhere, but he can only have one; his existing domicile continues until he acquires another and, *vice versa,* by acquiring a new domicile he relinquishes his former one. A person may have two places of residence for purposes of business or pleasure, but he can have but one *domicile.*

32 In some states the husband's share is less than the wife's, but most states treat husband and wife alike.

with the other one-half or two-thirds share going to the children. If there are no surviving children or issue,[33] the spouse usually takes the entire estate up to a certain fixed amount. If there is no surviving spouse, the children divide the entire estate equally; and the issue of any predeceased child (the intestate's grandchildren) take in place of their parents. Parents or other relatives of the decedent take no share as long as there are issue surviving.

In the absence of issue (and subject to the share of the surviving spouse) the parents are usually next in line. After the parents, the collateral[34] heirs come in—that is, the brothers and sisters, with the children of any deceased brothers and sisters (nephews and nieces of the intestate) taking the share that their parent would have taken, had he survived the intestate.

COMPUTING DEGREES OF KINDRED

If none of the relatives mentioned above survive the intestate, his property usually descends to his next of kin[35] as computed according to the method of the civil law. (See chart on facing page entitled RELATIONSHIPS AND DEGREES OF KINDRED ACCORDING TO THE CIVIL LAW.) Under that method the degree of relationship is determined by counting the number of steps (generations) back to the nearest common ancestor, and from such ancestor down to the particular

33 "Issue" means lineal descendants —those persons who have descended in a direct line from the decedent; the term refers to those persons who have *"issued"* from the decedent, that is, the children, grandchildren, and their children to the remotest degree.

34 "Collateral" heirs are those who descend from the same common ancestor and not from one another; they belong to the same ancestral stock but not in a direct line of descent. Thus, brothers, cousins, uncles, nephews, etc. are *collateral* kindred, whereas father, son, grandson, etc. are *lineal* kindred.

35 The term "next of kin" or "nearest of kin" means those persons nearest of kindred to the decedent, that is, the closest blood relatives. Ordinarily heirship is determined by the nearness of kindred only in cases where the decedent leaves no issue, parents, brothers or sisters.

RELATIONSHIPS AND DEGREES OF KINDRED

ACCORDING TO THE CIVIL LAW

To determine the degree of kindred, begin with the deceased and count the number of steps upward from him to the nearest common ancestor and from such ancestor down to the relative in question, reckoning a degree for each step.

relative in question, reckoning a degree for each step (generation).[36] The relative who stands in the lowest numerical degree of relationship to the intestate takes as next of kin. If several claimants are related in equal degree they share equally; but if they claim through different ancestors, those claiming through the nearer ancestor ordinarily take to the exclusion of those claiming through a more remote ancestor. For example, a first cousin (father's brother's child) and a great uncle (decedent's father's uncle) are both kindred of the fourth degree, but the first cousin, claiming through the nearer ancestor (the decedent's grandparents), would (in some states) take to the exclusion of the great uncle. Since distant collateral relatives often lack any real personal concern for the decedent, they are sometimes referred to as "laughing heirs."

Illegitimate and Adopted Children

At common law, a child born out of wedlock was considered to be the child of no one; such a child could not inherit from or through his mother or father and was considered to have no relatives except his own spouse and issue. The purpose of the common law rule was to restrain and control unlawful cohabitation by making lifetime embarrassments for the children.

The harshness of the treatment towards the innocent children of unmarried parents has been mitigated somewhat in all of the states today. Most states permit the illegitimate child to inherit from his mother; however, such child is usually excluded from his father's estate unless the parents later marry or the father acknowledges his paternity.

36 Another way of stating the rule is to count the steps from the intestate up to the common ancestor, and from the common ancestor down to the relative whose relationship is sought; the sum of these two counts is the degree of relationship between the intestate and the relative in question. For *example,* a first cousin once removed would be kindred in the *fifth* degree, since there are two degrees from the decedent back to the grandparent (common ancestor) and three more degrees down to the first cousin once removed—a total of five degrees.

In most states, by statute, adopted[37] children may take, by intestate succession, from the adopting parents as if they were natural children. And a majority of states allow the adopting parent to take by intestate succession from the adopted child; but in some of these it depends upon the *source* of the property.[38] As to whether an adopted child can inherit from his natural parents, or whether the natural parents can inherit from him, the states differ; they also differ as to whether an adopted child can inherit from the adopting parent's relatives.[39]

ESCHEAT

The statutes in most states declare that the property of a person who dies intestate and without heirs shall go to the state by *escheat.* You will recall that under the English feudal system, if the tenant died without heirs the land reverted or *escheated* to the overlord. Today the state is deemed to occupy the place of the feudal lord for this purpose, and the word "escheat" now signifies the right of the state to succeed to the property of one who dies intestate and without heirs.

SUMMARY

A will is an instrument by which a person makes a disposition of his property to take effect after his death; it is revocable during the maker's lifetime and operative for no purpose until death.

A person who dies leaving a valid will is said to have died *testate,* and is referred to as a *testator* (if a male) or a *testatrix* (if a female).

37 Although adoption was known to the Roman law and is said to have been known to the Athenians, and Spartans, and to other ancient peoples, it was unknown to the common law, and so the practice of adoption exists only by virtue of statute.

38 For instance, some states permit an adopting parent to take by intestate succession from an adopted child any property *except* property which came to the child from his natural parents or kindred.

39 A posthumous child will inherit as if he had been born in the intestate's lifetime. And in most states, kindred of the half blood inherit equally with those of the whole blood in the same degree.

A gift of real property by will is a *devise;* the recipient is referred to as a devisee. A gift of personal property by will is a *bequest* or *legacy,* and the recipient is referred to as a *legatee.*

The right to make a will is controlled by statute in every state. The minimum age varies from eighteen or less in some states to twenty one in others.

It is the rule in all states that in order to make an effective will the testator must be of *sound mind.* The requirement of a "sound mind" within the meaning of the term is generally met if at the time of executing the will, the testator can carry in his mind in a general way, the nature and extent of his property, those who are the natural objects of his bounty, and the practical effect of the will.

State statutes require that wills (except for nuncupative wills) shall be in writing and signed by the testator or by some person for him at his request and in his presence. Most states also require two witnesses to a will, although a few states require three.

A will is invalid if improperly executed or if the testator lacked the necessary mental capacity at the time the will was made. A will is also invalid if procured by undue influence or fraud.

"Undue influence" is persuasion carried to the point of coercion; it is such control over the testator as to destroy his free agency. Fraud exists when the testator has been intentionally deceived into doing what he would not otherwise have done.

An *holographic* will is one written entirely in the testator's own hand. In some states such wills need not be witnessed, while in other states they must be properly witnessed as in the case of ordinary wills.

A *nuncupative* will is an oral will, declared or dictated by the testator in his last sickness before a sufficient number of witnesses, and afterwards reduced to writing within a designated number of days.

A *joint* will is one in which the same instrument is made the will of two or more persons and is jointly signed by them. *Mutual* wills are the separate wills of two persons but containing mutual or reciprocal provisions.

A will may be revoked at any time before death. A will may be revoked by (1) its intentional destruction, (2) a later will or codicil, or (3) by operation of law resulting from changes in the condition and circumstances of the maker.

Afterborn children and children not mentioned in their parent's will are generally allowed to take an intestate share, unless it appears that the omission was intentional.

Before a will can become operative, it must be "probated"; that is, it must be proved or established in the probate court that the will was executed by a competent person and in the manner prescribed by law. Generally, a will may be contested by anyone who would be pecuniarily benefited by its disallowance.

If the language in a will is doubtful or ambiguous, the court will attempt to effectuate the intention of the testator as gathered from the language of the will when read as a whole.

If a person dies without having left a valid will, he is said to have died *intestate.* In such cases, the estate is distributed according to the laws of "intestate succession," also referred to as the "statutes of descent and distribution."

Although the statutes of intestate succession vary somewhat from state to state, they are designed to distribute the property in the manner in which the decedent would probably have done had he left a will; such distribution is based upon the presumption that the surviving spouse, and those in closest relationship to him, are the natural objects of his bounty.

Typically the surviving spouse takes a one-half or a one-third share, with the other one-half or two-thirds share going to the children. If there are no surviving children or issue, the spouse usually takes the entire estate up to a certain fixed amount. If there is no surviving spouse the children share the entire estate, with the issue of any predeceased child taking the share their parent would have taken. In the absence of issue (and subject to the share of the surviving spouse) the decedent's parents are next in line. After the parents come the decedent's brothers and sisters, and then the nephews and nieces. If none of the above relatives survives the intestate his property usually descends to his next of kin according to the method of the civil law. Under that method the degree of kindred is computed by counting the number of steps from the decedent up to the common ancestor, and from the ancestor down to the relative whose relationship is sought, reckoning a degree for each step; the relative who stands in the lowest numerical degree of relationship to the decedent takes as next of kin.

If the intestate leaves no spouse, issue, or next of kin, the property *escheats* to the state.

CHAPTER 10

DEEDS

INTRODUCTORY STATEMENT

There are four principal methods by which the ownership of real estate is transferred from one party to another: (1) transfer by adverse possession; (2) transfer on death by will; (3) transfer on death by intestate succession; and (4) voluntary transfer by a formal instrument of conveyance, that is, by *deed.* We have already considered the first three methods, and we turn our attention now to the fourth, and for our purposes, the most important method: transfer by deed.

HISTORICAL BACKGROUND

You will recall that under the early feudal system, landholding was based upon a *personal* relationship; a tenant was granted land because of the services he could render to the lord, and the lord was under a duty to protect the tenant. Naturally a lord who had a satisfactory tenant was not anxious to have another substituted in his place. Consequently, a tenant was not permitted to transfer his land to another without first obtaining the consent of his overlord. And even if such consent were granted, the tenant was required to make a money payment called a *fine.* It wasn't until about two hundred years after the Norman Conquest that tenants finally gained the right to transfer their land to another without permission of the overlord and without having to pay a fine.

The early method of transferring land from one person to another was by *"feoffment with livery of seisin"*. The *feoffment* was the transfer of the feudal tenement, which was accomplished by livery of (a delivery of) *seisin.*[1] In order to effect a transfer of seisin, the parties would go upon the land, and the grantor, in the presence of witnesses (usually neighbors), would point out or describe the land and also indicate the type of estate he wished to convey. The grantor would then formally "give" or "deliver" the seisin to the new owner by handing over to him a twig or lump of earth as a symbol of the transfer. Having made a symbolic delivery of the land, the grantor would then relinquish possession to the grantee, and the transfer was consummated. The livery of seisin operated to take the seisin out of the grantor and put it in the grantee.

By the end of the twelfth century it became customary for the grantor to furnish the grantee with a writing, called a deed or charter of feoffment.[2] But this was merely to furnish some permanent evidence of the completed transfer and the nature of the estate; the operative act was still the livery of seisin, not the giving of the charter or deed. In the course of time the reverse of this was to become true; the deed became essential and livery of seisin obsolete.[3]

In the sixteenth century the English parliament passed a statute (known as the Statute of Uses) which made possible new methods of conveyancing and gave impetus to our modern deed. The effect of this statute was to dispense with the necessity of the colorful but cumbersome ceremony of

1 At early common law, ownership could not exist apart from possession. A person who had possession coupled with a freehold interest was said to have the *seisin;* seisin was the feudal equivalent of our modern concept of ownership. In order to make an effective conveyance of the land, the seisin had to be transferred. This was accomplished through the livery of seisin; the seisin was "delivered" to the new owner.

2 These early charters or deeds were written in Latin and usually started out by calling to the attention of "all men present" the fact that a transfer had been made. They were quite brief, and simply stated who granted what to whom.

3 MOYNIHAN, INTRODUCTION TO THE LAW OF REAL PROPERTY 164 (1962).

livery of seisin; it cleared the way for a simple and efficient method of land transfer. After the passage of the Statute of Uses, a transfer of land could be accomplished by the mere execution of a written instrument (a deed), without the parties ever going upon or even near the property. Thus our modern system of land transfer was born. Today most states have statutes which specifically authorize the transfer of title by simple forms of deeds, without livery of seisin or other ceremony.

The word "deed" is subject to many definitions, but in the ordinary acceptance of the word, a deed is simply an instrument conveying real property. Although the essential elements of a valid conveyance vary somewhat from state to state, the modern deed, as we see it today, has evolved from the old common law charter of feoffment, and it still bears a striking resemblance to its ancient ancestor.

TYPES OF DEEDS

Generally

Although there is no one particular form of deed in use throughout the country, the general anatomy of a deed is substantially the same everywhere. There are two basic types: *warranty* and *quitclaim*. The warranty deed, which is the type most commonly used, contains personal covenants or "guarantees" by the grantor that his title is good. If the deed contains all of the usual warranties or covenants it is called a *general* warranty deed, but if it contains only some of them it is called a "special" or "limited" warranty deed.[4] The quitclaim deed merely purports to transfer whatever interest the grantor may presently have in the land without implying that he has a good title—or even that he has any title at all. By such deed the grantor warrants absolutely nothing; he merely transfers what title he has, *if any*.

[4] CRIBBET, THE LAW OF REAL PROPERTY 154 (1962).

The General Warranty Deed

A general warranty deed is one in which the grantor makes several personal guarantees as to the title. These guarantees are referred to as "covenants for title." The traditional or so-called "usual covenants" which appear in most general warranty deeds are:

(1) The covenant of *seisin*
(2) The covenant of *right to convey*
(3) The covenant *against encumbrances*
(4) The covenant for *quiet enjoyment*
(5) The covenant of *warranty*

The covenants of *seisin* and *right to convey* are considered as being practically the same thing. They are usually construed to mean that the grantor has an estate of the quantity and quality which he purports to convey. If at the time of the conveyance the grantor does not hold an estate of the quantity and quality which he purports to convey, there is a breach of both of these covenants.

The covenant *against encumbrances* is a guarantee that at the time of the conveyance there are no encumbrances on the property (other than those specifically mentioned), such as outstanding mortgages, leases, liens, taxes, covenants restricting the use of the land, easements, etc.[5]

The covenant for *quiet enjoyment* and the covenant of *warranty* are, for all practical purposes, the same, and are usually considered together. They amount to an assurance by the grantor that the grantee shall peaceably and quietly enjoy the premises, and that he will not be evicted by someone with a better title.[6] Under the covenant of warranty, the grantor promises to compensate the grantee for any loss he may

[5] The term *encumbrance* includes "every right to, or interest in, land which may subsist in another to the diminution of its value, but consistent with the passing of the fee." BLACK, LAW DICTIONARY (4th ed. 1951).

[6] For there to be a breach of these covenants there must be either an actual eviction or a surrender of possession following a court decision finding a paramount title in a third party.

sustain by virtue of a failure in the title. It is probably the most important covenant of all since it amounts to a continuing contract to defend the grantee's rightful possession against all lawful claims existing at the date of the conveyance.

Under the typical general warranty deed the grantor covenants that he will warrant and defend the title *against the lawful claims and demands of all persons.*[7] This means that he personally guarantees that the title is free of defects (not specifically mentioned in the deed), and that he will stand behind the title and, if need be, defend it against the lawful claims and demands of *all* persons, regardless of when such claims or defects originally arose—whether before or after he acquired the title.

If and when a covenant for title is broken, the person entitled to its benefit at the time may recover damages for breach of contract. But who may recover against whom? The covenant for quiet enjoyment and the covenant of warranty have always been considered as "future" or "continuing" covenants, since they are not broken until an eviction occurs; this may be several years and many grantees in the future. As continuing covenants, they continue to pass along with the land, as the title is transferred from one grantee to another, and so are said to "run with the land." This means that even though the land is transferred several times, a remote grantee who is evicted may maintain an action against any grantor in the chain of title who made such covenants. And it is not essential that all of the deeds in the chain be warranty deeds.

Example:

A conveys to B by warranty deed; B to C by warranty deed; C to D by quitclaim deed; and D to E by warranty deed. If E is evicted because of a failure in the title, he may sue A, B, or D on their continuing covenants, which

[7] The obligation does not exist with respect to unfounded claims, but only against *lawful* claims of ownership. Consequently, any time a grantee voluntarily pays a third party claimant without suit, he does so at his peril, since the warrantor may later deny the validity of the claim. CRIBBET, THE LAW OF REAL PROPERTY 211 (1962).

ran with the land, but he cannot sue C who gave no covenants for title.

At common law the covenants of seisin, right to convey, and the covenant against encumbrances did not run with the land. They were considered to be personal or present covenants in that they were breached, if at all, as soon as they were made—that is, when the deed was delivered. The grantor was either seised or he wasn't, he either had a right to convey or he didn't, and the property was either encumbered or it wasn't. A breach of any one of these covenants created in the immediate grantee a *personal* right to damages against *his* grantor. But at common law, *personal* rights were not transferable, and the result was that no *remote* grantee could sue on these covenants.[8]

Example:

A conveys to B by warranty deed; B to C by warranty deed; and C to D by warranty deed. At the time of the conveyance from A to B there was an undischarged mortgage, which D is required to pay in order to keep the land. Under the common law rule, and the rule in most states today, D may bring an action against C, his *immediate* grantor, but not against A or B, the remote grantors.[9]

Damages for Breach of Covenant

In the event of a breach of covenant, the law attempts to indemnify the aggrieved party by awarding him a sum of money which will put him in as good condition as if the covenant had not been broken. If there is a breach of the covenant of seisin which results in a failure of the title, the purchaser is entitled to recover the amount paid for the

8 *Id* at 209.

9 Although most states still follow this common law rule, it has been changed by statute in some states. In those states where the common law rule has been changed, a remote grantee may sue for breach of these personal covenants, and in the example above, D would be allowed to bring an action for breach of covenant not only against C, his immediate grantor, but also against the remote grantors—A or B.

property, plus interest from the time of payment. If the covenant is breached only with respect to a portion of the estate conveyed, the damages are limited to a proportionate part of the amount paid, plus interest.

If the breach is of a covenant against encumbrances, the damages are the amount actually paid to clear the title, but not exceeding the price paid. If the encumbrance is in the form of an easement, the damages are equal to the diminution of the value of the premises due to the encumbrance.

Where there has been a breach of warranty, most of the states confine the damages to the purchase price of the property, plus interest. However, in a few states the measure of damages is the actual *value* of the premises at the time of the eviction,[10] regardless of the purchase price, together with interest and the reasonable cost of defending the suit.[11]

The covenants for title do not assure the grantee that he will not lose the land;[12] they merely entitle him to money damages if the title fails. And, of course, even this protection is contingent upon the continued solvency of the person giving the guarantee.

After Acquired Title

A grantor who covenants that he will warrant and defend the title is, in effect, stipulating that he has the title which he purports to convey; and if he in fact does not own the property, the grantee may bring a legal action to recover damages for breach of the covenant. Suppose A "conveys" land that he does not own (either intentionally or unintentionally) to B by warranty deed, but at a later date A

10 In the case of a partial breach, the damages are based upon a proportionate share of the value, plus interest.

11 Where the buyer receives a lesser estate than the deed purports to convey (for example, a life estate rather than a fee simple), the damages are the price paid for the land, less the value of the estate actually received. Where a purchaser under a deed with covenants of title is required to defend the title in court, and loses the suit because his title was defective, he is entitled, in addition to regular damages, the reasonable cost of suit.

12 For this type of assurance the purchaser must look to the recording system, which is the subject matter of Chapter 12, *infra*.

does in fact acquire title to the land. Who then owns the land—A or B? It would appear that since A owned nothing at the time of the "conveyance" he could transfer nothing, leaving B with only a claim against A for money damages for breach of warranty. In such a case, however, A's after-acquired title automatically passes to B by operation of law. This is known as the doctrine of *estoppel by deed,* which holds that if a grantor purports to convey land which he does not then own, but which he subsequently acquires title to, such grantor's *after-acquired* title inures to the benefit of his grantee. It is called estoppel by deed because the grantor is estopped to deny that the title passed to his grantee, having represented at the time of the original conveyance that he owned the land. In other words, having previously guaranteed the title, the grantor is prevented by law from later denying it.

However, the doctrine only applies when the conveyance is by warranty deed. An after-acquired title will not pass to a grantee under a quitclaim deed because such deed usually purports to transfer only the grantor's *presently existing* interest in the land.

The Special or Limited Warranty Deed

If the covenant of warranty purports to protect the grantee against the claims of *all* persons, as in the case of the typical warranty deed, it is a covenant of *general warranty* and the deed is sometimes referred to as a general warranty deed. But if the warranty purports to protect the grantee only against the claims of certain persons, or against the claims of persons "claiming by, through, or under" the grantor, then it is a limited or special warranty. In most states such deeds are called *special* warranty deeds or *limited* warranty deeds; in a few states they are called quitclaim deeds even though they contain a covenant of limited warranty.

Under the special or limited warranty deed the grantor guarantees the title in a very limited way—that is, only against the claims of persons *"claiming by through or under"* him. In other words he guarantees the title only against defects arising since he himself acquired the land but not against defects or claims arising before that time. Under the special warranty deed the grantor merely transfers whatever present interest he has in the property and covenants that *he* has done nothing to impair the title since he became connected with the land.

Example:

> A purchases Blackacre in 1965 and conveys it to B in 1970 by *warranty deed;* B conveys it to C in 1975 by a special warranty deed. Later it is determined that the title is defective due to an undischarged mortgage given by A in 1968. Since the defect arose *prior* to B's acquisition of the land, his limited warranty has not been broken. However, C may sue A on his general warranty covenants which ran with the land.

The Quitclaim Deed

A quitclaim deed (sometimes called a release deed) is one in which the grantor warrants nothing; he merely releases whatever interest he may happen to have at the time—if any. At common law, a quitclaim deed was used merely to clear or perfect one's title in land; it was not considered a suitable instrument to actually transfer the title from one person to another. However, in most states today by statute, a quitclaim deed or deed of release will convey whatever estate the grantor has in the land as effectually as a general warranty deed. Although a release deed lacks the assurance and personal backing of a warranty deed, it is, nevertheless, a legitimate, though humble, member of the deed family.

FORMAL PARTS OF A DEED

Generally

Although the delivery of a written instrument has everywhere taken the place of the old common law livery of seisin, it is not the delivery of just any written instrument which will transfer title to real estate. To be effective as a legal conveyance the instrument must contain certain essential items. Generally, a deed must at least contain the names of the grantor and grantee, words of grant, a description of the land being conveyed, and the signature of the grantor; in some states witnesses are required, and in a few other states a seal is essential.

In addition to the items mentioned above, deeds almost invariably contain other parts which are customary but not essential. Although deed forms vary somewhat from state to state, the typical standard form deed usually consists of the following parts:

(1) The names of the parties and a statement of consideration
(2) A granting clause (operative words)
(3) Words of inheritance
(4) A description of the land being conveyed
(5) The habendum ("Have and to hold" clause)
(6) The grantor's covenants and warranties (if any)
(7) A release of the spouse's interest
(8) A testimonium clause
(9) The date, signature, and seal
(10) An acknowledgment

Names of the Parties

The ancient charter of feoffment told who granted what to whom, and the modern deed does the same thing. Following the introductory words "Know All Men by These Presents," the parties are named or otherwise identified. First the grantor is named, accompanied by a statement as to his or her residence.[13] After the identification of the grantor there is a statement of consideration, followed by the name of the grantee:

[13] Where no release of a spouse's dower or curtesy or other marital rights appears in the deed, it is customary at this point to also explain the grantor's marital status as either unmarried or widowed.

KNOW ALL MEN BY THESE PRESENTS

That I, ROBERT A. DOW, of Cape Elizabeth, in the County of Cumberland and State of Maine, in consideration of one dollar and other valuable consideration paid by JOHN D. FOSS and MARY N. FOSS, both of Rochester, County of Strafford and State of New Hampshire, the receipt whereof I do hereby acknowledge, . . .

It is a general rule of law that a deed which fails to name or otherwise identify the grantee is incomplete and inoperative to pass title. However, many states hold that if a deed is otherwise complete, the name of the grantee may be inserted, in the grantor's absence, by one acting under his oral authority, provided the grantee's name is inserted before delivery of the deed to him.

CONSIDERATION

Although a voluntary transfer of real estate is usually the result of a purchase and sale agreement, a conveyance itself is not a contract, and hence, no consideration is necessary or need be stated.

The practice of stating a consideration in deeds goes back to the sixteenth century; under the law in effect at that time, an actual consideration was essential to the operation of certain deeds. But now, for all practical purposes, a deed is good in most states even though made without consideration in fact or without any being expressed; today the customary recital of consideration has become a pure matter of form.[14]

THE GRANTING CLAUSE (operative words)

In order to transfer ownership from the grantor to the grantee, the grantor's intent to convey must be expressed in the deed by certain and definite words, called "operative

14 And it is customary to recite merely a nominal consideration ("one dollar and other valuable consideration") since most buyers do not wish to have the actual purchase price a matter of public record.

words." A deed containing no granting clause or "operative words" is void even though complete in all other respects.

Through long usage, each type of deed has acquired distinctive operating words. But no particular or technical words are necessary, provided the intent to convey is clearly expressed; in fact, one apt word is sufficient, although deeds usually contain more. In warranty deeds the operative words are usually "give, grant, bargain, sell and convey;" in quitclaim deeds the words "remise, release, bargain, sell and convey, and forever quitclaim" are frequently used. Although the operative words of conveyance may be placed in any part of the deed, they usually appear following the acknowledgment of consideration:

> . . . the receipt whereof I do hereby acknowledge, do hereby GIVE, GRANT, BARGAIN, SELL AND CONVEY unto the said JOHN D. FOSS and MARY N. FOSS, as joint tenants and not as tenants in common . . .[15]

(3) WORDS OF INHERITANCE

There is a natural tendency to think of ownership only in terms of the tangible, physical property, but as we have seen, ownership in real estate is really a concept; a person who "owns" land, more precisely, has an *interest in the* land—an interest called an *estate.* And so, following the granting clause are words which define the type of interest or estate that is to be conveyed.

You will recall that at common law, an estate in fee simple could not be transferred simply by designating it as an estate "in fee simple" or as an estate to last "forever." Being an estate of inheritance, it was absolutely essential that the transfer be to the grantee *"and his heirs."* These technical "words of inheritance" were not used to designate additional

15 At this point in the deed, if there are two or more grantees, the type of co-ownership is spelled out.

grantees, but rather, to designate or establish the quantum or type of estate conveyed—that is, an estate in *fee simple;* and no substitute words would suffice, regardless of how clearly they expressed an intent to convey a fee simple estate.[16]

Although just about all of the states have now dispensed with the common law rule requiring technical words of inheritance, such words are still generally used in most deed forms to describe a fee interest:

> . . . unto the said JOHN D. FOSS and MARY N. FOSS, as joint tenants and not as tenants in common, THEIR HEIRS AND ASSIGNS FOREVER . . .[17]

Description of the Land

Following the granting clause and the words of inheritance, the land to be conveyed is "described." The purpose of the legal description is to describe the land with such a degree of certainty as to identify it from all other land, and in such a way as to enable a competent person to locate it on the ground.

The test of the legal sufficiency of a description is this: Can a competent person, by referring to the deed, locate the land involved and determine its boundaries? This requirement is satisfied by any description which either identifies the property so that a competent person may locate it on the ground or by one which affords the *means* for such identification. Thus the description need not be in the deed itself, but may refer to a description appearing in some other instrument, such as a plot, map, or survey. In some states it is common practice to describe land "by adjoiners"—that is, by reference to the boundaries of adjoining owners, as for example: ". . . bounded on the North by land of Frank Rogers; on the East by Route 16; on the South by land of the heirs of A. I. Hall; and on the West by land now or formerly of Henry O. Brown."

16 3 AMERICAN LAW OF PROPERTY § 12.45 (Casner ed. 1952).

17 Where a life estate is being conveyed, the words "their heirs and assigns forever" are deleted and words appropriate to a life estate are inserted.

And a description may be valid though it is in general terms, such as "all of the land belonging to the grantor."[18] References to the property merely by name, such as "the Blackacre Estate," or as "my farm," or "my property,"[19] or even in some cases by street number, have been held to be sufficient. But although such imprecise descriptions are often upheld by the courts, their use should be avoided, for a description which is too general or vague may result in the creation of an unmarketable title.[20]

The Rectangular Survey System

Several methods of describing land are utilized in various parts of the country. The principal method used in most of the midwestern and western states is the so-called governmental or *rectangular survey system.* This system was adopted by the Continental Congress in 1785 and is now used in thirty states, namely all the states west of the Mississippi (except Texas), those states north of the Ohio River, and also the states of Alabama, Florida, and Mississippi.

The rectangular survey system is based upon a government survey made in preparation for the settlement of the vast areas west of the original thirteen colonies. The great survey divides the public domain into a grid of parallel lines running east and west, and meridians, running north and south; the distances between the parallels and meridians are twenty-four miles in each direction, resulting in units of land approximately twenty-four miles square, called "checks." Each check is

18 Such descriptions, sometimes called "Mother Hubbard" descriptions, are operative to convey all of the land owned by the grantor at the time of the conveyance.

19 But the words must refer to only *one* parcel of land. Thus, a reference to the property conveyed as "my farm" is usually sufficient if the grantor owns only one farm, but if he owns two farms, the deed itself furnishes no basis for identifying *which* farm is meant, and such descriptions are usually held to be invalid.

20 An "unmarketable" title is one which is subject to reasonable objections, and unless the parties have contracted otherwise, a purchaser may reject such title and recover back any partial payments made by him.

subdivided into sixteen units, each approximately six miles square,[21] called "townships."

The rows of townships running in an east and west direction are called *tiers;* the rows of townships running in a north and

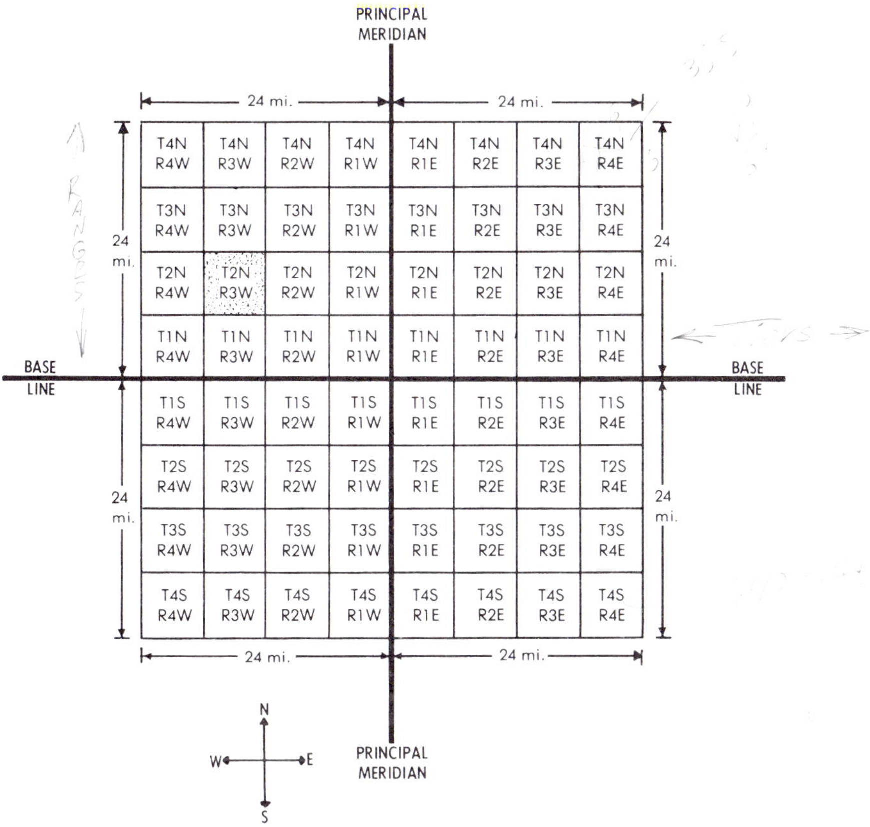

TOWNSHIP DESIGNATIONS

21 The townships are not exactly square since, due to the earth's curvature, the east and west boundary lines (the meridians) converge as they extend northward to the pole. Thus, the north boundary line of a township is approximately fifty feet shorter than the south boundary line. This discrepancy is minimized by establishing a "correction line" along every fourth tier of townships, that is, every twenty-four miles. At each correction line so-called "guide meridians" are established running due north for a distance of twenty-four miles to the next correction line. At each correction line the range lines (i.e. the east and west boundary lines of the townships) are "corrected" by again extending them a full six miles apart.

south direction are called *ranges.* The tiers are numbered with reference to certain parallels of latitude running east and west, designated as "base lines"; the ranges are numbered with reference to certain meridians running north and south and designated as "principal meridians." The tiers are numbered as being either north or south of the base line, and the ranges are numbered as being either east or west of a principal meridian. A particular township is identified as being so many tiers north or south of the base line and so many ranges east or west of the principal meridian. For example, in the illustration on page 205, the shaded township would be described as being T. 2 N., R. 3 W., meaning that it is located in the second tier north of the base line and in the third range west of the principal meridian.

Each township is further subdivided into thirty-six *sections,* each one mile square and containing 640 acres. These sections within the township are numbered consecutively beginning with section 1 in the northeast corner of each township and proceeding west to section 6 in the northwest corner, then dropping to the next row and proceeding from west to east and continuing alternately, from east to west and west to east, etc. until section 36 is reached in the southeast corner of the township.

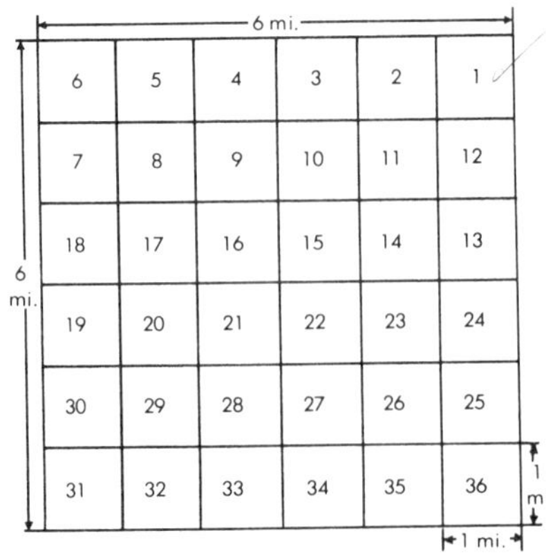

DIVISION OF TOWNSHIP INTO SECTIONS

The sections in a township are always numbered in the same sequence as that shown in the diagram on page 206. Any given section is located by indicating the section number and the township in which it is located. When describing a section it is customary to first state the section number and then the township in which it is located. For example, Section 12 in Township 2 North, Range 3 West would be written: Sec. 12, T. 2 N., R. 3 W.

The sections are generally marked on the ground by eight monuments or stakes, one located at each section corner and one set midway between each section corner thus marking the "quarter corners." For descriptive purposes involving parcels containing less than one section (640 acres), the section is further subdivided into half sections and quarter sections, and the quarter sections into quarter-quarter sections, etc. as illustrated below:

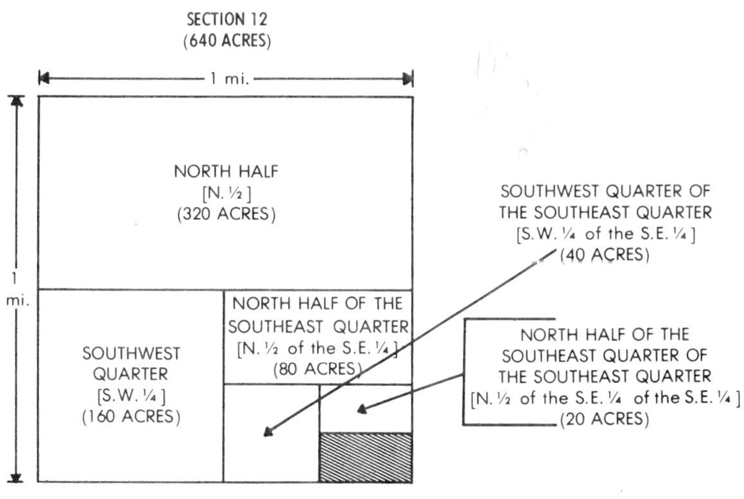

A SECTION OF 640 ACRES SUBDIVIDED INTO SMALLER PARTS

A particular parcel of land is described with reference to its location within a specified section of a designated township. For example, in the illustration on page 207 the shaded parcel would be described as: "The south half of the southeast quarter of the southeast quarter of section 12" of a designated township. The description would ordinarily be abbreviated as S. 1/2 of S. E. 1/4 of S. E. 1/4 of Sec. 12.

Rectangular descriptions are read or plotted backwards or in reverse order, that is,. from the general part of the description to the specific part at the beginning. For example, the "southeast quarter of the northeast quarter of the southeast quarter of the southeast quarter" of a square tract would be almost incomprehensible unless one were to first draw the square and set off the southeast quarter of it, then the southeast quarter of that, and then the northeast quarter of that, and lastly the southeast quarter of that. Although commonly used to describe large agricultural areas, the rectangular survey system is not adaptable to small or irregularly shaped parcels.

Description by Reference to a Plan or Map

Land may be described by reference to a recorded map or plan showing its location and boundaries.[22] For example, urban property is often surveyed into blocks which in turn are subdivided into lots. The lots are numbered on a map or plan which is recorded in the registry of deeds. Thereafter the lots may be described simply by referring to the plan and lot number such as:

> Lot 12, Block 5, of the Sunset Acres Development, surveyed by R. F. Young, August 23, 1943, and recorded in Plan Book 23, Page 16, of the Cumberland County Registry of Deeds.

Description by Metes and Bounds

The oldest method of describing land is by identifying its

[22] When land is described according to a recorded plan, to which reference is made in the deed, the plan becomes part of the description as if it were incorporated in the deed.

boundaries in detail. The boundaries are described by designating natural or artificial objects (called "monuments") along which the lines are to run, or by stating the "courses and distances" of such lines or both. This method is known as describing land by "metes and bounds" (meaning "measurements and boundaries"), and is in common use throughout most of the eastern part of the United States.[23] From a specified starting place, the tract is outlined by indicating the direction and length of each boundary line. The lines may run along natural or artificial boundaries, or they may be established by courses and distances; but they must be continuous—one must begin where the other leaves off, eventually returning to the point of beginning. A description which does not "close" is inadequate and the conveyance fails.

A metes and bounds description of the lot diagramed on the following page might be as follows:

> A certain lot or parcel of land, with the buildings thereon,[24] situated on the northerly side of Elm Street in the City of Portland, County of Cumberland, and State of Maine, bounded and described as follows:
>
> BEGINNING at an iron post set in the ground on the northerly side of said Elm Street, said post being located Two Hundred (200) feet westerly from the point of intersection of the northerly side line of Elm Street with the westerly side line of Maple Street; thence running North 25° 30′ East[25] by land now or formerly of Ralph Smith, a distance of One Hundred Seventy-five (175) feet to a certain point;

[23] The metes and bounds system is also used in conjunction with the rectangular survey system where the parcel described is irregularly shaped.

[24] It is not necessary to mention the land improvements in the description.

[25] Meaning a line which runs 25° 30′ east of due north.

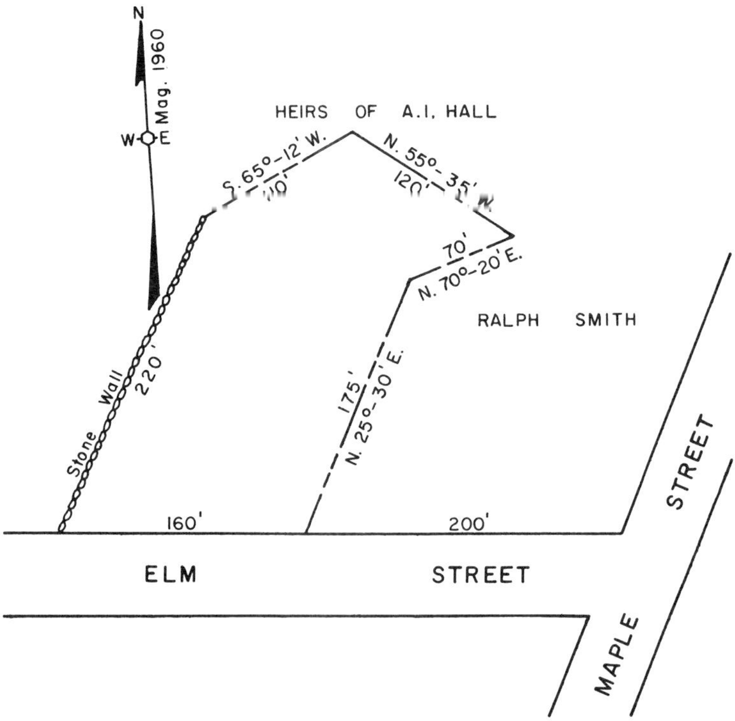

thence running North 70° 20′ East along said Smith land for a distance of Seventy (70) feet to a granite monument set in the ground; thence running North 55° 35′ West by land now or formerly of the heirs of A. I. Hall, One Hundred and Twenty (120) feet to an oak tree next to a large pine stump; thence South 65° 12′ West along land now or formerly of said Hall heirs, a distance of One Hundred and Ten (110) feet to a stone wall on the easterly side line of land formerly of George W. Jones; thence following along said stone wall for a distance of Two Hundred and Twenty (220) feet to a point where said wall intersects with the northerly side line of Elm Street; thence along the northerly side line of Elm Street a distance of One Hundred and Sixty (160) feet to the point of beginning. Said above described courses are magnetic and of the year 1960.

A conveyance of land described as bounded by a monument having width, usually carries title to the *center* of the monument (if the grantor owns to that extent), unless a contrary intent appears. This is most common in cases where the land conveyed is described as bounded on a highway, or to a highway, and thence by the highway. In such cases the grantee is presumed to take to the center of the highway subject to the public easement. This rule is based upon the theory that the grantor would not have intended to retain ownership in a long narrow strip of land with no apparent benefit to himself.[26] But when the *side* of the monument is expressly designated as the boundary line ("by the side of," or "along the side of") the title does not ordinarily carry to the center.

Where the land conveyed is bounded by a nonnavigable river or stream, the boundary line is presumed to extend to the center, or thread[27] of the stream, unless the deed expresses a contrary intent. Where the river is navigable or is subject to the ebb and flow of the tide, the general rule is that the line extends only to the high-water mark. The proper location of the boundary lines of land which borders on waters and watercourses depends largely upon who in fact owns the land underlying the waters—the individual or the government.[28] And the question of ownership may in turn depend upon whether the waters are tidal or nontidal and whether or not they are navigable. On this point there is much confusion and difference of opinion among the states. In the absence of a contrary intention appearing in the deed, there is a presumption that the grantor intended to convey all of the land owned by him under the water.

26 This is not an absolute rule of law but merely a principle of interpretation adopted for the purpose of finding out the true meaning of the words used. In construing deeds, the court will give effect, if possible, to the *intention* of the parties as expressed in the deed.

27 The "thread" of a stream is the middle line between the shores, irrespective of the depth of the channel.

28 Thus, under the general rule, the boundaries of lands abutting navigable lakes extend only to the low-water mark since the state ordinarily owns the bed of the lake.

At early common law all land on tide waters, between high and low-water mark, technically known as the "shore," belonged to the crown and was not the subject of private ownership. However, some states no longer follow this common law rule, and in these states the owner of land adjoining tidewater may own to the low-water mark. In a state where the common law rule prevails and the "sea" or the "shore" is named as the boundary, the line is usually determined to be the high-water mark. However, if the grantor in fact owns to the low-water mark his grantee is presumed to take to the low-water mark in the absence of a contrary intent.

A description referring to a boundary line as being "the shore" or "by the shore" may be ambiguous, leaving it doubtful whether the sea side or the land side of the shore was intended.[29] Generally, when the deed designates the boundary as "the sea" or "the ocean," nothing to the contrary appearing in the deed, the grant extends to the low-water mark if the grantor owns that far. Since the space between high and low-water mark is often considerable, descriptions involving land bounding on tidewater should be drafted with precision.[30]

29 "The shore is the strip of land lying between high-water mark and low-water mark. It is a band with two margins, an inner or landward margin corresponding with high-water mark and an outer or seaward margin corresponding with low-water mark. Whether in a given deed the one margin or the other marks the boundary depends upon all the calls in the deed and the particular circumstances and conditions of the case." Sinford v. Watts, 123 Me. 230, 122 Atl. 573 (1923).

30 *Accretion* and *Reliction.* What if the location of a water boundary changes due to the forces of nature; do the abutting property lines change also? Not if the shift is sudden or due to artificial means; but if the shift occurs *gradually,* by erosion, accretion, or reliction, the boundary of the abutting land is correspondingly shifted. When the line between land and water is changed due to the gradual deposit of soil (accretion) or by the imperceptible recession of the water (reliction), the owner becomes entitled to the new land. Conversely, if land bordering on water is gradually and imperceptibly worn away by the natural elements (erosion), or the water gradually encroaches, the owner loses such land. However, sudden or perceptible changes (avulsion) have no effect on the location of such boundary lines.

Ambiguous Descriptions

A legal description must identify the land with such certainty that the language used can only refer to but one possible tract. But what if the description is ambiguous;[31] does the deed fail? In such cases the courts attempt to resolve the ambiguity and, if at all possible, give effect to the intent of the parties as gathered from the whole instrument.[32] Although a description may be so vague as to make the deed void, the courts ordinarily go to extremes in an attempt to sustain the deed if at all possible.

In resolving ambiguities in descriptions, the courts have developed some general rules of construction designed to give effect to the probable intention of the parties. For example, among conflicting terms, natural monuments will ordinarily prevail over artificial monuments; either natural or artificial monuments take priority over maps, courses and distances, or statements as to quantity; courses control distances, and a description by courses and distances will usually prevail over one which describes the tract by name; statements as to quantity have the lowest priority when used with conflicting calls.

The words "more or less," following the quantity of land described in a deed, are words of safety and precaution; they are taken to mean "about," or "approximately," and are intended to cover reasonable variations in the stated quantity. They imply that the grantor does not warrant the precise quantity of land specified in the deed, but that it is approximately the amount stated. The qualifying words "more or less" will relieve the grantor from the obligation to make compensation for any deficiency, provided the deficit in

31 For instance, in a description by metes and bounds it is common to describe boundaries by referring to specific monuments on the ground coupled with a reference to their courses and distances. If a given course or distance does not coincide with the physical location of the monument there is, of course, an ambiguity. And there may be an ambiguity because a specified monument cannot be located, or because the acreage is incorrectly stated.

32 Ordinarily a deed will be construed most strongly against the grantor and most favorable to the grantee.

quantity is not unreasonable. But if there is a very material variation in quantity, coupled with fraud or misrepresentation on part of the grantor, the grantee will be allowed compensation for the deficiency.

Oftentimes a grantor will retain some interest in the land conveyed, usually in the form of an exception or reservation. For example, he may *exclude* from the conveyance a part of the land described, or the timber growth, or the mineral deposits; or he may convey the land but reserve a life estate or an easement in himself.[33] Any estate or other interest reserved by the grantor is usually embodied in the description, and is referred to as a *reddendum* (rendering or returning to).

Any other pertinent factors in connection with the conveyance, called "recitals," are usually placed at the end of the description. A "recital" is simply a statement of some fact concerning the conveyance, such as the source of the grantor's title, or the purposes for which the deed was made. Recitals are often used to give notice of any encumbrances on the property, and to state any restrictions, conditions, or other matters concerning the land.

All of the parts of a deed considered thus far are collectively referred to as "the premises." In fact, the technical meaning of the word "premises" in a deed is everything which precedes the *habendum*.

The Habendum

Following the legal description is the "to have and to hold" clause, or *habendum:*

> TO HAVE AND TO HOLD the foregranted and bargained premises, with all the privileges and

[33] There is a technical distinction between an exception and a reservation. By an exception the grantor completely excludes from the grant some part of the ownership, while in the case of a reservation, he transfers the entire property described but "recreates" in himself some specified interest in the land transferred. To put it another way, it is an *exception* when some part of the ownership is never parted with; it is a *reservation* when the grantor transfers the entire property described but creates or reserves some new thing to himself, out of the land transferred. 6 POWELL, REAL PROPERTY 224 (1975).

> appurtenances thereof, to the said John D. Foss and Mary N. Foss, as joint tenants and not as tenants in common, their heirs and assigns, to them and their use and behoof forever.

The purpose of the habendum clause is to again refer to the grantee by name and to indicate the type of estate conveyed.[34] The habendum may define, enlarge, or in some cases, diminish the estate granted; but any discrepancies between it and the granting clause will be reconciled, if possible, so as to give effect to the *intent of the parties* as expressed by the instrument as a whole.

The Grantor's Covenants

Immediately following the habendum clause are the grantor's covenants (if any):

> And I do covenant with the said grantees, their heirs and assigns, that I am lawfully seized in fee of the premises;[35] that they are free of all encumbrances except as aforesaid,[36] that I have good right to sell and convey the same to the said grantees to hold as aforesaid;[37] and that I and my heirs shall and will WARRANT AND DEFEND the same to the said grantees, their heirs and assigns forever, against the lawful claims and demands of all persons.[38]

Release of Spouse's Interest and Testimonium Clause

The testimonium clause ("In witness whereof," etc.), coupled with a release of the spouse's interest, form the concluding sentence of the deed:

34 Since this is ordinarily fully covered in the granting clause, the habendum is considered, in some states, to be a useless repetition and is often omitted from deed forms.

35 The covenant of *seisin.*

36 The covenant *against encumbrances.*

37 The covenant of *right to convey.*

38 The covenant of *warranty.*

IN WITNESS WHEREOF, I the said Robert A. Dow, and Nancy E. Dow, wife of the said Robert A. Dow, joining in this deed as grantor, and releasing and relinquishing all dower and homestead rights, and all other rights in the above-described premises, have hereunto set our hands and seals this 26th day of May in the year of our Lord one thousand nine hundred and seventy six.

Although it is a customary part of the deed, the testimonium clause is not really necessary. And there is no rule of law that requires a deed to be dated; the effective date is the date of delivery.[39]

Short Form Deeds

Several states have passed statutes which sanction the use of short form deeds. The shortening is accomplished by eliminating repetitious verbiage and by substituting certain short expressions for the traditional long form terminology. For example, such statutes typically provide that the expression "warranty covenants" in a deed shall have the same effect as if all the usual covenants of title had been written at length in the deed.

The purpose of short form deeds statutes is to avoid the unnecessary use of words in deeds. They provide short deed forms and declare that they shall have the same force and effect as the standard long forms. These statutes usually dispense with the necessity for technical words of inheritance or an habendum clause; they tend to prevent the registries of deeds from becoming unnecessarily bulky.

EXECUTION OF THE DEED

Grantor's Signature and Seal

Thus far, we have considered the two basic types of deeds

[39] But in the absence of other evidence, a deed is presumed to have been executed and delivered on the day of its date.

(warranty and quitclaim) and their essential and customary parts. But drafting the instrument is only part of the story; before a deed can be effective to transfer the ownership it must also be properly *executed.* "Execution" pertains to the mechanical acts necessary to make the deed effective as a conveyance; it relates to the old expression "signed, sealed, and delivered."

The various state statutes provide that a deed must be signed by the grantor. Unless the instrument bears some writing or symbol which is intended as the grantor's signature, it will be inoperative.[40] It is not essential that the grantor's signature be in his own handwriting; the signing may be by the grantor or by his authorized agent. Thus a grantor unable to write may verbally authorize the affixing of his name to the deed by another person.

The *grantee* need not sign the deed; his acceptance of the instrument makes it mutually binding.[41]

At common law deeds were sealed but not signed. The sealing, which was absolutely essential to the validity of a deed, was done by impressing a device on wax dropped on the paper. For many years the seal alone was sufficient to authenticate a deed and the grantor's signature was unnecessary. But in 1677 the English statute of frauds made a signing necessary. And although the statute did not dispense with the seal, its importance has gradually diminished over the years.

40 If one who is named as grantor acknowledges and delivers a deed to which his name has been affixed, no matter by whom, the deed is valid. The acknowledgment and delivery are acts of recognition and adoption, and will preclude the grantor from afterward denying his signature.

41 A deed which is executed by both the grantor and grantee is called a "deed by indenture," and one executed by the grantor only is called a "deed poll." The terms derive from the fact that originally "indenture" meant an indented deed. It was the custom to make two copies of the deed upon the same parchment, which was then cut in a waving or indented line, usually through the middle of a word. Each party kept part of the instrument which could be identified by matching the cut edges. In a "deed poll," there was only one copy, so the parchment was cut straight or "polled." Today almost all deeds are deeds poll. 5A THOMPSON, REAL PROPERTY § 2704 (repl. 1957).

At common law a seal consisted of an impression upon wax, but today the mere annexing of a wafer or other tenacious substance is sufficient to constitute a seal. However, most states have abolished the necessity for seals on deeds, although the custom of using them persists.[42]

Attestation and Acknowledgment

In some states it is essential that deeds be attested[43] by one or more witnesses, but no witnesses were required at common law and they are not required in most states. Nevertheless, it is customary to have the deed witnessed as a means of assuring proof of its authenticity. In many states, however, in order for a deed to be recorded in the registry of deeds it must be *acknowledged.* An "acknowledgment" amounts to a formal witnessing by a public officer, usually a notary public or justice of the peace; it is a declaration before some authorized public officer, by a person who has executed an instrument, that the instrument is his voluntary act and deed. A typical form of acknowledgment would be as follows:

> State of Maine, Cumberland, SS May 26, 1976
>
> Personally appeared the above-named Robert A. Dow, of Cape Elizabeth, County of Cumberland and State of Maine, and acknowledged the above instrument to be his free act and deed.
>
> Before me,
>
> ....
>
> Justice of the Peace

The acknowledgment is not technically part of the deed; it merely establishes the identity of the grantor and that the

42 Although the necessity for private seals on deeds has been abolished in most states as serving no useful purpose, the use of the seal continues to retain some of its significance, even today: "This venerable custom of sealing is a relic of ancient wisdom, and is not without its real use at this day. There is yet some degree of solemnity in this form of conveyance. A seal attracts attention, and excites caution in illiterate persons, and thereby operates as a security against fraud." Jackson *ex dem.* Gouch v. Wood, 12 Johns. (N.Y.) 73, 76 (1815).

43 "Attestation" refers to the act of witnessing the execution of a document and subscribing it as a witness.

instrument was duly signed. In most states a deed is valid, as between the parties, even though it was never acknowledged or recorded. However, as we shall see, an unrecorded title is a precarious one.

Delivery

Before a deed can become more than a piece of paper, it must not only be properly drafted and signed by the grantor, it must also be *delivered;* until delivery, a deed, though properly drafted, signed, and even recorded, is inoperative to pass title. The deed "speaks" only from the date of its delivery, [44] and this is the rule in every state. It is never the rule itself that is in doubt—it is whether there was *in fact* a delivery.

What amounts to a "delivery"? It has been defined as "the final and absolute transfer of a deed, properly executed, to the grantee, or to some person for his use, in such a manner that it cannot be recalled by the grantor."[45] No particular ceremony is necessary to constitute a delivery; it is sufficient if the grantor shows an intention to presently surrender all control over the title and vest it in the grantee. Ordinarily, delivery is accomplished simply by a manual transfer of the deed from the grantor to the grantee with the intent to convey the title. But an actual physical transfer of the instrument itself is not essential; a delivery will be effected if the grantor expresses, by word or conduct, an intention to make his deed presently operative so as to place title in the grantee. The controlling element is the grantor's *intention.*

Once there has been an effective delivery and ownership has passed to the grantee, a return of the deed to the grantor or its repossession by him has no effect, either to cancel the prior delivery or to reconvey the title to him.[46] In order to divest himself of ownership, the grantee must execute a new deed and deliver it.

44 The basic difference between a deed and a will is that a deed passes an interest to the grantee immediately upon delivery, while a will passes no interest until the death of the testator.

45 BLACK, LAW DICTIONARY (4th ed. 1951).

46 3 AMERICAN LAW OF PROPERTY § 12.64 (Casner ed. 1952).

To be effective, the delivery must be absolute in that the grantor must relinquish all control. If the grantor reserves the right to revoke or recall the deed at any time, there is no delivery; such a reservation would indicate a lack of intention to presently transfer the title. Thus, there is no delivery where a deed is given to the grantee with the intent that title shall pass only on condition that he perform certain agreements on his part.

The delivery must take effect during the grantor's lifetime, for a deed is not a will. For example, in a leading Massachusetts case,[47] the grantor executed a deed naming his grandson as grantee and placed the deed in a chest. The grantor died leaving a will which bequeathed the chest and its contents to the grandson. The court held that the deed was inoperative since it had not been delivered during the grantor's lifetime. Since the grantor could have changed or revoked his will at any time up to his death, he had never parted with *control* during his lifetime.

A deed may be placed in the hands of a third person to be delivered to the grantee upon the occurrence of a named event or upon the performance of stated conditions. This type of delivery is called *delivery in escrow.* A delivery in escrow places the deed beyond recall by the grantor, to be returned to him *only* if the event does not occur or there is a default in the performance of the conditions.[48] Prior to the happening of the event or the performance of the conditions, the grantor remains the technical owner of the land; but upon the happening of the named event or the performance of the stated conditions, the ownership will immediately pass to the grantee without the necessity of a "second" delivery by the escrow agent.

47 Parrott v. Avery, 159 Mass. 594, 35 N. E. 94 (1893).

48 In many parts of the country, the escrow arrangement is the usual vehicle for closing real estate transactions. The grantor deposits the deed with a third party (usually the bank or an attorney) to be held pending performance of the conditions (usually the payment of the purchase price). When the condition has been performed the escrow agent perfects the delivery by turning the deed over to the grantee.

However, for a delivery in escrow to be effective, the grantor must place the deed beyond recall. If he reserves the power to recall the deed, or retains control over the conditions or the happening of the event, regardless of whether exercised or not, there is no delivery.

Delivery of a deed to a third person, to be given to the grantee after the grantor's death,[49] will be sufficient to pass title if it clearly appears that the grantor parted with all control over the deed, and that he intended it to operate as a present conveyance, subject only to his life interest.[50] Conversely, a deed intended by the grantor to take effect only upon his death, and retained by him in his possession or within his control until his decease, passes no title from him to the grantee named in it. Such a transaction is referred to as an "attempted testamentary disposition" because the grantor's intent is to have the deed function as a will.

Where a deed is found in the possession of the grantee, there is a presumption that it was properly delivered, and only clear and convincing evidence can overcome the presumption. But there can be no delivery where the deed has come into the possession of the grantee by mistake, or for a special purpose apart from delivery; in such cases there has been no delivery whatever, conditional or otherwise, since there was never an *intent* on part of the grantor to part with control.

ACCEPTANCE

Theoretically, a deed does not pass title by delivery alone, since a grantor may not thrust his land upon an unwilling grantee; the grantee must expressly or impliedly *accept* the deed. However, in a commercial transaction, acceptance is normally predetermined, since the parties usually negotiate beforehand. In a gift transaction, which is a one-sided matter,

49 Technically such an arrangement differs from an escrow transaction in the fact that a delivery in escrow is dependent upon the happening of some event and not merely upon the lapse of time.

50 In this situation the grantor's death is merely the *occasion* upon which the third party is to hand over the deed; the actual delivery takes place when the deed is deposited with the third person.

acceptance is presumed when the deed is beneficial to the grantee. Thus, for all practical purposes, the requirement of acceptance has very little legal significance.

Real Estate Transfer Taxes

For many years prior to January 1, 1968, the Federal government had imposed a tax on real estate transfers in the amount of 55 cents for each $500, or fraction thereof, of the purchase price; the tax was paid through the purchase of special documentary stamps which were affixed to the deed. When the Federal tax was allowed to expire on December 31, 1967, most of the states took legislative action to fill the void by enacting their own real estate transfer tax laws. Most states today impose a tax on real estate transfers at either the same rate as the old Federal tax or at a rate reasonably close to it.

In most states (as was the case under the old Federal tax) the amount of the tax is computed on the consideration or value of the property *exclusive* of the amount of any pre-existing mortgage on the property at the time of the sale. In other words, when property is sold subject to an existing mortgage the unpaid balance of the mortgage is exempt and only the "equity" is subject to the tax.[51] However, this is not the rule in all the states. In a few states the tax is computed on the total consideration, *including* the amount of any pre-existing mortgages on the property at the time of sale.

The transfer tax is usually paid by affixing to the deed special tax stamps purchased at the registry at the time of recording the deed. Under the former Federal statute the transfer tax was customarily paid by the *grantor,* and most state statutes specify that the grantor shall be primarily responsible for the tax. However, failure to affix the proper stamps will not affect the validity of the deed, although such failure usually calls for the payment of a fine.

51 The "equity" as used here means the value of the property which *exceeds* the indebtedness against it. For example, if a $50,000 property is sold to a buyer who pays $10,000 in cash and assumes the seller's pre-existing mortgage in the amount of $40,000, only $10,000 (the "equity") is subject to the tax.

At the Federal level the real estate transfer tax was probably one of the least painful taxes ever imposed; and in the absence of any real increase in rate it should continue to be relatively painless as a state tax. Aside from being a modest revenue producer, the transfer tax serves another important purpose as well: it provides a useful source of statistical information for tax assessors, real estate appraisers, and others who are concerned with the evaluation of real estate. If the amount of stamps affixed to the deed[52] is a true reflection of the consideration paid, it will indicate (usually within $500) the sale price of the property, which is useful market information for evaluation purposes.

SUMMARY

A deed is an instrument conveying real property. There are two basic types: warranty and quitclaim. The warranty deed contains personal covenants or guarantees by the grantor that his title is good. If the deed contains all of the usual warranties or covenants it is called a *general* warranty deed; if it contains only some of them it is called a *special* warranty deed.

In a general warranty deed the grantor guarantees or "covenants" that he has an estate of the quantity and quality which he purports to convey (the covenants of *seisin* and *right to convey*); that there are no encumbrances on the property other than those specifically mentioned (the covenant *against encumbrances*); and that the grantee shall peaceably and quietly enjoy the premises and not be evicted by someone with a better title (the covenants of *quiet enjoyment* and *warranty*).

A grantor by general warranty deed promises to compensate the grantee for any loss he may sustain due to a defect in the title, whether the defect arose before or after the grantor acquired the title.

52 Although the transfer tax is ordinarily payable at the time the deed is recorded, in some states the stamps may be affixed to the deed either *before or after* recording. Of course, where this is permitted, affixing the stamps *after* recording avoids publicizing evidence of the purchase price, or the price paid for the equity, whichever the case may be.

The covenants for title "run with the land." This means that even though the land is transferred several times, a remote grantee may bring an action for breach of covenant against any grantor in the chain of title who made such covenants. The covenants for title do not assure the grantee that he will not lose the land, they merely entitle him to money damages if the title fails.

Where a grantor under a general warranty deed purports to convey land which he does not then own, but which he later acquires title to, such grantor's after-acquired title will automatically pass to his grantee by operation of law. But an after-acquired title will not pass to a grantee under a quitclaim deed, since such deed purports to transfer only the grantor's present interest in the land.

Under a special or limited warranty deed the grantor guarantees the title in a very limited way—that is, only against defects or claims arising since he himself acquired the land but not against defects or claims arising before that time.

Under a quitclaim deed (release deed) the grantor warrants absolutely nothing; he merely releases whatever interest he may presently have, if any.

Although deed forms vary somewhat from state to state, the typical standard form deed usually consists of the following parts:

(1) The names of the parties and a statement of consideration
(2) A granting clause (operative words)
(3) Words of inheritance
(4) A description of the land being conveyed
(5) The habendum ("Have and to hold" clause)
(6) The grantor's covenants and warranties (if any)
(7) A release of the spouse's interest
(8) A testimonium clause
(9) The date, signature, and seal
(10) An acknowledgment

A deed which fails to name the grantee is incomplete and inoperative to pass title; however, most states hold that if the deed is otherwise complete the grantee's name may be inserted, in the grantor's absence, by someone acting under his oral authority, provided the grantee's name is inserted before delivery of the deed to him.

Consideration is not essential to the validity of a deed; the practice of reciting a consideration has become a pure matter of form.

A deed must contain a granting clause expressing the grantor's intent to convey the property. Warranty deeds usually contain the words "give, grant, bargain, sell and convey"; in quitclaim deeds the words "remise, release, bargain, sell and convey" are frequently used. However, no particular words are necessary, provided the intent to convey is clearly expressed.

At common law, technical words of inheritance ("and his heirs") were absolutely essential to a conveyance of a fee simple estate. This common law rule has now been abolished in most states.

For a deed to be effective as a conveyance, it must describe the land with such a degree of certainty as to identify it from all other land, and in such a way as to enable a competent person to locate it on the ground.

There are several methods of describing land. The principal method used in most of the midwestern and western states is the so-called governmental or rectangular survey system. Land may also be described by reference to a recorded map or plan showing its location and boundaries. The oldest method of describing land is by "metes and bounds." It is the method in common use throughout most of the eastern part of the country. By this method, land is described by designating physical objects (called "monuments") along which the lines are to run, or by stating the courses and distances of such lines or both. From a specified point of beginning, the tract is outlined by indicating the direction and length of each boundary line; one line must begin where the other left off, eventually returning to the point of beginning.

The description must identify the land with such certainty that the language used can only refer to but one possible tract. If the description is ambiguous, the courts will attempt to resolve the ambiguity and, if possible, give effect to the intent of the parties as gathered from the entire deed.

Several states have statutes which sanction the use of "short form" deeds. The shortening is accomplished by substituting certain short expressions for the traditional long form terminology.

Before a deed can be effective to transfer ownership, it must be properly *executed*. Execution pertains to the mechanical acts necessary to make the deed effective as a conveyance; it relates to the old expression "signed, sealed, and delivered."

The various state statutes provide that a deed must be signed by the grantor or by his authorized agent. However, most states have abolished the necessity for seals on deeds. Some states require that deeds be witnessed, but witnesses were not required at common law and they are not required in most states. Nevertheless, it is customary to have deeds witnessed, and in many states in order for a deed to be recorded it must be "acknowledged." An "acknowledgment" is a declaration before an authorized public officer, by the grantor, that the instrument is his voluntary act and deed.

A deed, though properly drafted and signed by the grantor, passes no title until it is delivered. "Delivery" is the grantor's expression, by word or act, of his intention that the deed shall take effect as a transfer. No particular ceremony is necessary; it is sufficient if the grantor shows an intention to presently surrender all control over the title and vest it in the grantee.

A deed may be placed in the hands of a third person to be delivered to the grantee upon the occurrence of a named event or upon the performance of a stated condition. This type of delivery is called delivery in *escrow*. For a delivery in escrow to be effective, the grantor must place the deed beyond his control.

Delivery of a deed to a third person, to be given to the grantee upon the grantor's death is effective to pass title only if it clearly appears that the grantor parted with all control over the deed.

Most states impose a tax on real estate transfers at the rate of 50¢ or 55¢ for each $500 or fraction thereof of the purchase price, but the laws vary somewhat from state to state.

CHAPTER 11

MORTGAGES

HISTORICAL BACKGROUND

Seldom is the purchaser of real estate in a position to pay cash for the property; he ordinarily makes a down payment and borrows the balance over a period of time. This "financing" of the purchase price is usually accomplished through the use of the *mortgage*. A mortgage is a conditional conveyance of real estate as security for the payment of a debt or the performance of some other obligation. It is simply a *pledge* of real estate as security.

Under the early common law mortgage[1] the debtor (the pledgor—called the mortgagor) executed an outright deed to the lender (who was called the mortgagee) *upon condition*, however, that if the mortgagor-debtor repaid the debt by a certain time (known as the law day) he was entitled to a return of his land. However, if the mortgagor failed to make payment on the day set, the grantee (mortgagee) became the absolute owner; the defaulting mortgagor irrevocably lost (forfeited) his land. Since the value of the property usually exceeded the amount of the debt, mortgagees quite often

[1] At early common law the creditor-mortgagee took actual possession of the pledged land. And there were two types of land pledge: the "living gage" and the "dead gage." Under the "living gage" the mortgagee was required to satisfy his claim out of the rents and profits of the mortgaged land; under the "dead gage" the mortgagee was permitted to keep the rents and profits of the mortgaged land without applying them to the reduction of his claim, and hence, the land was "dead" to the debtor. The word mortgage derives from *mort gage* or "dead pledge." Under modern practice the mortgagor is allowed to retain possession of the mortgaged land. See 3 POWELL, REAL

became recipients of unconscionable windfalls at the expense of hapless mortgagors.

Because the strict enforcement of mortgages, as written, often worked a great hardship on borrowers, a change in the law was inevitable. By the seventeenth century the courts began to take the position that since the mortgage was intended merely as *security,* the summary forfeiture of the mortgaged land for a debt much less than its value was unjust. Thus the practice developed that even though the mortgagor failed to make payment on the very day set, if he could pay the amount of the debt plus interest within a *reasonable time* thereafter he would be entitled to the return of his property. This privilege of redeeming the property became known as the mortgagor's "equity of redemption." However, the practice of allowing mortgagors a "second chance" to redeem their property within a "reasonable time" after the law day placed mortgagees at an unfair disadvantage. As long as there was the possibility that the mortgagor would redeem, the land was unsaleable and the mortgagee could not realize on his security. Some time limit had to be imposed upon the mortgagor's right to redeem or the security function of the mortgage would disappear.

The need of the mortgagee to free himself eventually of the threat of having the property redeemed resulted in the *foreclosure suit*—a proceeding to bar or terminate the mortgagor's equity of redemption.[2] Upon default in the payment of the mortgage debt, the mortgagee would file a petition in court alleging that the mortgagor had defaulted on his mortgage. The court would then enter a decree ordering the mortgagor to pay the debt within a specified time (usually six months or a year) or be finally barred from redeeming. If the mortgagor failed to pay the debt within the time specified

PROPERTY 545-46 (1975).

2 *Foreclosure* means to shut out, to bar, to terminate or destroy an equity of redemption. Thus when reference is made to "foreclosing a mortgage," what is technically meant is that the mortgagor's *right to redeem* is foreclosed, not the mortgage.

in the decree, his right to redeem was forever barred and foreclosed. The effect of the foreclosure proceeding was to cut off the rights of the mortgagor and place title to the property absolutely in the mortgagee. This type of proceeding was known as *strict foreclosure.* Later, *foreclosure by sale* developed, whereby the mortgaged property was sold at public auction, with the proceeds used to pay off the mortgage debt and the surplus going to the mortgagor. Foreclosure by sale eventually became the most common method used. Although strict foreclosure is still found in many states today, it has been largely supplanted by foreclosure by sale. However, the methods of foreclosure are governed by the various state statutes which vary considerably from one state to another.

THE NATURE OF A MORTGAGE

The typical mortgage transaction involves the execution of two documents: (1) a *promissory note* and (2) a *mortgage deed.* The promissory note[3] is the primary instrument; it creates the legal obligation and makes the mortgagor personally liable for payment of the debt. The mortgage deed serves as collateral security for the loan; it is the secondary instrument and creates a *security* interest in the land.

Example:

A applies for a $10,000 bank loan. The bank is willing to make the loan but wants security. A owns Blackacre, worth $20,000; he signs a promissory note to the bank by which he promises to repay the $10,000 ten years from date with interest at 6%. In order to secure the repayment of the loan, A (the mortgagor) also gives the bank (the mortgagee) a mortgage on Blackacre. However, only the mortgage deed will be recorded in the registry of deeds.[4]

[3] A promissory note is an unconditional promise in writing, made by one person to another to pay a certain sum of money at a specified time.

[4] The promissory note itself is not recorded because it creates no interest in the land. Upon full performance of the conditions of the mortgage the

The modern mortgage deed, like its common law predecessor, is usually drawn in the form of an ordinary warranty deed, professing to convey the land outright; however, it contains a special provision, called a *defeasance clause,* which states, in effect, that if the debt is paid in accordance with the terms of the promissory note the conveyance shall become void and of no effect. So a mortgage is actually similar to a conveyance which is subject to a condition subsequent, the condition being the payment of the debt.[5]

Some states take the view that a mortgage deed actually transfers the legal title to the mortgagee, subject to the defeasance clause. This is known as the *title theory* of mortgages. Most of the states adopt the view that a mortgage does not convey the legal title to the mortgagee but merely gives him a *lien* on the property, known as the *lien theory* of mortgages. As a practical matter, however, the distinction between title-theory states and lien-theory states is largely academic since the mortgagee's interest is generally regarded as a security interest only.

Since a mortgage conveys an interest in real estate it must meet all the requirements of a valid deed. Along with the usual grantor's covenants for title, the typical mortgage deed usually contains additional covenants to the effect that the mortgagor promises: (1) to pay the indebtedness prescribed in the note, (2) to pay the taxes, liens and other assessments levied upon the property, (3) to keep the property insured in an appropriate amount for the benefit of the mortgagee, and (4) to keep the buildings in good repair and not suffer or commit any waste[6] of the mortgaged premises.

mortgagor is entitled to a cancellation of the note and a *discharge* of the mortgage.

5 In about a dozen states a device called a "trust deed" is used in place of the mortgage. In a trust deed, or "deed of trust" as it is also called, the conveyance is not to the mortgagee but to a third person who holds the title in trust for the benefit of the lender as security for the payment of the debt.

6 "Waste" is the doing of acts which cause permanent or lasting damage to the realty.

Most mortgages also contain a stipulation that upon the breach of any of the covenants in the mortgage (such as failure to make an installment payment or failure to pay taxes or keep the premises insured) the mortgagee may elect to declare the entire amount of the mortgage debt due and payable immediately. This is called an *acceleration clause* because it hastens or "accelerates" the time for the payment of the debt.[7]

Mortgages often contain a stipulation allowing the mortgagor the privilege of paying off the debt *before* maturity. This is called a *prepayment clause.* Unless the mortgage contains a prepayment clause, the mortgagor cannot insist upon making payment before maturity, even if the payment includes the interest to the date of maturity. The mortgagee is entitled to have his money remain invested at the stipulated rate of interest for the agreed period of time, in accordance with the terms of the note. Consequently, many mortgages contain penalty clauses which call for the payment of substantial amounts as a condition of accepting prepayment.

TYPES OF MORTGAGES

Term and Amortizing Mortgages

Mortgages may be classed as either *term mortgages* or *amortizing mortgages.* The *term* mortgage, which was common prior to the great depression of the thirties, usually called for quarterly or semi-annual payments of interest, with the principal debt payable in a lump sum at the end of the term, which was typically three to five years. If, at maturity, the mortgagee did not demand payment of the principal sum but was content to continue to receive interest payments only,

[7] A typical *acceleration clause* might read: ". . . and the Grantor agrees with the Grantee that in the event of a breach of any of the above covenants, the whole of the money, principal and interest hereby secured shall, at the election of said Grantee become immediately due and payable."

the mortgage was said to be "open." Such "open mortgages" were payable on demand.

The *amortizing* mortgage provides for a gradual liquidation of the mortgage debt through regular scheduled (usually monthly) payments of principal and interest. This type of mortgage enables the borrower to repay the debt over a comparatively long period of time while gradually building an equity in the property. The amortizing mortgage came into vogue after the depression, and today nearly all mortgages make some provision for amortizing the mortgage debt.

Budget and Package Mortgages

If the regular monthly mortgage payments of principal and interest also include one twelfth of the annual cost of the taxes and fire insurance, it is called a *budget* mortgage. And where mechanical equipment (including such items as refrigerators, ranges, dishwashers, and washing machines) is classified as realty and included in the mortgage loan, it is referred to as a *package* mortgage. The package mortgage enables a borrower to finance the initial purchase of major household appliances through his original real estate mortgage loan, usually at a lower rate and over a longer period of time than if purchased separately.

Blanket Mortgages

A mortgage which covers more than one parcel of real estate is called a *blanket* mortgage. Blanket mortgages are often used by builders and land developers who subdivide large tracts into lots for sale to individual purchasers. A partial release clause is usually incorporated into blanket mortgages in order to facilitate the sale of individual lots. The release clause usually sets out a schedule of lots to be released from the terms of the mortgage upon payment by the mortgagor of specified amounts per lot.

The Open-End Mortgage

An *open-end* mortgage transaction involves a contract

between the borrower and the lender which provides that the mortgaged real estate shall serve as security not only for the original loan but for *future* borrowings as well. The open-end mortgage functions as security for both the original loan and for any additional advances which may be made in the future.[8]

The open-end mortgage makes it possible for a borrower to secure future advances, up to a stated limit, through the expediency of executing a single mortgage. This saves interest and obviates the trouble and expense of executing a new mortgage each time funds are advanced. It is designed to serve the borrower who needs only a fraction of the loan to begin with but requires most of the funds in the form of deferred installments to suit his financial needs.[9]

SECOND MORTGAGES

A *second mortgage* is one which ranks second in a series of mortgages on the same property.[10] For example, let's assume that A owns land worth $20,000 and that it is already mortgaged to B for $10,000. A has an "equity" of $10,000.[11] A's equity could serve as security for an additional loan if someone were willing to accept a *second* mortgage on the land—that is, a mortgage subject to B's mortgage. Any mortgage which is subject or subordinate to another mortgage is also referred to as a "junior mortgage." Junior mortgages usually carry a rate of interest commensurate with the increased risk involved.[12]

Ordinarily mortgages are "first" or "second" according to

8 Do not confuse the "open-end" mortgage with an "open" mortgage. The term "open" mortgage refers to a mortgage that is past its due date.

9 Construction or improvement loans are a form of open-end mortgage. The mortgage is executed before the construction or improvement begins, but the funds are advanced as the work progresses, usually based upon various stages of completion.

10 A mortgage which ranks third is a third mortgage, etc.

11 "Equity" in this sense refers to the value of the property over and above the amount of the mortgage.

12 Second mortgages often contain provisions to the effect that a default in the first mortgage shall constitute a default in the second mortgage such as to permit its foreclosure. However, to complete his foreclosure the second mortgagee will be required to pay off the first mortgage.

the order in which they are recorded in the registry of deeds. And unless otherwise provided, when a first mortgage is discharged a second mortgage automatically becomes a first mortgage. This result is not always desirable, since it could prevent refinancing—that is, the placing of a new first mortgage. However, the order of priority may be controlled by a *subordination agreement* providing, in effect, that upon a discharge of the first mortgage the second mortgage will not become a first mortgage but will remain *subordinate* to any such new mortgage.

The Purchase Money Mortgage

Where a buyer lacks the full amount of the purchase price and is unable to obtain a loan elsewhere, the seller himself will sometimes "take back" a mortgage in lieu of the rest of the purchase price. Since the purpose of the mortgage is to secure the unpaid balance of the purchase price, it is known as a *purchase money mortgage.* In this situation, the seller, who is at once both the grantor and the mortgagee, is really financing the transaction.[13]

Installment Land Contracts

An *installment land contract* is a long-term contract for the purchase of real estate on an installment basis. It is sometimes used as a security device instead of the purchase money mortgage. Under an installment land contract the buyer is given possession but must make scheduled installment payments toward the purchase price. The legal title is retained by the seller as security for the payment of the purchase price; and the buyer does not receive a deed until the final installment is paid. Sometimes the installment contract is in the form of a sealed obligation under penalty on the part of the seller to convey a good title, in which case it is referred to as a "title bond" or a "bond for a deed."

13 In some states, any real estate mortgage given as security to finance part of the purchase price is referred to as a "purchase money mortgage," whether the loan is made by the seller, a third party, or by a lending institution.

The typical installment land contract or "bond for a deed" is a rather one-sided transaction in that if the purchaser defaults the seller may immediately repossess the land and keep all the payments made, with the purchaser having no right of redemption.[14] The harshness of this situation has been softened somewhat by legislation in some states.

MORTGAGE FORECLOSURE

As stated above, a mortgage is a conveyance of real estate as security for a debt. What if the mortgagor defaults in his payments, or breaches any of the other covenants in the mortgage—how does the mortgagee realize upon this security? At early common law there was no problem—immediately upon default the mortgagor forfeited his land and the mortgagee became the absolute owner. Later the mortgagor was given the right to redeem his land if, *within a reasonable time* after default, he paid the full amount of the debt plus interest. Consequently, before the mortgagee could realize upon his security he had to free himself of this equity of redemption. Thus developed the foreclosure suit—a proceeding to bar or terminate the equity of redemption.

Today foreclosure procedures are governed by the various state statutes. And although the procedures vary considerably from state to state, the object of foreclosure is the same everywhere: to terminate the mortgagor's equity of redemption.[15] There are four basic methods of foreclosure used throughout the United States: (1) Strict Foreclosure, (2)

[14] It isn't quite as one-sided as might first appear, however, since often times the installment payments roughly approximate the fair *rental* value of the property.

[15] A mortgage cannot be made irredeemable. The right of redemption is an integral part of any mortgage; it cannot be disannexed, even by an express agreement by the parties, and any stipulation purporting to do away with the mortgagor's right of redemption is void as against public policy.

A mortgagor may redeem the mortgaged property at any time within the redemption period by paying or tendering to the mortgagee the full amount of the debt plus interest and costs of foreclosure, and by performing all the other obligations set out in the mortgage.

Foreclosure by Entry and Possession, (3) Foreclosure by Judicial Sale, and (4) Foreclosure by Power of Sale.

Strict Foreclosure

"Strict foreclosure" is a legal proceeding under which the mortgagor, after default, is allowed a specified *period of time* in which to redeem his property by paying off the mortgage debt. If the mortgagor fails to redeem within the stipulated time period his rights in the property are forever barred and foreclosed. The effect of strict foreclosure is to place absolute ownership of the property in the mortgagee after the passage of the specified period of time, without the necessity of a sale of the property. Although permissible in several states, strict foreclosure is rarely used today.

Foreclosure by Entry and Possession

In a very few states (Maine, Massachusetts, New Hampshire and Rhode Island) a mortgage may be foreclosed by "entry and possession." Under this method the mortgagee, after default, enters into possession of the mortgaged property (either peaceably or under a court order) for the purpose of foreclosure. Once the mortgagee gains possession the mortgagor is then allowed a specified period of time in which to redeem the property; after that time his right of redemption is forever barred and foreclosed and the property is held absolutely and unconditionally by the foreclosing mortgagee.

Foreclosure by entry and possession is a form of strict foreclosure; the effect is to extinguish the mortgage debt to the extent of the fair market value[16] of the property at the time the foreclosure was completed, that is, when the equity of redemption expired. If at that time the value of the property is

16 "Fair market value" is that price which a property would likely bring on the open market, assuming an informed buyer, willing but not compelled to buy, and an informed seller, willing but not compelled to sell. When the issue is raised, "fair market value" is established by the testimony of competent real estate appraisers. However, the burden of proof is upon the mortgagor, who must establish the value of the mortgaged property at the time the foreclosure is completed.

less than the debt, the mortgagee is entitled to recover the deficiency.

Foreclosure by Judicial Sale

Foreclosure by judicial sale is the most generally used method of foreclosure in the United States today. Although the procedure varies considerably from state to state the typical action to foreclose by judicial sale begins by filing a legal complaint against the defaulting mortgagor and all other parties having any interest in the property. In order to determine the parties in interest it is necessary to make a preliminary search of the title in the registry of deeds. The complaint must allege that the mortgagor is in default and state the amount due on the mortgage; it must also intelligibly describe the mortgaged premises. A hearing is held and the court determines whether there has in fact been a default, and if so the total amount due on the mortgage. If the court determines that the mortgagor is in default it issues a decree or judgment of foreclosure, setting out the amount due and decreeing that if the mortgagor fails to make payment within a specified period of time (the equitable right of redemption) the property shall be sold at public auction. If the foreclosure sale brings more than the total amount due, the mortgagor is entitled to the surplus; however, if the sale brings less than the amount due, the mortgagee (in most states) is entitled to bring a further action against the mortgagor to recover the amount of the deficiency.

Foreclosure by Power of Sale

In several states it is the practice to insert in the mortgage instrument itself a provision giving the mortgagee the power to sell the property in the event of a default by the mortgagor, without resorting to formal foreclosure proceedings. The power of sale provision specifies what shall constitute a default, and in the event thereof authorizes the mortgagee to sell the property and to satisfy the debt out of the proceeds.

Since, under a power of sale, foreclosure is accomplished

without recourse to the courts it is less expensive and more expeditious than other methods of foreclosure. Although a few states forbid the power of sale as a method of foreclosure it is the predominant method used in nearly half of the states. Wherever the use of the power of sale is permitted, the procedure for conducting the sale is strictly regulated by statute in order to protect the mortgagor.

A foreclosure sale (either by judicial sale or by power of sale) terminates the mortgagor's equitable right of redemption. However, in over half of the states there are statutes which allow the mortgagor yet an additional period of time *after* the foreclosure sale in which to redeem the property. This additional redemption period varies among the states from two months to two years and is referred to as the *statutory* right of redemption.

The entire object of foreclosure is to extinguish the mortgagor's right of redemption. But whatever method[17] the mortgagee uses in his process of foreclosure, there must be strict compliance with the statute, otherwise the foreclosure will be ineffectual. And, if before the expiration of the right of redemption, the mortgagee accepts any payment to be applied to the mortgage debt, he is usually deemed to have waived his right to complete his foreclosure, *unless* there is a written agreement to the contrary.

The effect of completed foreclosure is to extinguish the mortgage debt to the extent of the value of the mortgaged property. If the value of the property (or the proceeds of the sale) proves to be less than the debt, the mortgagee (in most states) is entitled to recover the amount of the deficiency.

Deed in Lieu of Foreclosure

Although a mortgage may not be drafted in such a way as to

[17] In some states the mortgagee is relegated to a single method of foreclosure, but in most states he has a choice of methods. And in most states the mortgagee is not *required* to foreclose; he may, if the mortgagor has sufficient assets, sue directly on the promissory note. However, it is usually the mortgagor's lack of assets which brought about the default in the first place.

nullify the mortgagor's right to redeem, the mortgagor may sell the equity of redemption to the mortgagee *subsequent* to the execution of the mortgage. This is sometimes done when there has been a default and both parties wish to avoid the further expense of foreclosure proceedings. In this way the parties avoid the time and expense involved in a foreclosure action and the mortgagor avoids the possibility of a deficiency judgment.

When the mortgagee takes a deed from the mortgagor in satisfaction of the mortgage debt, the transaction is referred to as a "deed in lieu of foreclosure." However, the sale must be fair and free from fraud or oppression on the part of the mortgagee; if the mortgagee has taken unconscionable advantage of the mortgagor's position, the court will set the conveyance aside.[18]

THE TRANSFER OF MORTGAGED PROPERTY

You will recall that the typical mortgage transaction involves two elements: (1) the mortgagor's personal liability, evidenced by the promissory note, and (2) the lien on the land, evidenced by the mortgage deed. And, if upon completed foreclosure, the value of the land is inadequate to satisfy the debt, the mortgagor remains personally liable on the note for the amount of the deficiency.[19]

Usually when mortgaged real estate is sold it is refinanced —that is, the purchaser pays the full value of the property, as agreed upon, and the existing mortgage is paid off from the proceeds of the sale, at which time the seller is discharged from liability on his note. The purchaser, if he lacks the funds,

[18] Before the mortgagee can safely take a deed in lieu of foreclosure he must be careful to examine the title since any encumbrances recorded *after* the date of the mortgage will not be cut off as they would be by foreclosure.

[19] A few states have passed so-called anti-deficiency statutes which either limit or abolish the mortgagee's right to claim a deficiency under some circumstances.

then executes his own promissory note and places a new mortgage on the property as security.[20]

However, real estate is often sold without first paying off the existing mortgage—that is, the mortgagor merely sells his interest in the mortgaged property and the buyer continues to make the payments on the mortgage. Such a transaction is referred to as a sale of the "equity." The term "equity," as used here, is short for "equity of redemption," and means title subject to a mortgage. It is the traditional term used to describe the mortgagor's interest in the property. When a person speaks of his "equity" he is referring to the value of the property over and above the amount of the mortgage. Thus, the "equity" is the difference between the amount of the mortgage debt and the market value of the property.[21]

20 The payment of the purchase price, discharge of the old mortgage, delivery of the warranty deed and the execution of the new mortgage are all done concurrently at the closing.

21 There are situations in which, from the buyer's standpoint, the purchase of the seller's "equity" may be more desirable than refinancing. For instance, the existing mortgage may carry a rate of interest much lower than that presently obtainable, or the buyer's credit may be such that he is unable to secure his own financing. And by avoiding refinancing the buyer may reduce his "closing costs."

Ordinarily the mortgagor has an absolute right to transfer his interest ("equity") in the property. As a general rule courts will not enforce a covenant in a mortgage which flatly prohibits the mortgagor from selling his equity. Such restrictions have generally been held to be invalid as against public policy since they tend to impede the free transferability of land. However, in past years lending institutions have succeeded in circumventing this rule by inserting in the mortgage an *acceleration* clause to the effect that if the mortgagor sells his equity in the property without first obtaining the written consent of the lender, the entire balance of the mortgage shall become due and payable immediately, at the option of the lender. This type of acceleration clause is referred to as a "non-assumption" or "due-on-sale" clause.

"Due-on-sale" provisions have generally been upheld by the courts as a reasonable and legitimate method of protecting the mortgagee's security interest. The underlying reason for the "due-on-sale" clause is to insure that a responsible party is in possession, and also to allow the lender to take advantage of rising interest rates in the event the borrower transfers the security. Such clauses enable the lender to approve or disapprove the purchaser of the equity, charge an assumption fee, or demand an increase in the interest rate. "Due-on-sale" clauses first came about with rising interest rates. Although the courts generally sanction the use of "due-on-sale" clauses, the mortgagee's option to accelerate will usually be enforced only if he does so in good conscience and fairness to the mortgagor. In other words, the mortgagee must have a valid business reason for withholding consent to a transfer.

Example:

A owns Blackacre which has a market value of $15,000. The property is mortgaged to B and the balance of the mortgage debt is $10,000. A has a $5,000 "equity" in Blackacre.

In a "sale of the equity" the conveyance usually takes one of two forms: (1) Either the deed merely recites that the property is conveyed "subject to the mortgage,"[22] or (2) the deed provides that the property is conveyed subject to the mortgage *"which the purchaser assumes and agrees to pay."*[23]

TRANSFER "SUBJECT TO" THE MORTGAGE

Where the deed merely recites that the property is conveyed "subject to" the mortgage, the buyer merely recognizes the existence of the mortgage lien;[24] he does *not* become personally liable for the payment of the mortgage debt. If he does pay off the mortgage indebtedness, he will hold the land free and clear of the mortgage; if he fails to pay the mortgage, he runs the risk of losing the land through foreclosure. At any rate the most he can lose is the amount of his equity.

In a "subject to" sale, as between the grantor and the grantee, the mortgage debt is to be satisfied out of the land alone; the grantee merely takes subject to the mortgage lien—he incurs no *personal* liability, either to his grantor or to the mortgagee. Of course, in the event of a default, the *land* may be foreclosed upon, in which case the grantee will lose the property unless he pays the mortgage debt. But that is all he stands to lose; he will not be liable for any deficiency.

Example:

A owns Blackacre, worth $15,000. The property is

22 Referred to as a *"subject to"* clause.

23 Referred to as an *"assumption"* clause.

24 Actually, *any* conveyance of mortgaged property is "subject to" the mortgage if the mortgage has been recorded; and this is so whether the deed mentions the mortgage or not. A seller cannot transfer his land free of a recorded mortgage.

mortgaged to B and the balance of the mortgage debt is $12,000. A transfers his "equity" to C for $3,000 by deed which recites that the conveyance is made *"subject to"* the mortgage to B. C fails to meet the mortgage payments. Upon foreclosure the value of the property proves inadequate to satisfy the debt, accumulated interest, and cost of foreclosure, resulting in a $1,000 deficiency. C is not liable for the deficiency since he merely took "subject to" the mortgage. However, A is liable on his promissory note to B for the amount of the deficiency.[25]

TRANSFER WHERE BUYER ASSUMES THE MORTGAGE

Where the deed not only recites that the property is conveyed subject to a certain mortgage but states, in addition, that the grantee *"assumes and agrees to pay"*[26] the mortgage, such grantee becomes *personally* liable for the payment of the debt.[27] The grantee does not have to sign the deed to be bound by the provision; his mere acceptance of such a deed creates a binding contractual obligation to pay off the note, and it

25 A "subject to" transaction leaves the *mortgagee* (lender) in the same position as he was before the sale of the equity; he still has a personal claim against the mortgagor (seller of the equity) on his promissory note which is secured by the mortgage. And in the event of a default the mortgagee may foreclose and recover any deficiency from the mortgagor. However, in the event of a default the mortgagee, in most states, is not required to foreclose upon the mortgage; he may elect to sue the mortgagor (seller of the equity) on his promissory note, if he is solvent, and ignore the security. In the event that the mortgagee elects to ignore the security, and the mortgagor (seller of the equity) is required to pay off the note, he will be subrogated to the mortgagee's rights against the property and may obtain reimbursement through foreclosure. However, he may not recover for any *deficiency* against a purchaser of the equity who merely took "subject to" the mortgage, as in the case of C in the above example.

26 A typical assumption clause might read as follows: "Subject, however, to a certain mortgage executed by John B. Jones to Alfred H. Smith as mortgagee, which mortgage is dated October 15, 1976, and recorded in Cumberland County Registry of Deeds, Book 2321 Page 56, which said mortgage, and the obligation it secures, the grantee hereby *assumes and personally agrees to pay,* as part of the consideration for this conveyance."

Most transfers of mortgaged property involve an express assumption of the mortgage by the purchaser of the equity.

27 The buyer's promise to assume need not be incorporated into the deed itself. It may be express or implied; it may be evidenced by a separate instrument, or it may even be oral. Most commonly the promise to assume the mortgage is incorporated into the deed.

renders him liable not only to the grantor but to the mortgagee as well.

Example:

A conveys Blackacre to B by deed which recites that the conveyance is made subject to a certain mortgage held by the Second National Bank *"which mortgage the grantee assumes and agrees to pay."* B fails to meet the terms of the mortgage and the bank forecloses.[28] Upon completed foreclosure there is a deficiency. B is personally liable for the amount of the deficiency. In such a case the bank may obtain against B what is called a "deficiency judgment"; or it may bring an action against A on his promissory note.[29]

Thus when a purchaser of the equity accepts a deed which stipulates that he agrees to "assume and pay" the mortgage, he becomes personally liable to the mortgagee. And in the event of a default the mortgagee may sue either the mortgagor on his promissory note or sue the purchaser of the equity on his promise to pay off the mortgage indebtedness. If the mortgagee elects to foreclose and there is a deficiency, he may obtain a deficiency judgment against either the mortgagor or the assuming grantee.

But why should such mortgagee be allowed to enforce an agreement made between the buyer and seller—an agreement to which the mortgagee is not even a party? As a general proposition of law a person may not bring an action for breach of a contract unless he is a party to it. However, to that general rule of law there is an exception, known as the "third party beneficiary rule." The general principle of the third

28 If A has sufficient assets the bank may forego foreclosure proceedings and proceed directly against A in an action on the promissory note. In such a case A's payment of the note will result in his being "subrogated" to the bank's rights against B, the assuming grantee.

29 If A (the mortgagor) is required to pay the deficiency, he may obtain reimbursement from his assuming grantee (B) in an action for breach of contract.

party beneficiary rule[30] is that where two parties enter into a contract which will *benefit a third party,* such third party may himself, in certain instances, bring a direct action to enforce the contract.

Today the third party beneficiary doctrine is observed in just about all of the states and has been extended to mortgage assumption cases. In a mortgage assumption case, the "assuming" grantee's promise to pay the mortgage indebtedness constitutes a promise for the *benefit* of the mortgagee; and as such the mortgagee may enforce it even though he is not a party to the contract.

The *mortgagor* may compel payment of the mortgage debt by his assuming grantee, and this right extends to successive assuming grantees as well.

Example:

A conveys Blackacre to B who "assumes" the mortgage. Later B conveys to C who also "assumes" the mortgage. Still later C conveys to D who "assumes" the mortgage but later defaults. A may maintain an action against B, C, or D for breach of contract. An assuming grantee cannot relieve himself of the obligation to pay the mortgage by transferring the property to another who in turn assumes the mortgage; all successive assuming grantees remain liable even though they have parted with the property and though subsequent grantees have assumed the mortgage.

Similarly, under the third party beneficiary rule, each successive *assuming* grantee becomes and remains personally liable *to the mortgagee* for the payment of the mortgage debt.

Example:

A conveys Blackacre to B who "assumes" the mortgage, held by X Bank. B conveys to C who also "assumes" the mortgage. C conveys to D who merely

30 Also known as the Doctrine of *Lawrence v. Fox,* after an early New York case which adopted the rule. Lawrence v. Fox, 20 N. Y. 268 (1859).

takes "subject to" the mortgage. X Bank may recover against either A, B, or C.[31] D is not liable because he did not "assume" the mortgage indebtedness; the most he can lose is his "equity" in the property.[32]

SUMMARY

A mortgage is a conditional conveyance of real estate as *security* for the payment of a debt or the performance of some other obligation.

The typical mortgage transaction involves the execution of two documents: (1) a *promissory note* and (2) a *mortgage deed.* The promissory note creates the legal obligation; it makes the mortgagor personally liable for payment of the debt. The mortgage deed serves as collateral security for the loan.

The modern mortgage deed is drawn in the form of a warranty deed but containing a *defeasance clause*—that is, a provision which states, in effect, that if the debt is paid the conveyance shall become void and of no effect.

The typical mortgage deed contains the usual grantor's covenants found in most warranty deeds, plus additional covenants to the effect that the mortgagor promises: (1) to pay off the note, (2) to pay the real estate taxes, (3) to keep the property insured, and (4) to keep the property in good repair and not commit waste.

31 In a foreclosure action the mortgagee may join all of the assuming grantees together with the mortgagor so that the respective duties of the parties may be adjudicated in a single action. Of course the mortgagee is entitled to only one satisfaction of his claim.

32 The states are in disagreement as to whether an assuming grantee is liable after there has been a break in the chain of assumption. For example: A conveys to B who "assumes" the existing mortgage; B conveys to C who merely takes "subject to" the mortgage; later C conveys to D who "assumes" the mortgage. In some states D would *not* be held personally liable to the mortgagee because there has been a break in the chain of assumption; other states hold all the assuming grantees personally liable regardless of the break. Of course in no state would C (in the example above) be personally liable since he did not "assume" the mortgage.

A stipulation in a mortgage to the effect that upon breach of any of the mortgage covenants the mortgagee may elect to declare the entire amount of the debt due and payable immediately is called an *acceleration clause.*

A stipulation in a mortgage which gives the mortgagor the privilege of paying off the debt *before* maturity is called a *prepayment clause.*

Mortgages may be classed as either *term* or *amortizing.* A term mortgage is one which calls for periodic payments of interest, with the principal debt payable in a lump sum at the end of the term. If, at maturity, the mortgagee is content to continue to receive interest payments only, the mortgage is said to be "open." Such "open mortgages" are payable on demand. An *amortizing* mortgage provides for a gradual liquidation of the mortgage debt through regular (usually monthly) scheduled payments of principal and interest.

Where the regular monthly payments of principal and interest also include one twelfth of the annual cost of the taxes and insurance it is called a *budget* mortgage; where mechanical equipment is included in the mortgage it is referred to as a *package* mortgage. A mortgage which covers more than one parcel of real estate is called a *blanket* mortgage.

If the terms of the mortgage provide that the real estate shall serve as security not only for the original loan but for future borrowings as well, it is referred to as an *open-end* mortgage.

A *second* mortgage is one which ranks second in a series of mortgages on the same property; a mortgage which ranks third is a *third* mortgage, etc. Mortgages are "first," "second" or "third" according to the order in which they are recorded in the registry of deeds. When a first mortgage is discharged, a second mortgage automatically becomes a first mortgage. However, the order of priority may be controlled by a *subordination agreement*—an agreement by the parties to the effect that upon a discharge of the first mortgage the second mortgage will remain subordinate to any new mortgagc.

A mortgage which is given by the purchaser to the seller to secure the unpaid balance of the purchase price is called a *purchase money mortgage.*

An installment land contract or "bond for a deed" is a contract for the purchase of real estate on an installment basis. The legal title is retained by the seller until the final installment is paid, at which time a deed is delivered to the purchaser.

If the mortgagor defaults on his mortgage the mortgagee may realize upon his security by foreclosing. Today foreclosure procedures are governed by the various state statutes. The object of foreclosure is to terminate the mortgagor's equity of redemption.

There are four basic methods of foreclosure used in the United States: (1) Strict Foreclosure, (2) Foreclosure by Entry and Possession, (3) Foreclosure by Judicial Sale, and (4) Foreclosure by Power of Sale.

"Strict foreclosure" is a proceeding under which the mortgagor is allowed a specified *period of time* in which to redeem the property. If he fails to redeem within the stipulated period his equity of redemption is forever barred and foreclosed.

Under "foreclosure by entry and possession" the mortgagee takes possession of the mortgaged property, at which time the mortgagor is then allowed a specified period of time in which to redeem the property. If he fails to redeem within the specified time period the equity of redemption is forever barred and foreclosed.

In "foreclosure by judicial sale," the mortgagor, after default, is allowed a specified period of time in which to pay the total amount due on the mortgage. If he fails to make payment within the time specified, the property is sold at public auction.

Under "foreclosure by power of sale" the mortgage instrument itself contains a provision giving the mortgagee the power to sell the property in the event of a default and to satisfy the debt out of the proceeds.

The effect of completed foreclosure is to extinguish the mortgage debt to the extent of the value of the mortgaged property. If the value of the property proves to be less than the debt the mortgagee (in most states) is entitled to recover the deficiency.

Where, after default and in lieu of foreclosure, the mortgagee takes a deed from the mortgagor in satisfaction of the mortgage debt, the transaction is referred to as a *deed in lieu of foreclosure.* Such sale must be fair and free from fraud or oppression on the part of the mortgagee, or the court will set the conveyance aside.

When a seller transfers his interest in mortgaged property the transaction is referred to as a sale of the "equity." The term "equity" in this sense means title subject to a mortgage; it is the difference between the amount of the mortgage debt and the market value of the property.

In a "sale of the equity" the conveyance usually takes one of two forms: (1) Either the deed recites that the property is conveyed merely "subject to the mortgage," or (2) the deed provides that the grantee "assumes and agrees to pay" the mortgage.

Where the deed merely recites that the property is conveyed *"subject to"* the mortgage, the grantee does not become personally liable for the payment of the mortgage debt; the most he can lose is his equity.

Where the deed recites that the grantee *"assumes and agrees to pay"* the mortgage, the grantee becomes personally liable for the payment of the mortgage debt. Such grantee becomes liable not only to the grantor but to the mortgagee as well. And in the event of a default the mortgagee may sue either the original mortgagor on his promissory note or he may sue the "assuming" grantee. If thc mortgagee elects to foreclose and the value of the property is not sufficient to satisfy the debt, both the original mortgagor and the "assuming" grantee are liable for the deficiency.

The *mortgagor's* right to compel payment of the mortgage debt by his assuming grantee extends to successive assuming grantees; similarly, each successive assuming grantee becomes and remains personally liable to the *mortgagee* for the payment of the mortgage debt.

CHAPTER 12

RECORDING AND TITLE EXAMINATION

INTRODUCTORY STATEMENT

In the chapter on Deeds we examined the so-called "covenants for title" which are found in warranty deeds; we considered the nature of each of them, who could enforce them, and the measure of damages to be applied in the event of a breach of any one of them. But as a means of assuring a good title, the covenants have serious shortcomings. They do not assure the grantee that he will not lose the land; they merely entitle him to money damages if the title fails. And even this protection is contingent upon the continued availability and solvency of the warrantor. What the grantee really wants is assurance that he will not *lose* the property, but will be able to possess it peaceably as long as he wishes. The covenants for title give no such assurance. For that type of assurance the purchaser of real estate usually looks to the recording system of his particular state.

Recording systems are an attempt to provide a method by which the true status of land titles can be determined. The function of the recording laws is to provide a system whereby purchasers of real estate may protect themselves against secret unrecorded deeds and mortgages. This is accomplished by creating a permanent public record of land holding which can be examined by anyone wishing to determine the true status of the title.

Recording statutes vary somewhat from state to state, but they all have a common object: to protect subsequent innocent purchasers and mortgagees against previous unrecorded conveyances of the same land. Though worded differently, recording statutes proclaim, in effect, that "A conveyance shall not be valid against any person except the grantor, his heirs and devisees, and persons having actual notice of it, unless it is recorded."

HOW THE RECORDING SYSTEM WORKS

If there were no recording statute, priority of conveyances would simply be determined according to *time*—that is, according to the time when the interest was first acquired. For example, let us suppose A conveyed land to B and later conveyed the same land to C, an innocent purchaser without knowledge of A's prior transfer to B. Under such conditions C would take nothing for the simple reason that A had nothing to convey; he had already conveyed the land to B.[1]

You will recall from the chapter on Deeds that in most states a conveyance is valid, as between the grantor and grantee, even though it is not recorded; title passes from the grantor to the grantee as soon as the deed is *delivered*. In what way then do recording statutes affect land titles? Although it is true that failure to record an instrument does not render it void, the recording statutes declare, in effect, that an unrecorded instrument is binding *only* upon the grantor, his heirs and devisees, and persons having actual notice of it; as to all *other* persons an unrecorded instrument is without effect.

Thus an unrecorded title is a precarious one. To all grantees of an unrecorded interest in land, the recording statutes are saying: You may have a good title, but if you fail to record it you may *lose* it.

TYPES OF RECORDING STATUTES

Under what circumstances does a grantee lose his title by failing to record? It depends upon the particular state statute.

[1] In such a situation C would be relegated to an action for damages against A for breach of covenant.

Recording statutes in the United States are classified into three basic types: (1) *Pure Race,* (2) *Pure Notice,* and (3) *Race-Notice.*

Under the *"pure race"* type of statute the party who first records his instrument prevails, even though he took with notice of a prior unrecorded conveyance. Under this type of statute priority between successive grantees is determined solely by who wins the race to the recording office, hence they are called "race" type statutes. They exist in only a very few states.

Under the *"pure notice"* type of statute a subsequent purchaser who takes without notice of a prior unrecorded conveyance will prevail, regardless of who records first. In other words, an unrecorded conveyance is simply ineffective as against any subsequent purchaser who is without notice of the prior conveyance. This type of statute has the quality of inducing an early recording by the first purchaser in that, if he is to be protected, he must record his conveyance *before* the title gets into the hands of an innocent purchaser, regardless of who eventually records first.

Example:

A conveys Blackacre to B who does not then record his deed. Subsequently (and before B records) A conveys the same land to C who is an innocent purchaser without notice of the prior conveyance to B. Under a "pure notice" type statute C would prevail even though B were to later record his deed before C, or even if C did not record at all. B would lose his title by having failed to record his deed *before* the title passed into the hands of an innocent purchaser.

The *"race-notice"* type of statute is a combination of the other two types; priority of a subsequent purchaser depends upon *both* lack of notice *and* priority of record. Under this type of statute, in order to prevail, the subsequent purchaser must be without notice of the prior conveyance *and* he must record his instrument first. So if A conveys to B who does not record, and later conveys to C, an innocent purchaser without notice, B will nevertheless prevail if he records first.

Example:

A transfers Blackacre to B who fails to record his deed. A dies and his heirs, unaware of the conveyance to B, sell Blackacre to C, an innocent purchaser, who records his deed. Upon recording his deed C gets good title to the land. B *loses* his title by failing to record his deed.

Example:

A conveys to B who does not record. A then conveys the same land to C, an innocent purchaser, who also fails to record. Under the "race-notice" type statute, as between two *non-recording* innocent purchasers, the first in *time* (B in this case) would prevail. However, as between two non-recording innocent purchasers, the first one to eventually record his deed would prevail.

Example:

A conveys to B who does not record. A then conveys the same land to C, an innocent purchaser. C records and then B records. C prevails.

Example:

A conveys to B who does not record. A then conveys the same land to C, an innocent purchaser. B records and then C records. B prevails. Under the "race-notice" type statute, in order to prevail the subsequent purchaser must be without notice of the prior conveyance *and* he must record his instrument *first*.

Perhaps the question in your mind now is: How can a grantor pass an interest in land to anyone after having already conveyed the same land to someone else? At common law and in legal theory he cannot. However, the effect of the recording statutes is to take the title of the first grantee, who failed to record, and vest it in the subsequent grantee, provided he meets the requirements of the statute. So if the subsequent grantee is an innocent purchaser without notice of the prior conveyance (in a "pure-notice" state), or if he is an innocent purchaser without notice *and* records his deed first (in a "race-notice" state), title will vest in him by virtue of the recording statute.[2]

Persons Protected

The object of the recording statute is to protect innocent *purchasers* and mortgagees against conveyances which are not recorded. The statute does not protect persons who acquired the property as a gift or by will or inheritance; as to such persons a prior conveyance prevails even though not recorded.

Example:

A sells Blackacre to B who fails to record his deed. A later conveys Blackacre to C as a gift. Although C is without knowledge of the prior conveyance and records his deed, B will nevertheless prevail since C is not a *purchaser.*

To qualify as a "purchaser" it is not necessary that the consideration paid for the property be equal to its fair market value, or even that it be adequate. However, it must be more than nominal, and a mere recital of "value received" in a deed is not sufficient. A mortgagee is considered a "purchaser" and is entitled to the protection of the recording statutes.

To be protected under the recording statutes (except in the very few "pure race" states) a person must not only be a "purchaser" but he must also be an innocent purchaser without notice—that is, he must have purchased without knowledge of the prior unrecorded deed or mortgage. A purchaser who has notice of a prior unrecorded deed or

[2] *"Notice"* and *"race-notice"* statutes are almost equally divided among the states.

mortgage cannot gain good title by recording his instrument first; such person is not a good faith purchaser and does not fall within the protection of the recording statutes. A purchaser having notice of a prior unrecorded deed is affected in the same way as if the prior deed had actually been recorded.

Example:

A conveys land to B who does not record his deed. Thereafter A conveys the same land to C who has knowledge of the prior conveyance to B. C cannot, even by recording his deed first, gain title since he is not a purchaser *without notice.*

The "notice" need not amount to positive, certain knowledge of the prior conveyance; it may be *implied* from the circumstances. Thus, if a party has knowledge of such facts as would lead a fair and prudent person, using ordinary caution, to make further inquiries, and he avoids inquiring into the matter, he is chargeable with notice of the facts which by ordinary diligence he would have ascertained. This is sometimes referred to as "inquiry notice."[3]

The most common example of "implied" or "inquiry" notice is found in cases where the property is in the physical possession of someone other than the grantor. Such possession is sufficient to put any prospective purchaser on notice of a possible unrecorded interest in the occupant.

[3] Whatever puts a party upon inquiry amounts to notice, provided the inquiry would lead to a knowledge of the facts through the exercise of ordinary diligence. However, mere rumors received by the purchaser do not amount to "notice". And the burden of proof is on the grantee claiming title under an unrecorded deed to show that the purchaser of a subsequent recorded instrument had "notice" of the prior unrecorded deed.

A purchaser of real estate having notice of a prior unrecorded deed may, nevertheless, convey a good title to an innocent purchaser *without* notice. And if a purchaser *without* notice of a prior unrecorded deed conveys to one who *had* notice thereof, the latter will, nevertheless, receive good title; his title will not be impaired by the notice. In other words, once the land has passed to an innocent purchaser without notice, it is purged of its outstanding unrecorded interests. If this were not the case, an innocent purchaser without notice might never be able to sell his property.

Example:

A conveys or leases to B who takes possession but does not record his deed or lease. The mere fact that B is in physical possession of the premises is sufficient to charge a subsequent purchaser with "inquiry notice," thus obliging him to inquire into the nature and extent of B's interest. And this is the general rule even though the purchaser is in fact unaware of B's possession.[4]

The effect of "inquiry notice" is to charge the purchaser with notice of all the facts which a reasonable inquiry would have disclosed.

Example:

A conveys to B who takes possession but does not record his deed. Thereafter A conveys the same property to C, a purchaser without knowledge of the prior unrecorded conveyance to B. Although C records his deed B will nevertheless prevail, since C was not an innocent purchaser without notice. B's possession constituted an *implied* notice of his unrecorded title which C could have ascertained by reasonable diligence.

In some states any purchaser under a *quitclaim* deed is not an innocent purchaser *without notice*; because of the form of the deed he is automatically charged with *implied* notice of any adverse interest which may exist. Thus in these states a grantee under a quitclaim deed is not protected under the recording statute, even if he records his deed first; he takes at his peril, subject to any prior unrecorded instruments.

There are two reasons given for this rule: First, a quitclaim deed only purports to *release* whatever title the grantor may have *at the time;* and if the grantor has no title because of a

[4] The reason for this is that a reasonably prudent purchaser would first inspect a property before buying it, and in so doing would make inquiry as to the rights of any stranger occupying the premises. However, in a few states inquiry notice will not be imputed to a purchaser unless he has *actual knowledge* of the possession.

prior conveyance, even though unrecorded, his quitclaim grantee can take none—even if he records his deed. The other reason is that the mere *form* of the deed should indicate to the grantee that his grantor has little confidence in his title, and hence the quitclaim grantee is put on notice that he should make further inquiries.[5]

However, most states take the view that a quitclaim deed is considered as much a conveyance as it is a release, and that the mere form of the deed should not of itself suggest or imply a defective title. So under the majority rule—and the better rule—a purchaser under a quitclaim deed is as much protected by the recording statutes as a purchaser under a warranty deed.

TITLE EXAMINATION

WHY EXAMINE THE TITLE?

Merely because the seller of real estate is ready and willing to deliver a warranty deed is no assurance that he has good title to the land. He may have no title at all, or he may have title only to a portion of the land; he may or he may not own a fee simple absolute estate in the land; and even if he does, it may be encumbered by an undischarged mortgage, an easement, or a lien. There may be a cloud on the title[6] due to a vague legal description, or because of a defective instrument in the chain of title, or for any number of reasons. And if the title is *unmarketable* the buyer may be unable to re-sell the property at some future time. An "unmarketable title" is one with such defects as to cause a doubt in the mind of a reasonable purchaser sufficient to justify his refusal to take title to the property.[7]

[5] 4 AMERICAN LAW OF PROPERTY § 17.16 (Casner ed. 1952).

[6] A "cloud on the title" is anything such as a mortgage, deed or other instrument which, as a semblance of title, has some appearance of casting a valid objection over the true owner's title.

[7] For a title to be "marketable" or "merchantable" it need not be a perfectly clear title; but a title need not be wholly bad to be *un*marketable. A "marketable title" is a title free from reasonable doubt as to matters of law and fact. It is a title which a reasonable, prudent, well-informed purchaser, guided by competent legal advice,

A mortgagee will almost invariably insist upon an examination of the records to determine the true status of the title and for assurance that the security is sufficient from a title standpoint. The buyer's real protection (and the mortgagee's also) is to examine the records *before* the title passes because, except for the limited protection offered by the grantor's covenants for title, the full risk of title failure is assumed by the purchaser when he accepts the deed. The rule of *caveat emptor* applies: "Let a purchaser beware, who ought not to be ignorant that he is purchasing the rights of another."

Recording and Constructive Notice

The manner of recording, recording fees, what instruments may be recorded, and the method of keeping records are prescribed by the various state statutes. Recording statutes almost invariably provide that before an instrument may be accepted for recording it must be acknowledged.[8]

A person wishing to record a deed or any other instrument affecting the title merely presents it to the proper recording agency (usually referred to as the "recorder's office" or the "registry of deeds") in the county where the land is located. Upon receiving an instrument for recording the recording clerk certifies upon the instrument the day, hour and the minute it was received. An instrument is considered "recorded" at the time when it is received, and such time is entered on the record.

When an instrument is properly recorded the effect is to give legal notice to the world as to its existence. This "legal notice" which results from recording is called *constructive notice.*

would be willing to accept and take at its full value. A mere possibility or suspicion of a defect is not enough to render a title unmarketable if the title would satisfy the mythical well-informed purchaser. But a reasonable probability of litigation will render the title unmarketable.

8 You will recall that an "acknowledgment" is a formal witnessing by a public officer, usually a notary public or justice of the peace; it is a declaration before some authorized public officer, by a person who has executed an instrument, that the instrument is his voluntary act and deed.

Recording statutes operate to charge prospective purchasers and mortgagees with (constructive) notice of all prior *recorded* deeds and mortgages, and whether such persons actually examine the records or not, the law will presume that they have knowledge of everything they would have learned by such examination. A person will not be permitted to say he acted in ignorance of a recorded instrument, since constructive notice is a legal substitute for actual notice. However, the mere act of recording does not validate an instrument that was not valid to begin with. Thus if an instrument is void for such reasons as lack of delivery, fraud, forgery, insanity, etc., it does not gain validity by recording. Recording merely amounts to a public notice of the *existence* of the instrument.

The Registry Records

After an instrument has been submitted for recording it is copied in full (now done by photostatic means in most registries), and the copy is placed in a bound volume along with copies of other recorded documents. The pages of the volume are numbered and so is the volume itself. When one volume is filled with copies of instruments another volume is started; the volumes are numbered consecutively.

The recorded documents are located through a *grantor-grantee index* system. Under this system each recorded document is indexed both under the name of the grantor and under the name of the grantee, in alphabetical order. In addition to the names of the grantors and grantees, and the volume and page where the copied instruments appear, the *grantor-grantee index* usually indicates the location of the land, the type of instrument recorded and the date it was recorded.

The index is ordinarily contained in special individual volumes, with each volume covering a specified period, typically five or ten years. A section of a page in a grantor-grantee index volume covering the period from January 1,

1960 to January 1, 1965 might appear something like this:

GRANTOR — GRANTEE INDEX JAN. 1, 1960 - JAN. 1, 1965

NAME	LOCATION OF LAND	INSTRU-MENT	BOOK	PAGE GRANTOR	PAGE GRANTEE	DATE OF RECORD
CALDERWOOD, John T. / JORDAN, Edna E.	PORTLAND	WAR	2319		45	1/20 1961
CHISHOLM, Paul E. / SMITH, Frank D.	PORTLAND	MORT.	2360	231		5/11 1964
CONWAY, George A. / HARRISON, Harold A. &	SOUTH PORTLAND	WAR	2322		203	5/15 1961
CORRIGAN, Harold O. / KEEN, Alfred S.	FALMOUTH	QC	2292		126	3/23 1960
COSGROVE, Asa B. / POTVIN, Edward O.	CAPE ELIZABETH	WAR	2344	21		6/10 1963
CRAMM, Kenneth M. / ATKINSON, Neil D.	PORTLAND	DISCH.	2342		116	2/21 1963
CREEL, Robert G. & / ROBINSON, Frank S. &	SOUTH PORTLAND	WAR	2341		221	12/5 1962

From the above illustration you will note that John T. Calderwood was a grantee under a warranty deed involving land in Portland. The deed was recorded on January 20, 1961, a copy of which may be found on Page 45 of Volume numbered 2319. The grantor was Edna E. Jordan.

Also, that Paul E. Chisholm granted a mortgage of land in Portland to Frank D. Smith which was recorded on May 11, 1964, a copy of which appears in Volume 2360, Page 231; George A. Conway received a warranty deed to land in South Portland from Harold A. Harrison and others, recorded in Volume 2322 at Page 203; Harold O. Corrigan received a quitclaim deed to property in Falmouth from Alfred S. Keen; Asa B. Cosgrove conveyed land in Cape Elizabeth to Edward O. Potvin by warranty deed, etc.

In most registries the names of both grantors and grantees are listed alphabetically in a single index volume. If the page number of the book in which the document has been recorded appears in the grantor column, the party is a grantor, and if the page number appears in the grantee column the party is a grantee. In the illustration above Chisholm and Cosgrove were grantors and Calderwood, Conway, Corrigan, Cramm and Creel were grantees. In some registries the grantor-grantee index is arranged so that the grantors and the grantees are alphabetically listed in separate volumes.

The system of keeping the records varies considerably from state to state; it even varies somewhat from county to county within a single state. However, the two principal types of records to be consulted in the registry of deeds are those mentioned above: (1) the numbered volumes containing copies of the documents recorded and (2) the grantor-grantee index which indicates the names of the grantors and grantees in alphabetical order and in what volume and on what page the copied documents are located. And in addition there may be miscellaneous records which must also be consulted by the title examiner. For example, a deed often describes the land by reference to a recorded map or plan; these recorded maps or plans are generally kept in special volumes in a separate section of the registry. There may also be recorded in special volumes, depending upon the particular registry, such things as real estate attachments, mechanics' liens, notices of foreclosure, and tax liens. A search of the title will include an examination of all these records.

The Chain of Title

In order to determine the present status of the title to a given parcel of real estate the examiner must trace its "lineage." That is to say he must trace the historic ownership of the property—the circumstances under which it passed from one person to another. This succession of ownerships is referred to as the *chain of title.*

The name of each owner in the chain of title is checked out (in the grantor-grantee index) for that period during which he owned the property. The purpose is to determine what conveyances, if any, each successive owner may have made during his ownership, and to what extent such conveyances might have affected the title to the property. The process is known as *running the chain of title.* But how *far back* in the chain of title must the examiner go? What constitutes an adequate period of search?

In many parts of the country a typical title examination goes all the way back to the original source—a government or foreign grant to a private person.[9] In the eastern part of the country, title examinations do not ordinarily cover a period extending all the way back to the original grant; they are confined to a relatively short period, but sufficiently long to warrant a conclusion that there is no longer a reasonable probability of attack upon the title. This period varies from thirty to one hundred years, depending upon the particular state.

You will recall from the chapter on Adverse Possession that under the statute of limitations the right to recover lands adversely held by another is barred after a specified period of time, the period depending upon the particular state statute. Why, then, should it be necessary to trace the title back beyond the period of the statute of limitations? Why wouldn't the statutory period be sufficient? The reason is that under some circumstances the period of the statute is, in effect, lengthened. For instance, the statute of limitations will not run against a person who is under a legal disability.[10] Nor will it even begin to run against the owner of a future interest until he has the right to possession. And although an undischarged mortgage debt may have been barred by the statute of limitations, a part payment made after the statutory period will sometimes lift the protective bar of the statute and revive the mortgage. Also, deed restrictions or conditions placed upon the land may still be effective even though recorded beyond the statutory period.

However, the examination should be confined to a reasonable period of time or the cost of the search could be

9 Title to all land originates in a grant from a sovereignty. In most of the western states the first link in the chain of title is some form of a grant from our own federal government. In the south and southwest many titles originate from the sovereignties of Spain, France, and Mexico; and in the east from England and the thirteen original states. 4 AMERICAN LAW OF PROPERTY § 18.17. (Casner ed. 1952).

10 In most states a person is considered legally "disabled" if he is a minor, is insane, imprisoned, or is absent from the country.

prohibitive. Several states have passed statutes which limit the period of search by conclusively barring all outstanding interests after a gross period of time, typically forty years.

The Mechanics of Searching the Title[11]

Assume that George A. Conway is selling his residence to Robert O. Buyer. The parties have executed a purchase and sale agreement and Mr. Buyer's mortgage loan application has been approved by the bank. The bank's attorney is now about to search the title.

The first step in the process of searching the title is to trace the chain of title back a sufficient period of time and to the satisfaction of the searcher. The name of the present owner, George A. Conway, is used as a starting point. Although the title examiner is often furnished with a copy of the present owner's deed, in this case all he has is the full name of the owner and the legal description of the property.

Knowing that the present owner, George A. Conway, must have received the property from someone at some time past, the searcher consults the grantor-grantee index beginning with the most recent volume — January 1, 1975 to date. Since the name George A. Conway does not appear in that volume the searcher proceeds backward in time, consulting the index

11 Although the real estate broker will, on many occasions, consult the records at the registry of deeds, his use of them will ordinarily be for a limited purpose only—usually to copy a particular description in a deed, or to ascertain the selling price of a particular property as indicated by the transfer tax, or to analyze the wording of a certain restriction in a deed or check the terms of a lease, etc. The broker does not, of course, examine the records for the purpose of rendering an opinion on the status of the title; this function is necessarily confined to the legal profession.

However, the real estate broker should have a basic understanding of the recording system in his own state and a general idea of the mechanics of searching a title. A major part of the broker's function is to assist in the arrangement of financing, which is partly dependent upon the status of the title. When difficulties or delays arise in connection with the title the parties often seek an explanation from the broker who should be ready to explain the general nature of the difficulty and keep the parties accurately informed. He may even be able to suggest a solution and save an otherwise lost sale. At any rate, the more the broker knows about every aspect of a real estate transaction the better he serves his client and himself.

volume covering the period from 1970 to 1975 and then the volume covering the period from 1965 to 1970, with no results. However, when the searcher consults the index volume covering the period from 1960 to 1965 he finds that the name Conway, George A. appears therein as a grantee by warranty deed recorded on May 15, 1961, a copy of which may be found in Book 2322 Page 203. The grantors are listed as Harold A. Harrison and others.[12]

The searcher takes Book 2322 down from the shelf and turns to Page 203 in order to examine the copy of the deed from Harrison and others to George A. Conway. The searcher first checks the legal description in the recorded deed in order to make certain that it describes the same parcel of land as the one being searched.[13] The searcher then reads the deed carefully, noting its date, the names of the parties, the type of deed, whether it was properly signed and acknowledged, and whether it is complete in all other respects. He checks to see if the instrument purports to convey a fee simple absolute estate in the land or some lesser estate; he also determines whether or not the deed contains any restrictive covenants, easements, or other features that might constitute a cloud on the title. Having completed his examination of the deed from Harrison to Conway the searcher makes the following notations:

Harold A. and	War. Deed Book 2322 Page 203
Ethel B.	Dated 5-13-61
Harrison	Ack. 5-13-61
to	Rec. 5-15-61
George A. Conway	Rev. Stamps $24.20

12 See the illustration on page 261 *supra*.

13 If the land described in Book 2322 Page 203 turned out to be a different parcel from the one being searched, the examiner would continue his check of the grantor-grantee index under the name of George A. Conway until he found a conveyance to Conway which described the property being searched.

The next step is to find the grantor from whom the Harrisons acquired the property.[14] Since the Harrisons conveyed the property to Conway on May 13, 1961, they themselves must have been grantees of someone prior to that time. The searcher again consults the grantor-grantee index volume, this time under the name of Harrison, for the period covering January 1, 1960, to January 1, 1965.

Since the index shows no conveyance to Harrison during that period the searcher then consults the index volume covering the five year period from January 1, 1955, to January 1, 1960. The index volume covering this period shows three conveyances of property to the Harrisons. However a check of the descriptions in the deeds indicates that none of the conveyances concerns the parcel being searched.[15]

The searcher then proceeds backward, checking the grantor-grantee index volumes for the period covering 1950 to 1955 and for the period covering 1945 to 1950 with no results. However the index volume for 1940 to 1945 indicates a conveyance from James D. Bridges to Harold A. Harrison and others, which turns out to be the parcel being searched. This deed is dated June 2, 1942, and was recorded on June 10, 1942 in Book 1982 Page 34. After the deed is examined for completeness, etc., in the same manner as before, the searcher makes his notations and proceeds backward in time.

Since Bridges conveyed the property in 1942, he himself must have been a grantee of someone prior to that date.

14 Most modern deeds contain references stating from whom the grantor acquired the title and in what Book and Page the deed is recorded. For example: "Being the same premises conveyed to this grantor by deed of Robert C. and Mary H. Foss dated March 10, 1955 and recorded in Cumberland County Registry of Deeds in Book 2131 Page 208." The deed may recite title through a *will,* in which case the title examiner will proceed to the registry of probate and consult the will. These references or "recitals" usually follow the legal description. They obviate the necessity of checking the grantor-grantee index under the name of the grantor in order to find his predecessor in title; consequently they greatly facilitate the process of tracing back the chain of title.

15 Where an owner has conveyed several parcels at various times, the searcher must go through the sometimes tedious process of examining each deed to find which one describes the parcel being searched.

Again, the searcher consults the index volume—this time for the period 1940 to 1945 under the name of Bridges in order to find the grantor from whom *he* acquired the property. There is no record of a conveyance to James D. Bridges for the period 1940 to 1945 or for the period 1935 to 1940; but in the index volume for the period 1930 to 1935 the name of James D. Bridges does appear as a grantee. However, the type of instrument is coded "DEV" for *devise,* and the recording date is April 5, 1931. In the Book and Page number referred to there appears an abstract of the will of one Horace F. Bridges, listing James D. Bridges as the son of Horace F. Bridges and sole beneficiary under the will. The searcher then leaves the registry of deeds and goes into the registry of *probate* which is usually located in the same building.

In the registry of probate, estates are listed under the name of the decedent, so the searcher checks the probate index under the name of Horace F. Bridges.[16] There he obtains a docket number which directs him to a volume containing a list of the various documents relating to the estate of Horace F. Bridges who died on March 1, 1931. The searcher then examines the terms of the original will, petition for probate, inventory, account, and all other related documents. The searcher satisfies himself that James D. Bridges was in fact the sole beneficiary under the will of his father, that there are no outstanding interests or claims, and that the inheritance tax has been paid.

The searcher then returns to the registry of deeds and consults the grantor-grantee index under the name of the

[16] If the owner inherited the property from someone who died intestate (without a will) there may be no reference at all to that fact in the registry of deeds. Thus, if a search of the grantor-grantee index fails to disclose from whom the owner acquired the property the chances are that he inherited it through intestate succession. Since estates are indexed under the name of the decedent the searcher will go to the registry of probate and check the estates under the same name as the owner, on the theory that he inherited the property from an ancestor of the same name. If this brings no results the searcher may be able to find the name of the previous owner through the tax records or by making inquiries from older residents in the area. Tracing the chain of title often requires some detective work on the part of the title examiner.

father, Horace F. Bridges, in order to determine from whom *he* acquired the property. Proceeding backward from the date of death, nothing appears in the indexes until January 20, 1906; on that date the name of Horace F. Bridges appears as a grantee from Clarence J. Johnson and others by warranty deed recorded in Book 1120 Page 205. Again the searcher checks the legal description and examines the document in the same manner as before.

Having traced the chain of title backward a period of time considered adequate and to his satisfaction, the searcher now has a skeleton outline of the chain of title which looks something like this:

Clarence J. and Ellen B. Johnson to Horace F. Bridges	War. Deed Book 1120 p. 205 Dated 1-10-06 Ack. 1-10-06 Rec. 1-20-06
Horace F. Bridges to James D. Bridges	Devise Dock. No. 186243 Date of Death 3-1-31
James D. Bridges to Harold A. and Ethel B. Harrison	War. Deed Book 1982 p. 34 Dated 6-2-42 Ack. 6-2-42 Rec. 6-10-42 Stamps $13.20
Harold A. and Ethel B. Harrison to George A. Conway	War. Deed Book 2322 p. 203 Dated 5-13-61 Ack. 5-13-61 Rec. 5-15-61 Stamps $24.20

Having traced the chain of title back a sufficient period of time, the searcher must now check the grantor-grantee index under the name of each owner in the chain of title for that period of time during which he owned the property. This is done in order to see what conveyances, if any, were made by each owner during the time he owned the land. Through the process of "grantoring" out each owner during his period of ownership, the searcher can determine whether or not any of the parties in the chain of title conveyed the same property twice.[17] And by checking the grantor part of the index in this way, the searcher also compiles a list of recorded encumbrances, such as mortgages, liens, easements, etc. He must then ascertain from the records whether or not the mortgages have been discharged and what other encumbrances, if any, still remain on record. Depending upon the particular registry, it may also be necessary for the searcher to consult a separate special volume for attachments, mechanics' liens, tax liens and notices of foreclosure. And in order to determine the zoning and the current status of the real estate taxes, the searcher must consult the records of the city or town where the property is located.

So the searcher "grantors" each owner in the chain of title for that period during which he held title to the property, including, of course, the present owner right up to the time title actually passes. Since there is usually a period of a few days between the time when the examiner completes his search and the time title actually passes, a check of the registry must be made just prior to the delivery of the deed in order to make certain that nothing has been placed on the record in the interim that would affect the title.

Tract Indexes

Some states supplement the grantor-grantee index with a

17 The searcher must check out all transfers made by each of the owners in the chain of title. Thus the "grantoring" out process can be an extremely tedious task if the person being checked had made a large number of real estate transactions during his "holding period." Where the parcel being searched was once part of a larger tract under one ownership, and from which it was subdivided, the searcher must examine the deed descriptions relating to each of the various subdivided lots in order to insure that the grantor did not, inadvertently or otherwise, convey all or part of the lot being searched.

numerical or *tract* index. Under this system all recorded instruments are numerically keyed to a description of the land itself rather than indexed according to the names of the grantors and grantees.

The county is mapped and divided into blocks, which are further subdivided into separately owned lots. The lots and blocks are numbered and their boundaries are shown on maps located in the registry. There is a separate index for each block and a separate page in the index is assigned to each lot within a block. Appearing on that page is a list of all the recorded documents relating to that particular parcel of land, including a reference to the book and page wherein each document is recorded.

The title searcher merely consults the map to determine the lot and block number of his property. From there it is a simple matter to locate the page in the index listing all deeds, mortgages and other documents affecting that particular lot. Thereafter the title searcher proceeds to examine the title in the same manner as under the grantor-grantee system.

Abstracts and Certificates of Title

The person requesting the title search may wish to receive a complete *abstract of title*. An abstract of title is a condensed history of the title, consisting of a summary of the various recorded instruments in the chain of title, together with a statement of all liens or encumbrances to which the land is subject.

In many states, the furnishing of abstracts is often dispensed with and the general practice is to request of the examiner only a letter of opinion or his *certificate of title*. A certificate of title is simply the examiner's opinion of the title based upon his search and examination of the public records. No guarantee of the title is made, although the examiner will be liable for any loss occasioned by his negligence in searching the title.

Let us suppose the title search is complete and the

prospective owner or bank receives a letter of opinion or certificate of title indicating that the record title is clear according to the examiner. Can the parties then rest assured that the title is without defects? Certainly not, for there are several possible defects which even the most thorough examination would not disclose. For instance, aside from any actual errors in the record, it cannot be ascertained from the record itself whether a deed has been properly delivered or whether the grantor's signature was forged; in such cases no title passes regardless of what the record shows.[18] The land may be subject to a claim by adverse possession. Or a grantor in the chain of title may have lacked capacity due to minority or insanity; an instrument may have been procured by fraud or duress; there may be undisclosed heirs; or a deed may contain a misrepresentation as to the grantor's marital status, leaving open a claim by his spouse.

In the final analysis it should be said that, generally speaking, land titles are neither wholly good nor wholly bad. And since there is probably no such thing as a *perfect* title, a title examination is, in essence, an evaluation of possible risks.

TITLE INSURANCE

"Title insurance" is a fast-growing type of insurance which indemnifies the policyholder against loss resulting from defects in the title.[19] It affords the maximum in title protection since it provides compensation not only for loss due to

18 You will recall that recording adds nothing to the *validity* of an instrument. If for some reason the instrument was void before recording it will be void after recording. Recording merely amounts to a public notice of the *existence* of the instrument.

19 Title insurance indemnifies the policyholder only against defects in existence at the time the policy is issued; it does not protect against defects arising *after* that time.

The term "title insurance" could be somewhat misleading since titles are not actually *insured;* more accurately, policyholders are indemnified against monetary loss by reason of title failure.

Title companies usually issue three principal types of policies: (1) the *owner's* policy, which insures the owner's title, (2) the *mortgagee's* policy, which insures the title to the security interest of the mortgagee-lender, and (3) the *leasehold* policy, which insures the interest of the tenant under a long-term lease.

mistakes by the title examiner but also for "hidden" defects not disclosed by the public records. It also covers the cost of defending the title against attack, whether justified or not. However, there are some drawbacks. Like most insurance policies there are coverage limitations and exclusions. Premiums are fairly high and usually do not include the fee for searching the title. And although the premium is payable only once, the coverage extends only to those named in the policy. Generally title insurance policies are not transferable; if the property is sold the new owner must take out his own policy if he wishes to be covered.

Title insurance is available almost everywhere and is steadily increasing in favor throughout the United States. In many states it is as common as fire insurance and regarded by mortgage lenders as a prerequisite to financing. However, it is more prevalent in the west and midwest than in the northeast. In New England it appears to have gained general acceptance only in the larger cities.

THE TORRENS SYSTEM

The so-called *Torrens system* of land registration takes its name from Sir Robert Torrens, a British customs officer who first introduced the system in Australia. As a result of his experience with the ship registry system, Torrens conceived the idea that the title to real estate might be registered in much the same manner as registering the title to ships.[20] Torrens

20 "Under the English Merchants' Shipping Law a page in the registry was given to each ship registered, and on it appeared the name and description of the ship, the name of the owner and any liens or encumbrances. A duplicate of this page in the form of a certificate was given to the owner which was his evidence of ownership no matter where he might be. If there were several owners—and it was quite customary to have ships divided into shares of halfs, quarters, eighths, etc.—each owner received a certificate for his share. Any lien or claim against a ship was required to be noted on the registry page, so that it was possible for any interested person at a glance to see exactly the condition of the title. To make a transfer, it was necessary to assign the certificate and take it to the registry office whereupon the old certificate was cancelled, the old registry page closed, and a new page was opened. A duplicate certificate, that is, a copy of the new registry page, was given to the new owner. At no time was more than one certificate of the

concluded that, as in the case of ships, the ownership of real estate could be evidenced by an official *certificate of registration* showing on its face the state of the title and the person or persons in whom it is vested—something very similar to a motor vehicle registration certificate. The object of the system was to officially establish the ownership of real estate beyond any question and thereby pave the way for a simpler, quicker and cheaper method of transferring title. When the "Torrens" law was first enacted in Australia in 1858 it enjoyed immediate success, and with some modifications it has been adopted in England and several other countries, and to a limited extent in some of the American states.

In those states which have adopted the Torrens system, a person wishing to register his title first files an application for registration with the court. The names of all persons having or claiming to have any interest in the property are listed in the application. This is actually a legal proceeding in the nature of a suit to quiet title. The court then appoints an "examiner of titles" to investigate all the facts pertaining to the title. On the basis of the examiner's report the court issues a summons to all parties having or claiming any possible interest in or lien upon the property. If, after a hearing on the matter, the court is satisfied that the title should be registered, the applicant is issued a "certificate" of title. The certificate sets out the extent of the owner's title and any valid interests or claims outstanding against the property. The title thereupon becomes "registered," and in the absence of fraud or mistake the person named in the certificate holds the title free from all claims except those noted on the certificate.

The original certificate of title is kept in the office of the "registrar of titles" and the owner is furnished a "duplicate certificate." Mortgagees and lessees receive what are known

same interest outstanding, and it was not necessary to go back of the face of the outstanding certificate. There was no need to examine prior certificates, nor to scrutinize the legality of prior transactions." PATTON, *The Torrens System of Land Title Registration*, 19 MINN. L. REV. 519, n.2 (1935).

as mortgagee's and lessee's duplicates. Any interests less than a fee simple, together with mortgages, liens and other encumbrances, are listed in the original certificate and are referred to as "memorials." The "memorials" are also entered upon the owner's duplicate certificate. The certificate of title is kept current, always showing the status of the title and the person in whom it is vested.

Transferring ownership to registered land is a relatively simple process. The owner delivers a deed of the property, together with his certificate of title, to the grantee, who files them with the registrar of titles. The registrar then cancels the grantor's certificate of title and issues a new one to the grantee. In the case of registered land, the title does not pass when the deed is delivered; it passes with the cancelling of the old certificate and the issuance of a new one to the grantee.[21] Transfers by will or descent are made by the registrar in accordance with orders of the court directing him to do so.

For all practical purposes a Torrens certificate of title is conclusive proof that the title is as set out in the certificate. After a title has been registered no interest in the land may be acquired by prescription or adverse possession.

Under most Torrens statutes an assurance fund has been established to indemnify anyone damaged as a result of fraud or errors committed in the registration process.

To summarize, then, under the Torrens system of land registration the title is first adjudicated in a court proceeding and then "registered," whereupon the owner receives an

[21] The procedure for transferring a title which is registered under the Torrens system is very similar to transferring the ownership of stock in a corporation: The seller endorses his stock certificate over to the buyer, who sends the certificate to the company's transfer agent. The transfer agent cancels the old certificate and makes out a new one in the name of the new owner. If the owner of a 200 share certificate sells only 50 shares, then his endorsement signifies that only 50 shares are to be transferred to the buyer. The transfer agent then makes out two certificates, one for 150 shares in the old owner's name and the other for 50 shares in the name of the new owner.

The old certificate for 200 shares is cancelled. Title to the stock is not actually transferred to the new owner until the old certificate has been cancelled and a new certificate has been issued *and* until the names have been changed on the books of the company.

official "certificate of title." The certificate is kept current, always showing the status of the title and the person in whom it is vested. Because the certificate itself is conclusive proof of title, the title search becomes a simple matter; the examiner need only look at the certificate. Title is transferred by cancelling the grantor's certificate and issuing a new one to the grantee. The object of the Torrens system is to establish the ownership of land beyond question and to provide a quick, simple, and inexpensive method of transferring the title.

The fundamental difference between the Torrens system and the recording system is this: Under the Torrens system the *title* itself is *registered,* whereas under the recording system the *evidence* of the title (i.e., the deeds, mortgages, liens, etc.) is *recorded* and available for inspection, from which the title examiner must draw his own conclusion as to the state of the title.[22]

The Torrens system obviously has considerable merit. Indeed, at first blush it might seem to be the answer to our need for a simpler and more workable system. However, the Torrens system never gained a real foothold in this country. Although statutes permitting title registration were passed in nearly half of the states, the system never flourished. If anything it withered on the vine and eight states eventually repealed their statutes. Today the Torrens system exists only in Colorado, Georgia, Hawaii, Illinois, Massachusetts, Minnesota, New York, North Carolina, Ohio, Oregon, Virginia and Washington.[23] And even in these states the

[22] In a much quoted opinion of the Minnesota Court, Chief Justice Start put it thusly:

"The basic principle of this [Torrens] system is the registration of the *title* to land, instead of [recording]. . . the *evidence* of such title. In the one case [the Torrens system] only the ultimate fact or conclusion that a certain named party has title to a particular tract of land is registered, and a certificate thereof delivered to him. In the other [the recording system] the entire evidence, from which proposed purchasers must, at their peril, draw such conclusion, is [recorded]." State v. Westfall, 85 MINN. 437, 89 N.W. 175 (1902).

[23] 6 POWELL, REAL PROPERTY 306 (1975).

system remains optional and is used only to a limited extent.[24]

Various reasons have been advanced as to why the Torrens system failed in the United States. One reason is that when the Torrens system was introduced our present recording system had already become fairly well established, thus the new system was met with a natural reluctance to depart from proven ways. Moreover, the initial registration procedure was somewhat complex and costly. In addition, some of the early "Torrens" statutes were declared unconstitutional in that they deprived persons of their property without due process of law; and under some state statutes the certificate of title was regarded as not sufficiently conclusive. Also, title insurance and abstract companies, fearing they would be put out of business by the new system, vigorously opposed it. Indifference and skepticism also played a part in stunting the growth of the Torrens system in this country.

In retrospect it is perhaps unfortunate that the Torrens system never really took root here, for it is now apparent that our present system has failed to keep pace with American society. At the time when our recording acts were being adopted the country was new; title to land did not change hands often, and there was no pressing need for speedy transfers. However, with the spectacular growth of the country and the increased activity in land transactions our recording system has become inefficient and cumbersome. Each transfer lengthens the chain of title and adds to the burden of the search. "Every time land is bought and sold, it becomes the burdensome task of some examiner to trace the title back to its origin and pass judgment anew upon each link in the chain. How much longer can we continue to justify this practice? How insurmountable will be the complications half a century hence, or even a quarter of a century hence!"[25]

The most wasteful feature of our present system is the

[24] In some states it is used only to clear a title.

[25] BASYE, *Trends and Progress—The Marketable Title Acts,* 47 IOWA L. REV. 261 (1962).

necessity for repeated examinations of the same title. "[E]ach person dealing with the land must hire his own expert and each expert must perform the whole task over again. As the records swell with each transaction, the burden of examination becomes more oppressive."[26]

Dissatisfaction with our present recording system has been mounting for years. It has been characterized as "cumbersome," "time-consuming," "costly," "archaic" and "intolerable," among other things. In an attempt to make the recording system more workable, several states have adopted so-called "Marketable Title Acts." The purpose of these acts is to extinguish all claims and title defects automatically after a gross period of time (typically forty years or less) and thereby shorten the necessary period of search.[27]

Some reformers have suggested that the numerical or *tract* index system be used entirely, and that the unwieldy grantor-grantee index system be abandoned. Others have suggested a complete elimination of the present recording system in favor of the Torrens system. However it is difficult to make radical changes in a system as firmly entrenched as ours, and with each passing year the chances for sweeping reform become more remote. Perhaps at this late stage the "Marketable Title Acts" offer the best solution. At any rate, whatever corrective action we take we should take it soon, for the system seems destined to bury itself under an ever-thickening layer of conveyancing sediment.

SUMMARY

Recording systems are an attempt to provide, through the creation of permanent public records, a method by which the

26 BARNETT, *Marketable Title Acts—Panacea or Pandemonium?* 53 CORN. L. REV. 45 (1967).

27 "If the recording system is to be made workable it is necessary that the period of title search be radically reduced. This period should not exceed twenty years and ideally might be further shortened." PAYNE, *The Crisis in Conveyancing*, 19 MO. L. REV. 214 (1954).

true status of land titles can be determined. Their function is to protect innocent purchasers against secret unrecorded transfers.

Although a deed is valid as between grantor and grantee, even though not recorded, an unrecorded title is a precarious one. Under some circumstances a grantee who fails to record may *lose* his title.

There are three basic types of recording statutes in the United States: (1) *Pure Race* statutes, (2) *Pure Notice* statutes, and (3) *Race-Notice* statutes. Under the *pure race* type of statute the first party to record his instrument prevails, even though he took with notice of a prior unrecorded conveyance. Pure race statutes exist in only a very few states. Under the *pure notice* type statute a subsequent purchaser without notice will prevail regardless of who records first. The *race-notice* type of statute is a combination of the other two types; in order to prevail the subsequent purchaser must be without notice *and* he must record his instrument first.

The object of the recording statute is to protect innocent *purchasers* and *mortgagees* against previous unrecorded transfers. The statute does not protect persons who acquired their title by gift or inheritance; as to such persons a prior conveyance prevails even though not recorded.

To be protected under the recording statutes (except in the very few *pure race* states) a person must not only be a "purchaser" but he must also be an "innocent" purchaser, *without notice* of the prior unrecorded conveyance. A purchaser who has notice of a prior unrecorded deed or mortgage cannot gain good title, even though he records his instrument first; such person is not a good faith purchaser and does not fall within the protection of the recording statute. The "notice" need not amount to positive, certain knowledge of the prior conveyance; it may be implied from the circumstances.

The record should be examined before title passes because,

except for the limited protection offered by the grantor's covenants for title, the full risk of title failure is assumed by the purchaser when he accepts the deed.

The manner of recording and the system of keeping records varies somewhat from state to state. In most states a person wishing to record an instrument merely presents it, properly acknowledged, to the office of the register of deeds in the county where the land is located. An instrument is considered as recorded when it is received, and such time is entered on the record.

A recorded instrument constitutes legal notice to the world of its existence; this "legal notice" is called *constructive notice*. A person will not be permitted to say he acted in ignorance of a recorded instrument, since constructive notice is a legal substitute for actual notice.

When searching a title there are two principal types of records to be consulted in the registry of deeds: (1) numbered volumes containing copies of all documents recorded, and (2) the grantor-grantee index which indicates the names of the grantors and grantees in alphabetical order and in what volume and page the various documents appear. When ownership has passed through a will or by inheritance, a search of the title will include an examination of the *probate* records as well.

A title examination consists of tracing the historic ownership of the property as it passed from one person to another. The succession of ownerships is referred to as the *chain of title*. The records are examined under the name of each owner in the chain of title for that period of time during which he owned the property. The purpose is to determine what conveyances, if any, each successive owner may have made and if there exists any cloud on the title or other encumbrance which might affect the title to the property.

In many parts of the country a typical title examination goes all the way back to the original source—a government or foreign grant to a private person. In the eastern part of the country the examination usually involves tracing the chain of title back only thirty to one hundred years, depending upon the particular state.

The person requesting a title search may want a complete *abstract of title.* An abstract of title is a condensed history of the title, consisting of a summary of the various recorded instruments in the chain of title, together with a statement of all liens or encumbrances to which the land is subject. In many states it is the practice to obtain from the examiner only a letter of opinion or his certificate of title.

There are several possible "hidden" defects in a title which the record would not disclose. For instance, it cannot be ascertained from the record whether a deed has been properly delivered, or whether the grantor's signature was forged; in such cases no title passes regardless of what the record shows. Or a grantor in the chain of title may have lacked capacity due to minority or insanity; there may be heirs not disclosed by the record; a deed may contain a misrepresentation as to the grantor's marital status, etc.

There is probably no such thing as a *perfect* title; a title examination really amounts to an evaluation of possible risks. However, as an additional method of title protection, *title insurance* is available almost everywhere. "Title insurance" indemnifies the policyholder for any loss resulting from defects or failure of title; it provides monetary compensation not only for loss due to negligence in the title search itself but also for loss resulting from the "hidden" defects as well.

In a few states the *Torrens system* of land registration is used to a limited extent. Under the Torrens system the title is first adjudicated in a court proceeding and then "registered," whereupon the owner receives an official "certificate of title." For all practical purposes the certificate itself is conclusive proof of title. Title is transferred by cancelling the grantor's certificate and issuing a new one to the grantee. The object of the Torrens system is to establish the ownership of land beyond question and to provide a quick, simple and inexpensive method of transferring title.

CHAPTER 13

CONTRACTS

INTRODUCTORY STATEMENT

The sale of real estate usually involves at least three legal documents: the *deed,* the *mortgage,* and the *contract* to sell. The deed conveys the legal title, and the mortgage serves as a security device. But compared to the contract to sell, the deed and the mortgage are relatively simple instruments. The purchase and sale contract fixes the legal obligations of the parties with respect to the purchase price and all of the other terms of the sale. It serves as the "blueprint" of the transaction and is the fundamental instrument of the real estate business.

Of course the parties *could* transfer the title without first entering into a purchase and sale contract—much as one would purchase a kitchen appliance or a book. The buyer could simply pick out the property and pay the agreed price upon receiving the deed. However this is rarely done in practice, since there are usually several matters to be resolved before the title passes. For instance, there is the matter of title examination; before the buyer pays the purchase price he will want to verify the seller's interest in the property and ascertain whether or not the title is marketable. And most often there are financing arrangements to be made, which require time. Also there are a number of other details to consider, such as the type of deed to be delivered, the manner of payment, the date of possession, proration of taxes, the payment of mortgages, etc.

So, although the actual transfer of the legal title is accomplished by simply delivering the deed, in commercial transactions this final act is almost invariably preceded by a contract to sell. And in those transactions where a real estate broker is involved, it is often the broker who "drafts" the contract. Consequently it is essential that the broker possess at least a basic knowledge of the law of contracts, for when he undertakes the "drafting" of a contract he assumes a substantial responsibility.

CONTRACTS IN GENERAL

The term *contract* has been defined in many ways. It has been defined as "a promise or a set of promises for the breach of which the law gives a remedy, or the performance of which the law in some way recognizes as a duty."[1] It has also been defined as "a deliberate engagement between competent parties, upon a legal consideration, to do, or abstain from doing, some act."[2] It has been defined as "a binding enforceable agreement between two parties." And it has been defined in over a hundred other different ways. However, there is probably no one and only "correct" definition of the term *contract.* For our purposes a contract may be defined as *a promise or set of promises which the law will enforce.* And by further reducing the definition to its most elemental form, we could say that a contract is simply an enforceable promise. What do we mean by "enforceable"? We mean that the law will either make a party keep his promise or make him pay money damages to the other party for breaking the promise.

Of course not every promise is legally enforceable. For example, A's promise to take B to the theater would not

1 RESTATEMENT OF CONTRACTS § 1 (1932) [hereinafter cited as RESTATEMENT].

2 BLACK'S LAW DICTIONARY 394 (4th ed. 1951).

ordinarily be enforceable. A might have a moral duty to keep his promise but not a legal duty. And some promises are not even promises at all. For example, a businessman's letter to a wholesaler stating that "from now on I am going to purchase all my material from you" is a mere statement of intention and not a promise. And if A says to B, "I promise to buy such coal as I may wish to buy from you during the current year at $30 per ton," A in reality has not promised to buy any coal at all. Such statements are called "illusory" promises. So, in order for there to be a contract there must not only be a definite promise but it must be a promise which the law will enforce. And in order for there to be a promise which the law will enforce, certain basic elements must be present; otherwise no contract will result.

ESSENTIAL ELEMENTS OF A CONTRACT

For there to be a legally enforceable promise—that is, a *contract*—certain minimum requirements must be met:

(a) There must be an OFFER.

(b) The offer must be ACCEPTED.

(c) There must be CONSIDERATION.

The elements of *offer, acceptance,* and *consideration* are absolutely essential to the formation of any contract. If any one of these elements is lacking, no contract will result; together they form the supporting "skeleton" of all contracts, regardless of how simple or how complex their terms may be.

THE OFFER AND THE ACCEPTANCE

To create a contract there must be, among other things, a definite *offer*[3] by one party and an absolute and unequivocal

[3] There can be no contract for the sale of property unless there is first a definite *offer* of sale. Mere statements made with the intent to open negotiations do not constitute an offer. This is well illustrated in the leading case of Owen v. Tunison, 131 Me. 42, 158 Atl. 926 (1932). In that case the

acceptance of that offer by the other party.

An "offer" is simply a conditional promise—a promise conditional upon something to be done by the person to whom the offer is made. The condition may be the actual *performance* of an act or it may be the receiving of a return *promise* to pcrform thc act.

If the offer is conditional upon the doing of some *act* by the other party (the offeree), it is said to be an offer for a *unilateral* contract. Where the offer is conditional upon receiving a return *promise* to perform the act, it is said to be an offer for a *bilateral* contract.

For example, A says to B, "If you will mow my lawn I will pay you $5.00." A's offer (promise to pay) is conditional upon B's performing the *act* of mowing the lawn; this is an offer for a *unilateral* contract. It is *uni*lateral because there is only *one* promisor—A. B has made no return promise; he may accept A's offer by mowing the lawn, but he is under no obligation to do so. And if B does accept the offer by mowing the law, a contract will result and A's promise to pay the $5.00 will then become absolute and enforceable. Such contract is called *uni*lateral because only *one* party is legally obligated.

But if A says to B, "I will pay you $5.00 if you will *promise* to mow my lawn," the situation is different. Here A's offer

plaintiff wrote the defendant as follows: *"Will you sell me your store property which is located on Main St. in Bucksport, Me., running from Montgomery's Drug Store on one corner to a Grocery Store on the other, for the sum of $6,000.00?"* In answer the defendant wrote back as follows: *"Because of improvements which have been added and an expenditure of several thousand dollars it would not be possible for me to sell it unless I was to receive $16,000,00 cash."* Whereupon, the plaintiff at once sent the following message to the defendant: "ACCEPT YOUR OFFER FOR BRADLEY BLOCK BUCKSPORT TERMS SIXTEEN THOUSAND CASH. . . ."

The defendant decided not to sell and the plaintiff brought suit for breach of contract. The court held that there was no contract because there had been no definite *offer* to sell. The court said that the defendant's letter could not be construed to be an offer to sell his property, but rather, it merely contained statements of negotiation which might later lead to a sale. And since the defendant's letter did not constitute an offer to sell, the plaintiff's "acceptance" was ineffective and no contract resulted.

(promise to pay) is conditional, not upon B's actually performing the act, but rather upon B's *promise* to perform the act. B's return *promise* to perform will satisfy the condition of the offer and constitute an acceptance, resulting in a bilateral contract—*bi*lateral because by virtue of their mutual promises *both* parties become legally obligated. Here there are duties on both sides—a duty to perform on the one and a duty to pay on the other.

So, a *bilateral* contract consists of mutual promises made in exchange for each other by each of the parties; this results in mutual rights and mutual duties. In the case of a *unilateral* contract, however, the parties do not *exchange* promises —there is only *one* promisor and he is the only party legally obligated.

Most real estate brokers' "listing" agreements are of the unilateral type. That is, the property owner usually promises to pay the broker a commission in return for the *act* of producing a buyer who is ready, willing and able to purchase on the terms specified in the listing agreement. "Listing" contracts will be considered in the next chapter. In this chapter we are concerned chiefly with the contract for the purchase and sale of real estate (invariably of the bilateral type) where the parties exchange mutual promises—that is, a promise to buy in return for a promise to sell, upon the terms specified in the contract.

One who makes an offer (called the offeror) has a right to stipulate in his offer any conditions he wishes. And the person to whom the offer is made (called the offeree) can accept the offer only by satisfying all of the stipulated conditions. Until the offer is accepted, there can be no binding contract between the parties.

The acceptance must be clear and unequivocal, and it must be precisely in accordance with the terms of the offer. An "acceptance" which is equivocal or conditional, or which imposes new or different conditions, amounts to a rejection of the offer; for there to be a contract there must be a "meeting of the minds."[4] But once an offer is accepted, and the acceptance is communicated to the person making the offer, a contract arises and neither party can thereafter withdraw at pleasure.

Termination of Offers

Acceptance of an offer is possible only while the offer is "alive"—that is, the acceptance must occur before the offer is withdrawn or is otherwise terminated. Until an offer terminates, the person to whom the offer is made has the power to create a contract by accepting the offer. However, once the offer terminates, the power of acceptance is gone. But how long a period of time does the offeree have in which to accept—that is, how long does an offer last before it is too late to accept it?

By Lapse of Time

The person making the offer may specify the time within which acceptance must occur; he may make the duration of the offer as long or as brief as he wishes. If the offer is not accepted within the time specified, it will automatically terminate at the end of that time and acceptance thereafter will be ineffective. A late acceptance merely amounts to a new offer. If no time is specified in the offer it will terminate at the end of a reasonable time. What constitutes a "reasonable time" is a question of fact depending upon the circumstances existing at the time the offer and the attempted acceptance are made.

[4] Most everyone has heard the expression "meeting of the minds" in connection with the subject of contracts. What is really meant is not that there must be, literally, a meeting of the minds but rather that there must be a *manifestation of mutual assent* to the bargain. That is, the parties, in their dealings with each other, must *indicate* to each other through words or conduct or both that they are in mutual agreement as to the terms and conditions of the bargain. This manifestation of mutual assent or "meeting of the minds" expresses itself in the contractual elements of the offer and the acceptance.

By Revocation

A person who makes an offer may revoke it *at any time before it is accepted.* And this is so even though the person making the offer states that the offer will remain open for a definite period of time.

Example:

> A makes an offer to B and adds: "This is a firm offer which will remain open for thirty days." A may nevertheless revoke the offer at *any* time before acceptance.

Although offers may be withdrawn at any time before acceptance, they can be made irrevocable through a device known as an *option.* An option is a contract to keep an offer open. The offeror is paid a consideration in return for his promise to keep the offer open for a specified period of time. This payment of consideration in return for the promise not to withdraw the offer creates a collateral contract—a contract called an *option.* So an "option" may be defined as a contract by which an owner agrees to give another the privilege of buying the property at a fixed price within a specified period of time.[5]

By Rejection

An offer terminates when it is rejected. An offer is rejected when the person to whom it is made indicates by words or conduct that he intends not to accept the offer, or that he intends to give it further consideration.

A counter-offer constitutes a rejection of the original offer. An acceptance which differs in some respect from the terms of the original offer is a conditional acceptance; and a conditional acceptance is itself a counter-offer which operates as a rejection of the original offer.

[5] An option is not the same as a "first call" or "first refusal." One who has an option has a *right* to buy the property, while one who has a "first call" merely has the privilege of first refusal *if* and when the seller desires to sell, but the seller is not obligated to sell to anyone.

Once an offer has been rejected it ceases to exist and a later attempted acceptance will not be effective.

Example:

A makes an offer to B and adds: "This offer will remain open for a week." B rejects the offer the following day, but within a week from the making of the offer accepts it. Since B's rejection terminated A's offer, there could be no subsequent acceptance and so no contract.[6]

Example:

A offers to sell Blackacre to B for $5000, stating that the offer will remain open for thirty days. B replies, "I will pay $4800 for Blackacre," and on A's declining that, B writes, "I accept your offer to sell for $5000." There is no contract, although B's acceptance of these terms was made within the time limit originally fixed by A in his offer. Since B's counter-offer constituted a rejection of A's original offer, the attempted subsequent "acceptance" by B was of no effect.[7]

By Death or Insanity

An offer automatically terminates upon the subsequent death or insanity of the person making the offer. And the death or insanity of the person to whom the offer is made also has the effect of terminating the offer, since it thereby becomes impossible for that person to accept it. However, once an offer is accepted and a contract arises, the obligations under the contract (unless of a strictly personal nature) survive death and the contract remains enforceable by and against the deceased party's estate.

THE ACCEPTANCE MUST BE COMMUNICATED

In order to create a contract there must not only be a definite offer and an unequivocal acceptance—the acceptance

6 RESTATEMENT § 35, illustration 1.

7 *Id.* § 38, illustration 1.

must be *communicated* to the person making the offer. Until the acceptance is communicated to the person who made the offer there is no contract.

When the parties are in the presence of each other, or when they communicate by telephone, no problem of communication arises since spoken words are transmitted instantaneously. However, when the parties are at a distance from each other and communicate by mail or telegraph, there is a time lag between the sending and the receiving of a message. In such cases the question arises as to just *when* an acceptance is considered "communicated" so as to create a contract.

Acceptance by Correspondence

When the offer is made by correspondence, the acceptance takes effect at the moment it is *transmitted* by the means expressly or impliedly authorized by the offer.[8]

Example:

> A makes an offer to B by mail. B promptly mails an acceptance. The acceptance is considered "communicated" and a contract arises as soon as B's letter of acceptance is *posted in the mail.*[9]

However, if the person to whom the offer is made varies the authorized method of transmission, the acceptance takes effect only when it is actually *received.*

Example:

> A makes an offer to B by mail. B sends an acceptance by personal messenger. There is no acceptance and no contract until the acceptance is *received* by A.

Of course the person making the offer, if he wishes, may

[8] Thus, when an offer is transmitted by mail the implied mode of acceptance is by mail unless, of course, the offer specifies a different mode of communication.

[9] An acceptance is considered "mailed" when it is put in the control of the postal authorities. But in order for an acceptance by mail to take effect upon posting, it must be properly stamped and addressed.

make the formation of the contract dependent upon his actually receiving the notification of acceptance. In such a case no contract will arise until the acceptance is actually received.

According to the general rule a *revocation* or *rejection*, when sent from a distance, takes effect only when received.

Example:

A makes an offer to B by mail. The next day A, wishing to revoke his offer, sends B a letter to that effect. However, upon receiving A's offer, B immediately mails his acceptance, and two hours later receives A's letter of revocation. There is a contract since B's acceptance took place (by the act of posting) before he received A's revocation.

Example:

A makes an offer to B by mail. Upon receiving the offer B posts a letter of rejection. Two hours later B changes his mind and mails a letter of acceptance. In this situation B's letter of acceptance will not take effect until actually received by A. If the letter of acceptance reaches A before the rejection there will be a contract; however, if the letter of rejection reaches A first, no contract will result.

So, in summary, an acceptance by mail or telegraph, when that method of communication is authorized by the offer, takes effect when dispatched, but a communication which destroys or terminates an offer takes effect only when received.

CONSIDERATION

A contract is, in essence, a legally enforceable promise. But of course not all promises are legally enforceable. For instance, promises to make a gift are not enforceable even though clearly worded and indisputably proved. So the mere fact that a person makes a promise does not of itself impose a legal duty upon him to keep the promise. For a promise to be legally enforceable it must be accompanied by a factor known as *consideration*—that is, the person making the promise must receive something *in return* for his promise, something called "consideration."

Laymen usually equate *consideration* with *money*, but the term is much broader than that. Consideration, in the law of contracts, implies a bargain; it is the thing bargained for; it is something which is given as the agreed exchange for a promise. And that "something" may be the performance (or forbearance) of some act, it may be the receipt of a sum of money, or it may be the giving of a return promise. But without consideration a promise is not binding.[10]

In the unilateral contract situation, the consideration (the thing bargained for) is the performance of some *act;* in the bilateral contract situation, the consideration is a return *promise* to perform.[11] Consider again the following two simple examples:

10 "Consideration" in the law of contracts is also defined as anything which constitutes a *"benefit to the promisor"* or a *"detriment to the promisee."* By a "benefit to the promisor" is meant that the person making the offer (the promisor) must receive something in return for his promise—something which he was not previously entitled to receive. And by a "detriment to the promisee" is meant that the person to whom the promise is made (the promisee) must give up something in exchange for the promise—something which he was not previously obligated to give up. It does not matter how slight or inconsequential the requested act or return promise happens to be; if the act or forbearance or the return promise is something which the offeree is not obligated to do then it will constitute sufficient "consideration."

Neither the "benefit" to the promisor nor the "detriment" to the promisee need be actual; the terms are used in a technical, legal sense. For instance, the person who makes the promise (promisor) receives a "benefit" if, in exchange for his promise, he receives some performance, forbearance, or return promise which he was not previously entitled to receive. And it would constitute a legal "detriment" to the party to whom the promise is made (promisee) if, in exchange for the promise, he does or promises to do any act causing him the slightest inconvenience and which he was not obliged to do. For example, in a classic New York case the court held that a nephew's abstention from smoking and drinking for a specified period of time, though in fact a benefit to his health, constituted a legal "detriment" to him and so was sufficient consideration for his uncle's promise to pay the sum of $5000 in return for the nephew's abstinence. Hamer v. Sidway, 124 N.Y. 538, 27 N.E. 256 (1891).

11 For the distinction between bilateral and unilateral contracts, see page 285 *supra.*

Example:

A says to B, "If you will mow my lawn I will pay you $5.00." This is an offer for a unilateral contract. It is the *act* of mowing the lawn which is bargained for. And the act of mowing the lawn will constitute at once both the acceptance of the offer and the *consideration*.

Example:

A says to B, "I will pay you $5.00 if you will promise to mow my lawn." This is an offer for a bilateral contract. What is bargained for here is B's return *promise* to mow the lawn. B's return *promise* to perform will constitute the consideration for A's promise to pay, and a binding contract will result. The "consideration" consists of the mutual promises of the parties.

The typical real estate broker's "listing" contract is usually of the unilateral type, where the "consideration" is the broker's *act* of producing a ready, willing, and able buyer. However, contracts for the purchase and sale of real estate are almost invariably bilateral contracts, and the consideration takes the form of mutual promises; that is, the seller's promise to sell in return for the buyer's promise to buy, upon the terms stated in the contract. And although the buyer customarily makes an "earnest money" deposit upon the execution of the contract, such deposit is not essential to the *validity* of the contract because it is not the consideration; the *consideration* which supports the contract is the promise for a promise, that is, the promise to sell in exchange for the promise to buy.

TERMS MUST BE CERTAIN

In addition to the basic elements of offer, acceptance, and consideration, the *terms* of the agreement must be sufficiently definite and certain.[12] The court cannot *make* contracts for

[12] In order to make a binding contract, the "offer must be so definite in its terms, or require such definite terms in the acceptance, that the promises and performances to be rendered by each party are reasonably certain." RESTATEMENT § 32.

the parties; it can only *enforce* them. And the court will not enforce a contract unless it is first able to determine just what the parties agreed to do. Consequently, if the offer or the so-called "agreement" is so vague or indefinite as to make it impossible for the court to determine its meaning and fix the liability of the parties, no enforceable contract will result; the attempted contract will fail for lack of certainty. When a contract fails because of lack of certainty there is, technically speaking, no contract at all—the uncertainty of the terms will have prevented a contract from ever arising.

Although the terms of the agreement must be definite and certain, this does not mean that every single detail must be set forth. The court looks to substance rather than to form, and is reluctant to render a contract unenforceable if that result can be avoided. But where any of the *essential* terms are missing, the attempted contract will fail for lack of certainty. In the case of a contract for the sale of real estate the agreement must *at least* (a) state the names of the parties and their respective obligations under the contract, (b) describe the property sufficiently to identify it, and (c) state the purchase price. And if any of the terms are left open for future settlement, no contract will arise, for an agreement to agree in the future is in reality no agreement at all. Thus, where the parties agree to buy and sell "on terms to be arranged," or "at a price mutually satisfactory," there is no enforceable contract.

PARTIES MUST HAVE CONTRACTUAL CAPACITY

At common law a minor (a person under twenty-one years of age) was classified as an "infant," and as such, was conceived to be a person needing special legal protection because of his inexperience and immaturity. Such "infant" needed to be saved from unscrupulous persons who might take advantage of him; he even had to be protected from "his own improvident acts." Hence, at common law, the contracts of a minor could be rescinded or disaffirmed by him, *except* in cases where the contract was for "necessaries."[13]

The minor had an option; he could either disaffirm his contract and use his infancy as a defense, or he could, upon reaching twenty-one, ratify his contract and become legally bound by it. And this is still pretty much the law in the United States today, except that in many states the age of majority has been lowered. So any person dealing with a minor must do so at his peril. And although in many cases there may be hardships for an adult who transacts business with a minor, it usually requires but little investigation to ascertain whether or not one has reached his majority.

A person who is insane or who is lacking in mental capacity does not have the legal capacity to make a contract, and contracts made by such persons are voidable by them or by their legal representatives. Such person, upon regaining his sanity, may either ratify or disaffirm his contract.

A person may lack perfect mental soundness and still have capacity to contract. However, the mind must be of sufficient intelligence to be capable of comprehending the subject of the contract, its nature, and its probable consequences. Whether the mental infirmity has proceeded so far as to destroy that capability is a question of fact to be determined according to the circumstances in each case. But the burden of proving mental incapacity is upon the party alleging it.

The law places intoxicated persons in the same position as insane persons. If at the time of making the contract a party was so inebriated as to be incapable of understanding the nature and consequences of his act, then he may either ratify or disaffirm it when he becomes sober.

LEGALITY OF OBJECT

In order for a contract to be enforceable its objective must

[13] A minor was held liable for the "reasonable value" of any *necessaries* furnished him. "Necessaries" included such things as food, clothing, lodging, and medical care.

be *legal.* If the object of a contract is in violation of the law, or if it is contrary to public policy, the court will not enforce it. For example, any contract which *unreasonably* restrains a person from exercising his trade or business is against public policy and is illegal. An agreement in which the objective is to obstruct justice, or an agreement not to prosecute a person for a crime is void as against public policy. A loan contract calling for a rate of interest in excess of the rate permitted by statute (usury) is an illegal contract. And a contract made on Sunday, where the transaction of such business on Sunday is specifically prohibited by statute, is an illegal contract and unenforceable.

THE REQUIREMENT OF A WRITING —THE STATUTE OF FRAUDS

Generally

As we have seen, in order to create an enforceable contract there must be an offer and an acceptance, supported by consideration; also the terms of the agreement must be certain, the parties must have contractual capacity, and the object of the contract must be legal. All of these ingredients are necessary to the formation of *any* contract, whether it be verbal or in writing.[14] Moreover, with respect to some types of contracts, the law places the additional requirement that in order to be enforceable they must be *in writing* and *signed* by the party against whom the contract is to be enforced.

All the states have statutes which provide that certain types of contracts must be in writing to be enforceable. These statutes are referred to as "The Statute of Frauds." The original English statute of frauds was enacted in 1677 and was entitled "An Act for Prevention of Frauds and Perjuries." The act contained twenty-five sections and attempted to

[14] Most contracts are enforceable though not in writing; they are established through testimony. However, since oral contracts are not easily proved, contracts of any consequence are usually committed to writing even though the law may not require it.

prevent fraud in the proof of various types of legal transactions, principally by requiring them to be in writing. Nearly all of our state statutes are closely patterned after this famous English statute, although most states have modified it somewhat by either expanding or contracting its coverage. The primary purpose of the statute of frauds is to ensure reliable evidence of the contract and thus prevent a party from being compelled by oral and perhaps false testimony to be held responsible for a contract he claims he never made.

The various state statutes list several types of contracts which are not enforceable unless they are in *writing* and *signed* by the person against whom enforcement is sought. One type of contract required to be in writing in every state is the contract concerning the sale of an interest in *land.*[15] With some minor variations in wording the typical statute of frauds declares that

> "No action shall be brought upon any contract for the sale of land, or any interest concerning land, unless the promise, contract or agreement on which such action is brought, or some memorandum, or note thereof, is in writing and signed by the party to be charged."[16]

15 Other types of contracts, promises, or agreements which are required to be in writing to be enforceable in nearly all states are: (1) Promises by an executor or administrator to be *personally* answerable for the debts of the estate under his administration; (2) promises to answer for *another* person's debt or obligation; (3) contracts in which *marriage* is the consideration; (4) contracts which cannot be performed within one year.

Also, under the Uniform Commercial Code, adopted in most states, a contract for the sale of "goods" (things which are movable) *for the price of $500 or more* is not enforceable unless it is evidenced by some writing signed by the party against whom enforcement is sought.

16 In nearly all of the states the statute of frauds does not render oral contracts for the sale of land absolutely *void;* it merely renders them unenforceable against a party who refuses to perform. In other words, an oral contract for the sale of land may be avoided, but it is not void in itself. So if a buyer advances money under an oral contract to purchase land and later changes his mind, he cannot recover his down payment so long as the seller is able and willing to perform his part of the oral contract. And a seller who is ready and able to perform under an oral contract may recover on a check or a promissory note given as a down payment, even though he himself could not be compelled to perform because of the statute of frauds. But if the seller *refuses* to perform, the purchaser may recover his down payment.

What Is an Interest in Land?

An interest in land within the purview of the statute of frauds includes anything which is regarded by the law of property as real estate. Thus the statute includes any contract which concerns the transfer of an estate in land or any other permanent interest in land, such as an easement or a profit.

However, crops which require planting and cultivation ("emblements") do not constitute "an interest in land" within the meaning of the statute of frauds; consequently agreements concerning them need not be in writing to be enforceable. And in most states, contracts for the sale of growing timber, to be cut and removed from the land by the purchaser, are not construed as contracts for the sale of an "interest in land" and so are not within the statute of frauds.

Sufficiency of the Writing or Memorandum

The statute of frauds provides that a contract for the sale of land or any interest in land will not be enforceable ". . . unless the promise, contract or agreement on which such action is brought, or some memorandum or note thereof, is in writing and signed by the party to be charged." You will note that the statute gives an alternative; either the contract itself must be in writing *or* it must be evidenced by some "memorandum or note thereof."

No particular form is required as long as there is written evidence of the agreement. The note or memorandum may be a formally drafted document or it may consist of informal notes, letters, telegrams or receipts.[17] But to satisfy the statute, the writing or memorandum must contain within itself, or by reference to some other paper, the names of the parties and all the essential terms and conditions of the contract; and the terms and conditions must be expressed with

17 The note or memorandum may be made at any time between the formation of the contract and the commencement of the action to enforce it. Such memorandum or note does not constitute a new contract, it simply makes enforceable the original contract, although oral.

such reasonable certainty as may be understood from the memorandum without the aid of oral testimony.

So in order to satisfy the statute of frauds, the writing or memorandum must state with reasonable certainty: (1) each party to the contract, either by name or by such a description as will identify him, (2) the land or other subject matter of the contract,[18] and (3) all of the essential terms and conditions of the contract.[19]

In an old leading case,[20] the following memorandum was held sufficient to satisfy the statute of frauds:

> "Bath, April 10, 1890
>
> "Mary E. Nugent bought of Frances B. Smith, house and land on Winter Street, number 21, owned and occupied by said Frances B. Smith, for one thousand dollars. Paid one hundred dollars on account.
>
> Frances B. Smith."

Nugent was able to enforce the contract against Smith, who had signed the memorandum, but Smith would not have been able to enforce the contract against Nugent since Nugent had not *signed* the memorandum. The statute requires that the writing or memorandum be "signed by the party to be

18 In a contract for the sale of real estate the writing or memorandum must contain a description of the property sufficient to identify it; and it is sufficient if the memorandum furnishes a *means* of identification. If the memorandum itself furnishes some means or some basis for identification, supplementary oral evidence is admissible to *identify* the property but not to add to or in any way vary the description contained in the memorandum. For example, a description such as "my house," or "the property on Congress Street owned by the seller," or "my farm" has been held to be sufficient. However, if the description in the memorandum is equally applicable to two or more separate properties it will *not* be sufficient. For example, a description such as "The Harold Smith Farm" would be sufficient, but only if Harold Smith owned *one* farm; if Harold Smith owned two farms, oral testimony would be necessary to show *which* farm was meant.

19 To satisfy the requirements of the statute, the memorandum must contain all of the essential terms and conditions of the contract, *without recourse to oral testimony.* Since the *selling price* is an essential term in any contract for the sale of real estate it must be stated in the writing or memorandum.

20 Nugent v. Smith, 85 Me. 433, 27 Atl. 342 (1893).

charged'' or his authorized agent.[21] The ''party to be charged'' refers to the party against whom the contract is sought to be enforced.[22]

Separate Writings

The writing or memorandum need not be on a single sheet of paper; it may consist of several writings, letters, telegrams, or other pieces of paper. However, before they are allowed to be read together, the various papers must clearly refer to the same subject matter or transaction; and their connection must be apparent from a comparison of the writings themselves and cannot be shown by oral testimony—that is, the writings must show their connection by their own contents.

According to the general rule, the memorandum may consist of several writings, (a) if each writing is signed by the party to be charged, *or* (b) though only one writing is signed, if the signed writing is physically attached to the unsigned writing, or if it refers to the unsigned writing, or if it appears from an examination of all the writings that it was signed with reference to the unsigned writings.[23]

EXCEPTIONS TO THE STATUTE OF FRAUDS

Under some special circumstances the courts will enforce an *oral* contract for the sale of land notwithstanding the positive requirements of the statute of frauds. These special

21 The memorandum may be written by anyone, but it must be *signed* by the party to be charged or his authorized agent. The signature may be written, typewritten, printed or stamped; or it may be by mark or initials, so long as it was intended as a signature. And it need not be placed at the end of the writing, as a formal signature, but may appear anywhere in the body of the memorandum.

22 And an offer to purchase which is evidenced by a sufficient memorandum signed only by the buyer may be accepted verbally by the seller and enforced by him. However, in such a case the buyer could not enforce the contract against the seller who had not *signed* the memorandum.

23 RESTATEMENT § 208. Thus where an agreement concerning the sale of real estate is evidenced by two separate papers, only one of which is signed and neither of which contains in itself any reference to the other, oral testimony is generally not allowed to prove their connection.

circumstances involve situations where there has been a so-called "part performance" of the oral contract. Where the oral contract has been so far performed by one of the parties that fraud and injustice would result to him if the transaction were not completed, the court will usually compel the other party to perform the contract notwithstanding the statute of frauds. In such cases the contract is said to be "taken out" of the operation of the statute of frauds; the result is that the party against whom the contract is to be enforced is "estopped" from setting up the statute in defense.[24]

The states differ as to what constitutes a sufficient "part performance" to take an oral contract out of the operation of the statute. As a general rule, in order to take a contract out of the operation of the statute of frauds on the basis of part performance, one of the parties must have so irretrievably changed his position in reliance upon the oral contract that to deny enforcement would result in great hardship and constitute a fraud upon his rights.

In a great majority of the states a verbal contract to sell real estate will ordinarily be enforced under the doctrine of part performance where the buyer has:

(a) made substantial improvements to the realty in reliance upon the verbal agreement, *or*

(b) taken possession of the land pursuant to the verbal agreement *and has also* paid all or a portion of the purchase price.[25]

24 The basis for the rule is that the statute of frauds, having been enacted for the purpose of *preventing* frauds, should not be used fraudulently.

25 The general rule is correctly stated by the Supreme Court of Vermont: "[W]here the purchaser pays the whole or a part of the purchase money, and enters into possession of the premises, or does acts relying upon the agreement, that places him in such a position that the refusal by the seller to execute the contract on his part, will operate to his prejudice and injury, beyond the payment of money, so that the repayment of money, or the recovery of it, will not be an adequate remedy, then such acts will take the case out of the statute, and warrant

"Part performance" takes the contract out of the statute of frauds, not because it furnishes proof of the contract or because it makes the contract any stronger, but because it would be intolerable to permit the seller to escape performance after inducing the buyer to expend time, labor and money on the property. However, before an oral contract will be taken out of the operation of the statute of frauds, the proof of its part performance and the proof of the contract itself must be clear and convincing; the party seeking to take the case out of the operation of the statute must establish the existence of the oral contract by clear and positive evidence.

To summarize briefly then, in order to create a contract there must be an offer and an acceptance, and it must be supported by consideration. In addition, the terms of the agreement must be certain, the parties must have contractual capacity, and the object of the contract must be legal. And if the contract concerns the sale of an interest in land, in order to be enforceable it must be evidenced by some writing or memorandum containing all the essential terms of the contract and signed by the party to be charged. However, if the party seeking to enforce a verbal contract to sell land has taken possession of the property *and* paid all or a portion of the purchase price, or if he has made substantial improvements upon the realty, then the court will usually enforce the oral contract notwithstanding the positive requirements of the statute of frauds.

[the court] in decreeing a specific performance of the contract. A refusal under such circumstances to execute the contract, it is sometimes said in the books, operates as a fraud on the purchaser." Stark v. Wilder, 36 Vt. 752 (1864).

However, the payment of all or part of the purchase price must be coupled with a taking of possession; the mere payment of the purchase price alone will *not* take the contract out of the operation of the statute since the purchase price can be refunded. And in a few states part payment and possession alone will not take a verbal contract out of the statute of frauds; the buyer must *also* have made valuable improvements to the property.

In four states the doctrine of part performance has been wholly repudiated and is not followed. They are Kentucky, Mississippi, North Carolina and Tennessee.

CONTRACTS FOR THE SALE OF REAL ESTATE

INTRODUCTORY STATEMENT

Until now we have been concerned with the minimum requirements of contracts generally—that is, what *any* agreement must contain to be legally enforceable. Now we turn our attention to a special type of contract—the contract for the sale of real estate.

As we have seen, in addition to the basic elements of offer, acceptance, and consideration, the *terms* of the contract must be reasonably certain and definite. In the case of contracts for the sale of real estate, the essential terms include *at least* the names of the parties, an identification of the property, and the purchase price. And, of course, the statute of frauds requires that such contracts be in writing and signed by the party against whom they are to be enforced.

Contracts for the sale of real estate often require special drafting by an attorney. However, in those cases where a real estate broker is involved, and the transaction is uncomplicated, it is often the broker who prepares or "drafts" the contract. In such situations the parties often rely entirely upon the competency of the broker. Since a poorly drawn contract may cause financial loss or result in litigation, the drafting of sale contracts by brokers has been the source of increasing friction between lawyers and brokers throughout the country. The controversy centers around the unauthorized practice of law.[26] Some states prohibit brokers from preparing purchase and sale contracts on the ground that such services constitute an unauthorized practice of

26 The objection to the unauthorized practice of law is based upon the principle of *public protection* and not personal gain. The argument advanced is that where the parties are engaged in what is often one of the most important business transactions of their lives they should be represented by one who is, by profession, trained in solving the many potential legal problems connected with the transaction, and who owes to *them alone* an undivided duty of loyalty.

law.[27] Other states hold that such services do not constitute the practice of law *if* they are performed for no compensation other than the broker's commission. And still other states hold that the drafting of purchase and sale contracts by real estate brokers has become an established custom and is a necessary incident to their business.[28]

In a majority of states, the preparation of simple sale contracts by brokers has been more or less accepted as being a function incident to their business. There is no reason why this attitude should not persist so long as the brokers continue to maintain and demonstrate a degree of skill and knowledge commensurate with such an important undertaking. However, a sizable minority of states continue to prohibit the broker from actually drafting the contract.

In most states, a variety of printed contract *forms* are in use by real estate brokers who fill in the "blank spaces." In actuality the broker often does more than merely fill in the blank spaces of a contract form. Since the so-called "blanks"

27 After a long and costly dispute between the Chicago Bar Association and the Chicago Real Estate Board, the Supreme Court of Illinois, in a leading case, held that with respect to the preparation of purchase and sale contracts, real estate brokers were limited to merely "filling in the blanks" of standardized forms customarily used in the community, and to making "appropriate deletions" from such forms, and securing the signatures of the parties. And the case holds that the subject matter of the "blanks" which the brokers are allowed to fill in is confined to simple factual material such as the date, price, names of the parties, location of the property, date of giving possession, and the duration of the offer. The case prohibits explanation by the brokers of the provisions of the contract. Moreover, there was a strong dissenting opinion in the case to the effect that a real estate broker should not even be allowed to fill in the blanks of a standardized contract form: "The desired objective here is neither the preservation of business for lawyers nor commissions for brokers—it is the protection of the public. In my opinion this is best accomplished by entrusting the preparation of real estate contracts to those trained to recognize the substantial questions involved and competent to advise the parties regarding what, in many instances, is the most important investment they will ever make." Chicago Bar Association v. Quinland & Tyson, 34 Ill.2d 116, 214 N.E.2d 771 (1966).

28 After an Arizona decision holding that certain broker practices amounted to an unauthorized practice of law, the brokers of that state were successful in bringing about a constitutional amendment reversing the decision, ARIZ. CONST. art. 26, § 1.

usually require the insertion of terms which relate to such matters as the manner of payment, the apportionment of taxes, mortgage assumption agreements, conditions, etc., the broker, in those states which allow it, literally *drafts* the contract.

There is no special or required contract *form*; the types vary from state to state and even within a particular state or community. For instance, the instrument may be in the form of a bilateral agreement stating the terms and conditions of the sale. Or it may be prepared in the form of an *"offer to purchase"* upon stated terms, which offer is signed and submitted to the seller who signifies his "acceptance" by signing the instrument and returning a copy to the buyer. Sometimes the instrument is merely in the form of a broker's *"deposit receipt."* The typical "deposit receipt" acknowledges that a certain sum has been received by the broker as earnest money in part payment of the property, subject to the terms stated in the document. But regardless of what the instrument is *called,* if it contains all of the essential terms of the agreement and otherwise complies with the statute of frauds it becomes a binding contract when accepted.

Brokers in some areas use the so-called *"binder"* which is, in effect, both a deposit receipt and a written offer to purchase, subject to the seller's acceptance. The purpose of binders is often to bind a party quickly and before he can have second thoughts about the transaction. Sometimes they are enforceable as contracts and sometimes they are not. If the binder contains all of the essential terms of the agreement, it may constitute an enforceable contract when accepted by the seller. A binder will sometimes state that it is "subject to a formal contract" or otherwise indicate that the parties intend to execute a more formal contract later. If the terms of the binder indicate that it was not intended to be an enforceable contract, then no contract will result. However, it is not always possible to determine from the terms of the binder if the parties intended it as an enforceable contract or if they intended to be bound only upon the execution of a more formal instrument. In such cases only a lawsuit will supply the answer. Binders and other types of informal memoranda should be avoided, for they are breeders of controversy.

The contract fixes the legal obligations of the parties and serves as the "blueprint" of the transaction. Therefore, in the selection of a particular contract *form,* the real estate broker is concerned not only with what the document *must* contain, but what it *should* contain if it is to reflect the intent of the parties.[29] And although the form used should fully and clearly set out all of the terms and conditions of the contract, a broker who uses an unnecessarily lengthy form, or one containing overly legalistic sounding language, may be met with resistance from parties who are reluctant to sign something they do not fully understand. The purpose of the basic real estate contract is to set out who is selling what to whom, for how much, and under what terms. The degree of detail in which this is done should be kept to reasonable proportions.

STANDARD CONTRACT CLAUSES

THE PARTIES

Any contract for the sale of real estate must state the names of the parties and designate them as either buyer or seller. And although not strictly necessary, their complete addresses should also be included.

The seller's spouse should always be included as a party to the contract since, under the laws of most states, a spouse has

29 When a contract for the sale of real estate contains only the terms which are *essential* (the names of the parties, the property to be sold and the purchase price) it is said to be an "open" contract. It is called an open contract because it leaves the other terms "open"—terms such as the time for performance, the date of possession, risk of loss, etc. When terms are left open they will be implied by law rather than determined by the parties. No important term of the contract should be left open. The purchase and sale contract should state *all* of the terms of the sale, and they should be thoroughly understood by both parties.

certain marital rights (dower or curtesy, rights of descent, community property rights, homestead rights, etc.) in the real estate owned by the other spouse. If the seller's spouse has not signed the contract he or she may refuse to join in the deed, in which case the buyer can refuse to go through with the sale on the grounds that the seller is unable to deliver a marketable title.

Description of the Property

It is essential that the contract contain an adequate description of the land to be sold. The description need not be as precise as that required in a deed, but it must be sufficient to identify the property with reasonable certainty. Even a description by street number is generally held to be sufficient.

Ordinarily a description in a contract will be sufficient if it either identifies the property or supplies the "key" to its identification. Where the contract furnishes some basis for identification, such as "my house," or "the house now occupied by the seller," oral evidence is usually admissible to identify the property, but not to add to or in any way vary the description contained in the contract.[30]

Although the courts often go to extremes in upholding descriptions in contracts, if the premises are not sufficiently identified the contract will fail for lack of certainty. Therefore the broker should be very careful to adequately identify the property to be sold, if not by a formal legal description, then by reference to a description in a prior recorded deed, or by reference to a recorded map or plan, or at least by stating the complete address of the property, including the city and state.

Since fixtures[31] are part of the real estate they are automatically included in the sale by implication. However, if articles of personal property are to be included in the sale they should be itemized in the contract. And where there is some

30 *See* note 18 *supra.*

31 For the definition of a "fixture" *see* p. 4 *supra.*

doubt as to whether a particular item is personalty or realty, the question should be resolved by so specifying in the contract.

Purchase Price

The amount of the purchase price and the method of payment should be spelled out in detail.

Example:

The total purchase price is $20,000, payable as follows:

(a) $1000 upon the signing of this contract, receipt of which is hereby acknowledged.

(b) The balance of $19,000 in cash or by the purchaser's certified check upon delivery of the deed as hereinafter provided.

Example:

The total purchase price is $20,000, payable as follows:

(a) $1000 upon the signing of this contract, receipt of which is hereby acknowledged.

(b) $4000 in cash or by the purchaser's certified check upon delivery of the deed as hereinafter provided.

(c) The balance of the purchase price to be paid by assuming the existing first mortgage upon said premises held by the Third National Bank of Portland, Maine, recorded in Cumberland County Registry of Deeds, Book 2133 Page 201, the balance of which is $15,000 at the date of this contract.

(d) If between the date of this contract and the passing of title the abovementioned mortgage is reduced by one or more payments made by the seller, the amount of cash payable by the purchaser at the closing shall be increased by an amount equal to such principal payment or payments. The seller, however, is restricted to payments required under said mortgage.

If part of the purchase price is to be financed by the seller's taking back a purchase money mortgage,[32] the contract should specify the terms of the mortgage; otherwise the contract may fail for lack of certainty.

Type of Deed

What if the contract fails to specify the type of deed to be delivered—is it enforceable? Yes, and in most states the seller in such cases is required to give a warranty deed. However in several states, if a contract is silent as to the type of deed to be delivered the seller need only give a quitclaim deed, provided he has a marketable title. Because of the considerable difference between a warranty deed and a quitclaim deed, the contract should always specify the form of deed by which the conveyance is to be made.[33]

Marketable Title

Unless the sale contract specifically provides otherwise, the seller must convey what is called a "marketable title." A marketable title means a title free from reasonable doubt. To be marketable a title need not be *perfect.* A title may be marketable even though there is a possibility of a defect, provided such possibility is not enough to raise a reasonable doubt.

A marketable title is usually defined as one that is free from reasonable doubt—a title which a reasonably prudent and well-informed purchaser, guided by competent legal advice, would be willing to accept and pay the fair value for. A mere possibility or suspicion of a defect will not render the title unmarketable if it would satisfy the mythical, prudent and well-informed purchaser. But a reasonable probability of litigation will render the title unmarketable.

32 A "purchase money mortgage" is a mortgage given by a purchaser to the seller as security for all or part of the purchase price. *See* p. 235 *supra*.

33 For the difference between the various types of deeds, *see* pp. 193-199 *supra*.

Of course the parties may contract for something *less* than a marketable title if they wish. But if the contract is silent as to the character of the title and merely calls for a conveyance of the premises, the law will imply that a marketable title was intended.[34] However, most purchase and sale contracts expressly provide that the seller shall convey a "good title" or a "marketable title." The terms "clear title," "good title," "marketable title," "merchantable title," and "legally sufficient title" are considered to be synonymous.

Defects which render a title unmarketable may be defects in the chain of title or defects due to encumbrances or both. A defect in the chain of title might arise as a result of an improperly executed deed, or by the failure of a spouse to release his or her marital rights. It could arise as a result of the improper probate of a will through which the title was derived; or because there was a lack of delivery; or because a deed in the chain of title was executed by an incompetent grantor; or simply as a result of a misdescription of the property. Defects due to encumbrances are usually in the form of undischarged mortgages, liens, easements, restrictions, encroachments, attachments, or unpaid taxes.

Deed restrictions which control the use to which the land may be put, or which regulate the location or the character or kind of buildings to be erected on the land, constitute an encumbrance. However, restrictions which are imposed by law, such as zoning and building ordinances, do not render the title unmarketable because, as part of the law of the land, they affect *all* persons. But an existing *violation* of a zoning or building ordinance will ordinarily render the title unmarketable.

Encroachments which are substantial enough to interfere with the use and enjoyment of the premises constitute an

[34] A seller of real estate, in the absence of a provision otherwise, impliedly contracts to convey a marketable title. If he is unable to do so, the purchaser may rescind the contract and recover any partial payments made by him.

encumbrance and will render the title unmarketable. However, very slight encroachments will not render the title unmarketable, but each case must be determined on its own merits.

Unless the contract so specifies, the seller is under no obligation to furnish the purchaser with an abstract of title or to perform a title search; it is the obligation of the purchaser to determine the sufficiency of the title. If he chooses not to examine the title, he is relegated to the limited protection found in the warranties of his deed and in the other deeds in the chain of title. But if the purchaser determines that there are defects in the title, he cannot wait until the closing date and then refuse to go through with the sale on the ground that the title is unmarketable. He must seasonably notify the seller of any claimed defects in the title in order to allow him a reasonable opportunity to cure them if they can be cured.

With a few exceptions, once the transaction is closed and the deed is delivered, the purchaser can no longer rescind the contract if the title proves defective. In the absence of fraud or mistake the contract of sale becomes *merged* in the deed and the purchaser has no redress, except for that afforded him under the covenants in the deed.[35]

Encumbrances

Since the purchaser is entitled to a marketable title (unless the contract specifies otherwise), any existing encumbrances[36]

35 However, there are some exceptions to the merger rule. For instance, where the contract of sale calls for some collateral act to be performed after the transaction is closed, such as the erection of a building, or the installation of sewers and water mains, the collateral aspects of the contract survive and do not merge in the deed. And, of course, the contractual obligation of the purchaser to pay the agreed price for the property is not extinguished by the deed; if payment is not made prior to the delivery of the deed, the seller retains the right to recover the amount in accordance with the terms of the sale contract.

36 An *encumbrance* has been defined as "any right to, or interest in, the premises, subsisting in another, to the diminution of its value, although consistent with the passage of a fee by the conveyance." Olcott v. Southworth, 115 Vt. 421, 63 A.2d 189 (1949).

on the property must be specifically designated and *excepted.* Otherwise the seller will have breached this implied term in the contract and the purchaser, upon discovering the encumbrance, would be entitled to rescind the contract. Consequently contracts almost invariably contain a statement to the effect that the premises are sold *subject to* certain designated encumbrances or that the property is sold free of encumbrances *except* those specifically mentioned.[37]

Since deed restrictions often render a title unmarketable, a seller will sometimes wish to include a clause in the contract providing that the premises are sold "subject to covenants and restrictions of record, if any." A buyer who signs such a contract without first examining the title could end up with a pig in a poke.

Time For Performance

Ordinarily the exact *date* for performance (called the closing date) is not specified in the contract. The reason for this is that the closing date is usually dependent upon the schedule of whatever lending institution is to handle the transaction. The practice is to stipulate that the closing shall be *within* a specified number of days from the date of the contract, or that it shall be "on or before" a certain date. However if the contract is silent as to the time for performance, the law will imply that it is to be performed within a reasonable time. What constitutes a "reasonable time" depends upon the circumstances of the particular case.

Suppose the contract provides that the transaction shall be closed on a certain date or within a certain period of time, but one of the parties is unable to perform on or within the exact date specified. Will his failure to perform on or within that date constitute a breach of the agreement and thereby

37 For instance, a contract might provide that the premises are to be conveyed ". . . free from all encumbrances *except* an easement of access to and from the abutting premises, which easement is specifically set out in deed dated March 20, 1960, and recorded in Book 2510, Page 215 of the Cumberland County Registry of Deeds."

discharge the other party from his obligations under the contract? The early law took the position that if the contract specified a time for performance, then performance at that time was *essential,* unless the contract provided otherwise. This gave rise to the legal cliche *"time is of the essence of a contract."* It meant that a party who was unable to perform on the date specified was guilty of a breach of contract. In such cases the other party was not only excused from performing his part of the contract but he also had a cause of action for damages against the party who was unable to perform at the time specified.

The rule that time was "of the essence" in contracts for the sale of land created many hardships, especially when a buyer had to forfeit his down payment. And besides, the breach was often merely technical since the party who was unable to perform on the exact date specified was often prepared to make payment, clear the title, or otherwise perform his part of the contract within a few days.

The rule calling for performance on the exact date specified has been relaxed today. The general rule now is that in a contract for the sale of land, time is *not* of the essence, *unless* the contract so provides. So the mere fact that a time is fixed for performance does not *of itself* make "time of the essence." This means that the closing date specified in the contract is not vital and that each party will usually be allowed a reasonable time after such date to perform his part of the contract. The reason for this rule is that delays are frequent in land transactions and the damage caused by them is most often negligible.

However, if the time fixed for performance is of vital importance, either because of the nature of the transaction or because of the surrounding circumstances, then time *will* be of the essence. For example time is of the essence in *option* contracts. And time is usually of vital importance where the property under contract is subject to rapid fluctuations in value, or where the buyer has immediate need for the property and the seller is aware of such need. In such cases the time specified for performance is deemed to be essential to the contract. And of course time can be *made* "of the essence" by an express stipulation to that effect in the contract. Where such a provision is contained in the contract, the buyer is ordinarily excused from performance if the seller is not ready, willing, and able to perform on the date specified; and conversely, a buyer who is unable to perform at the time specified stands to lose all his rights under the contract, including the right to the return of money he has already paid in.[38]

Most contract forms contain a provision stating that "time shall be of the essence of this contract," or that "time is an essential part of this agreement." However, in the average purchase and sale situation it is difficult to see why, in the absence of special circumstances, such a provision should be included in the contract. Delays are a common occurrence in real estate transactions, the parties know this, and when they contract they usually do not intend to hold each other to a specific day. In fact, the parties themselves are often not even aware of the legal import of the "essence" clause. More often than not, an "essence" clause serves only to give a party who may have soured on the deal in the interim an option to renege with legal impunity if the other party is unable to perform precisely at the time specified.

It is even more difficult to imagine under what circumstances an "essence" clause could possibly be advantageous to the real estate broker who incorporates it in his contract form. The broker's function is to bring the parties together and effect a sale of the property; his ultimate objective is to close the deal and thereby earn a commission. If the transaction is not consummated because one of the parties

[38] Even where time is of the essence and there has been a default, the party to whom performance was to have been made may *waive* his right to terminate the contract because of the default, in which case the contract will remain mutually enforceable. Ordinarily a party must first tender his own performance before he can declare the other party in default of the contract.

is allowed to take advantage of an "essence" clause in the contract, the broker will have failed in his objective, notwithstanding the fact that he may be legally entitled to his commission.[39]

If an "essence" clause does not ordinarily reflect the true intent of the parties, and from the broker's standpoint only serves to militate against getting the deal through, why is it that most contract forms used by brokers contain a clause making time of the essence? Probably because such forms were originally prepared by lawyers, and the inclusion of an "essence" clause simply reflects the legal profession's traditional penchant for preciseness.[40]

Risk of Loss

It sometimes happens that during the interval between the making of the contract and the time for delivery of the deed the buildings are damaged or destroyed by fire, flood, windstorm, earthquake, hurricane, or other casualty. Most contracts contain a provision fixing the risk of loss in such cases. But what if the contract is silent on this point—who bears the loss, the buyer or the seller?[41]

In a majority of states, if the premises are accidentally damaged or destroyed between the date of the contract and the time for conveyance, the *purchaser* must bear the loss. And this is so even though the seller is in possession. The majority rule is based upon the legal concept that immediately upon the execution of an enforceable contract to sell, the beneficial or "equitable" title to the land passes to the

39 In such cases the broker is often forced to bring legal action in order to recover his commission.

40 For the purposes of illustration the sample contract forms set out in the Appendix *infra* contain an "essence" clause. However, it is suggested that before he adopts such a clause in his contract form, the broker should carefully consider, in each instance, whether such provision will in fact contribute something to the contract or merely hinder the ultimate objective of consummating the transaction.

41 We are concerned here with *accidental* loss. The burden of loss due to provable negligence falls upon the negligent party.

purchaser; thereafter the seller continues to hold the bare legal title only temporarily and in trust for the purchaser pending delivery of the deed. This concept is known as the doctrine of "equitable conversion" because, in legal theory, upon the execution of the contract the interests of the parties are reversed or *"converted"*; the purchaser is thereafter looked upon and treated as the owner of the land and the seller as the owner of the purchase money. Thus the majority rule holds that since a purchaser under a contract to sell is looked upon and treated as the beneficial "owner" of the property he should bear the risk of accidental loss.[42]

A sizable minority of states hold that where the premises are accidentally damaged or destroyed after the execution of the contract but before the delivery of the deed, the loss falls upon the *seller,* even though the purchaser is in possession. The minority rule is based upon the theory that in every contract for the sale of real estate there is an implied condition that the subject matter of the contract shall be *in existence* when the time for performance arrives. And if the subject matter has ceased to exist when that time comes, each party is discharged from his contract. Thus, under the minority rule, if the premises are accidentally damaged or destroyed before the title is conveyed, the purchaser may rescind the contract and recover his deposit and any partial payments made by him; but the damage to the property must be more than slight.

The minority rule is probably more logical since, in the typical situation, the seller already has the property insured and he usually remains in possession until the title passes. Besides, it seems more in keeping with common sense that a person should not bear the risk of loss until he becomes the legal owner. However, since both the buyer and seller have insurable interests they may protect themselves by insurance. An endorsement may be added to the seller's policy protecting

[42] Most states which place the risk of loss on the purchaser give him the benefit of the seller's insurance (if any), to be credited to the purchase price of the property. 3 AMERICAN LAW OF PROPERTY § 11.31 (Casner ed. 1952).

both him and the buyer as their interests may appear, or the purchaser may procure his own policy.[43]

Of course the risk of loss can be fixed by the terms of the contract, and this is usually done. A typical clause might read as follows: "The risk of loss or damage to the premises by fire or otherwise is assumed by the seller until delivery of the deed." And a provision in the contract that the seller shall deliver the premises "in the same condition as they now are," or words to that effect, places the risk of loss upon the seller.

Even in states which place the burden of loss upon the *seller* until the legal title passes (the minority view), most contracts contain an express provision to that effect anyway. This has merit even if it serves only to call to the attention of the parties that the premises should be adequately insured during the interim period.

Possession

Unless the contract specifies otherwise, the seller retains the right to possession and the right to the rents until delivery of the deed. And although the purchaser is entitled to the possession and rents at the time he receives the deed, in the sale of residential property it is customary to allow the seller a reasonable time after the closing to vacate the premises. Typical contracts usually stipulate that the purchaser is to receive possession on or before a certain date or within a specified number of days after the closing date. In sales of residential property the date of possession is often a major consideration in negotiating the contract.

Closing Adjustments

The typical purchase and sale contract usually makes provision for the prorating or apportionment of both the income and expenses of the property. Failure to provide in the

43 In some states, if the premises are accidentally damaged or destroyed after the execution of the contract but before the delivery of the deed, the loss falls upon the party *in possession,* whether he be buyer or seller.

contract for a fair division of the income and expenses can lead to inequities and dissatisfaction since, in the absence of any contractual provision, there is no legal requirement that the parties apportion anything. Ordinarily such items as taxes, rents, and utilities are apportioned as of the closing date, but the contract may specify any date which is agreeable to the parties.

Real estate tax adjustments are made on the basis of the fiscal tax year of the community, which in many areas does not coincide with the calendar year. It is customary to provide in the contract that the real estate taxes be prorated—usually as of the date of the passing of title.

In the case of income property, the contract usually provides that the rental income is to be apportioned as of the date of the closing. When the closing falls on a day when rents are payable in advance, no apportionment is necessary—the entire rent belongs to the buyer in accordance with the common law rule. Where the closing takes place *during* a rent period, and the entire rent for that period has been received by the seller, such income is usually prorated between the parties.

Contracts do not often provide for an insurance premium adjustment because, in most cases, the seller will cancel his insurance and the buyer will take out his own policy. However, where the policy is transferable and the buyer wishes to take over the seller's policy, the contract should provide for an apportionment of the premiums.

If the contract provides for an apportionment of fuel and utility costs, the buyer is usually charged with the estimated cost of fuel on the premises at the time of closing or at the date of possession. Utility costs are often apportioned on the basis of an official meter reading made shortly before the closing date. In the case of residential properties, the parties often arrive at an informal apportionment of fuel and utility costs based upon the past monthly averages; or they sometimes simply agree to advise the utility companies of the change of ownership as of a certain date, usually the date of possession.

Earnest Money

Although there is no legal requirement that there be a down payment,[44] contracts almost invariably contain a provision calling for a part payment or an "earnest money" deposit by the purchaser. The amount of the deposit is a matter of agreement between the parties, but it should be large enough to discourage the buyer from breaching the contract and also compensate the seller for having taken his property off the market. As a general rule the amount of the deposit varies from five to ten percent of the purchase price.

The contract usually provides that the earnest money deposit shall be held in escrow by the broker pending the closing. In this way the buyer should experience no delay in obtaining a return of his deposit in the event the seller is unable to perform.

Conditions

Contracts for the sale of real estate may be and often are made conditional upon any number of things. For example, the sale may be subject to the buyer's obtaining a mortgage in a specified amount, or upon his procuring a license or other permit to use the premises for a specified purpose, or upon his ability to secure a variance in the zoning ordinance. The sale may be conditional upon the buyer's selling his own property, or upon his obtaining an F.H.A. commitment for development, or upon the approval of a certain subdivision plan.

Whatever form the contingency may take, it should be carefully spelled out in the contract. For instance, if the sale is to be conditional upon the buyer's selling his own property, the contract should state the terms of such sale and place a time limit upon it. And if the sale is to be contingent upon the buyer's ability to obtain financing, the contract should specify such details as the type and amount of mortgage, the

[44] *See* p. 293 *supra.*

interest rate, and the terms of payment. If such details are omitted, as when the contract merely provides that the sale is "subject to financing," the court may declare the contract void for lack of certainty.

Where the contract is conditional upon the buyer's ability to procure a mortgage loan he must make reasonable efforts to do so. And although it is generally held that he need not apply to every available lending institution in the area, he must act in good faith and make bona fide efforts to obtain a mortgage. What constitutes "bona fide efforts" is a question of fact for the court to determine.

In contractual matters, the degree in which the pendulum of advantage swings in favor of one party or the other often depends not only upon the bargaining power of the parties themselves but also upon the skill of the person drafting the contract. Consequently it usually behooves a person to seek competent advice before he affixes his signature to a contract containing clauses, the legal effect of which he does not fully understand.

REMEDIES FOR BREACH OF CONTRACT

Generally

As we have seen, a contract is a promise or set of promises which the law will *enforce*. In the event that one of the parties is unable or refuses to perform his part of the contract, the other party ordinarily has a choice between three basic remedies: (a) He may rescind the contract; or (b) he may sue the other party for money damages; or (c) he may bring an action for specific performance. He will usually elect the remedy which is most favorable to his interests, unless his remedy is restricted by the terms of the contract itself.

Rescission

Rescission is, in effect, the unmaking of a contract. A party who chooses the remedy of rescission declares the contract terminated and both buyer and seller must then be restored to the same position they were in before the contract was made. The purpose of this remedy is to procure the cancellation of the contract.

A contract for the sale of real estate may be rescinded because it was induced by fraud,[45] duress, or undue influence, or because it was entered into through mistake.[46] The remedy of rescission in such cases is discretionary with the court and will be granted in accordance with what is reasonable and just under the circumstances. However, a contract may always be rescinded by mutual consent of the parties.

Rescission is not the same thing as forfeiture. In the case of a forfeiture (discussed later), the contract is terminated but the seller retains the buyer's payments; rescission also terminates the contract but the seller must return all payments

45 "Fraud" is a misrepresentation of a material fact known to be false and made with the intent to deceive the other party (or made with a reckless disregard of the truth), under circumstances where such other party is in fact deceived and damaged in reliance upon the misrepresentation. However, the misrepresentation must be as to a *fact* and not a mere expression of opinion. Representations as to the *value* of the property are usually considered as mere expressions of opinion. In sales of real estate the doctrine of *caveat emptor* usually applies, and the purchaser must examine, judge, and determine the facts for himself. However, a seller may not do anything to conceal or hide a material fact or defect or to lead the buyer to believe that certain facts exist when they do not. And in some cases even a seller's failure to disclose facts may constitute fraud if the circumstances are such that it would be unconscionable for him to remain silent about them. Thus, if a seller is aware of facts which are not reasonably discoverable by the purchaser, it is generally held that the seller is bound to disclose such facts, and failure to do so may constitute "misrepresentation by silence."

A contract obtained through false and fraudulent representations may be rescinded by the party defrauded, or he may elect to affirm the contract and sue for damages.

In an action for damages resulting from a sale procured by fraud, the damages are measured by the difference between the actual value of the property and its value had the property been as represented to be. But a party claiming fraud has the burden of proving it by clear and convincing evidence.

46 If there is an actual and honest mutual mistake as to any of the essential terms of the transaction, either party may rescind the contract, for a "contract" implies a meeting of the minds. For example, there may be a misunderstanding of the subject matter, as where a contract is executed for the sale of land on Maple Street in Portland when the purchaser thought he was buying a tract on another Maple Street in Portland but in no way connected with the tract mentioned in the agreement.

made by the buyer. A party rescinding a contract must do all that is practicable to place the other party in *status quo ante*—in the same position he occupied before the contract was made, otherwise he cannot maintain his action. Since rescission entitles a buyer to the return of his deposit money, he will usually choose this remedy in cases where there has been a drop in the value of the property.

Action For Damages

Either the seller or the buyer is entitled to bring an action for damages caused by the other's breach of the contract, unless of course, the amount of recovery is fixed by the contract itself in the form of agreed or liquidated damages. The object of this remedy is to place the non-breaching party in as good a position monetarily as he would have been had the other party performed the contract.

Where the Seller Breaches the Contract

In an action for damages for breach of contract to sell real estate, the general measure of damages may be stated as the difference between the contract price and the market value of the property at the time the deed was to be delivered. The difference represents the loss of the bargain. So where the *seller* refuses or is unable to convey according to his contract, the buyer may recover the difference between the contract price and the market value of the property at the time set for performance, plus any down payments already made by him.

Example:

The contract price is $50,000 and the seller breaches the contract. At the time scheduled for conveyance the property is worth $52,000. The buyer has paid $1,000 toward the purchase price. His damages are $3,000.

Example:

The contract price is $50,000 and the seller breaches the contract. At the time scheduled for conveyance the property is worth only $48,000. The buyer has paid $5,000 toward the purchase price. His damages are $3,000.

Where the market value of the property has *decreased,* as in the immediate example above, the buyer will choose the remedy of *rescission* rather than bring an action for damages; for by rescinding, the buyer would recover the full amount of his deposit, whereas if he brought an action for *damages* he would recover less than the amount of his deposit. But if the value of the property has *increased* since the making of the contract, the buyer will usually sue for damages.

In about half of the states, if the seller has acted in good faith but is unable to complete the sale because of a defect in the title, the buyer is *not* entitled to the loss of his bargain; all he can recover is his deposit plus any expenses incurred in searching the title. However, where the seller arbitrarily or in bad faith refuses to perform the contract, the buyer may recover damages for the loss of his bargain plus any deposits made by him. The other half of the states hold that the seller's good faith is immaterial, and if he is unable to perform the contract, for whatever reason, the buyer may recover for the loss of his bargain in accordance with the general rule of damages.

Where the Buyer Breaches the Contract

Where the *buyer* breaches the contract the seller may recover the loss of *his* bargain, if any; that is, the difference between the contract price and the market value of the property, less any payments already made by the buyer. But again, this assumes that there is no stipulation in the contract as to liquidated damages.

Example:

The contract price is $25,000 and the buyer breaches the contract. At the time scheduled for conveyance the property is worth $20,000. The buyer has already paid the seller $2,000 toward the purchase price. The seller's damages are $3,000.

Example:

The contract price is $25,000 and the buyer breaches the contract. At the time scheduled for conveyance the property is worth $23,000. The buyer has already made a $2,000 deposit. The seller's damages are nil

Specific Performance

Probably the most valuable remedy for breach of a contract to sell real estate is that of *specific performance.* A party will usually invoke the remedy of specific performance in cases where money damages would be inadequate, or where the contract concerns a property for which there is no satisfactory substitute of equal value. The remedy exists because there is no assurance that the land contracted for can be replaced by an equally satisfactory parcel at the same price. The law has long considered land to be "unique" in that there is really no monetary substitute for the particular property bargained for since it cannot be exactly duplicated in any other parcel.

Specific performance is a means of compelling a party to perform specifically that which he has contracted to do; it is a substitute for money damages when that remedy would be inadequate. The remedy is available to both the buyer and the seller. Where the *seller* refuses to perform, the court will compel him to convey the title;[47] where the *buyer* refuses to

[47] If the court directs a party to deliver a deed or perform any other specific act and the party fails to comply within the time specified, he stands in contempt of court and subjects himself to imprisonment under a contempt citation. In the rare event that a party might elect to languish in jail rather than comply with the court order, the Rules of Civil Procedure in most states provide that in the event that a party fails to deliver a deed or perform any other specific act directed by the court, the court may direct the act to be done by some other person appointed by the court, and the act when so done has the same legal effect as if done by the disobedient party.

If the seller dies before delivering the deed, the buyer may enforce specific performance against the seller's heirs, devisees, executors or administrators. And if the buyer dies before title passes, his heirs, devisees or other persons entitled to his estate may bring an action for specific performance against the seller.

perform the court will order him to pay the agreed purchase price.[48]

However, the remedy of specific performance is discretionary with the court, and whether it will be granted depends upon the circumstances of each particular case. It is an old legal maxim that a person seeking the extraordinary remedy of specific performance must come in with "clean hands." Thus, even though a contract will ordinarily be enforced regardless of whether the price is too high or too low, if there is a gross disparity between the price and the value, and this is coupled with the fact that a party has been taken advantage of due to his ignorance, age, or mental weakness, the court will usually refuse to grant specific performance. Generally speaking, the court will refuse to grant specific performance if it will cause disproportionate hardship or loss to the defendant, or if the terms of the contract are grossly unfair, or if the contract was induced by sharp practice or unethical conduct.[49] In such cases the party seeking to enforce the contract will be relegated to bringing an action for money damages.

Forfeiture and Liquidated Damages

Parties sometimes stipulate in advance as to the amount of damages to be recovered in the event of a breach by either one of them. A clause in a contract expressly fixing the amount of damages to be recovered in the event of a breach is called a "liquidated damages" clause. The court will enforce such a provision if the stipulated damages are reasonable in amount. However, if the sum agreed upon is disproportionate to the actual damages incurred, or if the purpose was to inflict a

48 Money damages are usually considered inadequate from the purchaser's standpoint because land is unique and cannot be duplicated. From the seller's standpoint money damages are sometimes inadequate because they only amount to the difference, if any, between the value of the land and the agreed price, which may be nominal. The seller will often prefer to collect the full purchase price and be rid of the property.

49 RESTATEMENT § 367.

penalty for nonperformance, the court will generally disregard the provision for liquidated damages and award an amount reflecting the actual damages.

Contracts for the sale of real estate often contain a stipulation to the effect that if the buyer fails to perform his part of the contract the earnest money deposit shall be "forfeited" and retained by the seller. Such a provision is called a *forfeiture* clause. But even in the absence of such a provision, a buyer who is in default cannot recover his earnest money from a seller who is ready, willing and able to perform his part of the agreement. In such a situation the seller may keep both his property *and* the buyer's deposit.[50] Moreover, the seller may retain the buyer's deposit and also bring an action for damages, but the amount of the deposit must be credited against the damages.

Contracts for the sale of real estate frequently provide that if the buyer fails to carry out the terms of the agreement his earnest money deposit shall be forfeited and "retained by the seller *as liquidated damages.*" Although a provision for liquidated damages ordinarily bars an action for *further* damages, such a clause will not preclude the seller from bringing an action for specific performance. However, if the contract is so drawn as to give the *buyer* a *choice* between performing the contract or forfeiting the deposit, the seller will be barred from seeking specific performance and will be relegated to keeping the deposit money as his sole remedy. Thus the buyer may *limit* his liability under a contract by insisting upon a clause to the effect that, in the event he defaults under the contract, the seller shall retain the down payment as liquidated damages, and the retention of such sum shall constitute the sole remedy of the seller. The effect of such a clause is to give the buyer the *option* of either carrying

50 And this is so even though the contract fails to comply with the statute of frauds, provided the seller is willing and able to perform his part of the oral contract. *See* note 16 *supra*.

out the contract or forfeiting the deposit as liquidated damages.[51]

ASSIGNMENT AND RECORDING

As we have seen, immediately upon the execution of a contract to sell real estate, the beneficial or "equitable" title to the property passes to the purchaser, and the seller continues to hold the legal title only temporarily and as security for the payment of the purchase price.[52] By virtue of the contract the buyer is entitled to receive a deed and the seller is entitled to the amount of the purchase price. And unless the contract expressly forbids it, either party may transfer these rights under the contract to a third person; the purchaser may transfer his right to receive the deed and the seller may transfer his right to the purchase money. Such a transfer is referred to as an *assignment*. The person who transfers his rights under a contract is called the "assignor," and the person to whom the rights are transferred is called the "assignee."[53]

When an assignment is made, the assignee succeeds to all the rights under the contract. Thus, if the buyer assigns his rights under the contract to another person, such person (the assignee) may enforce specific performance against the seller, but only if he, the assignee, complies with all of the terms of the contract.

Although a person may assign his rights under a contract, he may not thereby rid himself of his obligations; the parties remain liable notwithstanding an assignment. If this were not the case a person could avoid his contractual obligations

[51] The sample contracts in the Appendix *infra* give the *seller* a choice of either accepting the down payment as liquidated damages or bringing an action for specific performance.

[52] *See* p. 315 *supra*.

[53] An assignment may be effected by a simple endorsement on the contract similar to the following: "For value received I hereby assign to .... all my right, title and interest in and to the within contract of sale made by .... as seller and myself as purchaser."

merely by assigning the contract to someone without assets.

Although contracts for the sale of real estate may be recorded in the registry of deeds, this is seldom done except in the case of long-term installment contracts.[54] Recording is of no advantage to the seller but it protects the buyer from a possible transfer of the legal title to an innocent purchaser without notice of the contract.

An outstanding contract to sell constitutes an encumbrance on the title. Thus, whenever a contract to sell is recorded and the purchaser defaults, it is usually necessary to effectively terminate the interest of the defaulting purchaser in order to clear the record title. This may be accomplished by the seller's receiving a quitclaim deed from the defaulting purchaser or by his bringing an action to clear the title.

SUMMARY

A contract may be defined as a promise or set of promises which the law will enforce. Most simply stated, it is a legally enforceable promise.

For a promise to be legally enforceable, and therefore a contract, there must be a definite *offer* by one party and an absolute and unequivocal *acceptance* of that offer by the other party.

An offer is a conditional promise—a promise conditional upon something to be done by the person to whom the offer is made. The condition may be the actual *performance* of an act or it may be the receiving of a return *promise* to perform the act.

The acceptance must be precisely in accordance with the terms of the offer, and it must take place before the offer is withdrawn or is otherwise terminated.

54 As to long-term installment contracts, *see* p. 235 *supra*.

An offer may be terminated by:

(a) lapse of the time specified in the offer, and if no time is specified it will terminate at the end of a reasonable time;

(b) revocation by the person making the offer;

(c) rejection by the person to whom the offer is made; or

(d) the subsequent death or insanity of the person making the offer, or of the person to whom the offer is made.

In order for a contract to arise, the acceptance must be *communicated* to the person making the offer. When the offer is made by correspondence, the acceptance takes effect at the moment it is *transmitted* by the means authorized by the offer; however, if the person to whom the offer is made varies the authorized method of transmission, the acceptance takes effect only when actually *received.* A revocation or rejection, when made by correspondence, takes effect only when it is actually received.

To be enforceable, the promise must be supported by *consideration;* that is to say, the person making the promise must receive something *in exchange* for his promise. "Consideration" is that which is given as the agreed exchange for the promise. It may be the performance of an act, the receipt of a sum of money, or it may be a return promise. In contracts for the sale of real estate the consideration takes the form of mutual promises—that is, the seller's promise to sell in exchange for the buyer's promise to buy.

In addition to the elements of offer, acceptance, and consideration, the terms of the agreement must be sufficiently definite and certain. If any of the essential terms of the agreement are missing, the contract will fail for lack of certainty. In the case of contracts for the sale of real estate, the agreement must:

(a) state the names of the parties and their respective obligations under the contract;

(b) sufficiently identify the property to be sold; and

(c) state the purchase price.

In order for a contract to be enforceable the parties must have contractual capacity. In most cases, contracts are not enforceable against a minor unless ratified by him in writing after reaching the age of majority. A person who is insane or who is lacking in mental capacity does not have the legal capacity to make a contract; contracts made by such persons may be avoided by them or by their legal representatives.

If the object of a contract is illegal or is contrary to public policy, the court will not enforce it.

Under the statute of frauds, contracts concerning the sale of an interest in land are not enforceable unless evidenced by some writing or memorandum signed by the person against whom enforcement is sought. The writing or memorandum may be in any form, but it must contain within itself, or by reference to some other writing, the names of the parties and all the essential terms of the contract. The writing may be on separate papers provided they are all signed by the party to be charged, or that the unsigned papers are attached to or referred to in the signed paper.

Under some circumstances the court will enforce an oral contract for the sale of land notwithstanding the requirements of the statute of frauds. These circumstances involve situations where there has been such a "part performance" of the oral contract by one of the parties that fraud and injustice would result to him if the contract were not enforced. An oral contract for the sale of land will ordinarily be enforced under the doctrine of part performance if the party seeking to enforce the oral contract has:

(a) made substantial improvements to the realty in reliance upon the oral contract; or

(b) taken possession of the property and paid all or a part of the purchase price.

Contracts for the sale of real estate often require special drafting by an attorney, but in uncomplicated transactions it is often the real estate broker who prepares the contract. For this purpose a variety of contract forms are in general use by brokers who fill in the blank spaces and thus "draft" the contract. In the selection of a particular contract form, the broker is concerned not only with what the document *must* contain to be enforceable as a contract, but what it *should* contain if it is to properly reflect the intent of the parties. The purpose of the basic contract form is to set out who is selling what to whom, for how much, and under what terms.

Any contract for the sale of real estate must state the names of the parties and designate them as buyer or seller.

The contract must contain an adequate description of the property to be sold. The description need not be as precise as that required in a deed, but it must be sufficient to identify the property with reasonable certainty. And if articles of personalty are to be included in the sale they should be itemized in the contract. The amount of the purchase price and the method of payment should be spelled out in detail.

The contract should specify the type of deed by which the conveyance is to be made. Where the contract is silent as to the type of deed to be delivered, most states require the seller to give a warranty deed. However in several states, if the contract is silent as to the type of deed to be delivered the seller need only give a quitclaim deed, provided he has a marketable title.

Unless the contract provides otherwise, the seller must convey a "marketable title." A marketable title is a title free from reasonable doubt; it is a title which a reasonably prudent purchaser, guided by competent legal advice, would be willing to accept. Defects which render a title unmarketable may be defects in the chain of title or defects due to encumbrances or both. It is the obligation of the purchaser to determine the sufficiency of the title.

Since the buyer is entitled to a marketable title (unless the contract provides otherwise), any existing encumbrances on the property must be specifically designated and excepted. Otherwise, the seller will have breached this implied term in the contract.

In an ordinary contract for the sale of real estate, time is not "of the essence" unless the contract so specifies. But if the time fixed for performance is of vital importance due to the nature of the transaction or because of the surrounding circumstances, time *will* be of the essence. If the contract fails to specify the time for performance the law will imply that it be performed within a reasonable time.

If the premises are damaged or destroyed after the execution of the contract but before title passes, and the contract is silent as to who shall bear the loss in such case, the loss falls upon the purchaser in most states. However, in a sizable minority of states the loss falls upon the seller.

Unless the contract specifies otherwise, the purchaser is entitled to possession upon delivery of the deed.

Contracts for the sale of real estate usually provide for the apportionment of such items as real estate taxes, rental income, and cost of utilities. Real estate tax adjustments are made on the basis of the fiscal tax year of the taxing community. It is customary to provide in the contract that the real estate taxes be prorated as of the date when title passes.

Contracts almost invariably call for an "earnest money" deposit by the purchaser. The amount of the deposit should be large enough to discourage the buyer from breaching the contract and also compensate the seller for having taken his property off the market. The earnest money deposit is usually held in escrow by the real estate broker who, in most states, is required by statute to place all such deposits in a special trust account.

Contracts for the sale of real estate may be made contingent upon any number of things, such as the buyer's ability to sell other property owned by him, or his ability to obtain proper financing. Any contingency should be carefully spelled out in the contract.

If one of the parties fails or refuses to perform his part of the contract, the other party ordinarily has a choice between one of three remedies: (a) He may rescind the contract; or (b) he may sue the other party for money damages; or (c) he may bring an action for specific performance.

Rescission is, in effect, the cancellation of a contract. A party who chooses the remedy of rescission declares the contract terminated; both parties are then restored to the same position they were in before the contract was made. A contract may also be rescinded because it was induced by fraud, duress, or undue influence, or because of mistake. And a contract may always be rescinded by mutual consent.

The object of *money damages* is to put the non-breaching party in as good a position monetarily as he would have been had the other party performed the contract. The general measure of damages is the difference between the contract price and the market value of the property as of the time the deed was to be delivered. So where the seller breaches the contract, the buyer may recover the difference between the contract price and the market value of the property at the time set for performance, plus any down payments already made by him. Where the buyer breaches the contract, the seller may recover the difference between the contract price and the market value of the property, less any payments already made by the buyer.

The remedy of *specific performance* is a means of compelling a party to perform in accordance with the terms of the contract. It is a substitute for money damages when that remedy would be inadequate. However, the remedy of specific performance is discretionary with the court; if the terms of the contract are grossly unfair, or if the contract was induced by sharp practice or unethical conduct, the court will usually refuse to grant specific performance, in which case the party seeking to enforce the contract is relegated to an action for money damages.

A clause in a contract expressly fixing the amount of damages to be recovered in the event of a breach is called a "liquidated damages" clause. A stipulation to the effect that failure to perform shall cause a party to lose his rights under the contract and forfeit any payments already made is called a "forfeiture" clause.

Although a provision for liquidated damages will ordinarily prevent a seller from bringing an action for further damages, such a clause will not preclude him from bringing an action for specific performance, *unless* the contract is so worded as to give *the buyer a choice* between performing the contract or forfeiting the deposit. Where the contract allows the buyer to avoid carrying out the terms of the contract upon retention of the deposit by the seller, whether such retention is called a forfeiture or liquidated damages is not material; in either case the buyer has the option of either completing the purchase or forfeiting the deposit, and if he chooses not to complete the purchase his liability is limited to the amount of the deposit.

Unless the contract expressly forbids it, either party may transfer his rights under a contract to sell real estate. Such a transfer is called an *assignment;* the person who transfers his rights is called the "assignor" and the person to whom the rights are transferred is called the "assignee." Although a person may transfer his rights under a contract he may not, by assignment, rid himself of his obligations thereunder.

Although contracts for the sale of real estate may be recorded, this is seldom done except in the case of long-term installment contracts.

CHAPTER 14

REAL ESTATE BROKERAGE

NATURE OF THE BROKERAGE RELATIONSHIP

A "broker" may be defined as an *agent* who, for a commission, acts as a negotiator in bringing persons together to bargain, or who bargains for them.

Although a broker is an agent, he is an agent only in a limited sense. The word "agent" is a broader term than "broker." An agent is one who is authorized generally to represent and act for another (called the *principal)* under an employment arrangement which is more or less fixed and permanent.[1] A broker, on the other hand, has no permanent or continuing relationship with any one principal; he is similar to an independent contractor and holds himself out for employment by the general public. A broker is a *special agent,*

1 Agents may be classified as *actual* or *ostensible*. The agency is *actual* when the agent has in fact been employed and authorized by the principal to act for him; it is *ostensible* when the principal intentionally or by want of ordinary care leads a third person to believe another to be his agent who has not in fact been employed or authorized by him.

Agents may be *universal, general* or *special*. A *universal agent* is one authorized to do all acts for his principal which can lawfully be delegated to an agent. Such an agent has "universal" authority.

A *general agent* is one authorized to do all the acts pertaining to a business of a certain kind or at a particular place, or all the acts of a particular class or series.

A *special agent* is one authorized to perform a specified act or employed to conduct a particular transaction or piece of business for his principal. See 1 MECHEM, AGENCY §§ 57-61 (2d ed. (1914).

with limited authority, usually employed for a single object or transaction.[2]

Brokers are of many kinds, according to the nature of the transaction and the service which they perform. There are stockbrokers, insurance brokers, real estate brokers, produce brokers, ship brokers, merchandise brokers, and even marriage brokers, to name a few.

Real estate brokers are probably the most numerous class of brokers. A real estate broker is a person who is employed in negotiating the sale, purchase, or exchange of real property belonging to others. His compensation is usually in the form of a commission contingent upon success. Primarily, the real estate broker's function is to bring together potential buyers and sellers, and to act as negotiator between them in order to bring about a sale of the property. In addition, the real estate broker often performs other functions, such as procuring mortgage loans, collecting rents, and leasing and managing property.

A real estate broker is sometimes hired by a person wishing to *purchase* land, but this is relatively rare. Ordinarily he is hired by a landowner for the purpose of procuring a buyer who is ready, willing and able to purchase upon the terms prescribed by the owner. And although a real estate broker is often described as a "middleman," strictly speaking, he is not. A middleman is employed merely to bring parties together to deal for themselves—that is, to put the parties in a position where they may make their own deal. The middleman does not act as agent of either party but stands indifferent

[2] The terms "agent" and "broker" are distinguished in a leading Illinois case: "The word 'agent' is a broader term than 'broker,' more comprehensive in its legal scope, for while every broker is in a sense an agent, every agent is not a broker. A broker is distinguished from an agent in that a broker sustains no permanent employment by, or in relation to, any principal, but holds himself out for employment by the public generally, his employment in each instance being that of a special agent for a single object, whereas an agent sustains a fixed and permanent relation to the principal he represents and owes a permanent and continued allegiance." City of Chicago v. Barnett, 404 Ill. 136, 88 N.E.2d 477 (1949).

between them, whereas a broker is an *agent* of one of the parties, employed in a fiduciary capacity and bound to exert his best efforts in the interest of his employer. Since the relationship of a broker to his employer is that of agency, the rights and liabilities arising from this relationship are governed by the principles of the law of *agency.*[3]

CREATION OF THE BROKERAGE RELATIONSHIP

There Must Be a Hiring

The brokerage relationship is created by a contract of employment between the parties. The contract (unless required by statute to be in writing) may be express or implied,[4] but in order for a broker to be entitled to a commission he must have been hired by the person from whom he seeks to recover.

A broker who performs services without the express or implied consent of the owner is a mere "volunteer" and, as such, is not entitled to compensation, even though he may have brought the parties together and effectuated the sale. In most states the contract of employment may be verbal or in writing, but there must be a *hiring.*

If the broker is unable to establish the existence of an *express* contract of employment, he must prove facts from which a hiring can be *implied.* In order to establish an implied contract, it must appear from the facts and circumstances that the broker rendered services in behalf of the owner with his

[3] A real estate *salesman* is distinguishable from a real estate *broker* in that only the broker may enter into employment contracts in his own behalf. A real estate salesman is strictly speaking an *employee* of a broker and although such employee may in fact hold a broker's *license,* he is nevertheless a "salesman" while in the employ of another broker.

A "realtor" is a real estate broker who is a member of a local real estate board having membership in the "National Association of Real Estate Boards."

[4] An "express contract" is one in which the terms are expressly stated by the parties, either verbally or in writing. An "implied contract" is one which may be inferred from the *conduct* of the parties, though not expressed in words.

knowledge and consent. However, the mere consent by an owner to the rendition of unsolicited services by a real estate broker will not, by itself, give rise to an implied promise to pay a commission. A broker cannot by thrusting himself upon the owner expect to be paid for his unsolicited services, for the law will not assist a "volunteer." In order to raise an implied contract to pay a broker for services voluntarily rendered, such services must be beneficial to the owner, and he must have accepted them knowing or having reason to believe that they were rendered with the expectation of payment.[5]

If the owner so conducts himself in his dealings with the broker that the broker has reason to honestly believe that he has been employed to sell the property, the owner may be estopped to deny the employment. But the owner must, in some way, indicate that he accepted the broker as his agent. The mere statement by an owner to a broker that he desires to sell his property at a specified price is not of itself sufficient to create an agency relationship. And where a broker asks for and receives the terms under which an owner will sell, he does not thereby become the owner's agent, entitled to a commission if he produces a buyer. If the rule were otherwise, no owner would be safe in stating the price of his property within the hearing of a broker.[6]

5 It has been held in some states that if the owner knows he is dealing with a real estate broker and he accepts the broker's services in attempting to find a purchaser, such owner is charged with notice of the broker's expectation of getting paid for services rendered, and a promise to pay therefor will be implied. However, no promise to pay a brokerage commission will be implied if the owner is justified under the circumstances in presuming that the broker is representing the buyer or is himself a prospective buyer.

6 The general rule is well stated in the headnote to Summa v. Dereskiawicz, 82 Conn. 547, 74 Atl. 906 (1909): "A real estate broker, in order to recover a commission, must prove either an express contract or the existence of circumstances from which the law will imply a promise of payment. If he relies on an implied contract, he must prove, either that his services were rendered under a belief honestly entertained by him and reasonably induced by the defendant's conduct, that a request had been made of him by the defendant to render them, or, in the absence of such a request, under such circumstances as indicated an expectation of payment upon his part, and that the defendant, knowing such circumstances, had availed himself of the benefit of the services so rendered."

THE BROKER'S EMPLOYMENT ("LISTING") CONTRACT

NATURE OF THE CONTRACT

Since the brokerage relationship is created by a contract, either express or implied, the elements necessary to the formation of any contract must be present. There must be an offer and an acceptance, supported by consideration; and to insure a meeting of the minds as to essential matters, the terms of the agreement must be reasonably definite and certain.

Brokerage contracts, generally referred to as "listing" contracts, may be either bilateral or unilateral.[7] However, the typical broker's listing agreement is usually in the nature of a unilateral contract. The owner, in effect, promises to pay the broker a commission in return for his act of producing a buyer ready, willing and able to purchase on the owner's terms. The broker seldom promises in return that he will produce such a buyer, although he may promise to make diligent efforts to do so. Since the broker makes no promise that he can or will produce a buyer, he is under no legal obligation to do so; hence, the agreement is one-sided or "unilateral."

The owner's promise to pay a commission amounts to an offer of a unilateral contract which the broker can accept only by producing a buyer ready, willing and able to purchase on the owner's terms. When and if the broker is successful in producing such a buyer, the result will be a fully consummated unilateral contract, entitling the broker to his commission. But the broker does not earn his commission unless and until his efforts are successful; nor, in the absence

[7] You may recall from the chapter on contracts that a bilateral contract is one in which the parties exchange mutual promises, and that the consideration for the promise of one party is the return promise on the part of the other. In the case of a unilateral contract however, the parties do not exchange promises. In the unilateral situation only *one* of the parties makes a promise —a promise which is conditional upon the performance of some *act* by the other party. And it is the performance of the act which constitutes the consideration and makes the contract binding. *See* pp. 285-286 and pp. 292-293 *supra*.

of an agreement to the contrary, is he entitled to reimbursement for his expenses in a fruitless effort to find a buyer.[8]

Form of the Contract

A broker's employment contract or "listing" need not be in writing unless a written contract is required by statute. In most states the contract of employment may be either written or verbal, or it may be inferred from the conduct of the parties. However, in order to reduce the number of law suits between owners and brokers, several states have enacted statutes expressly declaring that all agreements concerning the employment of real estate brokers must be in writing. In these states a broker can recover his commission only if his listing agreement is in writing, notwithstanding the fact that he may have brought the parties together and successfully negotiated the sale.

Although the professed purpose of such statutes is to protect landowners from fraudulent claims by real estate brokers, they also have the effect of protecting brokers from the fraudulent conduct of unscrupulous owners seeking to avoid payment of commissions justly earned.

Statutes which require brokerage contracts to be in writing are merely extensions of the statute of frauds. What constitutes a sufficient writing or memorandum to satisfy the statute varies somewhat from state to state. Some states require the writing to set out the rate of commission while

[8] In the typical situation involving the employment of a real estate broker, compensation is conditional upon the achievement of a specified result. "In such cases, there is ordinarily no bilateral contract of employment between the principal and the broker; the principal in effect makes an offer which, in the absence of a manifestation of a contrary intent, is interpreted as a promise to pay the broker a commission in consideration of the production by the broker of a customer ready and willing to contract on the principal's terms and able to perform such a contract. The agent does not earn the commission unless his efforts are successful; nor, in the absence of an agreement to the contrary, is he entitled to recovery for the value of his services or to reimbursement for expenses he has incurred in the fruitless effort to find a customer." RESTATEMENT, AGENCY 2d § 445, comment c (1957).

other states hold that if the writing is sufficient in all other respects, the rate of commission need not appear, in which case the broker will be entitled to a "reasonable" commission. And although the property to be sold must be sufficiently identified, most states hold that the writing need not describe the property with the same precision and completeness as would be required in a contract of sale. The courts generally hold that the writing need not contain the purchase price to be obtained, or other detailed terms of the sale which would necessarily be embodied in a purchase and sale contract. Some statutes require that the writing state the duration of the broker's employment.

In order to avoid any misunderstanding, the listing agreement should contain (1) the names of the seller and the broker; (2) a description of the property; (3) the selling price; (4) any special conditions concerning the terms of the sale; (5) the rate of commission; (6) any special provisions concerning the exclusive character of the listing, if such is the case; (7) a provision authorizing the broker to hold earnest money deposits as escrow agent; (8) a provision authorizing the broker to place "for sale" signs on the property; and (9) the duration of the broker's employment.

TYPES OF LISTING CONTRACTS

The Open Listing

As we have seen, in order for a broker to be entitled to a commission he must have been employed by the person from whom he seeks to recover. There are various types of employment contracts, popularly referred to as "listings." An *open listing* is one in which the owner offers to pay the broker a commission if he procures a customer ready, willing and able to purchase at the price and on the terms specified by the owner.

Sometimes referred to as a "general listing" by the courts, an open listing merely amounts to an invitation to the broker to attempt to find a buyer. It is a "hiring" to be sure, but it is of the most flimsy type; it does not create a contractual relationship but approximates, rather, an offer by the owner which may be withdrawn by him at any time. And it leaves the owner free to list the property with other brokers, or to make a sale himself. In fact the very reason an owner gives an open listing is usually to afford himself the opportunity of selling the property through his own efforts, while at the same time keeping the sale "open" to the efforts of other brokers.

Under an open listing the owner may discharge the broker at any time, provided he does so in good faith and not for the purpose of depriving the broker of a commission virtually earned; and this is so notwithstanding the fact that the broker may have expended considerable effort and money in an attempt to find a buyer.

Where several brokers have an open listing on a property, a sale by either the owner himself or any one of the brokers amounts to an automatic revocation of the authority of all the other brokers, whether they have notice of the sale or not.[9] Actually, an open listing is analogous to an invitation to participate in a race; the rules are that the first broker to produce a buyer wins the commission, whereupon all the other contestants become disqualified. Obviously an open listing affords only a tenuous form of employment, since the broker's authority is always subject to the whim of the owner. And if the listing is terminated before the broker has produced a buyer, he will have worked for nothing.

Many landowners prefer the open listing arrangement; they feel that it is most advantageous to them since it allows them the privilege of employing several brokers at the same time, while still retaining the right to sell direct and save the commission. At first blush this would seem to be the case, but as a practical matter the presumed advantage of an open

[9] However, a few states hold that the broker's authority under an open listing is not terminated until he is actually notified of the sale.

listing often proves illusory. Most brokers are understandably reluctant to spend much time or money promoting the sale of a property when they know that their employment is subject to summary termination, either at the whim of the owner or as a result of a sale of the property by another broker or by the owner himself. Moreover, brokers do not usually relish the idea of competing with the owner in an attempt to find a buyer; such an arrangement can be embarrassing to the broker, especially if the owner himself advertises the property at a price less than the broker's listed price. Consequently an owner is often surprised to find that, after disseminating open listings to several brokers, he receives little, if any, action on his property as compared to an owner who has listed his property with one broker exclusively.

Many brokers refuse to accept open listings, and those who do are justifiably reluctant to devote the same time and effort promoting them as they would if the property were listed with them on an exclusive basis. The trend today is away from open listings and toward listings which give the broker more protection, such as the "exclusive agency" and the "exclusive right to sell."

The Exclusive Agency

The mere listing of property with a broker does not prevent the owner from employing other brokers. Unless he gives one broker the exclusive authority to sell the property, the owner may employ as many brokers as he wishes. When several brokers are so employed on a non-exclusive basis, the owner is liable to pay a commission only to the broker who first produces a buyer.

An *exclusive agency*[10] is a type of listing which protects the broker from competition by other brokers. When an owner gives an exclusive agency, he promises that during the life of

10 An exclusive agency is sometimes referred to as an "exclusive privilege to sell."

the contract he will not employ other brokers or sell the property to a purchaser procured through any other agent. However, such a listing does not preclude the owner from selling the property himself; it only prevents him from listing the property with other brokers.[11] In an exclusive agency contract the owner retains the right to sell the property himself without being liable to the broker for a commission. And if the owner effects a sale through his own efforts and before the broker has produced a purchaser, the exclusive agency will automatically terminate. Although a sale by the owner might work a hardship upon a broker who has gone to considerable expense in promoting the property, this is a chance the broker takes unless his listing contract protects him otherwise.

The Exclusive Right to Sell

The *exclusive right to sell* gives the broker the maximum protection. Not only does it make him the sole *agent* for the sale of the property, but it also precludes the owner from selling the property himself. When an owner gives an exclusive right to sell, he promises, in effect, that during the life of the contract he will not sell the property to any purchaser not procured by the listing broker. Thus a broker who has an exclusive right to sell is entitled to a commission from the owner, even though the owner himself effects the sale through his own efforts.

The exclusive right to sell is obviously the best type of listing from the broker's standpoint since it gives him a monopoly to sell. However, in order to create it, the terms of the listing must be clear and unequivocal. If the terms are at all ambiguous, the listing contract will be interpreted as an exclusive *agency* rather than an exclusive right to sell. The reason for this is that an owner's right to sell his own property

11 "A contract to give an 'exclusive agency' to deal with specified property is ordinarily interpreted as not precluding competition by the principal personally but only as precluding him from appointing another agent to accomplish the result." RESTATEMENT, AGENCY 2d § 449 (1957). *See* Appendix *infra* for sample form for "exclusive agency."

is an implied condition of every listing agreement, and unless expressly negatived, will prevail.

The mere fact that a listing is labeled as an "exclusive listing" or as an "exclusive right to sell" does not necessarily create such a listing; the label used is not controlling but must be considered along with all the other terms. Listings bearing such captions as "exclusive listing agreement," "exclusive right to handle the sale," and even "exclusive right to sell" have been construed to create only an exclusive agency. Conversely, listings captioned "exclusive agency" have, when read in their entirety, been held to create an exclusive right to sell.

In order to create an exclusive right to sell, the terms of the listing should expressly negate the owner's right to sell the property. This is usually accomplished by phraseology to the effect that the broker is to receive a full commission if, during the period of the listing, the property is sold by anyone, including the owner himself.[12]

The exclusive listing arrangement can be of benefit to the owner as well as to the broker. A broker who has an "exclusive" listing will ordinarily feel free to spend more time and money in an attempt to find a buyer, since he has some assurance that the property will not be sold out from under him before he has had a reasonable opportunity to perform. The principal disadvantage of the exclusive listing, from the owner's point of view, has always been that it limits the action to the efforts of a single broker. However, in practice the reverse of this is often true. If anything, exclusive listings have a tendency to foster cooperation among brokers; and with the advent of multiple listing services this once regarded disadvantage has all but disappeared. The trend toward the use of exclusive listing contracts has taken much of the

[12] For example: "You [the Broker] shall be entitled to the full amount of the commission stated herein if, during the term of this agreement, the subject property shall be sold or exchanged by you, or me, or anyone else." *See* Appendix *infra* for sample form for "exclusive right to sell."

"gamble" out of the brokerage business and thereby improved its stability and enhanced its professionalism.

Net Listings

The so-called *net listing* may be in the form of an open listing, an exclusive agency, or an exclusive right to sell. The "net" aspect has to do with the amount of the broker's compensation. The owner states the price he must receive for the property *net to him,* with the broker to receive as his commission all which he can get over and above that price. Under a net listing the broker will most likely receive either less than a fair commission or more than a fair commission. Because net listings breed contention they are not looked upon with favor, and in several states they are expressly prohibited by statute.

DURATION AND TERMINATION OF THE BROKER'S EMPLOYMENT

Duration of Employment

The duration of the broker's employment depends upon the intent of the parties as expressed or implied from the terms of the listing agreement. Where the duration is fixed by the listing agreement, the broker's authority automatically terminates at the expiration of the time specified, unless there is an extension of the time limit. Where no time is fixed for the duration of the agency, the general rule in the United States is that the broker's authority terminates after the expiration of a *reasonable* time, unless sooner terminated by the owner. What is a "reasonable" time depends upon the facts and circumstances of each particular case.

Termination of Employment Generally

Ordinarily the broker's employment terminates when the purpose of the agency is accomplished or when the time called for in the listing agreement expires. However, it may be terminated before that time, either by act or agreement of the parties or by operation of law. Termination by operation of law takes place upon the death or insanity of either party, upon the dissolution of the brokerage firm, or upon a change in the subject matter of the agency, such as loss or destruction of the property by fire.

Owner's Right to Terminate

You will recall that in the case of a general or "open" listing, the owner, acting in good faith, may discharge the broker at any time notwithstanding the fact that the broker may have spent considerable time and money attempting to find a buyer. However, where the listing is *exclusive,* the rules are different. Although the owner always has the *power* to terminate the agency at any time, even though the listing is "exclusive," he does not always have the legal *right* to do so. The owner's *power* to terminate is one thing; his *right* to do so without incurring liability to the broker for breach of contract is another.[13]

Where Exclusive Listing Specifies No Time

Where an exclusive listing specifies no definite period of employment, most states hold that the owner may revoke the agency at any time before the broker has procured a purchaser. However, the revocation must be in good faith; under no circumstances may an owner revoke the broker's authority as a mere device to escape payment of a commission virtually earned. For instance, the owner cannot wait until a prospect begins to nibble at the hook and then withdraw the listing in order to sell direct and avoid the commission.

A few states hold that where the listing is "exclusive" but

13 The owner always has the power (if not the right) to terminate the agent's authority *except* for the rare case in which the agent's authority is "coupled with an interest." If the agent has an interest in the property itself (as opposed to merely an interest in the proceeds from the sale of the property) his authority is said to be "coupled with an interest" and cannot be revoked.

no period of employment is specified, the broker is entitled to a *reasonable* time to perform. In these states the owner is not permitted to withdraw the agency until the broker has had a reasonable opportunity to find a purchaser, especially if he has incurred expense and spent time and labor in an attempt to perform. However, most states hold that even where the listing is "exclusive," if the listing specifies no period of employment the owner may withdraw the agency at will, provided he does so in good faith and before the broker has earned his commission.

Where Exclusive Listing is for a Specified Period

The fact that an owner gives a broker an exclusive listing for a specified period of time does not of itself legally bind the owner or prevent him from withdrawing the listing. For an owner to be legally bound there must be an enforceable contract. And, as we have seen, an essential element of any contract is "consideration"; the owner must receive some consideration for his promise to pay a commission. The mere listing of property with a broker for a specified period of time without consideration on the broker's part amounts only to a naked promise which the owner may revoke at any time. But what constitutes "consideration" in a brokerage contract?

If the listing agreement is in the form of a bilateral contract, wherein the owner and the broker exchange mutual promises, it is the *exchange of promises* which constitutes the consideration. In this situation a contract arises immediately upon the exchange of promises and both parties become bound. However, this is not the usual case. The ordinary listing agreement, at least when first entered into, is in the nature of an offer for a *unilateral* contract; the owner makes an offer which is, in effect, a promise to pay a commission in return for the broker's *act* of producing a purchaser.[14] Since

[14] You will recall that in a unilateral contract, the consideration does not take the form of mutual promises but consists of the performance of some *act* by one of the parties. It is the performance of the act which constitutes the consideration and makes the contract binding.

the broker does not promise in return that he can or will produce a purchaser, he is under no obligation to do so; hence the listing agreement lacks consideration and is unenforceable.[15] However, the broker can accept the owner's offer by performing the act of producing a purchaser. And if he does so within the time specified he will be entitled to a commission; his act of producing a purchaser will constitute at once both the acceptance of the offer and the *consideration* for the owner's promise to pay. The result will be a consummated unilateral contract.

Since the typical listing agreement merely amounts to a unilateral *offer* by the owner ("I offer you my promise to pay a commission for your act of producing a purchaser"), shouldn't such offer, like any other offer, be revocable at any time before it has been accepted? You will recall from the chapter on contracts that an offer may be revoked at any time before its acceptance, even though the person making the offer states that it shall remain open for a definite period of time.[16] Shouldn't the owner, therefore, have the right to withdraw his offer and thereby terminate the broker's employment at any time before a purchaser is actually produced? There are two general views in the United States on this point. Massachusetts and a minority of other states hold that an offer for a unilateral contract can only be accepted by full performance of the requested act, and until that time the unilateral offer, like any other offer, may be revoked. Under the minority rule the owner may revoke the broker's agency at any time before the broker has actually procured a purchaser; and this is so even though the listing is "exclusive" and for a fixed period of time, and notwithstanding the fact that the broker may have expended considerable time and money in an attempt to find a buyer.

A great majority of states have departed from this strict adherence to the unilateral contract theory. They hold that in

15 RESTATEMENT, AGENCY 2d § 445, comment c (1957).

16 See p. 288 *supra*.

the case of an offer for a unilateral contract, if the act requested necessarily requires time and expense to complete, a *part performance* of the requested act will render the offer irrevocable during the time fixed for performance. These states hold that part performance of the requested act furnishes both the "acceptance" and the "consideration" and turns the offer into a binding contract, conditional upon full performance within the time specified.[17] Under the majority rule an exclusive listing for a definite period becomes irrevocable after the broker has taken substantial steps to procure a purchaser.[18]

So under the majority rule, although the typical exclusive listing agreement when made is unilateral and unenforceable because it lacks consideration, this defect is cured the moment the broker has taken substantial steps to procure a purchaser, such as by advertising the property for sale, soliciting buyers,

17 In the leading case of Hutchinson v. Dobson-Bainbridge Realty Co., 31 Tenn. App. 490, 217 S.W.2d 6 (1946), the court said:

"Despite such hardship, many courts, in such a case as the one before us, hold that the principal has the right to revoke his offer and the broker's agency at any time before the broker has actually procured a purchaser. [cases cited.]

"A greater number of courts, however, hold that part performance of the consideration may make such an offer irrevocable, and that where the offeree or broker manifests his assent to the offer by entering upon performance and spending time and money in his efforts to perform, then the offer becomes irrevocable during the time stated and binding upon the principal according to its terms. [cases cited.]

"We think this is the better rule. The theoretical difficulties, formidable as they seem, are outweighed by the considerations of practical justice. This rule avoids hardship to the offeree, and yet does not hold the offeror beyond the terms of his promise. It is true by such terms he was to be bound only if the requested act was done; but this implies that he will let it be done, that he will keep his offer open till the offeree who has begun can finish doing it. At least this is so where the doing of it will necessarily require time and expense. In such a case it is but just to hold that the offeree's part performance furnishes the 'acceptance' and the 'consideration' for a binding subsidiary promise not to revoke the offer, or turns the offer into a presently binding contract conditional upon the offeree's full performance."

18 The rule does not apply to "open" listings where it is generally understood that more than one agent may be working on the property. In such cases the expenditure of money and effort by any one agent would not make the listing irrevocable; the first broker to produce a purchaser would still win the commission and the employment of all the other brokers would thereby terminate, not by revocation, but according to the implied terms of the listing.

or showing the property to prospective customers. The broker's expenditure of time or money in an attempt to find a buyer is considered a "part performance" of the requested act—it constitutes an "acceptance" of the owner's offer and furnishes the "consideration" for his promise to pay a commission; thereafter, the owner is no longer privileged to revoke the listing without rendering himself liable to the broker for breach of contract.[19] And although a commission is not earned until a purchaser is produced, this implies that the owner will let it be done—that he will not revoke the listing until the broker has been allowed the agreed time to find a buyer.

Certainly the majority rule is fairer. It avoids the hardship which would result if the owner were allowed to revoke the agency after the broker had expended his time and money in a good faith attempt to procure a purchaser. By preventing revocation and allowing the broker to finish what he has begun, the majority rule avoids such hardship to the broker and yet does not hold the owner beyond the terms of his promise.

The trend today is to draft listing agreements in the form of a bilateral contract wherein the owner and the broker exchange mutual promises; in return for the owner's promise to pay a commission for the procuring of a purchaser, the broker promises to list the property, advertise it, and to exert his best efforts to effect a sale. In such a case a contract arises immediately upon the exchange of promises and both parties become bound.

To summarize briefly then: the typical listing agreement is in the form of an offer by the owner to pay a commission for the broker's act of producing a buyer. The broker can accept

19 Even though a listing becomes irrevocable, in the case of the "exclusive *agency*" the owner still has the right to sell the property through his own efforts without being liable to the broker for a commission. In such case, a sale by the owner constitutes an automatic revocation of the listing; however, it is rightful since it is a revocation according to the terms of the listing contract.

the offer and earn a commission by producing a buyer within the time specified. Where the broker has not yet taken substantial steps to procure a purchaser, the owner may revoke the offer (listing) with impunity, even though it is "exclusive" and for a specified period of time. But *after* the broker has taken substantial steps to procure a purchaser, a great majority of states hold that the owner may not revoke the listing without rendering himself liable to the broker for a breach of contract. In a small minority of states the owner has a right to revoke the listing at any time before the broker has actually produced a buyer, notwithstanding the fact that the listing is "exclusive" and for a specified period, and regardless of the fact that the broker may have expended considerable time and money in an attempt to produce a buyer. Where the parties exchange mutual promises, a bilateral contract arises immediately and both parties become bound.

Damages for Wrongful Termination

If the owner wrongfully terminates the broker's listing contract before the time stipulated, he renders himself liable to the broker for damages. However, the law varies from state to state as to the *amount* of damages the broker is entitled to, and in a few states the law is unsettled on this point. Some states allow the broker to recover the full amount of the commission on the theory that performance by the broker was prevented by the owner. In other states the broker is only entitled to the amount of the commission if he can show that at the time his employment was terminated he could have produced a purchaser without incurring further expense. Still other states hold that where the owner wrongfully terminates the broker's employment, the broker is only entitled to recover the reasonable value of his services, measured by the expenses he incurred in an attempt to produce a purchaser.

Brokers sometimes include in their listing agreements a clause to the effect that the broker shall receive a full commission if, within the period specified in the listing, the owner *withdraws* the property from sale. However, owners are generally reluctant to make such a commitment. Of course, if the listing contract expressly provides that the broker shall receive a commission in the event the property is *sold* by anyone during the term of the listing (exclusive right to sell), then the broker is entitled to recover the full amount of the stipulated commission if the property is actually sold within that period.

PERFORMANCE AND THE RIGHT TO COMPENSATION

Introductory Statement

The broker's compensation is ordinarily a commission based on the gross selling price of the property. As a general rule, in order for a broker to be entitled to a commission he must not only have been hired by the person from whom he seeks to recover, he must also have *performed* his undertaking—that is, he must have accomplished what he undertook to do in his contract of employment.[20] If he has been unsuccessful he is not entitled to compensation, no matter how great his efforts or how meritorious his services.[21]

20 In addition to having performed his undertaking, the broker must have been duly *licensed* at the time he rendered the service; otherwise he cannot recover his commission.

21 The general rule has been well stated by the New York court: "It follows, as a necessary deduction from the established rule, that a broker is never entitled to commissions for unsuccessful efforts. The risk of failure is wholly his. The reward comes only with his success. That is the plain contract and contemplation of the parties. The broker may devote his time and labor, and expend his money with ever so much of devotion to the interest of his employer, and yet, if he fails, if without effecting an agreement or accomplishing a bargain, he abandons the effort, or his authority is fairly and in good faith terminated, he gains no right to commissions. He loses the labor and effort which was staked upon success. And in such event it matters not that after his failure, and the termination of his agency, what he has done proves of use and benefit to the principal. In a multitude of cases that must necessarily result. He may have introduced to each other parties who otherwise would have never met; he may have created impressions which, under later and more favorable circumstances, naturally lead to and materially assist in the consummation of a sale; he may have planted

WHAT CONSTITUTES PERFORMANCE GENERALLY

Just what constitutes "performance" depends upon the terms of the broker's employment contract. The broker and his principal are at liberty to make the payment of commissions dependent upon any conditions they wish; so if the listing contract provides that payment of the commission is contingent upon "consummation of the transaction," or "upon the transfer of title," the broker will not have earned his commission until the transfer is completed.[22] However, under the *usual* listing contract, the broker has performed his undertaking and is entitled to a commission when he *produces* a buyer who is *ready, willing* and *able* to purchase on the terms specified by the owner. The broker is deemed to have "produced" a buyer within the meaning of the rule if he:

(a) places such buyer in *communication* with the owner so that the owner and buyer have the opportunity to enter into a binding contract of sale,[23] *or*

the very seeds from which others reap the harvest; but all that gives him no claim. It was part of his risk that, failing himself, not successful in fulfilling his obligations, others might be left to some extent to avail themselves of the fruit of his labors." Sibbald v. Bethlehem Iron Co., 83 N. Y. 378, 38 Am. Rep. 441 (1880).

22 "For many cases no more satisfactory general rule can be laid down than to ascertain, 1. What did the broker undertake to do? 2. Has he completed that undertaking within the time and upon the terms stipulated? and 3. If not, is the default attributable to his own act or to the interference of the principal? If upon such an inquiry it be determined that the broker has performed within the time, and upon the terms, agreed upon, he is entitled to his commissions; if he has not, he is not so entitled, unless the performance was prevented by the principal under circumstances which gave him no right then and so to prevent it." 2 MECHEM, AGENCY § 2427 (2d ed. 1914).

23 Unless the listing contract specifies otherwise, it is not necessary that the broker complete the entire negotiations himself, or even that the sale be actually consummated. To be entitled to a commission the broker need only produce a purchaser who is ready, willing and able to buy on the terms prescribed by the owner. And when the broker *produces* such a person he is entitled to his commission even though the owner is unable to consummate the transaction or simply refuses to go through with the sale.

As was said by the Massachusetts court in an oft-cited case: "When the broker has produced a customer his duty is at an end; so far as his rights or his duties are concerned it is immaterial whether a contract is or is not made, or if made, whether it is or is not performed. The broker's right to a commission is no more dependent upon or affected by the fact that a contract is or is not drawn up and executed, than it is by the fact that the contract, if drawn up, is or is not carried into effect. Making or not making a con-

(b) obtains and delivers to the owner a written *offer* to purchase on the exact terms specified in the listing agreement, which offer the owner can immediately turn into a contract by accepting, *or*

(c) procures an unconditional and mutually binding *contract* between the parties.

In the absence of an express stipulation in the listing contract, it is not necessary for the broker to procure a binding written contract from his customer in order to be entitled to a commission; he need only *produce* a customer ready, willing and able to purchase on the terms prescribed by the owner, or upon modified terms acceptable to him. However, where the broker is employed to "effect a sale" of the property, or to "sell" the property (as distinguished from merely procuring a buyer), most courts hold that the broker is not entitled to his commission until he procures from his customer a binding contract of sale, unless, of course, failure to execute the contract was due to the fault of the owner.[24]

Buyer Must Be Ready, Willing and Able to Purchase

To be entitled to a commission the broker must produce a customer who is ready, willing, and able to purchase on the terms specified by the owner. A "ready" and "willing"

tract with the customer produced, enforcing or not enforcing a contract, if made, are matters for the broker's principal to do or not to do as his ability and inclination determine; they are matters with which the broker is not concerned, and on which his right to a commission is not dependent." Fitzpatrick v. Gilson, 176 Mass. 477, 57 N. E. 1000 (1900).

Although the broker is ordinarily entitled to his commission when he produces a purchaser who is ready, willing and able to buy on the terms prescribed by the owner, if the parties execute a sale contract which gives the buyer the *option* of either performing the contract or forfeiting his deposit, the broker will not be entitled to his commission unless the option is exercised and the sale consummated. See p. 357 *infra*.

24 A few courts refuse to distinguish between an employment to *find* a purchaser and an employment to *sell* the property. These courts regard such terms as "to sell" and "to procure a purchaser" as synonymous when used in listing contracts and hold that a broker employed to "sell" property has performed his undertaking and is entitled to his commission when he *produces* a buyer ready, willing and able to purchase on the terms specified by the owner.

customer is one who is prepared and willing to accept the terms offered by the owner and to enter into a binding contract of sale. And it must appear that the customer remained in the state of readiness and willingness long enough for the owner to have dealt with him.

The term "able" refers to financial ability. It is not necessary that the customer be in possession of the entire purchase price; it is sufficient if he is able to command the necessary funds within the time required to close the deal. Although an offer in writing may be good evidence of readiness and willingness, it may furnish no indication as to *ability*.

Where the broker produces a "ready" and "willing" customer but the owner refuses to consummate the sale, in order for the broker to recover his commission he must be prepared to *prove* that the customer was also financially "able" to pay the purchase price. However, according to the general rule in the United States, if the owner enters into a sales contract with the broker's customer, the question of the customer's financial ability becomes immaterial. Once the parties execute a contract of sale the broker is entitled to his commission, even if the customer later fails or refuses to carry out his contract. And this is so even though the customer's failure is due to his financial inability.[25] The basis of this rule is that the owner is not required to accept the customer without first making inquiry and satisfying himself as to the customer's financial ability. And if the owner accepts the customer and enters into a sales contract with him, he cannot later object on the ground that the customer was financially unable to carry out the contract.[26]

In order for the above rule to apply, the purchase and sale

25 And a subsequent release of the customer by the owner, or a cancellation or rescission of the contract, does not defeat the broker's right to the commission.

26 However, if the broker expressly warrants the buyer's financial ability to perform he is not entitled to a commission if the transaction fails due to the financial inability of the buyer.

contract must be *mutually enforceable;* that is, the contract must bind the purchaser *to make the purchase.* If the contract is conditional or if it gives the buyer the *option* of either making the purchase or forfeiting the down payment, it is not such a mutually enforceable contract as will entitle the broker to a commission, unless the purchase is actually consummated, or unless consummation is prevented by the seller. So a broker who procures no more than a conditional or an optional contract can recover a commission only if (a) an actual sale subsequently results, or (b) the purchaser attempts to exercise his option and is prevented from doing so by the seller.

The majority rule which permits a broker to recover a commission simply because his customer has entered into a *contract* with the owner is neither just nor logical. Nor is it realistic.

The majority rule casts upon the owner the burden of investigating the financial ability of the broker's customer. But as a practical matter a typical owner is neither inclined nor equipped to embark upon such an investigation; a buyer's financial ability is usually a matter to be resolved between him and his banker. If indeed there is an obligation to inquire into the financial status of a buyer, it should be the obligation of the broker who produced him. Also, when an owner lists property with a broker he usually expects to become liable for a commission only in the event a sale is actually consummated, unless of course the owner himself has prevented it. And it is generally expected that the commission money will come out of the proceeds of the sale. The signing of a purchase and sale contract is merely one of the steps toward consummating the transaction. If it later develops that the customer cannot or will not complete the sale, how can it be said that the broker has produced a ready, willing and able buyer?

In a 1967 landmark case, the Supreme Court of New Jersey *rejected* the proposition that whenever the owner enters into a contract with the broker's customer the broker's right to a commission is complete. After tracing the evolution of the law relating to a broker's right to commissions, the court concluded that over the years the majority rule had been perpetuated by precedent rather than logic. By rejecting the rule the court in effect repealed a century of New Jersey case law on the point. In delivering the opinion of the court, Justice Francis points out that

> "In a practical world, the true test of a willing buyer is not met when he signs an agreement to purchase; it is demonstrated at the time of closing of title, and if he unjustifiably refuses or is unable financially to perform *then,* the broker has not produced a willing buyer."[27]

Hopefully this far-reaching New Jersey decision will start a national trend away from the majority rule and eventually give it the burial it so richly deserves. However, at the present time the general rule in the country still is that once the owner enters into a binding contract with the broker's customer, the customer's financial ability is no longer open to question and the broker is entitled to his commission.

Must be on Terms Specified by Owner

The broker's customer must be ready, willing and able to purchase the property on the *terms* specified by the owner, or upon modified terms acceptable to him. A broker who produces a person who is willing to purchase only on different terms, or upon other conditions, has not performed according to his listing contract.[28]

27 Ellsworth Dobbs, Inc. v. Johnson, 50 N. J. 528, 236 A.2d 843 (1967).

28 Obviously a broker has not performed according to his listing contract when he produces a customer who offers *less* for the property than the price listed. And a broker employed to *"find a purchaser"* or to *"sell"* property is not entitled to a commission where he merely procures a customer to take an *option* on the property. An optional contract to purchase is not a compliance with the broker's undertaking to find a purchaser or to sell the property. In such cases the broker has not "performed" so as to be entitled to compensation unless the option is exercised, or unless the customer is willing to exercise the option but is prevented from doing so by the owner.

Where the broker produces a customer who makes an offer which is at variance with the terms prescribed by the owner, the owner is at liberty to either accept the modified terms or reject them. He has a perfect right to insist upon exact compliance with the terms of the listing agreement and is under no obligation to the broker to change or modify those terms. However, if as part of the same negotiations, and without terminating the agency, the owner accepts the modified terms, the broker will be entitled to the benefit of that variance if a sale to the broker's prospect results; in such case the broker will have performed his undertaking by producing a buyer ready, willing and able to purchase on terms satisfactory to the owner.[29]

Sale for Less than Listed Price

Ordinarily any variation (unless trivial) from the terms specified by the owner will preclude the broker's right to a commission if the owner rejects the offered terms. The most common type of variance usually involves the price of the property, or the method or medium of payment. Where the broker produces a customer who offers to purchase the property at less than the broker's listed price, the owner, of course, may either accept or reject the offer. If during the negotiations the owner voluntarily reduces the price and accepts the broker's customer, the broker is entitled to his commission based upon the sale price.[30]

A listing of property at a stipulated price, nothing being said as to terms, contemplates a *cash* sale. A "cash" sale is a sale conditioned on full payment concurrent with delivery of the deed, as distinguished from a sale where by agreement payment is deferred.

29 But where the sale is consummated after *termination* of the listing on different terms from those specified in the listing contract, the broker is usually held not entitled to a commission.

30 "In the ordinary situation in which the principal promises a broker a commission for finding a purchaser and the asking terms are stated to the broker, the usual interpretation is that the asking terms are intended merely to guide the broker in starting negotiations, and the broker is to have his commission if he produces a customer ready and willing to purchase on the asking

The owner has the right to insist upon the price listed with the broker and he may reject any lower offer presented to him. If the owner rejects a lower offer, the broker is not entitled to a commission, even though the owner later sells the property at a reduced price to the same purchaser; provided, of course, that the transaction is in good faith and not merely for the purpose of avoiding liability to the broker. In other words, although the broker may be the means of first bringing the parties together, if the negotiations fail to be productive and the parties in good faith withdraw and abandon the proposed sale, a subsequent renewal of negotiations followed by a sale at a lower price does not entitle the broker to a commission; in such a case he cannot be said to be the effective or procuring cause of the sale, though he may have contributed something.

Must be Within the Time Limited

The broker is not entitled to a commission unless he performs within the time specified in his listing contract.[31] Thus, if the broker's efforts do not produce a ready, willing and able buyer until *after* the listing has expired, he will not be entitled to his commission; and this is so even though the customer eventually buys the property. The broker must perform *within* the time period specified in his listing agreement, unless the delay was caused by the owner, or unless the owner voluntarily waives or extends the time period.

However, if a ready, willing and able purchaser is produced within the time specified, and negotiations continue to completion without interruption, the broker is

terms or on such modified terms as the principal may subsequently accept be fore the agency is revoked." RESTATEMENT, AGENCY 2d § 447, comment b (1957).

31 You will recall that in the case of an *"open"* listing, until the broker actually produces a customer ready willing and able to purchase, the owner, if acting in good faith, may *withdraw* the listing at any time. So in the case of an *open* listing the broker's right to a commission is fixed at the time of his discharge, if done in good faith. If at that time his efforts have not been successful, he has not earned his commission.

entitled to his commission even though the sale was not fully consummated until after the listing had expired. But the buyer must be *produced* within the time period; it is not enough that seeds are sown which later bear fruit in the production of a purchaser.

Exclusive listing contracts frequently contain a stipulation to the effect that the broker shall be entitled to a commission on any sale consummated within a specified time *after* the expiration of the listing *to any person with whom the broker has negotiated.*[32] Courts generally uphold such provisions and require the owner to pay a commission in the event of a sale to such person within the period specified.

Broker Must be Procuring Cause of Sale

Unless otherwise protected by the specific terms of his listing contract, in order for the broker to be entitled to a commission he must be the *procuring cause* of the sale. There are several other forms of expression which appear in the court decisions, apparently without any real difference in meaning. For example, the courts use such various terms as "procuring and inducing cause," "effective and producing cause," "efficient proximate cause," "immediate cause," "controlling cause," "proximate and procuring cause," etc. Basically the terms are synonymous.

Although the broker may have expended great effort and gone to considerable expense in promoting the property, unless his efforts were the procuring cause of the sale, he earns nothing. On the other hand, his efforts may have been slight, but if they produced the desired result, no more is required.

"Procuring cause" of the sale means that the broker must be the *primary* cause and not merely the contributing cause. It is not enough that the broker's effort was *one* of the causes

32 See sample listing form in Appendix *infra*.

of the sale or that he contributed to it in some way; he must have been the *effective* cause of the sale. His efforts need not be the sole cause but they must be the *predominating* cause.

Whether or not a broker is the procuring cause of a sale is a question of fact to be determined by the circumstances of each particular case. Generally speaking, it must appear that through the efforts of the broker a purchaser was brought into communication with the owner, and as a result thereof, and without a break in the causal relation between the broker's efforts and the sale, the object of the agency was accomplished.[33] In short, the broker must not only produce a purchaser but the sale must proceed from his efforts acting as a broker; his efforts must produce results.

To be the procuring cause of the sale, it is not necessary that the broker should personally have introduced the owner to the buyer; it is sufficient if the buyer was induced to apply to the owner through the means employed by the broker.[34] And it is not necessary that the broker himself should have conducted the negotiations between the parties, or that he should have participated in the negotiations, or even that he should have been present when the parties met or when the sale was made. It is sufficient if his efforts were the effective

33 The negotiations need not be without interruption but there must be some continuity in the broker's efforts to conclude the transaction. Thus if, in good faith, negotiations are broken off and months later the owner without the aid of the broker sells the property to the person with whom the broker had previously negotiated, the broker would not be considered the procuring cause of the sale. And if after bringing a customer into communication with the owner, the broker *abandons* his employment entirely, or if after introducing a prospect who proves unwilling to accept the owner's terms the broker simply ceases to make further efforts to negotiate with the prospect and negotiations are broken off and terminated, the broker will not be entitled to a commission if the owner later renews negotiations with the same prospect and concludes a sale without the aid of the broker.

34 Thus where the broker merely posts a "For Sale" sign on the premises, and the owner himself concludes a sale with a buyer who learned of the property through the sign, the broker is the "producing cause" of the sale even though the transaction is concluded without the broker's knowledge.

And a broker with whom the property has been listed is deemed to be the "procuring cause" of the sale where the property is sold to one who became interested through the efforts of the broker's *subagent*.

cause of the sale—that through his agency a purchaser was brought into communication with the owner resulting in a sale.[35]

Example:

A employs broker B to sell his residence. B advertises the property in a newspaper. C reads the ad, contacts the owner directly, and purchases the property. The broker is entitled to his commission. Although the sale was concluded without the broker's knowledge, he was nonetheless the procuring cause of the sale.

Example:

An owner employs broker B to sell his property. B sends a prospect directly to the owner, whereupon the prospect and the owner conclude the sale without the aid of the broker. The broker is, nevertheless, the procuring cause of the sale.

The mere fact, however, that the broker showed the property to a prospect or introduced him to the owner does not necessarily make him the procuring cause of the sale. But if such showing or introduction is the basis upon which negotiations are begun and the sale consummated, the broker may be deemed the procuring cause of the sale.

If the broker is the procuring cause of the sale he is entitled to his commission even though final negotiations are conducted by the owner, who, in order to make the sale, accepts less than the broker's listing price. But if negotiations fail, and the parties in good faith abandon the transaction, a subsequent renewal of negotiations followed by a sale at a lower price does not entitle the broker to a

[35] "It could not be ruled as a matter of law that the broker was not the efficient cause merely because he was not present at the execution of the contract or of the deed, and knew nothing about them until afterwards, nor because the final terms differed from those proposed during his negotiations. . . . Brokers have recovered commissions even where they took no part in the negotiations, never saw the purchaser, and did nothing except advertise the property." Corleto v. Prudential Ins. Co., 320 Mass. 612, 70 N. E. 2d 702 (1947).

commission; in such case the broker cannot be said to be the procuring cause of the sale.

Procuring cause of the sale means *proximate* cause and not remote cause. Thus if, after the broker has failed to effect a sale, and after his customer has decided not to buy, other persons persuade him to do so, the broker is not entitled to a commission. And where a person with whom the broker has unsuccessfully negotiated calls the property to the attention of another party who eventually buys it, the courts generally hold that the broker's efforts are not sufficiently direct to entitle him to a commission. With respect to the requirement of "proximate" cause, the Massachusetts court has said:

> "The general rule of law applicable to a case like this is, that, where there has been no direct communication between the broker and the purchaser, it must be shown affirmatively that the latter was induced to enter into the negotiations which resulted in the purchase through the means employed by the broker for that purpose. If the broker employed other persons to aid him, whether under pay or not, or if he put up maps, signs, notices, or otherwise advertised the property, by means of which a person was induced to open negotiations with the owner which resulted in his buying the property, the sale may be said to have been effected through the broker's instrumentality. But it must be made to appear that what the broker did was the immediate and efficient cause of such negotiations. If the broker merely talked about the property with different persons, and one of them, of his own accord, and not acting in behalf of the broker, mentioned to another that the property was for sale, and such last mentioned person thereupon looked into the matter and finally became the purchaser, the agency of the broker in inducing the sale was not sufficiently direct to entitle him to a commission."[36]

[36] Gleason v. Nelson, 162 Mass. 245, 38 N. E. 497 (1894).

Where Property is Listed with More than One Broker

As we have seen, where property is listed for sale with a number of brokers under an "open listing," the one who first produces a buyer wins the commission. Under an open listing arrangement it is not unusual for a single prospect to have been solicited by several brokers, sometimes resulting in a situation where two or more brokers each claim credit for having "produced" the same buyer. Where two or more brokers are involved in the same transaction, each contributing something to bring about the sale, each is not entitled to a share in the commission; only the broker who was the effective procuring cause of the sale is entitled to the commission. In such a case the court will never divide the commission among the brokers because there can be only one *predominating* cause. However, the rule is easier stated than applied, for it is often difficult to determine which of the brokers predominated in bringing about the sale.[37]

Ordinarily, where the buyer has been solicited by several brokers, the broker entitled to the commission is the one who succeeded in bringing the buyer and seller together, regardless of which broker *first* solicited the buyer. So if the first broker's efforts fail to bring about an agreement between his customer and the owner, and later a second broker succeeds in selling the property to the same customer, the second broker is entitled to the commission. But if the first broker brings about a substantial agreement between the parties, and a second broker merely works out the final details, the first broker is entitled to the commission. The broker who is the procuring or dominating cause of the sale is entitled to the commission even though the transaction is actually consummated through another broker.[38]

[37] In fact the New Hampshire court has said that "It is impossible to measure in quantitative units the efforts necessary to constitute the effective cause." Williams v. Walker, 95 N. H. 231, 61 A.2d 512 (1948).

[38] "*Where only one broker is employed.* If a person employs only one broker to procure a customer, the broker is ordinarily entitled to his commission . . . if he causes a customer to negotiate with the principal and the

Where Owner is Unaware that Buyer was Procured by Broker

Where a broker is in fact the procuring cause of the sale, most states hold that he will not be deprived of his commission merely because at the time of the sale the owner was not aware that the customer had been procured by the broker. However, a minority of states hold that if the owner sells the property in good faith and without knowledge that the customer had been procured through the efforts of the broker, the broker is *not* entitled to a commission. A few states have taken a middle course by adopting the majority rule but with modifications: They hold that the broker will not be deprived of his commission merely because the owner was unaware that the customer had been procured by the broker, *unless* by failing to so inform the owner the broker permits him, through ignorance, to either pay a commission to another broker or accept a lower price for the property on the assumption that the sale would be commission free. Thus it behooves the broker to keep the owner apprised of the names of all prospects to whom the property is shown.

customer makes a purchase without a substantial break in the ensuing negotiations. It is not necessary that the broker conduct the negotiation or even be an influential factor in persuading the customer to accept the terms; nor is it necessary that the broker should personally introduce the customer or bring the principal to his attention; he introduces the customer if, through any means which he uses to attract attention, the purchaser is led to the principal." RESTATEMENT, AGENCY 2d § 448, comment d (1957).

"*Where more than one broker is employed.* If the owner of property employs two or more brokers, not contracting that any of them shall have an exclusive agency, the broker who first secures the serious attention of the customer ordinarily is entitled to the commission. If, however, the first broker does not continue active negotiations, or if it appears that his negotiations are likely to prove fruitless, the principal is privileged to utilize the services of another broker for the purpose of accomplishing the transaction; if it is found that the services of such other broker predominate in producing the purchase, the principal has no duty to pay a commission to the first broker, and the second broker is entitled to the commission for his services. No more definite rule can be stated as to the conditions under which one or the other of the brokers is entitled to the commission." RESTATEMENT, AGENCY 2d § 448, comment e (1957).

Where the Listing is "Exclusive"

Of course where the broker has an "exclusive agency" or an "exclusive right to sell," he may recover a commission although the owner effects the sale through another broker, or, in the case of an exclusive right to sell, even if the owner sells the property himsclf; and the fact that the exclusive broker was not the procuring cause of the sale is immaterial. In such case the broker is entitled to his commission, not because he was the procuring cause of the sale, but by virtue of the special terms of his listing contract.[39]

BROKER'S AUTHORITY

Authority to Bind Principal

The ordinary real estate broker is a special agent with only limited authority; and he must keep within the bounds of that authority. If the broker exceeds his express or implied authority, the principal will not be held responsible. On the other hand, the principal is liable for such acts of his broker as are done within the scope of his authority.

Since the broker is ordinarily a mere negotiator between the parties, he has no implied authority to conclude a binding contract of sale on behalf of his employer. Such authority must be specially conferred upon him.

However, the broker is generally presumed to be invested with authority to perform those acts which are reasonably necessary to accomplish the purpose of his agency. Consequently, in most states representations by the broker concerning such matters as the character and condition of

39 "The usual listing agreement is so interpreted as to make compensation due only if the broker is the effective cause. There are, however, other agreements with brokers which make the rule inapplicable or vary the usual liabilities. . . . If the principal appoints the agent to an 'exclusive agency' or grants him an exclusive right to sell, and thereafter in the first case the result is accomplished by another agent, or in the second case even by the principal himself, the agent is entitled to damages. . . ." RESTATEMENT, AGENCY 2d 448, comment b (1957).

the soil, or the quantity of the land or status of the title are usually held binding upon the principal.

The principal will be held responsible for all the acts of his agent which are done within the scope of his authority whether such acts were authorized or not. Accordingly, the principal is liable to third parties for the fraudulent acts of his agent done within the scope of his authority, even though the principal himself is innocent. In such cases fraud by the agent is considered to be fraud by the principal. The rule is necessary to prevent fraud and to encourage confidence in dealing. And it is better that the principal should be bound by the fraud or misconduct of his own agent rather than that another should suffer.

The owner will ordinarily be liable for damages to third parties resulting from false representations of the broker regarding such matters as the existence of encumbrances or restrictions on the property, the location of boundary lines, the number of acres, the type and condition of the soil, the presence of minerals, the right to fixtures, the quantity of timber, and the adequacy of the water supply. The fact that the broker's misrepresentations were made under the mistaken belief that they were true is immaterial. And a provision in the sale contract to the effect that the seller will not be bound by any representations made by the broker unless such representations are set out in the contract will not relieve the owner from responsibility.

Authority to Accept Deposit

Ordinarily the broker has no *implied* authority to accept the purchase price or any part of it from the buyer on behalf of the seller; such authority must be expressly conferred by the terms of the listing agreement.[40] A buyer who makes

40 The broker's authority to receive payment will not be implied merely from the fact that he was hired to "sell" the property or to "negotiate a sale." Such authority must be expressly conferred by the listing agreement. The sample listing forms which appear in the Appendix *infra* expressly authorize the broker to accept earnest money deposits.

payment to a broker who has not been authorized to receive it does so at his own risk. In such case payment to the broker does not constitute payment to the owner, and the broker holds the money as agent for the buyer. So if the broker absconds or embezzles the money, the buyer must bear the loss, not the owner.

However, even if the broker receives payment without authority, an acceptance of the money by the owner would constitute a *ratification* of the broker's action. "Ratification" as used in the law of principal and agent is equivalent to a previous authorization and relates back to the time when the act ratified was done; it has the effect of conferring authority retroactively. Ratification of the broker's act may also result from the mere fact that the owner signs a purchase and sale contract reciting that earnest money deposits are being held by the broker. In such case the buyer would be entitled to recover the deposits from the owner in the event the money were wrongfully appropriated by the broker, or if the broker became insolvent without having remitted to the owner.

May Not Delegate Authority

Ordinarily an owner selects a real estate broker on the basis of his presumed knowledge and ability and because his character is such as to inspire trust and confidence. For this reason the authority conferred by the listing contract is deemed to be personal and therefore cannot be delegated to another so as to affect the rights of the owner without his express or implied consent.

Although the broker may not divest himself of his duties and responsibilities to the owner he may, nevertheless, properly delegate to others certain functions which do not require the exercise of discretion. For example, the broker may employ sub-agents to show the property to prospective purchasers or to otherwise interest them in the purchase of the property. The duties of the sub-agent under such circumstances are considered as being merely ministerial or mechanical, such functions not involving such an exercise of discretion that they may not be delegated to another. Thus the broker is generally held to be entitled to a commission upon a sale of the property by a sub-agent, regardless of whether or not the owner knew of the sub-agency.[41]

Since co-brokerage and multiple listing arrangements have now become an integral part of the real estate business, the utilization of sub-agents has become common practice. "Co-brokerage" is an arrangement whereby the listing broker agrees to share the commission with another broker (sub-agent) in the event that the other broker is able to produce a purchaser for the property. "Multiple listing" is simply a systematized method of co-brokerage. It is an arrangement whereby each member of the multiple listing service may bring his listings to the attention of the other members by furnishing them with a brief description of the property listed, together with the pertinent sales information. In the event that a member other than the listing broker sells the property, the commission is shared between the listing broker and the selling broker in accordance with a prearranged division. Because of the collective efforts of the member brokers, property listed with an active multiple listing service is likely to receive much greater exposure to the market than it would otherwise.

41 "As between principal and broker, it is generally considered immaterial that the purchaser of the real estate was secured through the efforts of a subagent, rather than by the personal efforts of the broker himself. Since the subagent cannot claim compensation from the owner, the fact that the broker agreed to divide the commissions with such subagent in no wise affects the broker's right to claim the whole compensation from the principal. Accordingly, where the agent for the sale of land has not attempted to divest himself of his functions or his responsibilities to his principal, he may recover a commission against the latter for bringing about a sale of the land, even though he has employed a subagent for the performance of mere ministerial duties connected with the negotiations." Philbrick v. Chase, 95 N. H. 82, 58 A.2d 317 (1948).

BROKER'S DUTIES AND LIABILITIES

Duties and Liabilities to Principal

It is the broker's duty to obey the instructions of his principal and to act strictly in accordance with the authority conferred upon him by the listing contract. Any violation of this duty renders the broker liable to the principal for any loss the latter may suffer as a result.

The broker is bound to exercise a reasonable degree of care and skill in the performance of his duties. And although he does not guarantee the success of his undertaking, the real estate broker holds himself out to the public as qualified to perform the important transaction entrusted to him. The law requires that he shall possess and exercise that degree of skill, care, knowledge and judgment ordinarily possessed and exercised by other real estate brokers in his community.

If a broker is guilty of negligence or incompetence, he not only becomes liable to his principal for any loss resulting, but he also forfeits his right to a commission. Moreover, the broker is not only liable for his own actions but for the actions of his sub-agents as well, provided they act within the scope of their authority. However, the broker will not be liable for a mistake in judgment which does not result from his failure to know or do that which a broker of ordinary prudence, in the same community and under the same circumstances, would know or do.

It is not the duty of the broker to give advice as to the legal sufficiency of the sale contract or to explain or construe the meaning of the terms used. However, where the broker undertakes to prepare the contract he may be held liable for any damages sustained by the principal if the transaction fails because of the broker's negligence or incompetence in drafting the instrument.

Broker is a Fiduciary

A real estate broker occupies a position of trust and confidence. He acts in a *fiduciary*[42] capacity and so is bound to exercise the utmost good faith and loyalty toward his principal.

This rule requires that the broker devote his entire skill and knowledge to the best interests of his employer, and to act with sole regard to those interests. Thus, the broker must not assume or continue the brokerage relationship if his own interests will, in any way, come into conflict with the interests of his principal. The broker may not act adversely to his client's interest by concealing or suppressing information; he is obligated to communicate all the information he may possess which may be either advantageous or detrimental to the interests of his employer. He must fully disclose to his principal at all times any interest of his own or of another client which may be antagonistic to that of the principal.

In short, the broker is bound to devote his sole, complete, and unqualified efforts to the advantage of his employer; to know no self-interest, and to act at all times as he thinks his employer would act if he were present. And this fiduciary duty applies to the listing broker's sub-agents as well. A broker who breaches his fiduciary duty becomes liable to his employer for any loss he may sustain and also forfeits all right to a commission.[43]

42 The term "fiduciary" generally applies to any person who occupies a position of special trust and confidence towards another.

43 "A real estate agent with whom property is listed for sale or exchange acts in a fiduciary capacity, if he accepts the proffered employment. It is his duty to obtain for his principal the largest price possible, or in case of an exchange the most advantageous trade. A secret agreement for compensation with the other party or his representative is inconsistent with such position of trust, and is a defense to an action by the agent to recover a commission from his own principal. The temptation is great under such circumstances for the agent to ignore the interests of his employer, and to press for the closing of such transaction as will be most advantageous to himself. Good faith demands a full and frank disclosure to his principal of any such arrangement." Devine v. Hudgins, 131 Me. 353, 163 Atl. 83 (1932).

A broker employed to sell property may not directly or indirectly purchase the property himself *unless* the principal has full knowledge of all the facts and consents to the transaction. If the broker, without the knowledge and consent of his employer, buys the property himself, the employer may repudiate the transaction and recover his property and any commissions paid to the broker. And it makes no difference that the broker acted in good faith and with an honest intent or motive; nothing short of full knowledge and consent of the employer will justify the broker in dealing with himself.[44]

And if a broker employed to sell property fraudulently purchases it for himself through a dummy, and later sells the property at a profit, he may be required to account to the principal for any profits he made on the transaction. Nor is the broker, under such circumstances, entitled to any commission. The law does not permit a broker to advance his own personal interests by making a secret profit at the expense of his employer.

The general rule that the broker may not purchase his principal's property without the latter's full knowledge and consent extends to purchases by near relatives and business associates of the broker. If the broker undertakes to sell to one to whom he is related, his natural inclination to favor his own might militate against the best interests of his employer. Consequently the broker has the duty to disclose that a prospective purchaser is a relative, partner or business associate. This duty of disclosure has been recognized in cases involving parents, wives, brothers and sisters, children, step-children, in-laws, partners, and business associates. The

44 "The agent's failure to reveal that he has an interest in the transaction is sometimes spoken of as fraudulent. If the agent intends to take advantage of the principal, the epithet, with its implication of immorality, is justified. But, irrespective of the words used to characterize the agent's conduct, such a transaction can be rescinded by the principal although the agent acts in good faith and without consciousness of wrong doing." RESTATEMENT, AGENCY 2d § 389, comment a (1957).

principal is entitled to assume that the broker is acting entirely in his best interest and will divulge all information which might possibly conflict with that interest, including the fact that a prospective buyer is related to the broker.

Acting for Both Parties

A real estate broker may not, without violating his duty of good faith, represent *both* the seller and the purchaser in a transaction, *unless* each has full knowledge of the double agency and consents to it. If the broker undertakes to represent both parties to a transaction, the party in ignorance of the dual agency may, upon discovering it, declare the contract void and recover from the broker any damage sustained plus all commissions paid. The obvious reason for this is that the interests of the buyer and seller are diametrically opposed; the seller naturally wants to receive the highest price possible for his property, while the buyer would prefer to purchase it at the lowest price possible. And since the broker is bound to obtain for his principal the most advantageous bargain possible, and because the principal is entitled to the *exclusive* benefit of the broker's skill, knowledge and best judgment in the furtherance of that end, it is apparent that the broker cannot serve at once both the buyer and the seller without violating his fiduciary duty to one or both of them.

The Duty of Full Disclosure

The broker's duty to exercise the utmost good faith and loyalty requires that he make a full and prompt disclosure to his employer of all facts within his knowledge which might affect the employer's interests. Neglect to do so renders the broker liable for whatever loss the employer sustains as a consequence, and also precludes the broker from compensation. Thus if the property has enhanced in value since the broker first listed it, it is his duty to inform his principal of that fact. It is also the duty of the selling broker to promptly communicate all offers submitted to him and to point out to the owner their advantages and disadvantages. And it is the broker's duty to inform his seller of all facts which might influence him in accepting or rejecting the offer, and to give him whatever information he has concerning the prospective buyer's financial status. So if the broker knows that his customer is resolved and prepared to pay a higher price than that submitted, it is his duty to communicate such fact to the owner; failure to do so constitutes a breach of good faith. A selling broker who withholds such information from the owner forfeits any claim to a commission; and this is so even though the owner eventually obtains the full price originally asked.[45] Conversely, a selling broker who discloses to a prospective purchaser the necessitous circumstances of his employer also violates his fiduciary duty.

As a general proposition of law, a selling broker violates his fiduciary duty if, *in bad faith,* he informs a prospective buyer that the property can be purchased for less than the listed price. However, courts are slow to find bad faith on the broker's part merely from the giving of such information. The primary function of the real estate broker is to bring potential buyers and sellers together in order to bring about a sale of the property. In his capacity as negotiator, the broker is required to make every effort to keep the parties interested in the transaction and to bring them eventually together. Therefore, statements by a broker to a prospective buyer to the effect that the property might possibly be purchased for less than the price quoted are

45 Where a selling broker is aware that his customer is resolved and prepared to pay the asking price, he should not send the customer to the owner to negotiate directly without first communicating such information to the owner. A selling broker withholding such information forfeits any claim to commissions, even though the owner obtains from the customer the full asking price.

generally regarded as statements of negotiation, or "dealer's talk."[46]

Duties and Liabilities to Third Persons

As we have seen, the ordinary real estate broker has no implied authority to conclude a binding contract on behalf of his principal. If the broker undertakes to contract on behalf of his principal without authority to do so, he becomes personally liable to the third party for any damages resulting from the unauthorized act.

However, the broker is sometimes granted special authority to contract in behalf of his principal. In such cases a broker who makes a contract for—and in the name of—his principal does not become personally liable upon the contract so long as the name of the principal is disclosed, or so long as the third party knows the broker is acting on behalf of that principal. But if the broker conceals the fact that he is acting as an agent for another, or if he fails to name the principal, he becomes personally liable on the contract. In such a case the third party is justified in assuming the broker intended to pledge his personal liability and responsibility in support of the contract.

So if the broker wants to avoid personal liability, he must disclose his principal at the time he makes the contract. The fact that the broker discloses his principal *after* the contract

46 Thus, in an Arizona case where the broker's salesman informed the purchaser that in all probability the property could be purchased for $8500 (although the listed price was $9500) Justice Udal said: "How can it be said that the effort of the broker in the instant case in attempting to interest a purchaser and bring the purchaser and the owner together by stating that the property might possibly be purchased for less than the quoted price (something which every prospective purchaser would be justified in assuming and which is a hope in the mind of every buyer) amounted to a breach of his duty to act for his principal's best interest? . . . It would be a most naive purchaser who would not know or assume without being told that the owner of realty might sell for less than the original asking price. In my opinion this broker's conduct does not disclose such bad faith or gross misconduct on his part as to warrant a forfeiture of all right to a commission." Haymes v. Rogers, 70 Ariz. 257, 219 P.2d 339 (1950).

is executed will not relieve him of his personal liability; in such case the third party has the option of proceeding against either the broker or against the after-disclosed principal.[47]

Liability for Earnest Money Deposits

If earnest money has been paid to the broker and the transaction fails because of the owner's inability to complete the sale, the broker is liable to the purchaser for the return of the deposit money, provided it still remains in his hands. In such a case the broker holds the money as a trustee, having no more title to it than the owner. However, the broker will not be liable if he has in good faith paid the money over to the owner.

The courts have uniformly rejected any contention by the broker that his right to a commission for procuring a purchaser entitles him to keep the earnest money deposit even when the owner fails to complete the deal.

Liability for Fraudulent Misrepresentations

A broker who induces a person to purchase property by means of fraudulent misrepresentations will be held personally responsible to that person for any loss he sustains due to such misrepresentations. And it is immaterial whether the fraudulent misrepresentations are committed through the medium of false statements or of conduct which is calculated to deceive or mislead.

Elements of Fraud

In order to maintain an action for fraudulent

[47] There is no *obligation* on the part of a broker to disclose the name of his principal, but failure to do so will render the broker personally liable on the contract. So where a broker enters into a contract without disclosing the name of his principal he becomes personally liable for any breach of the contract by the principal. And upon discovering the identity of the principal, the third party may bring an action against either the broker or his after-disclosed principal. But a broker who is required to pay damages as a result of a breach of the contract by his undisclosed principal is entitled to reimbursement from the principal.

misrepresentation, something more than the mere falsity of the statement must be shown. The complaining party must affirmatively prove: (1) that the representation was made as a statement of fact; (2) that it was false; (3) that it was known to be false by the party making it, or that it was made recklessly without knowledge of its truth or falsity; (4) that it was made with intent to deceive and for the purpose of inducing the other party to act upon it; (5) that the other party did in fact act and rely upon it; and (6) that he was damaged as a result. Each and every one of these elements must be proved or recovery will be denied, for as the Maine court has said:

> ". . . the action of deceit was not intended to be made easy to prove. Its purpose was to restrain law suits in commercial and trading transactions so that every time a party, through reliance upon opinion, or trade talk, or without taking pains to inquire for himself, got the bad end of a bargain he should not be permitted to fly to the courts for redress. Hence the purpose and form of the action, and proof of all the necessary elements, have always been adhered to with strictness, with the avowed design of abridging instead of enlarging the field of litigation."[48]

Liability for fraud may be predicated upon misrepresentations relating to such matters as the past or present income of the property, the volume of sales, the existence of encumbrances or restrictions on the property, the location of boundary lines, type and condition of the soil, the presence of minerals, number of acres, etc. However, to constitute actionable "fraud," the misrepresentation must concern a *fact* and not an opinion.

It is generally held that a statement concerning *future* profits or income is a mere prediction or opinion and not a statement of fact; consequently such statements will not

[48] Crossman v. Bacon & Robinson Co., 119 Me. 105, 109 Atl. 487 (1920).

support a claim for damages even though made with an intent to deceive. However, false statements concerning *past* profits or productiveness will constitute actionable fraud.

Representations that a property is worth so much, or that the owner paid so much for it, or that he has been offered so much for it, or has refused such a sum for it, are generally considered *not* to give rise to an action for fraud even though known to be false by the party making them and even though they were made with the intent to deceive. With regard to such representations, the maxim *caveat emptor* (let the purchaser beware) applies.

However, false representations concerning the location of boundary lines, the adequacy of the water supply, the quantity of hay cut on a farm in previous years, and the amount of acreage the property contained, have been held to constitute statements of *fact* which would support an action for fraud.

Fraud may be committed by the suppression or concealment of the truth as well as by false statements. For instance, it is the broker's duty, not only to the owner but also to the prospective purchaser, to promptly and truthfully communicate all offers to the owner; if the broker conceals an offer from the owner, or if he misrepresents to him the terms of an offer, the broker will be liable not only to the owner but to the offeror as well for any damages resulting therefrom.

To constitute actionable fraud, it is not necessary that the person making the statements actually knew them to be false; it is sufficient if he made them in reckless carelessness as to whether they were true or not.

However, the broker is generally held not liable for making false statements concerning rents, profits, or income where he merely repeats what the owner has told him and has no reason to doubt the owner's statements. It is the duty of the owner in describing the property committed to his agent for sale, to give a frank and honest statement as to all matters affecting its market value which are known to him, and particularly such matters as are peculiarly within his knowledge.

It must appear that the person complaining about the false statements *relied* upon them, for if he did not rely upon them he was not defrauded by them. So where one to whom false representations are made makes his own independent investigation as to the truth of the matter, and relies on his own investigation rather than on the representations made to him, he can have no cause of action for fraud. A false statement that had no influence on the decision of the party complaining does not constitute actionable "fraud." And a person to whom false statements are made will be denied recovery if he might have readily ascertained the truth by the exercise of ordinary care. Thus where a party has a reasonable opportunity to learn the facts he has no right to rely upon another's representations.

In order to sustain an action for fraud, the complaining party must not only have relied upon the false statement, he must have been *damaged* as a result.

A purchaser defrauded in a contract of sale may elect one of two remedies: (1) he may rescind the sale and recover the purchase price, or (2) he may sue in tort for deceit, in which case the measure of his damages is the difference between the actual value of the property at the time of the purchase and its value if it had been as represented.

It seems appropriate to conclude the chapter with a quote from the Florida court:

> "The real estate business is not an avenue by which one may practice the tricks of his trade or prey on the innocent and unsuspecting purchaser, nor is it a cloak to cover fraud and deception, or a means for designing persons to short-circuit those who would deal squarely and in good faith. It is indeed a highly respectable business or profession; its ethics are well defined and presumed to be known to those who patronize or engage

in that business. No business known to modern society has a longer or more respectable history. Real estate is a primary security for credit in all the civilized countries of the earth, and the real estate broker in our times [is] and long has been, the medium through which annually many millions of dollars in earnings and savings are secured or invested. He is the agent of his principal in every sense, and, when that relation is undertaken, a fiduciary relation is created which bars the agent from becoming interested in the business or property antagonistic to his principal without his knowledge or consent. Every man, in other words, to whom a business is intrusted by another, has a trust to perform; and every man is a trustee whose business is to advise concerning or to operate the business of another."[49]

SUMMARY

A real estate broker is a person who is employed in negotiating the sale, purchase, or exchange of real property belonging to others. His primary function is to bring potential buyers and sellers together and to act as negotiator between them. His compensation is usually in the form of a commission contingent upon success.

In order for a broker to be entitled to a commission he must have been employed by the person from whom he seeks to recover. Typically, the broker's employment or "listing" is in the nature of an offer for a unilateral contract; the owner, in effect, promises to pay the broker a commission for his act of finding a buyer.

There are three basic types of listings: (1) the "open listing," (2) the "exclusive agency," and (3) the "exclusive right to sell."

49 Quinn v. Phipps, 93 Fla. 805, 113 So. 419 (1927).

An *open listing* amounts to an invitation to the broker to find a buyer who is ready, willing and able to purchase on terms specified by the owner. Such a listing does not amount to a contract of employment; it leaves the owner free to list the property with other brokers or to sell it himself. The owner may withdraw an open listing at any time before the broker has produced a buyer.

An *exclusive agency* is a type of listing which protects the broker from competition by other brokers. Under an exclusive agency the owner agrees that during the term of the listing he will not employ other brokers or sell the property to a purchaser procured through another agent. However, under an exclusive agency the owner retains the right to sell the property himself without being liable to the broker for a commission.

An *exclusive right to sell* gives the broker a monopoly to sell; it not only makes the broker the sole agent for the sale of the property, it also precludes the owner from selling the property himself. Under an exclusive right to sell the broker is entitled to a commission if, during the life of the listing, the property is sold either through the efforts of another broker or the owner himself. In order to create an exclusive right to sell the terms of the listing must be clear and unequivocal.

The so-called *net listing* may be in the form of an open listing, an exclusive agency, or an exclusive right to sell. The "net" aspect has to do with the amount of the broker's commission. Under a net listing the owner specifies the price he must receive for the property *net* to him; the amount for which the property is sold in *excess* of that price constitutes the broker's commission.

Ordinarily the broker's employment terminates when the purpose of the agency is accomplished or when the term fixed in the listing agreement expires. The employment may also terminate by operation of law. Termination by operation of law takes place upon the death or insanity of either party, upon the dissolution of the brokerage firm, or upon the loss or destruction of the property by fire or other cause.

Under an "open" listing the owner may, in good faith, terminate the agency at any time before the broker has procured a purchaser. Where the listing is "exclusive" for a specified period, a minority of states hold that the owner may terminate the agency at any time before the broker produces a buyer, notwithstanding the fact that the broker may have spent money and effort in attempting to perform. However, a majority of states hold that an exclusive listing for a specified period becomes irrevocable during the time specified once the broker takes substantial steps to procure a purchaser, such as by advertising or showing the property.

If the owner wrongfully terminates the agency before the time stipulated, he renders himself liable to the broker for damages. The law varies from state to state as to the *amount* of damages the broker is entitled to in such case. In some states it is the full amount of the commission; in other states it is the reasonable value of the services rendered measured by the expenses incurred. In a few states the law is unsettled on this point. However, if the listing contract expressly provides for the payment of a commission in the event the property is sold by *anyone* during the listing period (exclusive right to sell), the broker will be entitled to the stipulated commission if the property is in fact sold within that period.

To be entitled to a commission, the broker must have *performed* his undertaking. What constitutes "performance" depends upon the terms of the employment contract, but usually it consists of producing a buyer who is ready, willing and able to purchase on the terms prescribed by the owner. The broker is deemed to have "produced" a buyer if he:

(a) places such buyer in *communication* with the owner so that the owner and buyer have the opportunity to enter into a binding contract, *or*

(b) obtains and delivers to the owner a written *offer* to purchase on the exact terms specified in the listing agreement, which offer the owner can immediately turn into a contract by accepting, *or*

(c) procures an unconditional and mutually binding *contract* between the parties.

Unless the listing contract so stipulates, it is not necessary that the broker procure a contract from his customer in order to be entitled to a commission; he need only produce a customer ready, willing and able to purchase on the terms prescribed by the owner, or upon modified terms acceptable to him. But if the broker is employed to *"effect a sale"* or to *"sell,"* as distinguished from a broker employed to find a purchaser, most states hold that the broker earns his commission only if he procures a binding contract of sale.

A ready and willing customer is one who is prepared and willing to accept the terms offered by the owner; the term "able" refers to financial ability. It is not necessary that the customer be in possession of the entire purchase price; it is sufficient if he is able to command the necessary funds within the time necessary to close the deal.

Once the parties enter into a mutually binding contract of sale, the broker is entitled to his commission even though his customer refuses to carry out the contract. But if the contract is drafted so as to give the buyer the *option* of either making the purchase or forfeiting the down payment, the broker will not be entitled to a commission unless the sale is actually consummated, or consummation is prevented by the seller.

The broker's customer must be ready, willing and able to purchase on the *terms* specified by the owner. However, if as part of the same negotiations, and without terminating the agency, the owner accepts modified terms offered to him by the broker's customer, the broker will be entitled to his commission.

The broker is not entitled to a commission unless he performs within the time specified in his listing contract. But if a buyer is produced within the time specified, the broker is entitled to a commission although the sale is not actually consummated until after the expiration of the listing period.

Unless he is otherwise protected by the terms of his listing contract, the broker must be the *procuring cause* of the sale or he will not be entitled to a commission. "Procuring cause" means that the broker must be the *primary* cause and not merely the contributing cause. His efforts need not be the sole cause of the sale but they must be the *predominating* cause.

To be the procuring cause of a sale it is not necessary that the broker should have introduced the owner to the buyer. It is sufficient if his efforts were the *effective* and *proximate* cause of the sale—that through the means employed by the broker, the purchaser was brought into communication with the owner resulting in a sale. And if the broker is the procuring cause of the sale, he is entitled to his commission even though final negotiations are conducted by the owner himself, who, in order to make the sale, accepts a price less than the listed price.

Where two or more brokers are involved in the same transaction, each contributing something to bring about the sale, each is not entitled to a share of the commission; only the broker who was the effective procuring cause of the sale is entitled to the commission, for there can be but one *predominating* cause.

If a broker is in fact the procuring cause of the sale, most states hold that he will not be deprived of his commission merely because the owner, at the time of sale, did not know the buyer had been procured by the broker. A minority of states hold that if the owner in good faith sells the property without knowledge that the purchaser has been procured through the efforts of the broker, the broker is *not* entitled to a commission. A few states have taken a middle course by holding that the broker will not be deprived of his commission merely because the owner did not know of the broker's instrumentality in procuring the purchaser, *unless,* by failing to inform him, the broker permits the owner through ignorance of the fact to (a) pay a commission to another broker, or (b) accept a lower price on the assumption that the sale would be commission free.

Where a broker is protected by an "exclusive" listing, he need not be the procuring cause of the sale to be entitled to a commission; in such case a broker may be entitled to a commission, not because he was the procuring cause of the sale, but by virtue of the special terms of his listing contract.

Although the ordinary real estate broker has no implied authority to conclude a binding contract on behalf of his employer, the broker is generally presumed to be invested with authority to perform those acts necessary to accomplish the purpose of his agency. And the principal will be held responsible for all acts of the agent which are done within the scope of his authority, whether such acts were authorized or not. The principal is also liable to third parties for the *fraudulent* acts of his agent done within the scope of his authority, even though the principal himself is innocent.

Ordinarily the broker has no implied authority to accept a deposit from the buyer; such authority must be expressly conferred upon him by the terms of the listing agreement. A buyer who makes payment to a broker who has no authority to accept it does so at his own risk; so if the broker later absconds or embezzles the money, the buyer must bear the loss, not the owner.

A real estate broker may not delegate his duties and responsibilities to another, although he may employ sub-agents to perform ministerial or mechanical functions which do not require the exercise of discretion.

The broker is bound to obey instructions and to exercise a reasonable degree of care and skill in the performance of his duties. The law requires that he shall possess and exercise that degree of skill, care, knowledge and judgment ordinarily possessed by other brokers in the community. A broker who is guilty of negligence or incompetence becomes liable to his principal for damages and forfeits all right to a commission.

The real estate broker acts in a fiduciary capacity; he occupies a position of trust and confidence and is bound to exercise the utmost good faith and loyalty toward his employer.

A broker employed to sell may not directly or indirectly purchase the property himself *unless* his employer has full knowledge of all the facts and consents to the transaction. And this applies also to the broker's near relatives and business associates; the broker has the duty to inform his employer if a prospective purchaser is a relative, partner or business associate.

A real estate broker may not represent *both* parties to a transaction *unless* each has full knowledge of the double agency and consents to it. If the broker undertakes to represent both the buyer and the seller, the party in ignorance of the dual agency may, upon discovering it, declare the contract void and recover from the broker any damages sustained plus all commissions paid.

The broker's duty to exercise the utmost good faith and loyalty requires that he make a full and prompt disclosure to his employer of all facts within his knowledge which might affect the employer's interests, or which might influence his decision to accept or reject an offer. Neglect to do so constitutes a breach of good faith and renders the broker liable for whatever loss the employer sustains as a consequence.

A broker who makes a contract in the name of his principal does not become personally liable upon the contract, provided he has authority to do so and so long as he discloses the name of his principal. But if the broker conceals the fact that he is acting as the agent of another, or if he fails to name the principal, he becomes personally liable on the contract.

If the broker is holding earnest money and the transaction fails because of the owner's inability to complete the sale, the broker is liable to the purchaser for the return of the money, regardless of the broker's right to a commission.

A broker who induces a person to purchase property by means of fraudulent misrepresentations will be held personally responsible to that person for any loss he sustains due to such misrepresentations. However, in order to maintain an action for fraudulent misrepresentation the complaining party must affirmatively prove: (1) that the representation made was a statement of *fact* and not an opinion; (2) that it was false; (3) that it was known to be false by the party making it, or was made recklessly without knowledge of its truth or falsity; (4) that it was made with the intent to deceive and for the purpose of inducing the other party to rely upon it; (5) that the other party did in fact rely upon it and was damaged as a result. Each and every one of the elements must be proved in order to sustain an action for fraud.

A purchaser who has been defrauded may elect one of two remedies: (1) he may rescind the sale and recover his purchase price, or (2) he may sue in tort for deceit, in which case the measure of damages is the difference between the actual value of the property at the time of the purchase and its value if it had been as represented.

APPENDIX

(Real Estate Forms)

Warranty Deed

Know All Men by these Presents,

That I, Robert A. DOW, of Cape Elizabeth, in the County of Cumberland and State of Maine,

in consideration of one dollar and other valuable consideration
paid by John D. FOSS and Mary N. FOSS, both of Rochester, County of Strafford and State of New Hampshire
the receipt whereof is hereby acknowledged, do hereby GIVE, GRANT, BARGAIN, SELL AND CONVEY, unto the said John D. FOSS and Mary N. FOSS, as joint tenants and not as tenants in common, their heirs and assigns forever,

A certain lot or parcel of land, with the buildings thereon, situated in the Town of Cape Elizabeth, County of Cumberland, and State of Maine, being LOT 12, BLOCK 5, of the Sunset Acres Development, surveyed by R.F. Young, August 23, 1943, and recorded in PLAN BOOK 23, PAGE 16, of the Cumberland County Registry of Deeds.

Being the same premises conveyed to this grantor by Alfred P. and Margaret N. Conway by deed dated June 15, 1958, and recorded in the Cumberland County Registry of Deeds, Book 2398, Page 66.

~~heirs and assigns forever.~~

To Have and to Hold the aforegranted and bargained premises with all the privileges and appurtenances thereof to the said John D. FOSS and Mary N. FOSS, as joint tenants and not as tenants in common,
their heirs and assigns, to them and their use and behoof forever.

And I do COVENANT with the said Grantees, their heirs and assigns, that I am lawfully seized in fee of the premises that they are free of all encumbrances; that I have good right to sell and convey the same to the said Grantees to hold as aforesaid; and that I and my heirs shall and will WARRANT and DEFEND the same to the said Grantees, heirs and assigns forever, against the lawful claims and demands of all persons.

In Witness Whereof, I the said Robert A. DOW and Nancy E. DOW, wife of the said Robert A. DOW,

joining in this deed as Grantor , and relinquishing and conveying all rights by descent and all other rights in the above described premises, have hereunto set our hands and seals this 26th day of May in the year of our Lord one thousand nine hundred and sixty-eight.

Signed, Sealed and Delivered in presence of

Kenneth C. Marks (signature)

Robert A. Dow (signature)
Nancy E. Dow (signature)

STATE OF MAINE

CUMBERLAND } ss. May 26, 19 68.

Personally appeared the above named Robert A. Dow
and acknowledged the above instrument to be his free act and deed.

Before me, Frank V. Robinson (signature)
Justice of the Peace.
~~Notary Public~~

STATE OF MAINE ss. Registry of Deeds

Received 19 at H., M., M., and recorded in

ATTEST: ______________________ Register.

Quit-Claim Deed

(With Covenant)

Know all Men by these Presents,

That I, ROBERT A. DOW, of Cape Elizabeth, in the County of Cumberland and State of Maine,

in consideration of one dollar and other valuable consideration

paid by John D. FOSS and Mary N. FOSS, both of Rochester, County of Strafford and State of New Hampshire,

the receipt whereof I do hereby acknowledge, do hereby **remise, release, bargain, sell and convey** and forever **quit-claim** unto the said John D. FOSS and Mary N. FOSS, as joint tenants and not as tenants in common, their heirs and assigns forever.

(DESCRIPTION)

To have and to hold, the same, together with all the privileges and appurtenances thereunto belonging, to them the said John D. FOSS and Mary N. FOSS, as joint tenants and not as tenants in common, their heirs and assigns forever.

And I do **covenant** with the said grantees, their heirs and assigns, that I will **warrant and forever defend** the premises to the said grantees, their heirs and assigns forever, against the lawful claims and demands of all persons claiming by, through, or under me.

In Witness Whereof, I the said ROBERT A. DOW and NANCY E. DOW, wife of the said ROBERT A. DOW, joining in this deed as Grantor, and relinquishing and conveying my right by descent and all other rights in the above described premises, have hereunto set our hands and seals this 26th day of May in the year of our Lord one thousand nine hundred and sixty-eight.

Signed, Sealed and Delivered in presence of

____________________ Robert A. Dow

____________________ Nancy E. Dow

____

State of Maine, CUMBERLAND } ss. May 26, 19 68

Personally appeared the above named ROBERT A. DOW and acknowledged the above instrument to be his free act and deed.

Before me,

Frank J. Robinson

Justice of the Peace.

Quit-Claim Deed

Without Covenant (Release)

Know all Men by these Presents,

That I, ROBERT A. DOW, of Cape Elizabeth, in the County of Cumberland and State of Maine,*

in consideration of one dollar and other valuable consideration

paid by JOHN D. FOSS and MARY N. FOSS, both of Rochester, County of Strafford and State of New Hampshire,

the receipt whereof I do hereby acknowledge, do hereby remise, release, bargain, sell and convey, and forever quit-claim unto the said JOHN D. FOSS and MARY N. FOSS, as joint tenants and not as tenants in common, their heirs and assigns forever,

(DESCRIPTION)

To have and to hold the same, together with all the privileges and appurtenances thereunto belonging, to them the said John D. FOSS and Mary N. FOSS, as joint tenants and not as tenants in common, their heirs and assigns forever.

In Witness Whereof, the said ROBERT A. DOW and NANCY E. DOW, wife of the said ROBERT A. DOW, ~~and~~

~~wife~~ ~~of the said~~

joining in this deed as Grantor , and relinquishing and conveying my right by descent and all other rights in the above described premises, have hereunto set our hands and seals this 26th day of May in the year of our Lord one thousand nine hundred and sixty-eight.

Signed, Sealed and Delivered
in presence of

Robert A. Dow
Nancy E. Dow

State of Maine,
CUMBERLAND } ss. May 26, 1968

Personally appeared the above named ROBERT A. DOW and acknowledged the above instrument to be his free act and deed.

Before me, Frank V. Robinson
Justice of the Peace.

Mortgage Deed

Know all Men by these Presents.

That,

in consideration of

paid by

the receipt whereof do hereby acknowledge, do hereby give, grant, bargain, sell and convey, unto the said

heirs and assigns forever.

(DESCRIPTION)

To Have and to Hold the aforesaid and bargained premises, with all the privileges and appurtenances thereof, to the said

heirs and assigns, to and their use and behoof forever.

And do **covenant** with the said Grantee heirs and assigns, that lawfully seized in fee of the premises; that they are free of all incumbrances; that have good right to sell and convey the same to the said Grantee to hold as aforesaid; and that and heirs, shall and will **Warrant and Defend** the same to the said

heirs and assigns forever, against the lawful claims and demands of all persons.

Provided Nevertheless, that if the said

heirs, executors or administrators pay to the said

heirs, executors, administrators or assigns, the sum of

from the day of the date hereof, with interest on said sum at the rate of per centum per annum, during said term and for such further time as said principal sum or any part thereof shall remain unpaid, payable annually, and until such payment shall pay all taxes and assessments on the granted premises, to whomsoever laid or assessed, and shall keep the buildings thereon insured against

fire in a sum not less than

dollars, for the benefit of the said Grantee , and executors, administrators and assigns, in such form and at such insurance offices as shall approve, and shall not commit nor suffer any strip or waste of the granted premises, nor commit any breach of any covenant herein contained, then this Deed, as also certain promissory note bearing even date with these presents, given by the said

to the said

to pay the sum and interest at the time aforesaid,

shall be void, otherwise shall remain in full force.

In Witness Whereof, the said

and

wife of the said

joining in this deed as Grantor , and relinquishing and conveying right by descent and all other rights in the above described premises, have hereunto set hand and seal this

day of in the year of our Lord one thousand nine hundred and

Signed, Sealed and Delivered in presence of

____________________ ____________________

____________________ ____________________

____________________ ____________________

____________________ ____________________

State of Maine. ss. 19

Personally appeared the above named

and acknowledged the above instrument

to be free act and deed.

Before me,

____

Justice of the Peace.

(Sample Listing Form)

NON EXCLUSIVE LISTING

Date.................................

I hereby authorize .... to procure a purchaser
(Broker)
for my property located at ....
.... for a price of $.................................
If during the term of this listing the broker produces a purchaser ready, willing, and able to purchase at the price and on the terms herein stated, he shall be entitled to a commission of .... percent of the above price or any other price which I may authorize or consent to.

Should the property be sold or exchanged within three months after the termination of this listing to any party with whom said broker has negotiated, and whose name has been furnished to me in writing by said broker during the period of this agreement, then the above commission shall be due and payable on demand.

Said Broker is hereby authorized to advertise the property for sale and accept earnest money deposits on the purchase price; and in the event of a sale of the property I agree to execute a good and sufficient Warranty Deed.

This is not an exclusive agency and nothing shall be construed herein as preventing me from listing the property with other Brokers or selling it myself. This listing is subject to prior sale by myself or other brokers.

This agreement shall expire on ...., except as to obligations which have accrued prior thereto.

OTHER SPECIAL CONDITIONS: ....
....
....

....

Broker's Signature Owner's Signature

I hereby acknowledge receipt of a copy of this listing.

....

....

Dated....................

(SAMPLE LISTING FORM)

EXCLUSIVE AGENCY

Date: ....

In consideration of your agreeing to list my property located at .... and described as: .... and further, in consideration of your immediate advertising and special effort in attempting to find a purchaser therefor, I, ... (owner) hereby give you, ... (broker), for the period of .... months from this date, terminating on ...., the EXCLUSIVE AGENCY to sell the above described real estate at a price of $........................ It is understood and agreed that if you procure a purchaser who is ready, willing, and able to purchase at the price and on the terms herein stated during the term of this agency, you shall receive a commission of .... percent of the above price or any lower price which I may accept.

Should the property be sold or exchanged within six months after the termination of this agreement to any party with whom you have negotiated, it shall be considered that you were the motivating factor and the commission shall be due and payable on demand.

You are authorized to hold all earnest money deposits as escrow agent, and to place your "For Sale" sign on the premises. In the event of sale, I agree to execute a good and sufficient Warranty Deed.

OTHER SPECIAL CONDITIONS: ....
....
....

....	....
Broker's Signature	Owner's Signature

I hereby acknowledge receipt of a copy hereof.

....
....
Owner
Dated..................

(SAMPLE LISTING FORM)

EXCLUSIVE RIGHT TO SELL

TO: .... Date ....
BROKER

In consideration of your efforts to procure a purchaser for my property located at

....

....

....

I hereby give you the EXCLUSIVE RIGHT TO SELL said real estate at a price of $........................... This listing agreement shall continue in effect for a period of .... months from this date, terminating on ...., with the understanding that if a purchaser is procured during said period by you, myself, or by anyone else, you shall receive a commission of .... percent of the above price or any other price that I shall accept.

And should the property be sold or exchanged within six months after the termination of this agreement to any party with whom you have had negotiations, the above commission shall be due and payable on demand.

You are authorized to accept all earnest money deposits and to place them in a special trust account as provided by law. You are also hereby authorized to place your sign upon the premises and to otherwise advertise the property for sale; and in the event of sale, I agree to convey the property by good and sufficient Warranty Deed.

OTHER SPECIAL CONDITIONS: ....

....

....

....
Broker's Signature Owner's Signature

Receipt of a copy of this listing is hereby acknowledged.

....

....
Owner
Dated: ....

(SAMPLE CONTRACT FORM)

CONTRACT FOR THE SALE OF REAL ESTATE

THIS AGREEMENT entered into by and between *John J. Jones and Mary E. Jones of Cape Elizabeth, Maine*

hereinafter called the SELLERS, and *Samuel S. Smith and June O. Smith of Newton, Massachusetts*

hereinafter called the PURCHASERS,

WITNESSETH as follows:

THAT on this *7th day of March 1969* the SELLERS agree to sell and the PURCHASERS agree to purchase the following described real estate:

Number 20 Elm Street, so called, in Cape Elizabeth, Maine, consisting of a lot of land together with the buildings thereon and more particularly described in deed from Frank F. Fuller to John J. Jones and Mary E. Jones dated September 2, 1945 recorded in Cumberland County Registry of Deeds, Book 2135 page 150.

for the total PRICE of *Ten Thousand ($10,000) Dollars*
to be paid as follows:

$1,000 upon the signing of this contract, receipt of which is hereby acknowledged, and the balance in cash or certified check upon delivery of the deed as hereinafter provided.

AND THE PARTIES HEREIN DO FURTHER AGREE AS FOLLOWS:

1. That the premises are to be conveyed by good and sufficient WARRANTY DEED which shall convey a marketable title thereto, free from all encumbrances EXCEPT: *(No Exceptions).*

2. That the transaction shall be closed with the delivery of the deed and the execution of all necessary documents to effectuate the terms of this agreement within *45* days from the date hereof, and that time shall be of the essence of this contract. However, if the title should prove defective, the SELLER shall have a reasonable time after notice of such fail to remedy the title. In the event that the SELLER is unable to remedy the title within said reasonable length of time or otherwise fails to fulfill any of the SELLER'S agreements herein, then the PURCHASERS may, at their option, withdraw all monies deposited by them under this agreement and be relieved of all obligations.

3. That risk of loss or damage to the premises by fire or otherwise until delivery of the deed is assumed by the SELLERS. Full possession of the premises is to be given over to the PURCHASERS on or before *15 days after delivery of the deed.*

4. That the following items shall be prorated as of *delivery of the deed: Real Estate Taxes for the current year.*

5. That the *$1,000* earnest money deposited hereunder on account of the purchase price, receipt of which has heretofore been acknowledged by the SELLERS, shall be placed in a special trust account by *GEORGE F. BABBIT* as escrow agent and held by him subject to the terms of this agreement, and said deposit shall be duly accounted for at the time for performance of this agreement.

6. If the PURCHASERS SHALL FAIL TO FULFILL any of the agreements herein, the SELLERS shall have the OPTION of either retaining all earnest money deposits made by the PURCHASERS as liquidated damages without recourse to either party, OR of employing all available legal and equitable remedies.

7. That there are no promises, verbal understandings, or agreements of any kind, pertaining to this contract other than specified herein.

8. AND FURTHER, that this agreement is subject to the following additional terms and conditions:

(a) If any part of the purchase price is to be obtained through a U.S. Government Federal Housing Administration insured loan it is expressly agreed that, notwithstanding any other provisions of this contract, the PURCHASER shall not be obligated to complete the purchase of the property described herein or to incur any penalty by forfeiture of earnest money deposits or otherwise unless the SELLER has delivered to the PURCHASER a written statement issued by the Federal Housing Commissioner setting forth the appraised value of the property for mortgage insurance purposes of not less than *$10,000.,* which statement the SELLER hereby agrees to deliver to the PURCHASER promptly after such appraised value statement is made available to the SELLER.

The PURCHASER shall, however, have the privilege and option of proceeding with the consummation of this contract without regard to the appraised valuation made by the Federal Housing Commissioner.

(b) Any further CONTINGENCIES or ADDITIONAL PROVISIONS:

This contract is contingent upon the purchasers' ability to secure a twenty year conventional mortgage loan in the amount of Seven Thousand Five Hundred ($7,500) Dollars at a rate of interest not in excess of seven (7%) percent.

....	....
WITNESS	SELLER
....	....
WITNESS	SELLER
	....
	PURCHASER
	....
	PURCHASER

This is a legally binding contract. If not understood seek legal advice.

(SAMPLE CONTRACT FORM)

CONTRACT FOR THE SALE OF REAL ESTATE

Cape Elizabeth, Maine
Dated: *March 7 1969*

Received of *Samuel S. Smith and June O. Smith of Newton, Massachusetts*
hereinafter called the purchasers, the sum of
One Thousand ($1000) Dollars
as earnest money and in part payment on account of the purchase price of the following described real estate:

Number 20 Elm Street in Cape, Elizabeth, Maine, consisting of a lot of land together with the buildings thereon and more particularly described in deed from Frank F. Fuller to John J. Jones and Mary E. Jones dated September 2, 1945 and recorded in Cumberland County Registry of Deeds, Book 2135 page 150.

for the total price of *Ten Thousand ($10,000) Dollars*
to be paid as follows: *One Thousand ($1000) Dollars with the signing of this contract, receipt of which has been acknowledged, and the balance in cash or certified check upon delivery of the deed as hereinafter provided.*

Said earnest money deposit is received and held by *George F. Babbit* broker, subject to the following conditions:

1. That the said *$1000* earnest money deposited hereunder on account of the purchase price shall be placed in a special trust account by said broker and held by him as escrow agent until the date of closing, subject to the terms of this agreement. If the sellers fail to accept this offer within *3* days from date said earnest money deposit shall be promptly returned to the purchasers.
2. That the premises are to be conveyed by good and sufficient WARRANTY DEED which shall convey a marketable title thereto, free from all encumbrances EXCEPT: *(No Exceptions).*

3. That the transaction shall be closed with the delivery of the deed and the execution of all necessary documents to effectuate the terms of this agreement within *45* days from the date hereof, and that time shall be of the essence of this contract. However, if the title should prove defective, the SELLER shall have a reasonable time after notice of such fact to remedy the title. In the event that the SELLER is unable to remedy the title within said reasonable length of time or otherwise fails to fulfill any of the SELLER'S agreements herein, then the PURCHASERS may, at their opition, withdraw all monies deposited by them under this agreement and be relieved of all obligations.

4. That risk of loss or damage to the premises by fire or otherwise until delivery of the deed is assumed by the SELLERS. Full possession of the premises is to be given over to the PURCHASERS on or before *15 days after delivery of the deed.*

5. That the following items shall be prorated as of *delivery of the deed: Real Estate Taxes for the current year.*

6. If the PURCHASERS SHALL FAIL TO FULFILL any of the agreements herein, the SELLERS shall have the OPTION of either retaining all earnest money deposits made by the PURCHASERS as liquidated damages without recourse to either party, OR of employing all available legal and equitable remedies.

7. That there are no promises, verbal understandings, or agreements of any kind, pertaining to this contract other than specified herein.

8. AND FURTHER, that this agreement is subject to the following additional terms and conditions:

   (a) If any part of the purchase price is to be obtained through a U.S. Government Federal Housing Administration insured loan it is expressly agreed that, notwithstanding any other provisions of this contract, the PURCHASER shall not be obligated to complete the purchase of the property described herein or to incur any penalty by forfeiture of earnest money deposits or otherwise unless the SELLER has delivered to the PURCHASER a written statement issued by the Federal Housing Commissioner setting forth the appraised value of the property for mortgage insurance purposes of not less than *$10,000.*, which statement the SELLER hereby agrees to deliver to the PURCHASER promptly after such appraised value statement is made available to the SELLER.

The PURCHASER shall, however, have the privilege and option of proceeding with the consummation of this contract without regard to the appraised valuation made by the Federal Housing Commissioner.

(b) Any further CONTINGENCIES or ADDITIONAL PROVISIONS:

This contract is contingent upon the purchasers' ability to secure a twenty year conventional mortgage loan in the amount of Seven Thousand Five Hundred ($7,500) Dollars at a rate of interest not in excess of seven (7%) percent.

by..

BROKER

We hereby agree to purchase the above-described real estate at the price and upon the terms and conditions set forth above.

WITNESS:

....

PURCHASER

....

PURCHASER

We hereby accept this offer in accordance with the terms and conditions set forth above.

SIGNED THIS *7th* DAY OF *March 1969.*

WITNESS:

....

SELLER

....

SELLER

INDEX

A

B

G

H

I

J

K

L

Z